T0340222

HOW TO RULE?

A guide through history for those perplexed about the fate of democracy and the government of diverse societies. In war and in peace, amid disruptive change and during reconstruction, a government of people and events will always be called for. But in this age of anxiety and uncertainty, people on the left and the right are losing confidence in governments, elections and politicians. Many ask whether democracy has failed, and ponder alternatives. Knowing how to govern, and how to be governed, are necessary for solving collectively our pressing social and ecological problems.

This book rediscovers diverse models of government, including the successful statecraft and drastic mistakes of past rulers and their advisers. From ancient to modern times, what methods of government have arisen and succeeded, or what were their fatal flaws? What ethical and political ideas informed the rulers and the ruled? How have states dealt with unexpected calamities or with cultural and religious differences? And what kept things (more or less) running smoothly? Amid rapid change and political dissent, it's timely to re-examine the ideas and practices that governed large populations and guided their rulers. In an age of political distrust, disruptive populism and global crises, we need to rearm ourselves with knowledge of history and diverse political ideas to better address contemporary problems.

This book will appeal to students in political theory, political history, or history of government and public policy.

Grant Duncan is a university teacher, political theorist and media commentator living in Auckland, New Zealand, and working at Massey University. (www.grantduncan.com)

HOW TO RULE?

The Arts of Government from Antiquity to the Present

Grant Duncan

Routledge
Taylor & Francis Group

LONDON AND NEW YORK

First published 2022
by Routledge
2 Park Square, Milton Park, Abingdon, Oxon OX14 4RN

and by Routledge
605 Third Avenue, New York, NY 10158

Routledge is an imprint of the Taylor & Francis Group, an informa business

© 2022 Grant Duncan

British Library Cataloguing-in-Publication Data
A catalogue record for this book is available from the British Library

Library of Congress Cataloging-in-Publication Data
A catalog record has been requested for this book

ISBN: 978-0-367-76449-4 (hbk)
ISBN: 978-0-367-76448-7 (pbk)
ISBN: 978-1-003-16695-5 (ebk)

DOI: 10.4324/9781003166955

Typeset in Bembo
by codeMantra

This book is dedicated to the memory of Margaret Lorraine Duncan, née Clift, 1932–2021.

CONTENTS

ACKNOWLEDGEMENTS

It was in August 2018 that I drafted a plan for the present book. At that time, political scientists were concerned about the rise of populism and the consequences of the Brexit referendum and the Trump presidency. As my draft was in progress, my own normally peaceful country suffered a horrific terrorist attack, and in the following year, the whole world was hit by a pandemic. So, even as I was seeking lessons in the arts of government from the distant past, the present times were dishing them out faster than I could keep up.

I utilised geographical isolation and pandemic lockdown to look at the history of government around the world in a different way. But I was drawn back to the words of Jean-Jacques Rousseau in *The Social Contract* referring to his native Geneva: 'Whenever I think about governments, happily I always find in my studies new reasons to love that of my own country.'

In teaching public policy and political thought, the classroom includes people with diverse opinions which they may or may not keep to themselves. Similarly, when speaking in the media, one addresses an invisible audience including the full spectrum of political values. The art is to speak with confidence in a way that can be heard with interest, rather than cynicism, by as wide a range of people as possible. Teaching and commenting have schooled me in a kind of realism which looks first at what *is* the case, rather than what ought to be, and allows those who read or listen to make up their own minds.

The first people to thank are the many students who have been an audience. Whatever criticisms they may have had they've kept largely to themselves. But teaching them has taught me an approach that is reflected in this book.

The quality of written English here owes very much to the exacting professional editorship of Kai Jensen. Any remaining errors and infelicities reflect on me. I am also much indebted to Kathy Troup for advice on Roman history.

I am fortunate to be surrounded by academic colleagues who have (sometimes unwittingly) advised me in the writing of this book, including (in no particular order) Adam Claasen, Damien Rogers, Barbara Anderson, Nicolas Pirsoul, Mac Tofilau, Peter Lineham, Parisa Kooshesh, Anastasia Bakogianni, Tracey Nicholls, Graeme Macrae, Amy Whitehead, James Liu, Sarah Choi, David Belgrave and Michael Belgrave. I greatly appreciate the assistance of librarians Vanessa Gibson and Tom Vadrevu.

My sister Gail Duncan gave helpful feedback on some early draft pages. I am especially grateful to my daughter and academic colleague, Pansy Duncan, who gave us a beautiful boy in October 2019. This book is about the past, but it's written for Wolfie's future.

Auckland
February 2021

1
THE ARTS OF GOVERNMENT

It was October 2019, and it looked as if the wheels were falling off that rickety vehicle called Democracy. It was some three years since the dual anti-establishment shocks of the Brexit referendum and the election of President Donald Trump, and there had been dire warnings from respectable political scientists that democracy was broken and in decline – perhaps terminal decline.[1] Boris Johnson was the prime minister of the United Kingdom, but he lacked a working majority in the House of Commons. The Supreme Court overrode his plan to prorogue the parliament. He had promised Brexit by 31 October but couldn't get a revised deal approved by parliament in time; so, like a disorganised student, he requested another extension. And he called an election for the coming December. The constitution of the United Kingdom looked as if it had broken down, however. Brexit supporters were furious that 'the will of the people', as expressed in a referendum result that favoured leaving the European Union, was being subverted by their representatives. Many of those who had voted to remain in the European Union just wanted the drawn-out and acrimonious divorce and the economic uncertainty to be over and done with. Others insisted on a second referendum. British public life descended to levels of incivility not witnessed in recent history. People questioned the system of political representation itself and asked whether Britain's unwritten constitution needed an overhaul.

Meanwhile, in Washington, DC, the House of Representatives initiated impeachment proceedings against President Trump. It was alleged that the president had violated the law by asking the leader of a foreign state, as a 'favour', to order an investigation into the son of Trump's leading political rival, with the alleged goal of aiding Trump's campaign for re-election. The delivery of $400 million in military aid, granted by Congress, happened to be stalled by the White House while the foreign leader, President Zelensky of Ukraine, made up his mind. Mr Trump defended himself by saying he had put 'no pressure' on the Ukrainian

DOI: 10.4324/9781003166955-1

leader. In that same month, Trump upset many Republicans (among others) by unexpectedly ordering the withdrawal of US troops from Kurdish-held territory in Syria, creating a power vacuum into which Turkish forces quickly moved, supported by the Russians.[2] The office of the president and indeed the Constitution were undergoing a severe stress test. The political disagreement was about more than the conduct of the incumbent president; there was a fundamental disagreement about political legitimacy.[3] It became a common tactic to describe political opponents as unpatriotic, treasonous or insane, as if to rule them out of the game altogether. Many of those who watched in dismay were losing their trust in politicians and in the system of government itself.

In Hong Kong, pro-democracy protestors were openly defying Chinese rule; in Chile, rioters burned subway stations and looted supermarkets; in Barcelona, Catalonian separatists protested violently against prison sentences handed down on nine representatives who had backed a pro-independence referendum. And in Poland, the conservative Law and Justice Party – responsible for undermining freedom of the press and the independence of the judiciary – was returned to office with increased support in an election that also saw an increase in voter turnout. Indeed, elections throughout Europe had seen the rise of parties that openly challenged internationally accepted norms of human rights, especially those regarding minority groups and migrants – and they did so in the name of 'the nation'. In Hungary, this meant a politically dominant hybrid of *illiberal* democracy that thrived on perceived threats from arrivals of refugees and migrants. In western Europe, party-political fragmentation, the weaknesses of mainstream centre-left and centre-right parties, and the strength of far-right populist parties meant that governments were being cobbled together from unlikely coalitions.[4] Italy's short-lived coalition between the 5-Star Movement and the far-right Lega was one particularly dysfunctional example. The future was looking bleak for democracy – particularly for *liberal* democracy. Liberalism itself had become in many people's vocabulary a dirty word that evoked either (for the left) the *neo*liberalism that had caused social dislocation and inequality, or (for the right) the big-city elites who seemed arrogant, condescending and smugly cosmopolitan.

And yet outstanding global issues, including climate change, economic inequalities and poverty, and the online proliferation of extremist ideologies were needing urgently to be addressed. More than ever in history, humanity needed solutions to problems requiring *global* collective action, but governments weren't trusted to address them effectively at the national level, let alone the international. Indeed, in the case of online propaganda, some state actors and political parties were taking advantage of the problems. Had something gone terribly wrong with *systems* of government? Apparently there *was* a major problem, but *what* exactly was it? And if we could agree on a diagnosis of the problem, then what could be done about it?

And then in 2020, a novel coronavirus caused a pandemic. Respiratory disease and death ran rampant as health-care systems were overwhelmed with critical cases. The wealthiest and most advanced countries of the world, notably the United States, United Kingdom and countries of the European Union, suffered massive human and economic losses. The everyday norms of government and of private and commercial life had to be suspended. Temporary emergency powers were invoked to protect public health. To control transmission of the virus, whole populations were placed under compulsory lockdown, overriding their civil and economic liberties. Communities became divided (roughly) between those who were willing to sacrifice liberties in order to control disease and prevent death, and those who would risk death rather than sacrifice their liberties – between those who saw government as protective and those who saw it as a threat. Either way, there could be no return to the *status quo*. For better or worse, government was undergoing another round of transformation.

Where had we gone wrong?

In a contemporary system of representative government, ideally, the competitors for power attain, retain or lose office as an outcome of free and fair elections based on a universal adult franchise. Losers concede defeat peacefully; the armed forces remain in their barracks; career public servants will implement the voter-mandated policy platform of the incoming government. Between elections, the opinions and voices of 'the public' will be heeded – if only with an eye to success at the next election. But this is not – and, I will later argue, was never really intended to be – 'rule *by* the people' in the direct and substantial sense. At elections those who turn out to vote wield a *momentary* power – only to entrust the powers to pass and execute laws to a tiny minority of people (as representatives) who are mostly beholden to the political parties that preselected them as candidates. The voters' trust is only conditional, of course, as elected offices are constitutionally limited in scope and tenure. We've learned, after all, to trust no one with ill-defined or unlimited powers. So in a representative system, 'the people' retain an electoral veto on any government, and hence they hold them to account. A relatively small swing in voters' choices away from governing parties and towards opposing parties often suffices to change the government, or at least to change its composition. The true political change agents are thus a relatively small proportion of 'swing' voters. Political party membership and loyalty have declined in recent decades; polarisation and electoral volatility have risen.

Moreover, on social media and on university campuses, a strange inversion had occurred. Many on the left were calling for their opponents to be silenced or banned. They demanded restrictions on freedom of speech on the grounds that vulnerable minorities were at risk. Silencing voices is, however, a tactic of authoritarian politics. Meanwhile, those on the right were borrowing the old tactics of the left. Realising the power of victimhood, the right complained about suppression due to left-wing 'political correctness', and they adopted unconventional forms of protest and (mis)information campaigns. For instance, the

German far-right sought recognition for the victims of the bombing of Dresden in World War II. The right had adopted the previously left-wing tactic of disrupting politics-as-usual through protest.

Many hard-working white folks were feeling under siege and began fighting back. Donald Trump led their fight precisely because he was a rule-breaker, not a rule-follower. His willingness to flout laws and conventions, repeatedly and shamelessly, proclaimed that this was a route to success. Freedom-loving mavericks at last could stand proud; he implicitly handed a get-out-of-jail-free card to other disruptive rule-breakers. His propensity to follow one transgression unapologetically by performing another violated norms of political leadership. Scandals that would normally have terminated a political career didn't block his pathway to the presidency as his life had always been openly scandalous. His supporters saw him as authentic, even honest, and not hypocritical, unlike 'normal' politicians. Trump also showed disdain for experts and administrators. But this particular trend had begun even before the attack on 'big government' by Ronald Reagan.[5] Public-service professionals and bureaucrats were often derided as self-interested empire-builders who resisted innovation and lagged behind private enterprise. Disdain for experts and administrators had long been widely shared as people turned away from public life saying that they didn't trust politicians or government. This trend against administration and regulation, combined with misinformation and conspiracy theories, left the United States less well prepared than it could have been to deal with the Covid-19 pandemic.[6]

Leading western countries were witnessing a decline in public trust in government and a disinclination to engage in public affairs. The Aristotelian principle of citizenship (learn how to rule well, and how to *be ruled* well) was off the table. Worse still, there was an assault on public confidence in commonly accepted sources of knowledge (especially mainstream media) as the maximisation of scepticism and disbelief became a political strategy. The atmosphere became so polarised that it was politically unwise for members of opposing sides to reach out to, let alone cooperate with, one another. Aiding and abetting 'the enemy' would invite severe backlash from one's own allies. Society was set at odds with itself, and political progress became almost impossible. A fundamental system change had occurred. Something had lifted the lid off the least civil and most hostile collective emotions. Social media enabled this, but they couldn't have been entirely to blame on their own, as worse forms of disorder – not to mention civil war – had occurred in the past, well before the inception of mass media and the internet. There has never been a golden age of politics, guided entirely by truth and justice; the popular idea of '*post*-truth politics' ignores history. But the internet and social media accelerated the proliferation of falsehoods[7] and exacerbated the present discontents.

Looking back to a time just before the internet age, in the early 1990s, one prominent analyst of representative government[8] observed that, in the era of 'audience democracy' (characterised by broadcast media, opinion polling and a wide 'division of labour' between leading political actors and voters), public news outlets did convey certain biases or distortions (through agenda-setting, framing and editing), but they were largely politically neutral and non-partisan.[9] While people disagreed over policies and crises, there was basic agreement about what were the problems and the essential facts. The subject matter in contention, or the field on which a battle was fought, such as in the Watergate crisis, was largely agreed by the major contestants.[10] With the internet and social media, however, there was a proliferation of channels of news and opinion, all of which compete for attention, but not all of which have high standards of reporting. And the perception of the facts and issues themselves became highly contestable, to the extent that one person's fact was another's misinformation. Even when a fact was agreed upon, the interpretations thereof differed wildly. Norms about what counts as evidence and rational debate were no longer agreed. This was exacerbated as the global reach and communication speeds of the internet had greatly accelerated the distribution of misinformation and controversy, and so multiplied the available interpretations.

All the same, such a basic dysfunction wasn't historically unprecedented. Political controversy or confusion over the very disposition of the ground of debate itself, to the extent that people believe untruths or doubt well-founded facts, had occurred before – well before modern media.[11] How had people faced such problems in the past? How had societies succeeded – or failed – in regulating them? How, then, could the present discontents be better navigated so that the urgent tasks of governing serious global problems could proceed more effectively?

Today we face problems of a kind and global scale that humans have never before faced. Three such sets of problems are extreme economic inequalities, climate change and artificial intelligence. The gross and morally repugnant inequality of wealth that divides the world's richest from the world's poorest is well recorded.[12] Inequality also manifests itself in more localised forms such as unemployment, precarious or insecure employment, high costs of housing and human trafficking. Climate change could result in large areas of the (presently) habitable world being inundated by rising seas, made desert or deprived of water, causing mass migration, crop failures, malnutrition and social unrest. And while many of us struggle to keep up with new digital technologies, intelligent machines are beginning to influence or even to master our personal and political choices, while criminal activities and extremist politics flourish online.

These kinds of problems are sometimes referred to as 'wicked problems'. That is, they're characterised by uncertainty in terms of causes, consequences and remedies; many people question whether they're even problems; they're highly contestable politically and culturally; they're intractable, yet neither can they be ignored. Intractability means that they don't admit of solutions that will eradicate them. Smallpox can be eradicated; climate change can't. The fact that wicked problems are ineradicable, however, doesn't mean that they can't be addressed. Indeed, there are morally and politically compelling reasons, supported by empirical evidence, that should convince us to address them through governmental policymaking and collective action.

But the premise of this book is that government *too* is a wicked problem which humans have addressed repeatedly and yet never succeeded in solving. 'Governing' is a complex, contestable and intractable problem that can't be ignored. But if those who govern can't govern effectively, then humankind can't effectively address the global problems of inequalities, climate change and artificial intelligence either, as all these problems demand concerted collective actions.

Reflecting the character of government *per se* as a wicked problem, if not the wickedest of all wicked problems, there's been speculation about the demise of representative democracy, and controversy about whether modern systems of government are broken, 'rigged' or untrustworthy – with a cynicism that reaches deeper than a dislike of individual politicians or parties. Competitive political systems attract careerists whose aim is to become re-elected, rather than to undertake the painstaking tasks of governing in the long-term interests of the people. Along with widespread cynicism, however, there comes a readiness for 'strong' leaders who are prepared to break the norms of established politics. Cynicism and disruption prevent the building of consensus about how best to govern one's country and address global problems; they fuel anti-establishment rejection of the conventional ways in which we've been governed. Modern states lose their authoritative grasp of the arts of governing while crises loom. The arts of government are part of the problem; yet they were supposed to supply the solutions. How did we get here? Is there a way out? Reconsidering the historical arts of government is an essential step towards comprehending the problem. In the following sections, I outline the basic concepts that have guided this study.

To rule and to govern

This book is about ruling – and rulers – and about governing. So, what do we mean by *rule* and by *government*? Every society has rules, written or unwritten. They govern actions according to what we should or shouldn't do in certain circumstances. We can include the grammar of the language we speak and our customary obligations as to who owes what to whom. For much of our lives, we're living by such rules without thinking about them. They often become so ingrained or habitual that we don't ask, 'What should I say or do now?' In familiar situations the answer is self-evident, the question isn't put, and so we speak or act. If, however, someone breaks a rule, or we find ourselves in an unexpected or unfamiliar situation, then we become conscious of rules, or our ignorance of them, or a lack of them. We may want to enforce an existing rule, learn what the rule is or invent a new one. Or existing rules may be unclear, and we debate whether a rule was followed or was broken, or needs to change.

A set of rules implies some obligation to follow them in the right circumstances, and an opportunity, if not a desire, to break them. But, despite our historical search for an ultimate authority, there's no meta-rule that determines how to follow rules, or how to tell the difference exactly between rule-following and transgression. Given the dramatic political histories of disobedience, civil strife, uprisings and revolutions, humans have a strong propensity to break rules as well as follow them, or to fight over what's right and wrong. The heroes of America's war of independence, for instance, were once considered traitors. And today, those condemned as terrorists by one person, may be freedom fighters for another. It's too glib simply to assert: 'Human beings are rule-following animals by nature; they are born to conform to the social norms they see around them.'[13] If we're 'born to conform', then paradoxically we're also born to *transgress*. But can we always tell the difference? People regularly (and metaphorically) bend and break rules, and not only by mistake. Often there are good reasons for it. There's always an informal zone in which recognised law goes unobserved, over-looked or unenforced, even by law-enforcement agents; every set of laws has a paradoxical exception that suspends the law, often for necessity's sake – such as self-defence. If rule-following were somehow 'natural' to us as humans, or ge-netically programmed, then how could it be that *breaking* rules is often important to us for security, creativity and personal dignity, and for the achievement of political change and social progress? During mass protest or civil disobedience, paradoxically, the rule-breaker rules. And yet, rules exist, and we can observe people following or breaking them, despite the lack of meta-rules to set with absolute clarity the boundaries between obedience and disobedience.

If anything is natural to humans, it's the need and the ability to belong and cooperate in groups. To do that, people adopt norms – which may become for-malised into rituals, laws or organised routines. People also need ways of identi-fying those who belong to other groups or who need to be ostracised, and norm violations are at the heart of such differentiation or exclusion. The question of what life might be like without norms or rules is pointlessly speculative, as such a life could only be solitary and hence not fully human. Simply learning to speak a native language is itself the adoption of rules and norms of grammar and meaning. So, rather than say that humans are innately rule-followers, it's sounder to say that we're innately social and communicative, and that rules condition and maintain our association, cohesion and belonging. Rules that become in-stitutionalised and enforced as law in particular communities are elaborations of basic means by which we live safely and cohesively and act collectively. But also, complaining, petitioning and protesting in groups, even to the point of break-ing rules, are important means of sorting out with whom we belong and what our rules ought to be. We don't need to posit a rule-following gene; nothing is 'hard-wired'. Rather than begin with individuals' rule-following as the primary concern, as if it were a trait, we can put relationship and belonging first and see rule-following and rule-breaking as indispensable means of keeping people to-gether and distinguishing one group from another.

Then what about *rulers*, or the people who make the rules? The truly despotic ruler's word was regarded as law – but never in a social vacuum. Despots always call for executioners and administrators to put their words into action, and for subjects to obey them. Masters can't be masters without servants. But one of the great historical struggles has been to subordinate those who rule to an impersonal rule of law. Government by the arbitrary will of rulers gives way gradually to government by law. Such law should be understood by and applicable to all those belonging to (or visiting) that state. Those who make the rules become subject to them along with everyone else. Similarly, the legitimacy of government, from early times, has been judged by how well it serves the interests or wellbeing of the people, and not exclusively the interests of the rulers. The best rulers, legislators or governors act in the common interest, not in self-interest – a principle that's older than Socrates and Confucius (Chapter 2). Over the course of history, written law subordinates the lawmaker, whose powers are thus limited. But in spite of this, rulership or (nowadays) leadership is still significant in itself, in a way that exceeds any law. Even in the best of democracies, people still care about political leadership; they're fascinated, inspired or dismayed by leaders, even though their powers are constitutionally limited. The personal qualities of prime ministers or presidents, and our feelings towards them, influence how we vote – and how we protest.

There's an anecdote about the communist dictator – one of the most ruthless in recent history – Joseph Stalin (1878–1953). When Stalin's son Vasily used the family name for personal advantage, Stalin is reported to have rebuked him by saying, 'You're not Stalin and I'm not Stalin. Stalin is Soviet power. Stalin is what he is in the newspapers and the portraits, not you, no not even me!'[14] Certainly, Stalin's image was used to reinforce a cult of personality, to personify a total state and to project dictatorial rule across a vast union of republics. That he could see a gulf between his likeness and himself shows perhaps some ironic self-awareness. But idolisation (and its flipside, demonisation) of leaders occurs also in democracies. The opposing and impassioned reactions to Obama and Trump are recent examples. The ruler or leader, as perceived by the people, is something other than, or more than, the mere human who sits in the country's highest office. Subordination to a constitutional rule of law certainly alters, but doesn't obliterate, a common fascination with the leader.

Government

Over the centuries, the point where the arts of government take over from the singular decree of the sovereign has shifted, if unevenly, in favour of the former. And so we should ask what is meant by *government*. The word may evoke the institutions that reside in capital cities, including assemblies, political cabinets and bureaucracies, from which we see law and administration emerge. This is a static, hierarchical and almost abstract view. But we can also think of government as processes or sets of actions that we perform to change or regulate our own and others' actions, making the social environment more predictable and secure. That is, to govern is to act upon the actions of others and upon oneself.[15]

In Shakespeare's *Much Ado About Nothing* (IV, i), Hero – daughter of Leonato, governor of Messina – is falsely accused of 'vile encounters', or pre-marital sexual infidelity. As one of her accusers puts it, 'I am sorry for thy much misgovernment', encompassing several senses of 'government'. The ruler, Leonato, should govern the community; parents should govern their families; individuals, especially those of ruling families, should be raised to govern themselves morally. Here 'government' is seen as a process or a sequence of actions and reactions: how the young are raised and disciplined; how adults conduct themselves and others, and how they eschew misconduct. But the distinction between appropriate government and misgovernment is made 'in the eyes of others', as people judge what should and shouldn't be done. In Hero's case, some of the onlookers have been deceived into making a gross misjudgement.

In John Locke's *Second Treatise of Government*, we find this maxim: 'The subjection of a minor places in the father a temporary government.'[16] As minors, our 'government' resided in our parents; as adults, however, we rationally consent to be ruled by the majority under a civil government. In Locke's time, government had a broader social scope or context than we normally mean today. Like Shakespeare, Locke encompasses the education and discipline of the young. It was common for well-off households to hire a governess as a resident educator of the household's children. We govern the young to become autonomous and to exercise their own will, but within morally self-governed and legally governed limits. If that young person is a royal heir-apparent, there's a long tradition of 'mirror of princes' texts that seek to train, constrain and refine the up-and-coming ruler's conduct, examples of which are considered in this book.

Government, then, can be regarded as the many and varied things people *do* to make their own and others' conduct correct, predictable and productive, to achieve commonly valued or necessary aims. And government is what people do collectively to regulate their actions in order to deal with or avert disasters, to defend common interests and to live well. The good conduct or self-government of those who govern, moreover, is a matter of the highest political concern – captured (and surveyed) nowadays in terms such as competence, honesty and trustworthiness. The 'good' government of ourselves and others resides in the ways in which people can readily answer the question, 'How should we act?' How do we decide what's best for ourselves, our family or a whole population, be it under stable and predictable conditions or amid uncertainty and crisis? In routine and unexceptional circumstances the question 'How should we act?' has an answer that's so self-evident we don't even have to ask it. The right action becomes habitual or bureaucratically regulated, and the 'veneer of civilisation' appears unbreakable. Motorists stop at red lights; officials prepare next year's budget. Questions may be asked about destinations or priorities, but the patterns of conduct are thus effectively *governed*.

If a crisis occurs, the normative ways and means of governing ourselves and others are disturbed and challenged and may prove to be inadequate. Emergency powers may be called for, followed by new laws and policy aims. An absence of governmental rule (anarchism) does not take hold, and a government of the new situation arises, but not spontaneously. This book looks at numerous historical examples of, and themes in, the government of peoples and of states. It examines how they were established and sustained, and less so their disruption due to war, revolution or systemic failure. The focus here is on the secure regulation or the 'making habitual' – in spite of uncertainties – in short, the arts of government. Government and public policy aren't institutionalised achievements, they are never-ending processes.

The state

All societies are governed in the broader sense described above. For the purposes of this book, no society is 'primitive' in the sense of being original, close to nature, rudimentary or undeveloped. All have languages with complex grammars, social norms about 'who owes what to whom' (or reciprocity), hierarchies of authority that determine whose word should be heeded, sanctions against misconduct and regulated customs. But not all societies are governed as *states*. The features that characterised early states included written language and hence law codes and records of debts, walled urban centres, social stratification and palaces and/or temples that stood out from other structures. Food surpluses were collected centrally and used to support priests, tradespeople, administrators, soldiers and others. This meant having people who collected and recorded taxes. Dues were paid in various 'currencies': measures of grain, livestock, furs, days of labour, military service or in the sovereign's own coin, if there was one. There are exceptions to these particulars, such as the Incas, who had no written language but did have a method of record-keeping using knotted threads. And if the urban centre is constructed on islands, such as Venice, then defensive walls are unnecessary.

The appearance of the state as a stable socio-governmental formation is controversial, however. Why did it happen, and who benefited from it? Early signs of transitions from hunting and gathering to settlements with domestication of plants and animals and regulated farming practices have been found in the Fertile Crescent (which arches from the Levant around to the Persian Gulf) dating back as far as the ninth millennium BCE. From then, but only very gradually, farming practices spread, towns and cities grew, wealth accumulated and societies became stratified. The first city-states were those of Sumeria, southern Mesopotamia, between the rivers Tigris and Euphrates, dating to the fourth millennium BCE. The leading city of that era, Uruk, reached a population of 50,000 by about 2900 BCE when the cuneiform written language was well established.[17] There's controversy, however, over whether this emergence of the state represented 'progress' for the majority of its members. Walled cities were crowded and unhygienic, enabling the spread of infectious diseases. Large-scale agriculture with relatively few grains as staple foods meant less dietary variety than hunter-gatherers were accustomed to, and it risked crop failure. It required disciplined labour forces on a narrow diet. Were the hunter-gatherers better off than the city-dwellers? Did the advent of urban civilisation mean the elevation of humankind, or the oppression of captive labourers, or perhaps both, depending on status? Were early labour forces coerced to serve the interests of rulers and priests? Or did they sometimes seek the protection of cities and their rulers for security, or for religious devotion? The pressures caused by changing climates and environmental conditions, notably aridity, moreover, may have been instrumental in driving relatively dense populations that were already using fixed-field agriculture into the state form. Early states were characterised by the forcible organisation of land and people to produce grain surpluses that paid and fed an urban elite and their taxmen, guards and makers of specialist goods.[18]

Other peoples who continued to live as hunter-gatherers or pastoral nomads weren't always keen to join civil-urban cultures, and many actively resisted or escaped them. On the other hand, the conquests of settled societies by nomadic peoples have often seen the latter settle into the urban lifestyle, desiring its wealth and luxury themselves, as observed by the fourteenth-century author Ibn Khaldun (Chapter 5). Farming and urbanisation led to economic specialisation and social stratification, and hence to the accumulation of wealth and technical advancements. These achievements created desirable targets for non-settled peoples who were accustomed to raiding others. Through the long course of history, they also led to forms of technological superiority that enabled greater mobility and hence imperialist expansion. The relationships between the nomadic and the settled peoples are dialectical and not one-dimensional. But most of the literally 'hard' archaeological evidence from ancient times consists of urban ruins, while written documents were produced only by states. People who were nomadic and those who lived in temporary or small settlements made of perishable materials left little behind them by way of enduring remains. Ancient states, therefore, unwittingly bequeathed us far more information about themselves, skewing the record in their favour.[19] For this book that isn't a big problem, as state-based government is our main concern, although we'll also explore the mobile statecraft of nomads (Chapter 5). We shouldn't jump to any conclusion, however, about the reasons for early state formation, nor assume that it represented unalloyed progress.

Surpassing the bounds of the city-states, the first known *empire* was the Akkadian, created initially by Sargon, who ruled from 2334 to 2279 BCE. It stretched from the Mediterranean coast through Mesopotamia to the Persian Gulf. An empire is a political entity that's geographically extensive and encompasses diverse peoples and cultures. The logic of empire, driven by the needs of its agricultural base, is to expand – although it does eventually collapse. The arguments over the origins of the state form and the rise and fall of empires are far from over. Given the meagre evidence from those times, however, theories about the origins of the state may reveal more about present-day political beliefs than about what actually happened and why.

Development mythology

Equally controversial are theories about an inexorable development, progress or purpose of states and empires that treat the past as a pathway towards the present. Again, when the partial evidence we have to hand is interpreted retrospectively, our thinking may be prone to preconceived views. For example, Finer's impressive *History of Government* demonstrates that the history of governmental forms isn't historically linear, and yet he asserts that 'the European modern state – the territorial nation-state that proclaims democratic and secular values – has become the model for the entire contemporary world.'[20] One may admire the achievements of many contemporary European states, and one notes the adoption and imposition of European forms of government elsewhere in the world, but the phrase 'has become' lends a sense of finality that may instead be falsified by future events. A more widely cited example was Francis Fukuyama's announcement that the western formula of liberal democracy plus free markets represented 'the end of history'.[21] The models of government set by the European Union and the United States were treated as ideals to which all others aspired, or even as an ultimate realisation of world-historical progress.

As a counter-example, China's past, present and (presumably) future are misunderstood if we take the European liberal-democratic state as its model.[22] The sections on China in this book should help the reader understand why. Similarly, struggles for indigenous self-determination and governance must deal with, but shouldn't be subsumed into, the model of the European nation-state as some kind of ultimate achievement. For some that model was the problem, not the solution. So I don't share the 'central question' that Finer poses: 'How do states come to be what they are?'[23] Like strong theories about the origins of states, explanatory theories of evolution or development – and decline – may be shaped by the values of the present and of the particular author.[24] Instances of government or misgovernment may, of course, have contributed to a state's emergence or demise, but we should be cautious about presuming these are steps in a long developmental pathway.

While new technologies do propel politically significant changes, as we observe today, their uses may not make humans smarter or better as rulers or governors. Indeed, the opposite could be the case, as, the lower the level of technology, the more multi-skilled and resourceful people may have to be to succeed. We shouldn't confuse technological advancement with political skill. Many ancient theories of government still make sense to us today, revealing that this is a field that doesn't 'advance' in anything like the manner that technology and natural sciences do. Fundamentally we may be neither more nor less wise today about the ethics of good government than the ancient philosophers and their rulers when viewed in their historical context. So the past shouldn't be treated as 'less developed' in an ethical and political understanding of government and rulership. Accordingly, I avoid narratives of adaptation and 'fitness', which propose, for example in Fukuyama's words, that:

> Political institutions develop, often slowly and painfully, over time, as human societies strive to organize themselves to master their environments. But political decay occurs when political systems fail to adjust to changing circumstances.[25]

States are affected by changing climates, environments, competitors or other circumstances, and people do make efforts to adapt, and often fail to do so, but we shouldn't presume that political institutions and government are subject to a 'natural selection' process arising from environmental pressures and adaptations. That thinking gets us into circularities where past facts are made to fit a pseudo-Darwinian theory, framed retrospectively as development and decay in a long march towards higher civilisation.

Hence this book isn't a narrative of origins, development or evolution, nor does it propose a typology of states. It bypasses the hazards of assuming that some forms of government are highly developed or superior, while others must therefore be somehow lower forms. Its concern is instead with human efforts to regulate human conduct in different historical contexts. It is about *what people do to (try to) keep things running smoothly*. While instances of historical change or imperial rise and fall are of course important, this book is more concerned with efforts to regulate. War and revolution are naturally relevant, but we will look at what happened 'in between', and at the government of people and events despite disasters. The choices of themes for the chapters, and of countries and historical eras to illustrate those themes, isn't intended to create a typology. It's to explore different ways of governing. And many relevant examples, such as Japan, have regrettably been left out.

Given the cautions expressed above, the historical narratives in this book show how 'government' and 'rule' happen in many different ways. Over the long course of history, personal rule by monarchs from palace-households, or (while on campaign) from tents or horseback, gives way to impersonal rule of law and regulated administration. But we should be careful not to overestimate the extent to which the personal will of the monarch pervaded ancient empires, on a day-to-day basis, given the slow speed of communication and the reliance on ministers, local nobility and so on. While technology has more recently en-abled greater uses of impersonal rule-based (or algorithm-based) administration through pervasive methods of cyber-government, the figure of 'the leader' re-mains a strong presence in people's minds. So neither should we underestimate the symbolic effects, amplified by social media, of 'personality'.

Public policy

This book is also a history of public policy. A typical textbook defines public policy as 'the sum total of government action, from signals of intent to the fi-nal outcomes'.[26] And public policy is itself an academic discipline. So the term encompasses theories and practices, including underlying social values, political decisions and public services, and their consequences. The emergence of the ac-ademic discipline of public policy is normally traced back to the post-World War II era and the seminal work of the American political scientist Harold Lasswell (1902–78) (Chapter 8, Part 3), although histories of the discipline may make brief references to examples from earlier centuries.[27] Yet the term 'public policy' has a much older meaning in English, referring to the legal principle 'that prospective injury to the public good is a basis for refusing to enforce a contract which would otherwise be valid'.[28] And governmental practices that we could call 'public policy' date back to ancient times, as documented herein through numerous examples. I go further, however, to point out that the theoretical study of public policy (the study of how we govern) is at least as old as Confucius. One only has to compare the *Analects* of Confucius with *The Book of Lord Shang*, from the fifth and fourth centuries BCE, respectively, to see that ancient Chinese authors were asking 'How to rule and to govern?' and offering radically differing prescriptions (Chapter 2, Part 1). The reader will find herein further references to theoretical and practical treatises, dating from antiquity to recent times, about successful and unsuccessful statecraft and rulership, and how best to conduct oneself as a ruler, governor or political leader (notably the mirror of princes tradition). Hence this book fleshes out accounts of the history of public policy that one finds in standard textbooks.

Chapter outlines

This book considers themes, illustrations and examples in the history of government; it's not intended to be a comprehensive world history. It proceeds roughly but not consistently in chronological order, and so there's some back and forth between the ages. The next chapter moves from east to west, from China to India to Greece, to survey some of the key ideas from antiquity that continue to stimulate our minds. These ideas aren't treated in the abstract, however, but are described within their historical and political contexts. And they're *enduring* ideas. The Chinese desire for unity and harmony, the pragmatism of India's manuals of statecraft and the rational optimism of the Greeks remain with us.

When we had nothing faster at our service than the horse, how did we manage to rule over physically vast realms and culturally diverse populations? The third chapter moves from west to east, from Rome to Persia and back to China. Then, the Judeo-Christian and Islamic traditions bring monotheistic religions into the question of how to rule. Chapter 4 looks back to the ancient Jewish kingdoms and the example they set; to Byzantium, especially during the age of Justinian I; and then to the major rivals of the Christian empires, the Islamic caliphates. These empires produced many important ideas about statecraft and rulership. At the same time, they had to contend with nomadic conquerors; hence Chapter 5 looks at the government of people on the move and how they interacted with settled civilisations and their established practices.

The modern era saw a significant change in maritime and military technologies, propelling an era of European imperialism across oceans and deep into distant continents. This disrupted many forms of indigenous government, inaugurated colonial government and rebounded back upon the European monarchies, forcing them to revise their own ideas and practices. This is the main theme of Chapter 6. Out of these struggles emerged a greater emphasis on 'the people' as the basis and the object of good government. The idea of a republic and the uses of representation were by no means new, but they became crucial to modern government, as covered in Chapter 7. The same chapter also looks at the reformation of government amid the revolutionary over-turning of an unpopular government. Chapter 8 considers the ancient art of civil administration and the uses of bureaucracy. This also poses the ideal of a science of administration. Chapter 9 covers the major conflicts of the twentieth century in terms of competing models of government: socialist, fascist and liberal-democratic, with special attention to neoliberalism. The chapter concludes by asking how 'democratic' the representative systems that we have today really are.

There's a particular sense of crisis in the government of our times. An appreciation of the history of statecraft and rulership, however, shows us that the problem of government is far from new. It shows us how much we have achieved (and ruined) and yet how little we've learned. Renaissance humanist opinion often held that history is 'life's teacher', as knowing the past 'fosters prudence'.[29] It may also foster humility as we discover that present-day problems aren't unique and that our proposed solutions aren't very original. But G.W.F. Hegel expressed the deeper insight that we learn from history that governments learn nothing from history.[30] To govern means to deal with concrete questions in the thick of unfolding events, with uncertain consequences. The aim is to create predictable routines – despite unpredictable people and events – but the successes of government are always at risk from unexpected events, unintended consequences and sheer bad luck. There's always more to come – the unexpected and the unthinkable – that could derail the normalised government of things, defeating our aims to mitigate uncertainty, prevent disaster and maximise regularity. We can look at the past and at various ways in which people have thought about and practically determined how to rule and govern. The trouble may be that we become wise only after the fact; we walk backwards into an unknowable future. Past experiences accumulate before our eyes but reveal nothing that can save us from tripping up. Something as unexpected and inhuman as a virus could change our fate, our government and our consciousness of ourselves.

Notes

1 Abramowitz, 2018; Hetherington & Rudolf, 2015; Levitsky & Ziblatt, 2018; Mounk, 2018; Pew Research, 2017; Runciman, 2018.
2 President Trump wrote a bizarre letter (dated 9 October 2019) to President Erdogan of Turkey, a NATO ally, warning him to do a 'deal' or see his country's economy get destroyed. Trump admonished him in unpresidential language: 'Don't be tough guy. Don't be a fool!'
3 Pepinsky, 2019.
4 Grzymala-Busse, 2019; Mudde, 2019.
5 Niskanen, 1971.
6 Graff, 2020.

7 Vosoughi, Roy & Aral, 2018.
8 Manin, 1997.
9 There were exceptions, notably British tabloids. Newton, 2019.
10 Manin, 1997, p. 229.
11 As a historical example of such intractable controversy, Manin refers to the Drey-fus affair in France (1894–1906), in which whole sections of French society became committed to entrenched positions on a man's unjust conviction for espionage. In the seventeenth century, Thomas Hobbes was concerned about preachers and political pretenders misleading gullible people.
12 See https://inequality.org/facts/.
13 Fukuyama, 2011, p. 7.
14 Stalin, quoted in Montefiore, 2003, p. 4.
15 'In the sixteenth century, "government" did not refer only to political structures or to the management of states; rather, it designated the way in which the conduct of individuals or of groups might be directed: the government of children, of souls, of communities, of families, of the sick.' Foucault, 1982, p. 790, abridged.
16 Locke, 1980, p. 37, §67, italics added.
17 Haywood, 2005.
18 Scott, 2017.
19 Scott, 2017, makes an important case against the standard narrative of a Neolithic 'revolution' and then a 'breakthrough' to urbanisation and hence to civilisation.
20 Finer, 1999, vol. I, p. 94. In fairness to the late Professor Finer (1915–93), he didn't witness some of the recent crises in Europe, especially those since 2016.
21 This supposed 'end of history' would represent 'the end point of mankind's ideologi-cal evolution and the universalization of Western liberal democracy as the final form of human government.' Fukuyama, 1989, p. 4.
22 Jacques, 2012.
23 Finer, 1999, vol. I, p. 9.
24 There are interesting efforts to quantify and mathematically model the dynamics and long-term cycles of the rise and fall of empires. These could help to reduce presentist interpretation and to quantify such cycles. But so far, they do not produce original theories. See, for example, Turchin, 2018.
25 Fukuyama, 2011, p. 7.
26 Cairney, 2012, p. 5.
27 DeLeon, 2008.
28 Oxford English Dictionary online, accessed May 2020. For example, G. Wilson, 1770: 'This court constantly sets aside such bargains, upon the principles of public policy.' For legal history, see Ghodoosi, 2015.
29 Letter from Isotta Nogarola (1418–66) to Feltrino Boiardo, 1438. Nogarola, Robin & King, 2004, p. 77.
30 'Rulers, statesmen and nations are often advised to learn the lesson of historical ex-perience. But what experience and history teach us is this — that nations and govern-ments have never learned anything from history or acted upon any lessons they might have drawn from it. Each age and each nation finds itself in such peculiar circum-stances, in such a unique situation, that it can and must make decisions with respect to itself alone.' Hegel, 1975 [1828], p. 21.

References

Abramowitz, Michael J. 2018. *Freedom in the World 2018*. Washington, DC: Freedom House.
Cairney, Paul. 2012. *Understanding Public Policy: Theories and Issues*. Houndmills: Palgrave Macmillan.

DeLeon, Peter. 2008. 'The Historical Roots of the Field.' In *The Oxford Handbook of Public Policy*, by Robert E. Goodin, Michael Moran and Martin Rein, 39–57. Oxford: Oxford University Press.

Finer, S.E. 1999. *The History of Government*. Oxford: Oxford University Press.

Foucault, Michel. 1982. 'The Subject and Power.' *Critical Inquiry* 8 (4): 777–95.

Fukuyama, Francis. 1989. 'The End of History?' *The National Interest*, 3–18.

———. 2011. *The Origins of Political Order: From Prehuman Times to the French Revolution*. London: Profile Books.

Ghodoosi, Farshad. 2015. 'The Concept of Public Policy in Law: Revisiting the Role of the Public Policy Doctrine in the Enforcement of Private Legal Arrangements.' *Nebraska Law Review* 94 (3): 685–736.

Graff, Garrett M. 2020. 'Trump Broke the Agencies That Were Supposed To Stop the Covid-19 Epidemic.' *Politico*. 4 7. Accessed November 9, 2020. https://www.politico.com/news/magazine/2020/04/07/trump-dismantled-the-very-jobs-meant-to-stop-the-covid-19-epidemic-173347.

Grzymala-Busse, Anna. 2019. 'The Failure of Europe's Mainstream Parties.' *Journal of Democracy* 30 (4): 35–47.

Haywood, John. 2005. *The Penguin Historical Atlas of Ancient Civilizations*. London: Penguin.

Hegel, G.W.F. 1975. *Lectures on the Philosophy of World History*. Cambridge: Cambridge University Press.

Hetherington, Marc, and Thomas J. Rudolph. 2015. *Why Washington Won't Work: Polarization, Political Trust, and the Governing Crisis*. Chicago, IL: University of Chicago Press.

Jacques, Martin. 2012. *When China Rules the World: The End of the Western World and the Birth of a New Global Order*. New York, NY: Penguin.

Levitsky, Steven, and Daniel Ziblatt. 2018. *How Democracies Die*. New York, NY: Crown.

Locke, John. 1980. *Second Treatise of Government*. Indianapolis, IN: Hackett.

Manin, Bernard. 1997. *The Principles of Representative Government*. Cambridge: Cambridge University Press.

Montefiore, Simon Sebag. 2003. *Stalin: The Court of the Red Tsar*. London: Weidenfeld & Nicolson.

Mounk, Yascha. 2018. *The People vs. Democracy: Why Our Freedom Is in Danger and How to Save It*. Cambridge, MA: Yale University Press.

Mudde, Cas. 2019. 'The 2019 EU Elections: Moving the Center.' *Journal of Democracy* 30 (4): 20–34.

Newton, Kenneth. 2019. *Surprising News: How the Media Affect – and Do Not Affect – Politics*. Boulder, CO: Lynne Rienner.

Niskanen, William A. 1971. *Bureaucracy and Representative Government*. New York, NY: Transaction.

Nogarola, Isotta, Diana Maury Robin, and Margaret L. King. 2004. *Complete Writings: Letterbook, Dialogue on Adam and Eve, Orations*. Chicago, IL: University of Chicago Press.

Pepinsky, Thomas. 2019. 'Why the Impeachment Fight Is Even Scarier Than You Think.' *Politico Magazine*. October 31. Accessed November 3, 2019. https://www.politico.com/magazine/story/2019/10/31/regime-cleavage-229895.

Pew Research Center. 2017. 'Public Trust in Government: 1958–2017.' *Pew Research*. December 14. Accessed November 8, 2018. http://www.people-press.org/2017/12/14/public-trust-in-government-1958-2017/.

Runciman, David. 2018. *How Democracy Ends.* Chicago, IL: Basic Books.

Scott, James C. 2017. *Against the Grain: A Deep History of the Earliest States.* New Haven, CT: Yale University Press.

Turchin, Peter. 2018. *Historical Dynamics: Why States Rise and Fall.* Princeton, NJ: Princeton University Press.

Vosoughi, Soroush, Deb Roy, and Sinan Aral. 2018. 'The Spread of True and False News Online.' *Science* 359 (6380): 1146–51.

2
ENDURING IDEAS

Justice, law, virtuous rulership and successful government have been our practical concerns since at least the earliest written records of the Sumerian and Egyptian civilisations. The present account begins somewhat later, however, in the sixth century BCE. It journeys through ancient China, India and Greece. Learning about early ideas and practices puts into historical perspective some of the problems with which we struggle today, but we shouldn't expect to find here an ancient wisdom that applies to all times and places. This chapter surveys prominent early texts on constitutions, statecraft and advice to rulers, placing them in their historical contexts and revealing differences and similarities across the three civilisations. Ancient political thought was sophisticated and varied, and ranged from practical questions of administration to speculation about destiny and about virtuous conduct in challenging political circumstances.

Part 1: China

The outstanding feature of Chinese history is the resilience of the dynastic-imperial model, albeit punctuated by periods of conflict and division. Following the fall of each dynasty, a new one would replace it,[1] ruling its vast territory, although not always under ethnically Chinese rulers. A unified monarchical-civilisational model (All-under-Heaven, *tianxia*) was fought for and sustained for over two millennia.[2] The question wasn't whether a unified empire was desirable, but who had the mandate of heaven to rule it – and whether strict laws or revered customs should inform this government.

Since the earliest dynasties four millennia ago, China was divided into many distinct polities, but their numbers declined over the centuries. In 1045 BCE, the Shang dynasty of the lower Yellow River basin was defeated by the Western Zhou. The latter formed a new kingdom and divided their territory into fiefdoms

DOI: 10.4324/9781003166955-2

for loyal family members and followers. This inaugurated a dynasty that was to last for about 800 years. The king's legitimacy, as against rival family members or dynasties, relied upon Heaven's Mandate (*tian ming*). Only the legitimate ruler could consult Heaven directly, through divination, and the rites performed by him were vital for the harmony and wellbeing of the realm. But his and his successors' mandate was finite, contingent upon their personal virtue. The king (or, later, emperor) was both Son of Heaven and father of the people. To what extent this implied an absolute centralised power of the ruler, or a decentralised authority with benevolent concern for all subjects would be continually contested.

The Western Zhou capital, Xi'an, was vulnerable to external attack, and the ruling family shifted its base eastwards to Luoyang in 770 BCE. This meant that the king's domain was smaller, however, and surrounded by fiefdoms that increasingly acted independently. Thus began the Spring and Autumn Period (770–481 BCE), followed by the Warring States Period (480–221 BCE). By 256 BCE, there were seven competing states left, embroiled in warfare – but peace and stability required political unity. Eventually, the stronger states conquered the weaker, and the strongest proved to be the western state of Qin.[3]

Political and administrative changes during this period were profound. At the beginning of the seventh century BCE, hereditary fiefs began to be replaced by centrally administered counties and commanderies overseen by (respective) magistrates and governors appointed and paid by the state. Commanderies (or prefectures) were created for the military administration of newly conquered or vulnerable territories, but by the third century, they became superordinate units divided into counties. Central government relied increasingly on quantitative methods such as censuses, tax registers and crop records, and on specialised offices with professional appointees. Codified laws and punishments had appeared by the sixth century BCE, and these began to replace unwritten customary norms and rituals. Feudal land tenure (with service in kind or tithes to overlords) gave way to buying and selling. Peasants who couldn't afford to own land became tenant-farmers or wage-labourers, and taxes were imposed by central government. Landowners and officials thus rose in social status.[4] In addition, there arose a class of influential educated gentlemen – often itinerant – many of whom found favour as advisers to rulers. Amid the chaos of wars and the desire for political unity and harmony, these scholars addressed the practical questions of ethical conduct and rulership.

Despite the patriarchal traditions and the near absence of women in the writings of leading intellectuals, there were powerful women – for example, Qin Xuan (c. 324–265 BCE), who rose from court concubine to become dowager empress of Qin after helping to install her son as heir to the throne.[5] This semi-barbarous upstart state of Qin had during the reign of King Xiao (361–338 BCE) adopted new techniques of government, promoted by his adviser Shang Yang (c. 390–338 BCE).[6] Their reforms included the centralisation of administrative power, the division of Qin into 31 counties, more flexible land tenure, standardisation of weights and measures, and the enforcement of laws regardless of rank. 'The population was divided into units of five or ten families each, within which all members were held collectively responsible for the wrongdoing of any individual.'[7] This rewarded denunciation by kin or close community members and broke familial loyalties. The aim was to produce a militaristic agrarian society, with formal recognition of status based more on merit than on pedigree. The ultimate political success of Qin owed much to 'efficiency, precision, and fixed routine in administrative procedure, exact quantification, improvement of agricultural production and conserving of natural resources.'[8] It was King Zheng of Qin (259–210 BCE)[9] who achieved, by aggressive force of arms and autocratic rule, the first unification of China in 221 BCE, taking the title of Shi Huangdi or First August Emperor. He and his successors were unpopular, however, leading to a revolt. After a period of civil war, imperial rule passed over to the Han dynasty, which lasted from 206 BCE to 220 CE (Chapter 3, Part 3).

Schools of thought

The principles that guided Chinese political thought were diverse and were formed well before imperial unification, especially during the Warring States Period. Stability through unity was widely desired, and most authors agreed that a powerful monarch was essential.[10] A key problem for Chinese political thinkers, then, concerned the qualities of the virtuous ruler. Gaining the Mandate of Heaven and the trust of the people – *who* should do so, and *how* – were hotly contested. Any contending ruler, no matter how strong militarily, needed good advisers. And the leading intellectuals or teachers of the literate class of gentlemen sought their patronage. Hence while the independent states were at war, intellectual life flourished. Although there's little historically reliable information about him, the most renowned is Kong Qiu or, in English, Confucius (551–479 BCE). Confucian ideas weren't always 'the ruling ideas', however; there were alternative and rival traditions that we need to consider.[11] The spectrum of ancient Chinese political thought may be divided roughly into competing schools – although these weren't formal academic institutions. Moreover, none of the texts of these times comes down to us 'in one piece'; they're amalgams and collations, not necessarily written entirely (if at all) by their named authors. I'll outline below four schools of thought: Confucian, Mohist, Daoist and legalist.

Across these differing schools, we find four basic domains: above all, the pattern or will of Heaven, upon which the tenure and legitimacy of the ruler depended; then the natural world, which reflected the will of Heaven, notably when natural disasters signified the loss of a ruler's mandate; the common people in whose interests the monarch ruled, and whose collective mood (rebellious or contented) also reflected upon the ruler; a ruling class, including the monarch, whose observance of ritual, as communion with Heaven, was vital for the state's continuity and cohesion. The unity and harmony of these four realms were the basic aims of good rulership. But there were competing ideas about how best to achieve this.

Confucians

Confucius was concerned with the continuation of ancient rites, manners and civility that honoured parents and ancestors and kept people on rightful and orderly pathways. The duty to maintain benevolent and harmonious conduct was incumbent upon those responsible for families, communities and especially states. This included formal religious ceremonial and correct conduct (*li*), grounded in ethics of benevolence or humaneness (*ren*), or 'observance of the rites through overcoming the self'.[12] *Ren* guides justice with empathy: 'Do not impose on others what you yourself do not desire.'[13] The nobleman acts rightly by conforming with ancient traditions and the will of Heaven. For good government Confucius advises: 'Give them enough food, give them enough arms, and the common people will have trust in you.' When asked which of the three (food, arms or trust) should be given up first, if need be, he replies, 'Give up arms.' The next to be relinquished is food. Trust, however, is indispensable. 'Death has always been with us ... but, when there is no trust, the common people will have nothing to stand on.'[14] Where there's a foundation of trust, coercion is unnecessary. 'To govern (*cheng*) is to correct (*cheng*),' and the scholar, nobleman or ruler should set the example, to cast a beneficial influence over others.[15] Hence morally good leadership exerts its own benevolent power and is far superior to edicts and punishments.[16] While Confucius revered the ancient Zhou rulers, he also envisaged individual and collective learning and progress.

Confucius became the leading historical figure, but others inspired by him followed their own paths. Mengzi, or Mencius (c. 372–289 BCE), had an optimistic view of human goodness and a strong sense of moral conduct, acquired from his widowed mother, the celebrated Mother Meng (c. 400–350 BCE).[17] Everyone possesses the potential for benevolent, compassionate and just conduct, but it needs to be nurtured. While the ultimate source of all moral goodness is Heaven, its realisation depends on human actions and education, and this calls for lower taxes, lighter punishments and distribution of basic goods. The good of the people is the highest priority, so government needs to be guided by benevolence and rightness rather than by calculated results, because 'if profit is put before rightness, there is no satisfaction short of total usurpation.'[18] Hence the good ruler acts for the people, out of benevolence – just as the good parent does for the child who, in return, owes obedience. And as empathy is innate, even a cruel ruler can learn its benefits. Nevertheless, rulers who harm the people, through selfishness or injustice, could legitimately be deposed.[19] This latter idea didn't take hold under Chinese autocratic and bureaucratic government, but Mencius' argument that the emperor exists for the sake of the people – not vice versa – did last.[20]

Xunzi (c. 310–c. 220 BCE) held a more pessimistic view of human nature. Freedom to follow our natural self-regarding inclinations leads to disorder, and hence we need moral improvement and education, and effective rulers who foster 'ordered communities structured by moral rules'.[21] Xunzi argued that 'ritual principles must not be neglected even for a moment'[22] because they engender obedience, reduce quarrelling and reinforce social hierarchy and order. The ordinary ruler should apply punishments when needed, especially to those who act in bad faith; whereas the 'true king' is followed faithfully, without the force of arms, due to his superior benevolence, righteousness and authority. In turn, the ruler's legitimacy depends upon the wellbeing and tranquillity of the people. Appointments to official posts should be on merit and not on family pedigree.[23]

The fundamental value of education is shared by the Confucian thinkers, even though they differ over the innate trustworthiness of humans. Confucian virtue is relational and practical rather than governed by abstract principles or laws; social harmony is a concert of differences, not uniformity. And the state is analogous to, if not continuous with, the extended family. Filial piety is a norm of family life, but it permits remonstrating with parents (or with rulers) when they're ethically wrong. There was debate as to whether one's loyalty to family should come before loyalty to state or emperor, or vice versa. For some later rulers, filial piety justified obedience to an absolute monarch, but this isn't explicitly supported by older Confucian texts.[24]

Rival schools

About Mozi, namesake of the Mohist school, little is known, but he is thought to have lived in the fifth century BCE. Rather than seek the continuation of the ancient ritual practices of the ruling class, Mozi spoke against them and had more concern for the suffering experienced by the common people, especially farmers. His advice to rulers included principles of meritocracy, frugality and impartiality. Before there were rulers and governments, there were disharmony, conflict and chaos. Hence there needed to be a ruler to determine right and wrong and to dish out rewards and punishments. But struggles between states and between powerful families, oppression of the weak and lack of benevolence caused suffering and harm. The best policy for eliminating such harms was impartial care or universal love, by which one treats one's friend as if oneself, and one's friend's father as if he were one's own father, and so on, in submission to the will of Heaven. 'If there is universal mutual love in the world, then there is order.'[25] States should eliminate wasteful expenditure on funerals and musical events, and offensive warfare should be avoided, as they neither help the poor nor provide stability. Mohists, however, would assist states in building their defences. Although Mozi is most concerned for the welfare of the common people, his view of the just social order is nonetheless hierarchical and monarchical, and all order ultimately resides in 'the will of Heaven'. 'Heaven is broad and unselfish in its actions and is generous in its bestowing without considering itself virtuous. Therefore, the sage kings took it as the standard.'[26] Heaven commands benevolent and righteous conduct of rulers and punishes those who fail.

Daoism is traced back mainly to two ancient texts, the *Laozi* or *Doadejing* (On Virtue and the Way) and the *Zhuangzi* (named after its author, Master

Zhuang, 369–298 BCE). Daoist texts use allusive and paradoxical propositions and provocative anecdotes to disrupt assumptions and free us from attachments to worldly concerns and moral conventions – and even from the supposed wisdom of sages. Suffering and happiness result from habits of thought and action – which can be overcome, if we follow 'the Way' (*dao*), or let things occur in tune with their nature. *Dao* may also be translated as 'method' or 'path'. It refers to the underlying spontaneous nature or order of things, in accordance with which we should strive to live.[27] The ethic of Daoism is thus a kind of *in*action, or a noncoercive action. Harsh government is deplored and the wise nobleman refuses any offer to take the throne. The ideal ruler is restrained, non-assertive and inscrutable, reveals neither desires nor plans, ignores manipulative or self-interested advice, and doesn't initiate conflict, but does allow communities to prosper in their own way.[28] Daoism suggests a form of anarchism or 'government by non-government'.[29]

Legalism, in stark contrast, rejected virtuous benevolence; it advocated strict laws and harsh punishments, without leniency. The oldest extant legalist text, by the Qin minister Shang Yang, is highly prescriptive and pragmatic, if not amoral, promoting state power based on military and agricultural efficiency. *The Book of Lord Shang* prescribes a total state that unrelentingly applies rewards and punishments to force the people to farm and to fight, and ultimately to serve the interests of the ruler.

> The True Monarch inflicts punishments on about-to-be-committed transgressions: then major wickedness will not be born. He rewards those who inform about the depraved: then even minor transgressions are not lost. When, in ordering the people, you can prevent depravity from being born and minor transgressions from being lost, the state is well ordered. When the state is well ordered, you are powerful.[30]

The king should get rid of scholarly advisers who are merely talkative parasites. He should promote only those who engage in agriculture and warfare to produce surpluses that feed soldiers who will then conquer more arable lands.

The legalist school examined 'how to preserve and strengthen the state',[31] beginning with clear methods of government and personnel management that could be recorded and learned. The legalist philosopher Han Fei (c. 280–233 BCE), who served the king of Qin,[32] advised naming each office or duty, describing its correct performance, checking whether each official is actually performing as prescribed, and punishing those who fail to do so. If all is effectively ordered, the officials serve 'a virtually transcendent ruler whose power is absolute because he is silent, mysterious, but always holding in his hands the ultimate weapons of control, cutting back the powers of others who become too prominent.'[33] There's little need to exert his powers forcefully if the king reveals no inner thoughts or desires, and thus his ministers are unable to pre-empt what he wants. 'Discard wisdom, forswear ability, so that your subordinates cannot guess what you are about.'[34] The king can't trust those around him, as they're all potential traitors. He should suppress self-interested actions of subordinates and enforce obedience to laws, applying them to all regardless of rank. He should keep strict and impartial control of rewards and punishments and not allow himself to be compromised by special pleading. Officials should unquestioningly obey their superiors; commoners should mind their own business. 'Honorable and humble do not get in each other's way, and stupid and wise find their proper place. This is the perfection of good government.'[35] Legalist government was pragmatically focussed on present-day problems, and rejected traditions received from an idealised past.

The first emperor

It was legalism, rather than Confucian virtues, that informed the policies of the first emperor (r. 221–210 BCE).[36] He refused to allocate distant conquered domains to heirs but divided the empire into 36 commanderies, each with an appointed triumvirate of civil governor, military commander and imperial inspector, under whom were counties administered by appointed magistrates. He applied strict laws and impersonal administrative methods, and rejected the model of feudal loyalty and ancient rites. Former royal families, nobles and officials of the conquered states were removed to the imperial capital and housed under surveillance in new palaces. Advantage trumped benevolence.

The emperor oversaw the simplification and universalisation of Chinese characters,[37] the empire-wide application of Qin's punitive legal code; and the standardisation of weights and measures, metal currency and the gauge of wheeled vehicles. Unification allowed for mobilisation of huge workforces for the construction of imperial highways, canals and defensive walls, the development of new agricultural lands and the building of palaces and the emperor's mausoleum. Convicts, reprobates and the disfavoured, along with their families, were assembled in the tens of thousands and sent to colonise new territories or to work on the emperor's massive projects.[38]

These policies ignored the ideals of the ancient dynasties of Shang and Zhou which the Confucians had revered. The new emperor placed administrative and military abilities ahead of ancestry when it came to appointments and honours. Apparently fed up with those who invoked the past in order to criticise the present, and who thus stirred up dissent, an imperial decree ordered the burning of books (other than those considered useful) and the execution of 460 scholars.[39] Confucian and Daoist ideas weren't completely suppressed, however, as elements of these philosophies were sometimes expressed by the emperor himself. He accepted legalism for political necessity, but sometimes included 'Confucian notions of a rather elementary sort.'[40]

The first emperor failed to plan an orderly succession, however, and he died (in 210 BCE) while on a tour of the empire, rather than peacefully in his palace. The deceased emperor's own advisers engineered the suicide of his eldest son and the succession of a younger son. The latter was also bullied into killing himself. Rebellions broke out, the capital was occupied by rebel forces in 207, and the first of the subsequent Han dynasty was installed in 202. Explanations for the short duration of the first empire include its lack of benevolence, disrespect for customs, refusal to follow the example of ancient sage-kings, incompetence of successors, the costs of centralised state bureaucratic control over such vast territory, the harshness of the new legal code and popular resistance to forced labour and censorship. Nonetheless, many of its reforms, such as meritocracy, standardisation and bureaucratisation, were adopted and developed by subsequent dynasties, albeit with greater respect for Confucian heritage.[41]

> It is the legalist–Confucian symbiosis evolved during the Han dynasty, with administrative controls at the top merging into self-administered behavioural standards below, that gave to the Chinese state the necessary combination of firmness and flexibility that enabled it to survive.[42]

A distinctive imperial model had begun: a (theoretically) omnipotent monarch possessing the mandate of Heaven, moderated by skilled and learned officials, and always wary of the disruptive potential of mass rebellion.

Part 2: India

Ancient Indian Vedic thought and ritual practices are narrated and taught through a vast collection of texts, the oldest surviving being the *Rigveda*, dating back to the second millennium BCE. This corpus of philosophical and religious texts, including the *Upanishads*, was compiled in writing by about 600 BCE. They taught knowledge of self, cosmology and correct ritual. Doctrines of karma gave moral instruction on the consequences of our actions, including reincarnation, and on right or lawful conduct in the broader spiritual and social senses. The epic *Bhagavad Gita* depicted the spiritual principles that guided the warrior-ruler towards selfless action in accordance with destiny. These texts also reveal a social stratification into four castes – priest, warrior, merchant-tradesman and servant – with differentiated gender roles and duties. The *raja* was originally an elected warrior-chief of a clan but may be called 'king' as societies became more complex. He was drawn from the powerful warrior caste (*kshatriya*), but paid respect to scholar-priests (*brāhmana*). The raja wielded power but the brahman legitimised it through ritual.[43]

The Vedic tradition, its priesthood and caste-based social order were opposed, however, by the Buddhist and Jainist sects which had emerged by the fifth century BCE. Following the teaching of Mahavira, Jainism required radical ascetic renunciation as a way towards ultimate knowledge and liberation from the cycle of reincarnation. Buddhism advocated a middle way. Monks and nuns 'renounced social obligations to take on an alternative life' in a community or assembly of equals, supported by lay followers.[44] Both Mahavira and the

Buddha were born into *kshatriya* families in clan-based republics (*gana-sanghas*) in which decision-making was shared among the patriarchs of leading families. Caste privileges and rituals were undercut by their teachings. 'Substantial parts of early Buddhist and Jainist literatures contain expositions of protest and resistance,' including arguments for 'human equality' and against claims of priestly superiority.[45] Buddhist political theory saw the origins of government in the need for just solutions to social conflicts over land-ownership. In monarchies that followed Vedic scripture, on the other hand, kings were regarded as having divine origins.[46]

Buddhism

Gautama Buddha (or Siddhartha Gautama) is said to have been born in northeast India or Nepal, possibly in the later sixth century BCE, while he died possibly as late as the end of the fifth. He was a prince of a ruling family in the ancient town of Kapilavastu – the exact site of which is uncertain. At the age of 29, he left the protective life of the palace and saw for the first time the nature of human suffering, after which he renounced worldly things to become a mendicant and teacher. The community of monks created around the Buddha in his lifetime was egalitarian, as one's caste and family were no longer significant, and decision-making was shared. Spiritual advancement was based upon disciplined meditational achievements. A high-born brahmin had to undertake the same practices as anyone else. Women had an equal capacity for spiritual awakening,[47] and nuns enjoyed relative independence and respect.

As Buddhism teaches non-attachment to the world and non-existence of the self, and its meditational disciplines aim to transcend life's sufferings and desires, politics and government may seem unimportant. Nonetheless, ideas about law and monarchy are found in early Buddhist texts.[48] The king should support agriculture and make sure that powerful members of his court don't exploit or over-tax farmers. Prosperous farmers will be able to support mendicant Buddhist monks, especially if devoting fewer resources to Vedic rites. A virtuous ruler will rule impartially, with the consent or at least acquiescence of his subjects, and without resorting to violence. In the parable of the Wheel-Turning Monarch, the ruler was a great conqueror but was himself ruled by 'principle'. 'A wheel-turning monarch knows what is right, knows principle, knows moderation, knows the right time, and knows the assembly.'[49] When the wheel-treasure appeared to a new king, he then became the next wheel-turning monarch. Following the wheel across the land, other rulers accepted his protection. He prohibited killing living creatures, lying, stealing, sexual misconduct and alcohol; he maintained the current level of taxation. When eventually this virtuous line of monarchs is broken by an heir who fails to adopt the duties of a wheel-turning monarch, the kingdom declines into disorder as the injunctions are disobeyed, one after another. As he fails to give to the poor and to provide protection and security, but rules according to his own ideas, a cycle of punishment and dishonesty commences, and human vices become common as the social order degenerates.[50] So a righteous ruler is better than a corrupt one, but ultimately the choice to follow the path to enlightenment is paramount, and this applies regardless of the political order.[51]

The first Buddhist council following the death of the Buddha was convened in Magadha, a kingdom on the Gangetic Plain that had been expanding by defeating neighbouring states. Buddhism and other non-Vedic sects gained strong followings among the mercantile *vaishya* caste at this time, and their political importance grew further in the Mauryan era.[52]

The Mauryan empire

Before the rise of the Mauryan empire in the late fourth century BCE, northern India consisted of numerous kingdoms and republics with advanced systems of administration and taxation. From the sixth century, the Indus valley belonged to the Achaemenian Persian empire (Chapter 3, Part 2) until the conquests of Alexander of Macedon in 327 BCE. His departure from Punjab created a power vacuum to the northwest, however. It was from this side of the Magadha kingdom that Chandragupta Maurya (r. 320–298 BCE) emerged to seize the throne. Late in life, tradition has it, Chandragupta renounced everything to become a Jain monk. His grandson Ashoka (304–232 BCE) inherited the throne in 269 and subdued most of the subcontinent.

The Edicts of Ashoka are a remarkable set of documents found in numerous locations around the subcontinent, literally carved in stone, mainly in the Prakrit language. (Some in the northeast of the empire are in Aramaic and Greek.) While many points are repeated, each of the carved edicts is unique and addresses issues arising in the particular location, seemingly dictated by the king himself. They were to be read aloud for the benefit of largely illiterate local audiences. They include exhortations to the highest ethical standards of public conduct and only rarely threaten punishment. It isn't possible to judge how closely they were actually followed 'on the ground', but they demonstrate how an imperial ruler once sought to promulgate principles of justice and improve the wellbeing of his subjects.

The Edicts call on all officials and subjects to live according to the *dhamma*[53] which is described as 'having few faults and many good deeds, mercy, charity, truthfulness, and purity'.[54] The king's rural officers and magistrates are entrusted with independent authority to judge and punish, but they must administer justice uniformly, fairly and impartially and work for the welfare and happiness of the people. The king promises to be always available to receive reports and to send teams of inspectors every few years to see how well his plan for the people is going. He repeats the principle of non-injury and calls for an end to the killing of animals. All subjects are enjoined to obey their parents, respect family and treat brahmins, ascetics and mendicants respectfully and generously. Ashoka had joined the Buddhist community, but the Edicts don't impose particular doctrines, and they call for mutual respect between the religions. He expresses remorse for the death, grief and dislocation caused by his wars of conquest and promises to reign without doing any further harm. All would be done according to the *dhamma*, as a unifying principle of justice and good, for the happiness of all subjects and for their progress towards heaven. The Edicts describe Ashoka as the father of the people. The principle of his rule thus combined benign paternalism with religious toleration and universal principles of justice in order to gain the loyalty of all castes to the centralised administration of his vast territory. One Edict expressed confidence that persuasion and admonition would improve adherence to *dhamma*, and that legislation and punishment would only be used reluctantly. Special officers of *dhamma* were appointed to work with the religious sects, distribute charity and praise acts of virtue. These officers didn't, however, replace tax-collectors, superintendents and magistrates.

We don't know how effective Ashoka was in bringing about tangible improvements in public administration, social order and wellbeing. There's no consensus about the extent to which imperial administration was effectively centralised around the capital, Pataliputra, nor how many of the pre-conquest regional rulers, laws and customs remained in place. Given the size and diversity of the subcontinent, it seems improbable that there could have been a uniform system of law and administration across all regions, down to the level of villages and farms. The Edicts mention pockets of resistance from forest people.

This idealised reign of social responsibility, toleration and justice coincided, it is said, with 30 years of peace and economic progress.[55] But the Mauryan dynasty collapsed within 50 years of Ashoka's death, even though there was no major catastrophe or economic decline to precipitate it. Contributing factors could have included the series of short-lived successors and the division of the empire into two, leaving the north-western frontier harder to defend from the successors of Alexander. The Mauryan regime depended heavily on the virtues and abilities of the ruler himself. It lacked a fully regulated state apparatus and system of laws, the constraints of which could have ensured a succession of principled, or at least harmless, rulers. Moreover, the selection of administrators appears to have been made personally by the ruler and would have been liable to substantial changes by successors. New appointees may have been less familiar with or committed to the original Ashokan principles of just conduct. Ashoka created a special cadre of officials whose job was to ensure that the *dhamma* was being practised and the welfare of the people was protected, with powers to enter households of any ethnic group, religion, caste or status. These officers could have become officious and overbearing, and hence unwelcome and counterproductive. Given the size of the empire, its administration would often have been slow and ineffective, and demands for greater self-determination or self-rule may have arisen.[56]

Arthashāstra

Indian literature preserves accounts of good government, in particular the Law Code of Manu (or *Manusmriti*) and the *Arthashāstra* of Kautilya. Neither should be taken to represent actual conduct of rulers, nor law and policy in the normative sense. They're better regarded as treatises or textbooks for education or advice, presenting ideal types, not real-world examples. Furthermore, they're compiled from pre-existing sources and/or drawn from lengthy traditions in politics and government, most of which are now lost.[57] They address two of the three main areas of human enterprise: *dharma* (law, justice) and *artha* (success, or statecraft) – the third being *kāma* (pleasure).

We find a pragmatic and detailed account of government in the *Arthashāstra*. Although this treatise on statecraft is a composite text, it was sometimes identified with Chanakya, chief minister of Chandragupta Maurya.[58] It describes in the abstract an ideal or typical monarchy rather than that of any identifiable state or region. While the descriptions of monarchy and fortified cities are in line with historical and archaeological evidence, we can't assume that it describes the actual statecraft of its times. It does however give us an outline or a set of intellectual coordinates, within which government (as practical imperatives and activities) could be thought in this classical age. Good policy, it advises, leads to success in the exertion of labour and the secure enjoyment of the fruits of one's labour. But good policy requires the appropriate use of punishment, and government is by definition the administration of punishment (the rod). Punishment that's too severe terrifies people, while lenience breeds contempt. Failure to punish leads to 'the law of the fish', where the strong devour the weak. Appropriate punishment, however, based on training and facts rather than passions, breeds respect.

As a monarchy, the success of the state depends on the training and self-discipline of the king. The ideal king has 'desire to learn, attentive listening, grasping, retention, comprehension, reasoning, rejection, and devotion to truth.' A rigorous education 'produces a keen intellect, a keen intellect produces disciplined performance, and disciplined performance produces the exemplary qualities of the self.' The ultimate aim of the king's education is 'mastery over the senses', accomplished 'by giving up passion, anger, greed, pride, conceit, and excitement.' The ultimate enemies of the king are his own sensations and emotions. If he lacks control of the senses, he will perish.[59] The king can't, however, carry out or supervise all undertakings, so he appoints and ranks advisers and ministers. This should be based on their capabilities, including their loyalty. The key adviser is the counsellor chaplain, who should be 'a man who comes from a very distinguished family and has an equally distinguished character, who is thoroughly trained in the Veda.' The king should follow his advice 'as a pupil his teacher, a son his father, and a servant his master.'[60]

The many practical concerns include the geographical and administrative organisation of the state, supervision of officials, collection of taxes, adjudication of disputes, waging war and forging alliances. The *Arthashāstra* advises on the uses and conduct of spies, informants and secret agents. To test the loyalty of high officials, the king may send an agent to tempt them into seeking his overthrow. One suggested approach is a honey-trap. The officials who refuse these offers have integrity. The *Arthashāstra* advises that the king's agents should infiltrate all parts of the realm as well as rival territories, and it sets out methods for recruiting disaffected people, foiling plots and detecting crime and tax evasion. The aim is 'success'. Righteousness is only affordable once the state is functioning securely and successfully.

Manusmriti

The Law Code of Manu is a treatise that mainly concerns *dharma*, or righteous and just conduct.[61] Of most interest for present purposes, however, is the chapter on rulers and government or the law for the king (*rājadharma*). This part 'drew extensively from' the *Arthashāstra*, but with greater concern for the divinity and spiritual progress of kings.[62] The king, according to Manu, is 'a great deity in human form'. He's likened to fire, and should never be regarded as 'just a human being'.[63] But the king has a dual nature, analogous with animals.

> He should hide his limbs like a tortoise and conceal his own weak points. He should ponder over his affairs like a heron, dart off like a rabbit, snatch like a wolf, and attack like a lion.[64]

His primary purpose is punishment, and hence protection of the people. The divinely given power to punish was created for the king, and the world would be corrupted and overturned without it. Basic policy aims are acquisition, preservation, augmentation and distribution.

> What he has not acquired, he should seek to acquire with military force; what he has acquired, he should preserve with vigilance; what he has preserved, he should augment through profitable investments; and what he has augmented, he should distribute through gifts.[65]

Hence his basic means are conquest, surveillance, investment and donation. All is ultimately the concern of the king, supported by advisers, officials and armed forces.

This sketches some of the evidence that remains from a vast subcontinent which saw diverse republics, kingdoms and empires and produced sophisticated literary, intellectual and religious traditions. Although unified empires did appear (and disappear) in India, this model didn't persist historically as it did in China. Extant Indian literature shows a sophisticated appreciation of public administration, military strategy, taxation, adjudication and surveillance. The personal attributes, conduct and training of the king are a central concern. The *Arthashāstra* shows an ability to think of government in purely secular terms. The Vedic tradition and the pre-eminence of the brahmin caste continued, however, while rulers were chosen normally from the warrior caste. Indian states relied mainly on monarchy, and hence on the personal attributes, self-discipline and trustworthiness of the king and his closest advisers.

Part 3: Greece

Whereas Chinese and Indian imperial expansion occupied vast continental spaces, the Greeks, due to over-population in their mountainous homelands, colonised many islands and coastal locations around the Mediterranean and Black Seas, stretching from (what we now call) Marseille to Crimea. They saw themselves as a culturally distinct Hellenic people with a common polytheistic religion but held no strong desire for imperial unity as in China. They remained in relatively small, independently governed city-states which forged alliances when needed. Aristotle claimed that the Greeks had 'the best constitutions', and that, if they united under one constitution, they would be 'capable of ruling all other people.'[66] But, perhaps because of their political disunity, Greek culture and philosophy were vibrant and innovative.

The Greek *polis* was both a territory and a community or city-state. It typically encompassed a relatively small area, governed from an urban centre protected by walls. The walled city formed the commercial, social and cultural centre of the *polis*. The Homeric epics of the eighth century BCE portray the *polis* as headed by a king, supported by a council of elders drawn from powerful families. By the fourth century, a wide variety of constitutions had evolved. Inherited kingship generally gave way to rule by magistrates appointed by councils of aristocrats who in turn consulted assemblies of citizens. In some cases, the citizens (*polites*), including the poorer ones, took a greater part due to their landholding (however small) and/or their military duties as hoplites (armoured infantrymen). The relative balance of powers between these three classes (kings, councillors and citizens at large) varied among the states. The politically active citizens didn't include women, foreigners or slaves, but a citizen's eligibility to participate in the governance of the *polis*, rather than simply to live as a subject, is one of the innovations of Greek public life. With the advent of lawgivers (notably Lycurgus of Sparta and Solon of Athens[67]) and the establishment of colonies, it appeared moreover that states could be designed along rational lines, rather than just evolve out of power struggles, ancient traditions or religious edicts. Greek intellectuals began to speculate rationally about different kinds of constitution and government, about virtuous statesmanship and about individual and collective wellbeing, thus creating the first comprehensive *political* philosophy.[68]

The Greeks became locked in a struggle, however, with their powerful eastern neighbour: the Achaemenian Persian Empire (Chapter 3, Part 2). The Ionian Greek cities of western Asia Minor were conquered by the Persians in 545 BCE. Revolts against Persian rule led to two Persian expeditions onto the Greek mainland in 490 and 480 BCE. The latter resulted in the evacuation and destruction of Athens, but the Persians were forced to withdraw after being defeated at the naval battle of Salamis and then on land at Plataea. From 478, Athens took the leading role in the Delian League to expel the Persians. Athenian imperial ambitions grew due to overconfidence within their democratic polity, and war with the Peloponnesian League, led by Sparta, followed in 431. The Athenians suffered a major defeat after attacking Syracuse (in Sicily) in 415. Eleven years later they surrendered to the Spartans, who appointed a short-lived oligarchy ('the thirty tyrants') to govern Athens. Democracy was restored to Athens in 403. Sparta was defeated, in its turn, by a Theban-led alliance in 371. The disunity of the Greek city-states left them ill-prepared to counteract the expansion of the Macedonian king, Philip II. Following the battle of Chaeronea in 338, the Macedonians took command of Greece and mounted an expedition against Persia, resulting in the extraordinary conquests by Alexander (who died in Babylon in 323) and a legacy of Hellenistic rulership and cultural influence as far east as the Indus Valley in today's Pakistan. How, then, were the two most powerful Greek states governed?

Sparta

Sparta was a diarchy, having two kings from parallel dynasties who ruled in tandem. The kings had priestly and judicial roles, but most importantly one of them would lead the army on campaign. The reforms of Lycurgus had instituted a magistracy, sharing executive powers with the kings and consisting of five *ephors* chosen annually by an assembly of citizens. There was also a council of elders (*gerousia*) of 28 members (men aged 60 and over) who were elected for life by the assembly, plus the two kings *ex officio*. Male citizens were landowners and treated as political equals. All citizens 30 years and older belonged to the assembly, but this only heard matters that were forwarded by the council and had little power to initiate policy or amend executive decrees. Moreover, the vast majority of the population of Sparta and its vassal state Messenia were serfs (*helots*) who did household and agricultural work and thus sustained citizens in their public and military duties. There were numerous other neighbouring communities (*perioikoi*) that had been conquered by the Spartans and retained their local government and ways of life – but were subjects and obligatory allies of Sparta. The Spartan citizens were a small minority compared to the conquered population.

Life for Spartan males was devoted to rigorous military training, beginning at age seven, and full military service from 21 to 60 years of age. Spartan women were relatively independent and leisured compared to women elsewhere in Greece at that time. They were educated and engaged in athletic, equestrian and cultural activities. Their physical training was much the same as men's, but less arduous – on the assumption that strong healthy women would produce strong children. According to Aristotle, 'something like two-fifths of all the land [was] possessed by women.'[69] The Spartans' self-discipline and devotion to law made them a formidable military force, widely admired, if mythologised, through the centuries since.[70] But the relative equality observed among the landowning Spartans was bought at the expense of the *helots*.[71]

Athens

Athens was Sparta's main strategic rival, and the two had completely different constitutions. Both were patriarchal, but Athenian women lacked the freedoms and relative equality of Spartan women. In Athens, girls were raised indoors, received no formal education and were trained to be silent.

> [Female citizens] were excluded from politics, had to have a male legal guardian who spoke for them in court, and were not legally entitled to make large financial transactions on their own. They could, however, control property and have their financial interests protected in law suits.[72]

Whereas the Spartans relied entirely on serf labour, in the Athenian household (*oikos*), women's productivity and management were economically important, for instance in weaving. Poorer women worked outside the home. Slavery was common, especially in mining and manufacturing, but only a minority of households could afford a slave.

Public political action and dialogue were the exclusive domain of free males – estimated to be as little as ten to twenty percent of the total resident population. Athens is rightly regarded as the birthplace of direct democracy, but it wasn't a representative system with elected lawmakers acting on behalf of their constituencies, as known today (Chapter 7, Part 2). The following account covers the reforms of Cleisthenes from 507 BCE. Those reforms were the result of dynastic rivalry between an oligarchic faction backed by Sparta and others who supported the blueprint for a new democratic constitution. It took a coup and a counter-coup (backed by a popular uprising) to transfer powers to 'the people'. Apart from two brief periods of oligarchy in 411 and 404, democracy in Athens lasted until its destruction by the Macedonians in 322.

The best way to understand the Athenian constitution is from the bottom up, as Cleisthenes proposed a radical restructuring from the grassroots. Local government, military recruitment and the classification of citizens had previously been based on ancient clan or tribal associations, favouring selection for offices on grounds of wealth and pedigree. The traditional tribes were abolished as administrative units and replaced by a system based on the local *deme*, which could be a village or settlement or (in the city of Athens itself) ward or neighbourhood, of which altogether there are estimated to have been 139. Each *deme* had its own leader and assembly. Membership of the *deme* was for life and passed on to children,[73] even if one moved outside of it. Each member, regardless of wealth or pedigree, became identified with the *deme* as a citizen; local participation was enhanced through its religious cults and ceremonies.

The *polis* (city of Athens, port of Piraeus and surrounding territory of Attica) was divided into ten 'tribes', each of which incorporated a portion of the coastal, inland and urban regions, thus creating new political units each of which encompassed a social and geographical cross-section, and which broke up the old alliances. Each tribe recruited a contingent of cavalry and infantrymen and elected a general.[74] In the 500-member council, each tribe held an equal share of seats (50), to which each *deme* contributed its proportional share. Membership of the council was chosen by lots annually from among (male) citizens 30 or over, but with an income qualification that excluded the poorer half. No one was allowed to serve two consecutive one-year terms or more than twice in a lifetime. One of the 50-member tribal groups would preside over the council, and this role circulated around all the ten tribes, each for one-tenth of the year. The rapid turnover of membership and presidency of the council prevented it from becoming an oligarchy and widened involvement. The council initiated and managed the agenda of the assembly, and executed its decisions, including financial orders. It ordered the flow of business and protected the assembly from being 'ambushed' by proposals from the floor.

All male citizens 20 and over could sit, speak and vote in the assembly ('the controlling body of the state'[75]), and hence have a share in passing laws and decrees. The assembly approved the ten generals (one from each tribe) and other military leaders by show of hands. The numerous administrative magistrates (who oversaw courts, public services and accounts) and jurors (who were also, in effect, judges) were chosen by lot from among citizen-volunteers 30 years and older. There were also paid secretaries and under-secretaries, the latter role being open to foreigners and slaves. So the popular assembly was the sovereign decision-making body. But not every one of the thousands of citizens would have spoken. One could hire speech-writers and orators for the courts or the assembly. Political influence required the rhetorical skill to win the confidence of the mass of citizens in an open forum – and that required education.[76] A wider stratum of 'middling' citizens became more politically active in the latter half of the fifth century BCE, due to social mobility;[77] but wealthy slave-owners with more leisure-time enjoyed a distinct advantage. Free labourers with no education would have had little say. Nonetheless, the level of power-sharing was relatively high.

Any eligible citizen could put a proposal to or speak at the assembly (although probably only a minority did so in practice) or put himself forward for service in the courts. With the use of lots for many official roles, any candidate stood an equal chance; thus, political professionalism was minimised and there was a high rate of rotation.[78] This energised the citizenry and boosted their commitment to the common defence, as witnessed especially during the Persian wars. But wealth still mattered, as social status and informal influence would have favoured those wealthy individuals and families who could afford entertainments, donations and monuments. Training in rhetoric was in high demand, given the forum-style government, also favouring the rich. The reforms of Cleisthenes preserved, moreover, the ancient tribunal, or Areopagus, as a 'guardian of the laws' to which senior magistrates were admitted on retirement, although its powers diminished over time.

An unusual example of the arts of government was Athenian ostracism. This could be undertaken once in any year if the assembly voted to do so, on a minimum of 6000 votes. Each voter scratched the name of the person he wanted to be banished on a potsherd (*ostraca*) and the person named on the largest number of them had to quit Attica and not come back for ten years – although with no loss of property. This severe punishment was inflicted on several occasions to expel a leader (often a general) who had attracted great public disapproval.[79] It counts as a practice of government as it restrained the conduct of prominent individuals and factions, and it was an executive action of the sovereign assembly. As a decision of an assembly, and not a monarch or magistrate, this shows the character of Athenian democracy: citizens collectively governed, in this case by making an example of someone. The sovereign power over life can mean in practice the termination of biological life (execution) or the suspension of civil life (banishment), and ostracism was the latter.

Socrates and Plato

So what was wrong with democracy, according to Athens' leading intellectuals? We can start with Socrates, who was condemned to death for corrupting the young and dishonouring the gods. He bowed to the sentence and voluntarily drank deadly poisonous hemlock on the grounds (as Plato records in *The Apology of Socrates*) that we can't pick and choose between those actions of the state that we approve of and those we don't. The *polis* wasn't a prison, as he had been free to leave it. Having chosen to stay, he was obliged to accept all its judgements, not just those that suited him.

Socrates died in 399 BCE when his most famous follower, Plato (427–347 BCE), was 28. Plato's *Republic* is a dialogue in which Socrates portrays an ideal *polis* founded on the principle of justice as harmony. The conversation gets heated when the intemperate Thrasymachus tells Socrates that justice, even if codified in law, is basically that which serves the interests of the strong. Can Socrates convince us that justice means doing what's inherently right, and that it makes us better off than seeking advantage over others?

Socrates argues that there exist abstract and eternal 'forms' which are the true essences behind qualities such as beauty, equality and the good, and which underlie our differing perceptions and conflicting opinions. There exists a realm of harmonious and unchanging lawfulness that we can discover by using reason and which should guide our actions. But it takes a lengthy philosophical education to acquire knowledge of this ultimate truth – the form of the good. The wisest and most learned (who may equally be women or men) have seen the form of the good; they understand what's right and just: so they should be the ones who rule. Rulership shouldn't be a prerogative of the high-born, the wealthy or the powerful, let alone the many, but reserved for philosopher-kings. These ideal rulers would be denied private wealth, property and family associations, and they would live communally, so that they would rule impartially for the whole *polis* and not out of self-interest. Society would be strictly divided into three classes: the ruling philosopher-kings (Guardians), the military (Auxiliaries) and the farmers and artisans.

Aiming for justice as harmony and for the rule of reason (over wealth, honour or hedonism), Socrates portrays a *polis* that's closer to Spartan communalism than Athenian egalitarianism and openness. He wasn't convinced of the benefits of democracy, which he describes as 'an agreeable anarchic form of society, with plenty of variety, which treats all men as equals, whether they are equal or not'.[80] People accustomed to democracy complain about the slightest affront to their liberties. But 'an excessive desire for liberty undermines democracy and leads to the demand for tyranny [or] a reaction to an extreme of subjection.'[81] Democracy, or rule by the majority of free citizens, was disharmonious.

The good person and the wise ruler not only do what's right and just, they also get much more *eudaimonia* than the tyrant, Socrates argues. *Eudaimonia* may be translated as prosperity, wellbeing, happiness or flourishing. It was best judged when looking back at a person's whole life. Power and wealth that are acquired by dishonest or unjust means only lead to misery. We should therefore establish justice within our souls and within the city – and there exists an eternal 'template' to guide us in doing so. This universalism contrasts starkly with the actual discord of democratic politics and the diversity of the city-states. But it implies that a harmonious and just order of things is at least conceivable. Socrates' prescription, however, requires citizens to abandon many freedoms, such as the formation of one's own family and the enjoyment of poetry. (Poets are to be excluded from the republic because poetry, being based on illusions, is inherently immoral.) In *The Republic*, the philosopher-kings are sage-like virtuous rulers, who presumably never disagree with one another and whom the lower classes unquestioningly trust. Even Plato's less utopian dialogue *The Laws* – which advocates a stronger role for law as well as wise rulership – disapproves of change, and says that those who oversee the law shouldn't be questioned.

Aristotle

Aristotle (384–322 BC) differs greatly from Plato, offering a more pragmatic and down-to-earth approach. His description of *eudaimonia* isn't altogether different from the qualities of life advocated in contemporary happiness literature. Hedonistic pleasures and wealth alone don't suffice. Moderate wealth is necessary for a good life, but accumulation for its own sake is 'unnatural'. Good relationships of love or friendship (*philía*) are essential for the best quality of life – and the noblest kind of *philía* involves generosity and the love of others for their own sake, not for pleasure or for their usefulness. The best way of life includes leisure time for higher thought or contemplation. *Eudaimonia* is an activity of the soul (*psyche*), and we achieve it best by using the rational, ethical mind. Emotions did matter to Aristotle, but he wouldn't agree with our modern mantras about following our feelings or being passionate about everything we do.

Aristotle noticed that animals express pain and pleasure, and they associate in herds, flocks and so on. Humans too are sentient social animals, and belonging to a community is necessary for their sustenance. But because humans have the faculties of speech and of reason, they must deliberate on matters of justice and equality. 'Man is a political animal' – that is, an animal destined by nature to live 'civilly', in a *polis* and not a mere herd. Justice is a defining feature of the *polis*, and the state's purpose is to advance the ultimate aim of the individuals who compose it – to maximise their opportunities for *eudaimonia*.[82]

Unlike Plato, Aristotle doesn't propose an ideal state, but looks for a practically possible compromise, considering real-world political claims and class interests. A state's constitution (*politeia*) includes the sovereign power, the distribution of its public offices, and the aims to which these give effect. So what kind of constitution is the most conducive to achieving *eudaimonia*? In proper or correct constitutions, the rulers aim for the common good; in incorrect or 'deviant' ones, they seek their own advantage. This polarity is then divided by three, depending on whether the state is ruled by one, by a few or by the many. Monarchies and aristocracies are 'correct', as compared with the 'deviant' forms of tyranny and oligarchy, respectively. Democracy is considered 'deviant' because the poor majority rule in their own interests, alienating the wealthy and high-born. In the worst of democracies, according to Aristotle, the people rule by decree and not by law, and they end up following a demagogue. The demagogue is to the people what the flatterer is to the tyrant; such a democracy is tyranny by the people.[83] In the best of democracies, however, the property-owning males elect the wealthier or more capable citizens to the top offices to govern on their behalf. These magistrates will behave well, he says, as the populace can hold them to account without taking too much time away from making their own living. This sounds close to modern representation, but Aristotle recommended a middle way between democracy (rule by the majority) and oligarchy (rule by a wealthy minority). This 'polity' would permit participation by the majority of middle-strata citizens, limited to those who own arms – thus imposing a property qualification, as the weapons and armour required for the infantry (the hoplites) were costly. The higher public offices would be limited to those with greater wealth or ability. This constitution, Aristotle argued, had the best chance of stability, being a compromise between the class interests of the wealthy few and the middle-ranking male citizens.

Athenian democracy is sometimes idealised as the original or pure form of democracy, as it was more direct and it inducted all citizens into its offices. But there was bitter rivalry between elite families. The wealthy were more likely to be heard, either because they had education and oratorical skills or because they could afford the best orators to speak on their behalf. Women, slaves and resident foreigners (including Aristotle as a Macedonian) played no part. Sparta too has often been idealised as a disciplined and martial society in which women had much more freedom. But both city-states were harsh overlords to their weaker neighbours, treating others as inherently inferior slave labour. The enduring brilliance of the Greeks, however, lies in their willingness to experiment and reform, and then to record in writing their history and ideas. The reforms of

Cleisthenes and the more ancient lawgivers show that they could imagine and design a better form of polity or constitution. The Greeks' rationalism insisted that our individual and collective fate and prosperity aren't due to the whims of the gods but lie within ourselves. The idea of mixed government, derived from Aristotle's categorisation into three (rule by one, by a few or by the many), influenced political theorists, Christian and Muslim, for many centuries.

Conclusion

This chapter has outlined practices and ideas that arose in three of the great ancient civilisations, revealing the diversity of arts of government and locating a wide range of intellectual 'survey pegs' within which rulership and statecraft were understood. One may begin with rulers themselves, or 'how to govern oneself'. As the *Arthashāstra* tells us, the king who lacks control of his own senses and feelings will perish. The ancient Greek and Chinese philosophers similarly condemned rulers who lacked self-discipline. Furthermore, government addresses the question of how to guide or manage others, often across long distances and in large populations, and to regulate activities and control the flow of information. Although the communication technologies of those times were limited to handwriting and horsepower, enduring techniques of government were well developed: written laws (that were publicly communicated), archives, policing, taxation, money, public works and distribution of basic goods. This regulation of civil and economic life was legitimised by all-encompassing principles with deep symbolic efficacy, such as Heaven, *dharma*, justice, harmony, benevolence, virtue and *eudaimonia*, among others. And day-to-day government necessitated collective efforts to maintain respect for customs, enforce laws, punish transgressors, distribute rewards and honours, and standardise terminologies, weights, measures and daily, monthly and annual timetables. Information had to be gathered (often covertly) and the flow of money into and out of treasuries maintained and strictly monitored. Armed forces had to be marshalled, equipped and trained. These enduring arts of government were already well understood in ancient times.

Looked at from one angle, there's been little change in the fundamentals of government since ancient times. A basic 'grammar' of politics, rulership and statecraft persists. While Aristotle's natural science is of interest only to specialists nowadays, his observations about ethics and politics still make sense. We reject his views about slaves, but his assertion that states exist for the purpose of improving the chances of living well, collectively and individually, sounds familiar. Aristotle's logic was utterly different from ancient Chinese thought, but the abiding questions of Chinese philosophy ('what type of person is fit to govern and lead others; how can we create order in society'[84]) were familiar to both Plato and Aristotle. They still make sense today, as we question the character and integrity of political leaders and witness political polarisation and protest.

Notes

1 The main exception is the period of disunion from the end of the Han dynasty in 220 CE through to 600 CE.
2 In contrast, the Europeans, excepting the era of imperial Roman rule, were politically and culturally disunited, often violently.
3 Bodde, 1986; Finer, 1999; Keay, 2011; Pines, 2012.
4 Bodde, 1986.
5 Bennett Peterson, 2000.
6 Shang Yang, 2019, trans. Yuri Pines.
7 Bodde, 1986, p. 36.
8 Ibid., p. 52, abridged.
9 Known for the terracotta warriors.
10

> The idea that "All-under-Heaven" should be unified under the aegis of the single monarch predated the imperial unification of 221 BCE and directly contributed to it. Indeed, it may be argued that this belief remains the single most important legacy of the traditional political culture well into our own day.
>
> Pines, 2012, pp. 11–12, abridged

11 Nivison, 1999.
12 Confucius, 1979, p. 112, XII.1, trans. D.C. Lau.
13 Ibid., p. 112, XII.2.
14 Ibid., p. 113, XII.8.
15 Ibid., p. 115, XII.17–9.
16 Ibid., p. 63, II.3.
17 Bennett Peterson, 2000; Raphals, 1998.
18 Mencius, 1984, p. 3; Book I, part A, §1.
19 'If the prince made serious mistakes, they [ministers of royal blood] would remonstrate with him. But if repeated remonstrations fell on deaf ears, they would depose him.' Mencius, 1984, p. 219; Book V, part B, §9. See also Sterckx, 2019.
20 D.C. Lau, Introduction, in Mencius, 1984, p. xxxv.
21 Nivison, 1999, p. 796.
22 Xunzi, 2003, p. 48, trans. Burton Watson.
23 Ibid.
24 Tan, 2002.
25 Mo Di and Johnston, 2010, p. 135. Confucians couldn't accept this idea, as 'by loving everyone equally, one fails to acknowledge the ethical significance of family relationships and thereby sinks to the level of beasts.' Tan, 2002, p. 173.
26 Mo Di and Johnston, 2010, p. 27.
27 Sterckx, 2019.
28 Nivison, 1999; Zhuangzi, 2013, trans. Burton Watson.
29 Ames, 1994, p. 46.
30 Shang Yang, 2019, p. 158.
31 Burton Watson, 'Introduction', in Feizi, 2003, p. 5.
32 Unfortunately for Han Fei, the minister Li Si advised the king of Qin that Han Fei shouldn't be trusted. He was imprisoned, and Li Si is said to have persuaded him to end his own life with poison.
33 Nivison, 1999, p. 804.
34 Feizi, 2003, p. 17.
35 Ibid., p. 25.
36 Finer, 1999, vol. II.
37 Of all the cultural factors that advanced political unity, 'there is little question that the uniformity of written language (in contrast to the diversity of the spoken dialects) has been more influential than any other.' Bodde, 1986, p. 58.

38 Ibid., pp. 59–66.
39 Ibid., pp. 69–72.
40 Ibid., p. 81.
41 Ibid., pp. 85–90.
42 Ibid., p. 90.
43 Thapar, 2002.
44 Ibid., p. 172.
45 Sen, 2005, p. 10.
46 Thapar, 2002.
47 With the significant reservation that 'the body of a Buddha is always sexed as male.' Balkwill, 2018, p. 2.
48 Moore, 2016.
49 'Wielding Power'. Sutta Central. Retrieved from https://suttacentral.net/an5.131/en/sujato on 16 November 2020.
50 'The Wheel-Turning Monarch'. Sutta Central. Retrieved from https://suttacentral.net/dn26/ on September 30 2018.
51 Moore, 2016.
52 Keay, 2010, p. 89.
53 The Prakrit equivalent of *dharma*.
54 Translations of the Edicts are from Thapar, 2012, Appendix V.
55 A 'contemporary cult' has recently emerged around the historical figure of Ashoka. Thapar, 2012, p. 269.
56 Ibid.
57 Chousalkar, 2018.
58 Olivelle dates it much later, between 50 and 125 CE. See: Olivelle, 2013, p. 29. The extant manuscript itself came to light only in 1905, and its scholarship is still evolving.
59 Ibid., pp. 69–71.
60 Ibid., p. 74.
61 The Code of Manu became controversial in modern times, as it was adopted in 1772 by British administrators in India as a primary source of laws for Hindus, alongside *sharia* for Muslims. This anachronistic appropriation of the (sometimes inconsistent) prescriptions found in the Code ignored long traditions of local judicial practices and unwritten legal precepts. It has been blamed for impeding progress by assuming one version of the caste system and for perpetuating the subordination of women. The Code sets out detailed and exacting prescriptions for the brahmin, with strict divisions of labour between castes. The shudra are limited to the service of those of higher birth, and they are said to be barred from accumulation of wealth. And a woman, it says, 'must never seek to live independently. She must never want to separate herself from her father, husband, or sons; for by separating herself from them, a woman brings disgrace on both families.' Olivelle, 2004, Ch 5, §149. See also: Rocher, 1993; Tharoor, 2017, ch. 4.
62 McClish, 2017, p. 264.
63 Code of Manu, Olivelle, 2004, ch. 7, §8.
64 Ibid., ch. 7, §105–6.
65 Ibid., ch. 7, §101.
66 Aristotle, 1999, p. 410, §1327b 32.
67 Lycurgus is possibly a figure of legend only, but is reputed to have laid down the communistic and militaristic constitution of Sparta in the ninth century BCE. In 494/3 BCE, Solon was appointed as *archon* or chief magistrate and reformed Athens' constitution to make wealth, rather than noble birth, the criterion of eligibility for office-holding, and to devolve some powers to the assembly.
68 Finer, 1999, vol. I; Mitchell, 2015.
69 Aristotle, 1999, p. 144, §1270a. 'The wealthiest women in mainland Greece were Spartans.' Pomeroy, 2002, p. 82.
70 Hodgkinson and Morris, 2012.

71 Finer, 1999, vol. I.
72 Ibid.
73 Following a law of 451 BCE,

> citizenship would be conferred only on children whose mother and father both were Athenians. Previously, the offspring of Athenian men who married non-Athenian women were granted citizenship. Aristocratic men in particular had tended to marry rich foreign women. This new law enhanced the status of Athenian mothers and made Athenian citizenship a more exclusive category.
>
> Martin, n.d., abridged

74 Not by lot in this case, for obvious reasons; and generals had to be approved by the assembly.
75 Thorley, 2004, p. 34.
76 Finer, 1999, vol. I; Mitchell, 2015; Thorley, 2004.
77 Paillard, 2014.
78 Manin, 1997.
79 'The ostracism was seen as something of a farce.' Thorley, 2004, pp. 44–5. It wasn't used after 417, when Hyperbolos called for it but saw it used against him (ibid., p. 90). In historical hindsight, ostracism was sometimes unjustified.
80 Plato, 2007, p. 294.
81 Ibid., pp. 299, 301, abridged.
82 Aristotle, 1999, p. 60, I, ii.
83 Ibid., p. 251, IV, iv.
84 Sterckx, 2019, p. xii.

References

Ames, Roger. 1994. *The Art of Rulership: A Study of Ancient Chinese Political Thought.* Albany: State University of New York Press.

Aristotle. 1999. *The Politics.* Edited by T.A. Sinclair and T.J. Saunders (trans). London: Penguin.

Balkwill, Stephanie. 2018. 'Why Does a Woman Need to Become a Man in Order to Become a Buddha?: Past Investigations, New Leads.' *Religion Compass* 12 (8): e12270.

Bennett Peterson, Barbara. 2000. *Notable Women of China.* New York, NY: Routledge.

Bodde, D. 1986. 'The State and Empire of Ch'in.' In *The Cambridge History of China*, by Denis Twitchett and Michael Loewe, 20–102. Cambridge: Cambridge University Press.

Chousalkar, Ashok S. 2018. *Revisiting the Political Thought of Ancient India: Pre-Kautilyan Arthashastra Tradition.* New Delhi, India: Sage.

Confucius. 1979. *The Analects.* London: Penguin

Feizi, Han. 2003. *Han Feizi: Basic Writings.* Edited by Burton Watson. New York, NY: Columbia University Press.

Finer, S.E. 1999. *The History of Government.* Oxford: Oxford University Press.

Hodkinson, Stephen, and Ian Macgregor Morris. 2012. *Sparta in Modern Thought: Politics, History and Culture.* Swansea: Classical Press of Wales.

Keay, John. 2011. *China: A History.* New York, NY: Basic Books.

———. 2010. *India: A History.* New York, NY: Grove Press.

Manin, Bernard. 1997. *The Principles of Representative Government.* Cambridge: Cambridge University Press.

Martin, Thomas R. n.d. 'An Overview of Classical Greek History from Mycenae to Alexander.' *Perseus Digital Library.* Accessed April 10, 2020. http://www.perseus.tufts.edu/hopper/text?doc=Perseus:text:1999.04.0009.

McClish, Mark. 2017. 'King.' In *The Oxford History of Hinduism: Hindu Law: A New History of Dharmaśāstra*, by Patrick Olivelle and Donald R. Davis, 257–72. Oxford: Oxford University Press.

Mencius. 1984. *Mencius*. Edited by D.C. Lau. Hong Kong: The Chinese University Press.

Mitchell, Thomas N. 2015. *Democracy's Beginning: The Athenian Story*. New Haven, CT: Yale University Press.

Mo Di, and Ian Johnston. 2010. *The Mozi: A Complete Translation*. Hong Kong: The Chinese University of Hong Kong Press.

Moore, Matthew J. 2016. *Buddhism and Political Theory*. New York, NY: Oxford University Press.

Nivison, David Shepherd. 1999. 'The Classical Philosophical Writings.' In *The Cambridge History of Ancient China: From the Origins of Civilization to 221 BC*, by Michael Loewe and Edward L. Shaughnessy, 745–812. Cambridge: Cambridge University Press.

Olivelle, Patrick. 2013. *King, Governance, and Law in Ancient India: Kautilya's Arthasastra*. New York, NY: Oxford University Press.

———. 2004. *The Law Code of Manu*. Oxford: Oxford University Press.

Paillard, Elodie. 2014. 'The Structural Evolution of Fifth-Century Athenian Society: Archaeological Evidence and Literary Sources.' *Mediterranean Archaeology* 27: 77–84.

Pines, Yuri. 2012. *The Everlasting Empire: The Political Culture of Ancient China and Its Imperial Legacy*. Princeton, NJ: Princeton University Press.

Plato. 2007. *The Republic*. Edited by Desmond Lee (trans). London: Penguin.

Pomeroy, Sarah B. 2002. *Spartan Women*. Oxford: Oxford University Press.

Raphals, Lisa. 1998. *Sharing the Light: Representations of Women and Virtue in Early China*. Albany: State University of New York Press.

Rocher, Ludo. 1993. 'Law Books in an Oral Culture: The Indian "Dharmaśāstras".' *Proceedings of the American Philosophical Society* 137 (2): 254–67.

Sen, Amartya. 2005. *The Argumentative Indian: Writings on Indian History, Culture and Identity*. London: Penguin/Allen Lane.

Shang, Yang. 2019. *The Book of Lord Shang: Apologetics of State Power in Early China*. Edited by Yuri Pine. Chicago, IL: Columbia University Press.

Sterckx, Roel. 2019. *Chinese Thought from Confucius to Cook Ding*. London: Penguin.

Tan, Sor-Hoon. 2002. 'Between Family and State Relational Tensions in Confucian Ethics.' In *Mencius : Contexts and Interpretations*, by Alan K. Chan, 169–88. Honolulu: University of Hawaii Press.

Thapar, Romila. 2012. *Aśoka and the Decline of the Mauryas*. Oxford: Oxford University Press.

———. 2002. *Early India: From the Origins to AD 1300*. London: Allen Lane.

Tharoor, Shashi. 2017. *Inglorious Empire: What the British Did to India*. Melbourne, Australia: Scribe.

Thorley, John. 2004. *Athenian Democracy*. London: Routledge.

Xunzi. 2003. *Xunzi; Basic Writings*. Edited by Burton Watson. New York, NY: Columbia University Press.

Zhuangzi. 2013. *The Complete Works of Zhuangzi*. Edited by Burton Watson. New York, NY: Columbia University Press.

3

THE GREAT EMPIRES

Rome, Persia and China

In 343 BCE, Aristotle of Stagira left his studies in Athens to tutor prince Alexander of Macedon. After the Macedonians' victory over the Greeks in 338, Aristotle returned to Athens to establish his own school at the Lyceum.[1] He was a foreign resident of Athens, not a citizen. Then in 323 Alexander of Macedon, after a short but stellar career conquering the Persian empire, died in Babylon. Once the news of Alexander's death reached Athens, Aristotle left again due to anti-Macedonian sentiment. He had made (or led) a major study of constitutions, including those of Athens, Crete and Carthage. By that time Rome had expanded beyond its city-state boundaries to conquer the Etruscan town of Veii to the north (in 396 BCE), and south to conquer Greek colonies and establish some of its own in Campania, thus making Rome the dominant Latin city. No one yet knew that this rising power on the western side of the Italian peninsula would become the capital of a great empire.

While the last chapter looked at the formative political ideas of three ancient civilisations, the present one considers the practices of government in three full-fledged empires. The word *empire* descends from the Latin *imperium*, meaning the sovereign or magisterial powers invested in a person or office. In contemporary English, an empire is an extensive polity encompassing numerous peoples or nations, ruled from a metropolitan capital. This chapter goes from west to east, beginning with the republican Roman constitution and its eventual subordination by emperors. Did the sheer pressure of Rome's expansion and wealth overturn the political ethics of service to the republic that had evolved over four centuries? Then we turn to Persia's Achaemenian and Sassanian empires; then to China under the Han dynasty. We consider how these large and diverse empires were able to operate relatively cohesively. Although this chapter is more about practices than theories, we'll encounter ideas about 'ethics of self-mastery' for emperors and statesmen including a remarkable Chinese textbook on how to rule.

DOI: 10.4324/9781003166955-3

Part 1: Rome

Aristotle would have noted some interesting features of the Roman constitution. The founding line of kings had come to an end in 509 BCE, to be replaced by a *res publica* – an entity or thing of the people. The former monarchical power (*imperium*) was divided among a number of magistrates subject to popular assemblies, checks and balances, veto powers and informal conventions. This complex constitution developed gradually through conflicts between the common plebeian class and the ruling patricians, to give the plebeians greater access to public offices, influence over law-making and the right to marry into patrician families. 'By 300 B.C., the plebeian élite had largely achieved equality with the patricians;'[2] but this was a co-opted minority of the plebs. Although the assembly of the plebeians could elect tribunes with sweeping powers, no poor citizen had a hope of becoming a tribune: the costs of acquiring and maintaining high office were too great. As imperial adventures created extreme wealth for the few, political violence and class conflict only intensified.

The republic

The Roman constitution arose initially to end monarchy and manage class conflict, rather than to limit powers by separating different branches of government. It was never fully codified in writing and was always a work in progress, so any portrayal of it, especially such a brief one as this, is necessarily partial. But we begin with the assemblies, followed by the executive and judicial magistrates.

The senate was a policy advisory or consultative body of former top magistrates, nominated for life, that met only when summoned by a consul or praetor (see below) and spoke only to those matters put to it. It had no particular legal authorisation, but by convention, it was 'the central steering authority of the republic'.[3] Three popular assemblies could pass laws, but only met when summoned; they only voted on propositions handed to them, on a yes or no basis, with no formal debate. The *comitia centuriata* was an assembly of the citizen army, arranged in 'centuries', each stratified according to wealth, and with votes weighted towards the wealthy. It elected annually the higher magistrates who would rule for the coming year. The *comitia tributa* consisted of the same people, but with equal voting weight. It decided on war and peace. The *concilium plebis* was a popular assembly, organised like the *comitia tributa* but with a countervailing power, as it excluded the patricians and was overseen by the lower magistrates it elected – the plebeian tribunes and aediles.

As for the magistracies, the most distinguished were the two censors, who were former consuls elected for five-year terms. They acted jointly, primarily to undertake the census, classifying persons as slave or free, citizen or non-citizen, and assigning each citizen to a class based on wealth. This latter classification could advance or block a political career. The highest executive office with *imperium* was the consulship. There were two consuls as joint heads of state and commanders-in-chief, but only for one year. Re-election was only possible once in a lifetime, and only following a ten-year stand-down – although with important exceptions. The praetors, whose number grew to six, had delegated powers of *imperium*, primarily judicial and law-making for Rome itself or its provinces, or in command of armies. There were two pairs of aediles whose tasks were urban governance and market supervision within Rome; they also provided or paid personally for games and other entertainments. Under those magistrates with *imperium* (the consuls and praetors) there were the quaestors (numbering eventually 20), who managed the treasury, public revenues and archives. The tribunes of the plebs, elected by the *concilium plebis*, wielded considerable powers of veto over the other magistrates and could intercede on behalf of any plebeian aggrieved by a magistrate's actions – but they lacked any share of *imperium*. They grew in number from two to ten, and the main formal check on their quite sweeping powers was the veto of a fellow tribune.[4]

Due to dissent, Rome's oligarchs had been forced to compromise with the plebs and to share decision-making in order to maintain popular commitment to the common defence and expansion of the republic. Ancient authors, notably the Greek historian Polybius (c. 200–118 BCE) and the Roman lawyer Marcus Tullius Cicero (106–43 BCE),[5] believed that the republican government that included the three main social classes was the factor that gave Rome its unity of purpose. Niccolò Machiavelli (1469–1527 CE) would also later argue that this mixed government of 'princely' consuls, the aristocratic senate, and the plebeian assemblies and tribunes produced stability and led to success, 'since all three kinds of government there had their part.'[6] In addition, Machiavelli believed that the Romans' religion was essential for their civilisation and for the discipline of armies. Their fear of breaking oaths and respect for omens and auspices were indispensable, he claimed, and we may agree that these customs effectively bound people to duties and mutual obligations. Rome's successes included expansions into Sicily, Sardinia and the Iberian Peninsula (by 200 BCE), and victory in the Punic wars against Carthage (sacked in 146 BCE). The Romans didn't simply replicate their city-state republican model in their colonies and conquered provinces. Adaptations were made to an extent that 'a map of the states of Italy in 264 B.C. compiled on the basis of their juridical relationship to Rome looks like a rather confusing mosaic.'[7] Cities such as Capua (in Campania, south of Rome) were incorporated on the grounds that the people would have rights and duties as Roman citizens but without the vote (*cives sine suffragio*), creating a 'municipality' that allowed autonomous local administration. Nonetheless Rome placed limits on conquered peoples, and some rebelled against such 'second-class' citizenship. Other colonies were created as Latin settlements, meaning that Romans and those from other allied cities of Latium were included. This gave Rome solid bases from which to extend military, economic and cultural influence, and to increase manpower while opening opportunities for poorer Romans who were willing to emigrate. Other rival states formed treaties with Rome on differing terms depending on how readily they capitulated.[8]

Governance of distant provinces meant slow and hazardous travel. Outside Rome 'commanders did not face nearly as many restrictions on their official powers [as within Rome], and subordinates might often find themselves in semi-independent positions, without effective oversight.'[9] Magistrates appointed as commanders of distant provinces were initially given *imperium* over that territory but, during the second century BCE, the senate took over their appointments (so they were no longer elected by the people) and increasingly supervised them, including transits to and from their posts. Commanders were not to lead expeditions outside of the provinces to which they were appointed; nonetheless, they possessed considerable powers as judges and arbitrators within them. Appointments were normally for one year but with possible 'prorogation' for a second year. Laws were introduced to control their succession, to guard against treason and to hold them responsible for their subordinates' conduct.[10] The provinces went from being thinly administered military commands to more defined territorial entities with defensible borders. The convention developed that consuls and praetors should spend their year's magistracy entirely within Rome, and then have extended *imperium* to command a province and its army for one year.

Rome didn't have a permanent bureaucracy, although magistrates had a small salaried staff to carry out orders.[11] As the annual turnover of magistrates was relatively high, continuity and institutional memory resided in the Senate. This didn't prevent provincial governors from plundering and exploiting the provinces for their own and their friends' enrichment, then evading prosecution by being well connected in the capital. On the other hand, courts and laws were in place to compensate foreigners for theft and extortion. As Cicero demonstrated, there was genuine concern for justice and impartiality in government.

> The men chosen to rule [Rome] in ancient times were those who enjoyed a great popular reputation for justice; and if they were believed to be intelligent as well, there was no limit to the advantages people expected to obtain under their leadership. But the main thing the leaders had to provide was justice. Indeed it is a quality that must be cultivated and maintained by every possible means. This must be done for its own sake – for that is what justice means, its very essence. But it is also true that just dealings add honour and glory to one's reputation.[12]

All the same, an informal *realpolitik* had evolved that made the formal constitution look like 'a sham'.[13] What really counted was a general's vast personal following (*clientela*) including sometimes whole communities who owed him *fides* or loyalty. And the most powerful and transformative leaders, such as Sulla, Pompey and the Caesars, bent or changed the rules.[14]

Roman women were neither secluded in the home nor segregated socially from the male company as Athenian women were, and they enjoyed some independent legal rights after the death of their fathers. But no woman ever held public office. Cornelia Africana (c. 195–115 BCE) is remembered, however, as a model Roman woman of learning and virtue. After the death of her husband, she remained a widow and refused a proposal of marriage from Egypt's Ptolemy VIII, devoting herself instead to the education of her children – particularly her sons, Tiberius and Gaius Gracchus, who were elected tribunes by the people's assembly in 133 and 123 BCE, respectively. They were popular champions of reforms that would redistribute land to poorer Romans and subsidise grain – and they were both murdered, along with thousands of their followers, by members of the senatorial elite.[15] The gloves came off; politics became factionalised, violent and unscrupulous. Civil war ensued, extending to many Italian states who sought either to free themselves from Roman domination or to gain full citizenship. But 'Rome was able to secure victory as soon as she made the political concession of extending citizenship to all the inhabitants of Italy south of the Po Valley (90/89 B.C.).'[16] This in turn led to new administrative problems for the census and the popular assemblies. Worse though, the strict distinctions between civil and military, or citizen and enemy, began in practice to break down. The traditional republican virtues of loyalty and sacrifice to the community and to one's allies were abandoned by a new class of adventurers.

Fall of the republic

Lucius Cornelius Sulla Felix (c. 138–78 BCE), known as Sulla, led the forces under his command against a rival general, perpetuating civil war. He was supported by Gnaeus Pompeius (106–48 BCE), or Pompey, who had unlawfully raised a private army. After marching on Rome in 82 BCE, Sulla was appointed 'dictator with supreme power to reorganise the state'. The ancient republican office of 'dictator' didn't originally have the negative connotations we assume today. It was a temporary post for times of military emergency, the most celebrated instance being the dictatorship (in the 490s BCE) of Cincinnatus, who is reputed to have taken command of the Roman forces, led them to victory and then retired nobly back to his farm. Neither Sulla nor Pompey was so self-effacing. Sulla reformed the Roman constitution by increasing the size of the senate to 600 and restoring its centrality, reducing the power of the council of the plebs, and reorganising the courts. He also carried out a systematic purge of those he deemed enemies of the state, executing and seizing the property of thousands of members of the nobility. A pattern set in of Romans fighting Romans. The rivalry led in 60 BCE to the first triumvirate, an informal alliance between Julius Caesar, Pompey and Crassus.[17] After Caesar's successful campaign in Gaul, his famous crossing of the Rubicon at the northern boundary of Italy in 49 BCE led to a confrontation with Pompey, whom he defeated at Pharsalus, Greece. Pompey was subsequently assassinated in Egypt. Caesar was declared *dictator perpetuus* (dictator for life) but was himself assassinated in 44. His great-nephew (and adopted son) Octavian then helped to defeat Caesar's leading assassins, Brutus and Cassius. As Cicero put it, 'while there are such vastly lucrative rewards, civil war will never end.' He lamented that 'the real Rome' – the republic he had fought to preserve – had come to an end.[18]

The second triumvirate, formed in 43 BCE, was an alliance between Octavian, Marcus Antonius (Mark Antony) and Marcus Aemilius Lepidus. It lasted until 33 BCE. Unlike the first, it was a legally established institution with *imperium maius,* superior to all other magistrates including consuls. By 31 BCE, however, Mark Antony was defeated and then committed suicide (along with Cleopatra), while Lepidus was marginalised. Octavian was repeatedly re-elected as consul and later styled himself *princeps* (first citizen, from which is derived the English word *prince*) and Augustus (Revered). The transition from the republic's divided *imperium* to the new autocracy was confirmed through a surprising reciprocal exchange. In 27 BCE, Octavian announced that he was giving all his military, legal and administrative authority back to the senate – which duly persuaded him to accept proconsular authority over Spain, Gaul and Syria, effectively giving him command of the majority of the legions, while allowing him to seek re-election as consul in Rome. The Republican government was 'restored', but the emperor's powers, especially over armies, were confirmed. Octavian couldn't govern without the senate, nor could he alienate too many of the republican traditionalists who feared one-man rule. His legitimacy derived from ending the civil war, restoring rule of law and re-establishing central government, while preserving existing institutions. He relied also on an empire-wide *clientela* – a network of personal connections, followers and loyalties, with attendant obligations and rewards, that he had built up himself or inherited from his adoptive father and Mark Antony. Octavian had usurped *imperium maius* as commander-in-chief, supreme judge and high priest (*pontifex maximus*); the senate, assemblies and magistrates now looked up to him.[19]

Was it inevitable that 'the price of empire' would be an autocratic emperor?[20] As the empire grew along with its administrative challenges, the republican constitution (made for a city-state) was too unwieldy for such vast territory, and it lacked continuity due to the high turnover of magistrates. The imperial lure of easy wealth, and the corruption that went with it, undermined the republic's traditions of moral restraint, political compromise and popular participation. While Rome didn't have formal political parties, the underlying social antagonism between *optimates* (elites) and *populares* (democrats) represented a wide (possibly irreconcilable) divergence in political aims and desired reforms. Julius Caesar was a populist reformer on land and grain distribution.[21] His assassins ostensibly wished to preserve traditional republican liberties, but they were defending the privileges of the wealthiest Romans, including themselves. We shouldn't assume that none of them would have seized power for himself if fortune had favoured him. Soldiers, on the other hand, were willing to march on Rome because of their grievances. Military recruitment of landless Romans and of non-Romans had become common out of necessity. Hence many soldiers no longer saw themselves as defending the security of the *res publica* and their own landholdings, and they expected material rewards for service, be they booty, citizenship and/or land. Their allegiance shifted from the state towards 'the successful general who led them'.[22]

The downfall of the republic was often attributed to the morally corrupting effect of 'avarice and ambition'[23] over traditional simplicity. 'The country had been transformed, and there was nothing left of the fine old Roman character,' according to Tacitus (ca 55–117 CE).[24] In favour of Augustus, some said that he had acted out of filial piety towards Julius Caesar, that Rome was in a state of emergency, that government by one man was the only cure, and that peace for the majority was his only aim. The sceptics replied that these were pretexts for his 'lust for power', in pursuit of which he had eliminated all rivals. Augustus' reign was lengthy (27 BCE–14 CE) and order was indeed restored. By the time he died, then, any suggestion of a return to a government 'by the combined efforts of a greater number' did not convince enough senators, and Augustus was succeeded by his step-son Tiberius (r. 14–37 CE).[25] A contagion of accusations, trials and executions occurred during Tiberius' reign, leading to an indiscriminate massacre. He and subsequent emperors, notably Nero and Caligula, set examples of extremely bad rulership if anything.[26] But, as Tacitus put it, the deeds of the emperors, 'however distasteful', and the litany of 'cruel orders, unremitting accusations, treacherous friendships [and] innocent men ruined' had to be recorded so that readers would learn to distinguish right from wrong.[27] The achievement of high offices and rewards no longer arose from excellence, as they had under the republic, but depended instead on servility before the new autocrats. Public service and Ciceronian justice had given way to lies, accusations and bribery.[28] The tyranny of Nero produced a monotonous and depressing series of trials and forced suicides. Even if many died honorably, their sheer numbers betrayed a 'slavish passivity' among the Roman elite.[29]

How could one conduct oneself with any integrity under such dictators? Many educated Romans found guidance in the Stoic tradition inherited from the Greeks. Stoicism taught emotional restraint and indifference in the face of Fortune (good or bad) as it's 'up to us' how we face or react to the circumstances into which fate delivers us. What matters most is virtue, not how much we achieve nor how happy (or miserable) we feel, nor wealth nor even health. Life only seems short to those who fail to live it with virtue, said Seneca (4–65 CE).[30] He who is master of himself will never feel like a prisoner. 'For what can be above the man who is above Fortune?'[31] As part of a purge of conspirators, Nero ordered Seneca, his close adviser, to kill himself. Seneca obliged and his wife joined him. Such deaths could be regarded as the opposite of servitude: those who had the courage to oppose a tyrant sacrificed themselves for others. Or were these individual martyrdoms a wasteful loss and a failure of collective courage?

Roman authors wrote about the actions of individuals viewed as exemplars, good or bad. They were interested in the conduct of each emperor, his family members and the senate, and in the mutual loyalty or trust (*fides*) that was gained or lost between them. They left us with no general models of rulership and statecraft, nor innovations in political theory.[32] Tacitus mentioned different forms of constitution derived from Aristotle, but only to point out that Rome had become an autocracy. Rationally designing and building a Platonic ideal state or an Aristotelian best-practice polity was apparently beyond the Romans' imagination. Instead, the transition to imperial government occurred through bloody and chaotic events over many decades. And yet autocracy may seem (in hindsight) to have been necessary, if not logical. The ancient republic had overthrown monarchy; four centuries later the empire needed an emperor. Such thinking is circular and retrospectively self-justifying. And a major problem, shared by all monarchies, was in the succession. Many emperors were assassinated and there was rarely a straightforward father-to-natural-son transition. Being proclaimed emperor by the troops under one's command was often the essential first step, followed by a costly civil war against rivals, as was the case for Constantine the Great (r. 306–37 CE). Arguably this had the advantage of competitive selection; whereas unchallenged inheritors could be incompetent. Emperors relied on loyal armed forces to gain and keep the throne; they often ruled by inspiring fear and cultivating sycophants. The former republican sense of shared responsibility among a larger ruling class of senators and magistrates was lost, even though the offices of the republic remained in place.

Imperial government

High-level politics didn't necessarily concern the soldiers and citizens, and the empire grew in spite of bad emperors. It thrived best, however, with good ones. Under emperor Marcus Aurelius (d. 180 CE) Roman territory included France, Spain, Italy, the Balkans, Greece, Turkey, the Levant, Egypt, the North African coast and most of Britain. By his time peace and prosperity had been largely achieved.[33] Marcus is remembered as the fifth of 'the five good emperors', all of whom, as Machiavelli noted, gained the throne through adoption and not hereditary succession, and who between them oversaw eight decades of self-restrained and just government in which proper authorities were respected.[34] Marcus Aurelius's *Meditations* is one of the classics of stoic philosophy. It's a series of deeply reflective 'notes to self' or personal spiritual reminders and admonitions, the modesty and humaneness of which belie the fact that its author was emperor. His thoughts on the government of oneself could apply to anyone. He doesn't directly refer to great events of his time. When he refers to the state, he combines it with metaphysical matters and only hints at his powers and duties as emperor.

> Revere the ultimate power in the universe: this is what makes use of all things and directs all things. But similarly revere the ultimate power in yourself: this is akin to that other power. In you too this is what makes use of all else, and your life is governed by it.
>
> What is not harmful to the city does not harm the citizen either. Whenever you imagine you have been harmed, apply this criterion: if the city

is not harmed by this, then I have not been harmed either. If on the other hand harm is done to the city, you should not be angry, but demonstrate to the doer of this harm what he has failed to see himself.[35]

The second century CE saw the height of Roman imperial rule, with stable, established borders. Those under its rule could conduct their business freely, so long as they remained obedient. Disobedience and rebellion were dealt with violently and cruelly. By 'Roman' we should now think of a style of governance, and not just the city or the natives of Rome itself, as citizenship was extended to wider populations of free men who could appeal to Roman law. The central (and most costly) imperial institution and the model for government itself was the army. It provided career paths for ambitious and talented men, kept the peace and supported provincial governors. Violence and civil disorder weren't uncommon in Roman provinces, and there was no police force (as we understand it today) dedicated to keeping communities safe and orderly.[36] Households and communities often had to protect themselves from bandits, and only the more civilised provinces had established councils with night watches and guards.

Roman civil governance and military force overlapped considerably, therefore – especially in those provinces where there was little or no tradition of formal law and administration. In provinces where effective institutions had existed before the Roman conquest, especially in the Hellenistic east and Egypt, political customs (such as assemblies) could continue but they relinquished supreme military authority – although the large city of Alexandria and the province of Egypt were governed more centrally by the emperor through a viceroy. In general Roman rule meant that 'pre-existing local hierarchies were transformed into hierarchies that served Rome, and the power of local leaders was harnessed to the needs of the imperial ruler.'[37] Rome overlaid a 'government without bureaucracy'[38] and a court of appeal for the cities. 'The chief magistrates of many communities were shadows of Roman consuls, "two men" (*duoviri* or *duumviri*) serving as co-mayors for one year, assisted by the same types of attendants as consuls in Rome.'[39] High public office was often more of an expense than a source of revenue, but conspicuous expenditure conferred status and honour. Local elites vied therefore to hold civic offices and to sponsor public amenities such as baths, circuses and shrines in the Roman style. In addition, Roman military encampments provided economic opportunities, as settlements and markets formed around them. Latin and (in the east) Greek were official languages of administration. In the absence of a paid professional bureaucracy, the local oligarchs, as magistrates and councils, often assisted by public slaves, took care of civic administration and supervised markets including weights and measures. They levied troops and raised taxes for the imperial government. Rome didn't interfere with local culture and religion, provided that the emperor was honoured and obeyed. The persecution of Christians only arose because they refused to worship emperors, were intolerant of other faiths and repudiated the pagan gods who had protected cities.

Roman provincial governors were appointed with instructions from the emperor, along with a small personal staff that included soldiers promoted to administrative functions. In peaceful provinces, most of a governor's time would be taken up in settling local legal disputes, while a common task for soldiers was recapturing fugitive slaves. Something resembling a civil service did start to emerge in the second century. This meant less reliance on the slaves or freedmen within the household of emperor or governor. Instead, slaves and freedmen staffed a permanent administrative support structure. Administrative prefectures (below the magistracies reserved for senators) were occupied by the *equites*, the affluent class of 'knights'. Their functions included city police (*vigiles*), corn supply, finance and secretarial services in Rome and throughout the empire.[40] The highest office knights could aspire to was the prefecture of the praetorian guard. But knights and senators were amateurs in public office; they didn't become a permanent professional workforce. In the second and third centuries, emperors also sent out special soldiers called *frumentarii*. The name suggests that they originated from those whose job was grain acquisition, but they came to perform special operations such as arrests, assassinations and domestic espionage, and they worked across all levels of the Roman government.[41] Graft and misappropriation were rife, and Roman officers were often guilty of cruelty and abuse of powers, but there were also laws to punish egregious offenders. Roman law gave citizens rights *against* the state and some protections of due process – although more so in commercial than criminal matters. Roman rule, then, meant peace, stability, law-bound administration and opportunities for wealthy provincials to gain citizenship and political advancement. It abandoned the original exclusivity of Roman citizenship to create an imperial way of life that was impartial towards one's ethno-religious heritage. Autocracy at the center was balanced with local civic autonomy, backed by the relentless force of arms.[42]

But the empire suffered rebellions and invasions in the mid-third century and became difficult to control. Diocletian (r. 284–305) reorganised it into four autonomous territories with four emperors, presided over by himself. Constantine (r. 324–37) formalised a division into two halves, east and west, establishing Constantinople as a 'second Rome' (Chapter 4, Part 2). This is not the place to retell the story of the fall of the western empire in the fifth century. The present question is how the imperial government worked when it did work. The Roman system was a peculiar amalgam. In the course of his career, a member of the governing class could be a pagan priest, military commander, public orator, judge, senator and sponsor of public events. Ancient republican offices and assemblies in Rome were coupled with an efficient military machine and a complex system of arrangements and treaties with distant municipalities or tribes, but with little bureaucracy. It had traditions, rites, laws and a strong code of honour, but no shared political ideology beyond loyalty to Rome and its greater glory. The Romans understood their government through the actuality of its history and its great men and women, not through ideas about a better world.

Part 2: Persia

The Romans' greatest adversaries lay to their east – in Persia. Despite many efforts, the Romans never managed to subdue Persia beyond Asia Minor, other than the short-lived occupations of Armenia and Mesopotamia. Indeed, one of Rome's most humiliating defeats was against the Parthians at Carrhae in 53 BCE, while in 260 CE the Persians captured the Roman emperor Valerian at a battle near Edessa.[43] Sadly, the history of that vast territory stretching from Asia Minor to the Hindu Kush is little known to most 'western' readers. The Greeks wrote histories, while ancient Persian culture was mainly oral, and so the received knowledge of Persia largely derives from unreliable or biased Greek authors such as Herodotus.

In the sixth century BCE, Babylon had re-established itself as an imperial capital after a revolt against the Assyrians in 609 BCE. To the east of Mesopotamia was the Median Empire. The Medes had joined the Babylonians in defeating the Assyrians and were overlords of the Persians who occupied the south-west of today's Iran. Then a king called Cyrus inherited the Persian throne in about 559 BCE. The Achaemenian Persian Empire emerged around 550 BCE when Cyrus defeated the Medes. In 546 he overtook Asia Minor, including the Ionian Greek cities, and then the Babylonian Empire in 539. His son Cambyses (r. 529–522) conquered Egypt and Libya. After Cambyses, a usurper of the throne, Darius I (r. 521–486), took the Indus Valley in the east and Thrace in south-eastern Europe in 513. In response to Athenian support for revolts in Ionian Greek cities, Darius sent a force against Athens but was defeated at Marathon in 491. His son Xerxes was defeated in the naval battle of Salamis in 480. When the Macedonians and Greeks joined forces and marched east in 334, led by Alexander the Great, the Achaemenid dynasty fell. Following Alexander's death in 324, his generals divided the conquered Persian territories between them, Antigonus taking Asia Minor and the Levant; Ptolemy, Egypt; and Seleucus, Babylon and greater Persia. The Seleucid dynasty lasted from 312 to 63 BCE when it was defeated by the Parthians, who were originally a nomadic Central Asian tribe. To the west in Asia Minor the Kingdom of Pontus, ruled by the Parthian Mithridatic dynasty, emerged in the early third century. It was conquered by the Romans after a series of hard-fought wars.

The Kings of Persis (in south-west Iran) also arose in the third century BCE, originally as governors under Seleucid imperial rule, and then under the Parthians. They overturned the Parthians in about 224 CE and established the Sassanian empire, with its capital at Ctesiphon,[44] lasting until 651 CE. The Sassanids were the last pre-Islamic dynasty in Iran. The Achaemenian and Sassanian Empires are the main focus of this part.

Zoroastrianism

To understand pre-Islamic Persia, we should understand its principal religion. It isn't known when the prophet Zarathustra (or Zoroaster) lived, but it may have been as early as 1500 BCE. Zoroastrianism is a quasi-monotheistic faith that worships a lord of wisdom, Ahura Mazdā, and believes there's a cosmic struggle between light and dark, or truth and falsehood. Opposed to Ahura Mazdā, and representing violence, evil and death, is the spirit Angra Mainyu, who will be defeated at the end of time. Each person chooses between the two. The righteous way is symbolised by fire, and each soul will be judged after death.[45] Zoroastrianism became the main (but not exclusive) religion of the Persians. It was administered by a priesthood, the Magi, who were largely peripheral to Achaemenid politics and exerted no effective constraint on the monarch.[46] Inscriptions of Darius I, however, demonstrate his worship of Ahura Mazdā as creator, king-maker and protector of the realm. Rebellion by the people is attributed to evil, or the lie, as a distinct force. Liars should be punished. The king, of course, desires and represents truth, and this involves his self-control of emotion. One of Darius's inscriptions (probably intended to justify retrospectively his usurpation of the throne) boasts of his self-restraint:

> I am not a friend to the man who is a liar. I am not hot-tempered. What things arise in my anger, I hold firmly under control by my mind. I am firmly ruling over my own impulses.[47]

Although Zoroastrianism recognised a supreme being, it included numerous other deities and spirits.[48] It didn't preach asceticism, nor did it condemn other religions. Achaemenid rule was remarkable for its official toleration of diverse ethno-religious groups.[49] Cyrus the Great allowed exiled Jews to return to Jerusalem and rebuild the Temple, and he restored the Babylonian cults. Allowing for the propaganda inherent in official inscriptions, a relatively tolerant attitude towards local customs (compared with the Assyrians) may help to explain how Cyrus so rapidly conquered Media and Babylon.[50]

Achaemenian government

While Persian kings weren't worshipped as deities, they represented themselves as recipients of absolute sovereignty from Ahura Mazdā. A king would call councils of nobles or judges when needed, but his word was binding, including upon successors.[51] Darius I is said to have had six wives and a large harem, while the king's mother held a dominant position within the court. 'Royal women enjoyed a position which allowed them free disposition of the produce of their estates reflected in their ability to give their own orders to officials, to use their own seal and to employ their own bureaucratic staff.'[52] Palace workforces, including women and men, acted as officials, assistants and scribes. The court was run as the king's (very large) household, including his personal officers. The commander of his bodyguard became the first minister and controlled access to him. There's also evidence of an officer who controlled the flow of household goods.[53]

Reform of the Achaemenian state occurred in the reign of Darius I. The empire was divided into satrapies – originally 20, according to Herodotus, with fixed tributes. The satraps or 'protectors' were governors of provinces and were mainly Persians. They had their own palaces which attracted local Persian nobility. In some cases, the satrapies were handed from father to son and risked becoming principalities. 'Their jurisdiction embraced the spheres of civil and military action; they seem to have been responsible for the payment of the annual tribute, the raising of military levies, and for justice and security.'[54] The satraps' loyalty to the king must have relied heavily on shared lineage and culture, intermarriage and material rewards.[55] Prime farming land was often granted in fief to Persian nobility, while much of the mountainous country remained relatively independent or even outside the reach of Persian law. The economic model was based on the centralised accumulation of wealth through tribute. Imperial and satrapal coinages were minted (apparently only for the western regions, however), but many payments, even to royalty, were in kind, such as wine, grain or livestock.[56] Although there are known to have been rebellions that were suppressed, for example in Egypt and Ionia, the Achaemenids maintained peace through most of their realm.

It's surprising that such a vast and diverse empire, the largest ever at that time, in which the quickest mode of transport was the horse, lasted as long as it did – over 200 years. Other large ancient empires that were formed through rapid conquests broke up soon after the death of the conqueror.[57] The secret of the Achaemenid dynasty's longevity was probably *not* to standardise things (unlike China's first emperor), but to remain a 'night-watchman state' for which the two basic elements were 'tribute and obedience'. The satraps collected the tribute and kept the peace locally.[58] Local traditions, hierarchies and governance were allowed to continue, however, using their local languages. In spite of their lack of literature, the Persians had a civilising influence by maintaining peace and building infrastructure such as roads with regular posting stations, canals and ports. But their army failed to adapt to the effectiveness of the Greek infantry. They had hired Greeks as mercenaries, even to fight other Greeks,[59] but Alexander's expeditionary force destroyed an empire that was comparatively stable. The Greek generals divided the territory after Alexander's death and didn't restore the unity that the Achaemenids had sustained. Unlike the Greeks – who looked down on 'barbarians' and whose city-states excluded outsiders from citizenship – the Achaemenian Empire was diverse and inclusive, although demanding of tribute and intolerant of rebellion.

The Sassanian empire

We now leap forward in time to the third century CE. Ardashir I (180–242 CE) founded the Sassanian Empire after defeating the Parthians in 224. The Sassanids' territory was never as extensive as the Achaemenids', despite a will to restore it. Moreover, Sassanian rule tended towards centralisation, and they faced quite different internal and external threats. In the region of Asia Minor and upper Mesopotamia, the Sassanians had ongoing conflicts with the eastern Roman

Empire (Byzantium), and in the east, they had to deal with the semi-nomadic tribal Hephthalites. There were also internal religious challenges which meant that the Sassanids weren't as tolerant as the Achaemenids.

The king of kings (*shahanshah*) was supported by a council of the royal family and one of the nobles, and a well-organised system of law and administration. The institution of self-governing 'free' cities and semi-independent dynasts had survived through the Seleucid and Parthian eras but gradually came to an end under the Sassanids. The cities instead were governed by appointees of the central government who also held important positions in the court of the *shahanshah*. There was a well-developed judiciary,[60] and the central government was served in the cities by judges and officials who dealt with state property and taxes. In the later Sassanian era, the realm was divided into four vice-regencies, with 37 districts for taxation purposes. Matters to do with the state and those to do with the temple were assigned to separate officials and separate branches of administration. There was a poll tax and also a land tax, and hence a land survey was performed in the sixth century when the system was reformed. A key economic resource, however, was trade, as Persia controlled important routes between east and west. There was revenue from customs duties at borders and city gates, and some commodities were restricted or monopolised for political reasons. Silks were especially important as they could be used as currency (for instance to pay tributes) and as diplomatic gifts.[61]

Heterodoxy

While Zoroastrianism remained the principal religion, the Sassanian period saw two important heterodox socio-religious movements, Manichaeism and Mazdakism. The prophet Mani (216–274 CE) came from an Iranian family resident in Babylon. He preached a new revelation, and eventually gained an audience with the king, Shāpūr I (r. 240–270). In spite of resistance from religious authorities, Shāpūr permitted Mani to preach within the empire and made him a royal retainer. But in 274 Bahrām I summoned him and, with some lobbying from Zoroastrian priests, condemned and arrested him. Mani died in prison. Manichaeism is akin to Zoroastrianism in that it shares the dualistic opposition of light/dark or truth/lie, but tends further towards monotheism by opposing God and matter and putting good above evil, rather than treating the opposing principles as primeval twins. It has a redemptive theology and also recognises Jesus as a messenger of revelation. It spread west through the Roman Empire but was condemned by Diocletian in 297.[62] Manichaeism also spread east via trade routes through Samarkand and Tashkent and was adopted by the Turkic Uighur tribes in the eighth century.[63]

The Mazdakites followed a gnostic[64] interpretation of Zoroastrianism which sought social justice. As an early form of socialism, it gained support from peasants, artisans and other poorer sections of society – although it didn't advocate liberation of slaves. Mazdak (d. 520s CE) promoted reforms to address poverty, including land redistribution, progressive taxation and the communal sharing of resources. It's often alleged that Mazdakites shared women in common, but it's more plausible that they sought to abolish polygyny, concubinage and harems, to allow women to marry outside of their class, and to liberalise the rules of levirate marriage.[65] Relaxation of the laws of inheritance and marriage, however, was a threat to traditional class distinctions and lineages, and hence was opposed by the nobility. Mazdakism flourished under Kavād (r. 488–496, 498–531 CE), who saw political advantage in challenging the privileges of the nobility and clergy. Kavād was deposed and only regained the throne with the backing of the Hephthalites. The Mazdakites were violently suppressed by his successor, Khusrau I (r. 531–579).[66]

Jews and Christians

Zoroastrianism became more closely associated with the monarchy as a state religion, and a stricter orthodoxy evolved. Jewish and Christian communities had some autonomy under the Sassanians, but there were times of conflict and persecution and some discriminatory policies. The universalism and messianism of the monotheistic religions were bound to clash from time to time with the interests of the Zoroastrian priesthood.

Jewish communities were established in Mesopotamia well before Iranian rule. A wave of Jewish exiles arrived in 722 BCE and another, following the destruction of the Temple, in 587 BCE. The Babylonian exilarch was the head of the Jewish community and was recognised by the Sassanian court. The early Sassanids were minded to convert non-Zoroastrians, however, and they revoked the self-governance rights of Jewish communities. But a compromise was reached in 261 CE whereby Jewish courts would recognise Persian laws, taxes and land tenure policies. Jews enjoyed 'the same legal rights as everyone else'.[67] Hence they had more freedom than Christians, and the Persian environment stimulated the development of the Babylonian Talmud.

> The single most important event in the history of the Jews and of Judaism was the formation of the Babylonian Talmud [third to fifth centuries CE] upon the foundations of Babylonian Jewish political, cultural and religious life. In a less cosmopolitan and accommodating civilization, that document probably could not have emerged. The Iranians primarily contributed not doctrines or other sorts of 'influence', but the opportunity for Jewry to work out its own affairs in its own way.[68]

Early Christian missionary activity in Persia began under the tolerant (if not indifferent) Parthian rulers, and so Christian communities were well established by the time of the Sassanid takeover in 224 CE. Christians were also captured during wars with the Romans and relocated to Persia. Toleration became strained, however, during the reign of the Roman emperor Constantine (324–37 CE), as the Persians' enemy was now a Christian, and the loyalty of Christians in Persia was put into question. Moreover Shāpūr II (r. 309–379 CE) 'needed money for his army to attack the Romans, so taxes on Christians were doubled to provide extra revenues.'[69] Naturally, Christians objected – and persecution occurred until Shāpūr II's death. Setting aside this period and some other incidents of sectarian violence, the Sassanian emperors were largely tolerant of Christians, and Christians served in the imperial army.

In 424 CE, the Church of the East in Persia broke away from the authority of Byzantine priests. Furthermore, the theology of Nestorius (Patriarch of Constantinople, 428–431)[70] was deemed heretical at the councils of Ephesus (in 431) and Chalcedon (in 451). Followers of Nestorian doctrine relocated to Persia and joined the Church of the East. Subsequently, the only Christians officially tolerated by the Sassanids were Nestorians, as their beliefs were closer to Zoroastrianism and were rejected in Byzantium. In 562, however, the religious freedom of Christians in Persia was curtailed when proselytising was made a capital offence.[71]

Sassanian state reform

The revolutionary Mazdakite movement and its violent suppression by Khusrau I in the sixth century highlight a class struggle that led to reforms which centralised government and restructured the class system. Khusrau's tax reforms bypassed the large landowning nobility and delivered a more reliable revenue to the central treasury. The role of the nobility in raising (and hence controlling) regiments was also reduced. A new class of knights (smaller landowners or *dekhāns*) were raised to noble status. They were equipped and paid for military service directly from the centre, thus buying loyalty to the *shahanshah* rather than the local aristocrat. Civil administration and military service became more meritocratic as a result, and the army became more efficient.[72]

The ongoing wars between the Sassanian and Byzantine empires were largely inconclusive and exhausted both sides. The power vacuum that arose in the Levant and Mesopotamia in the seventh century provided the opportunity for fast-moving Arab warriors, inspired by a new monotheistic faith, to invade and conquer. In return, though, Persian administrators civilised their new Muslim masters by providing them with ready-made techniques of administration suited to their newly acquired multi-ethnic empire. The Persians also supplied a concept of kingship that helped to develop the caliphs – who had begun as relatively egalitarian tribesmen of the desert – into absolute monarchs. Although the religious toleration and diversity of past Persian empires were overridden by the universalism of Islam, conversions were often voluntary, motivated by this new religion's espousal of principles of social justice. But as we'll see in the next chapter, conversion also reduced the subject's tax liability. The next two chapters include Islamic rulers, and we'll see how Persian traditions of government and Persian political thinkers were indispensable to their success.

Part 3: The Han dynasty

We now return to China. The previous chapter covered the formation of the Chinese state and the reign of the first emperor – whose dynasty ended soon after his death in 210 BCE. One of the leaders in the civil war that followed, Liu Bang (256–195 BCE), was a man of peasant origin who adopted the name Han for his dynasty. Emerging as undisputed victor, he was 'induced by his confederates to accept the title of emperor' in 202 BCE and designated Gaozu (Great Progenitor).[73] The Han dynasty is divided historically into two major periods: the Western or Former Han (206 BCE–9 CE) and the Eastern or Later Han (25–220 CE). The short-lived Xin dynasty (9–23 CE), ruled by Wang Mang, a former commander of the armed forces, separates the Former and Later Han. The present section covers only the Former Han.

The Han dynasty set the standard for rulership and government in China. The first Han emperor, Gaozu, largely adopted legalism: 'meritorious service must be encouraged by rewards, and infringement of the law must be punished.'[74] Legalism put the practical aims of the state first, rather than cultivating exemplary virtuous leaders. The exception to legalist practice under Gaozu was the allocation of governorships, as fiefs were granted in some areas to commanders who had seized territory and declared themselves kings. They had supported Liu Bang's war, and he needed to maintain that support and prevent bids for independence.[75] Over time, Confucian scholarship (banned by the Qin emperor) was rehabilitated and became the basis of education and selection in the imperial bureaucracy. This strand of thought put correct conduct, respectful relationships and the betterment of society first, based on learning and benevolence rather than strict enforcement of law.[76] Hence, an ideological debate emerged between those who advocated materialist pragmatism and those who sought a conservative Confucian style of government – although both sides accepted the unified monarchical-imperial model and the primary economic importance of agriculture.

The imperial court

Unlike their Roman counterparts, the Chinese emperors weren't active rulers and commanders. The Han emperor upheld the bond between temporal and supernatural realms on which the legitimacy of the dynasty and its government depended. His personality and preferences did make a difference, but his role was comparatively formal and passive.

> Institutionally speaking, the emperor was omnipotent, omniscient, and omnipresent – in other words, all but divine. Personally, however, it was tacitly recognized that his abilities might be limited and his morality flawed, and that his individual input in political processes should therefore remain circumscribed.[77]

He remained in the inner palace, aloof from civil servants, approving measures that were put before him rather than initiating policy. This Chinese bureaucratic version of 'checks and balances' (which lasted until 1912 CE) prevented most emperors from becoming genuine despots and made it feasible to govern even when the emperor was an infant or incapacitated. He had three senior statesmen as advisers. The most senior was the chancellor or head of the administration. The imperial counsellor provided a check on the chancellor and was concerned with implementation of policy and the performance of the bureaucracy. The supreme commander led the military, but this post was eventually discontinued. Below these senior officials were nine ministers in charge of administrative branches of government with their own staff of officials. Furthermore, a private secretariat evolved around the emperor and empress, headed by a nominated marshal of state, allowing them to bypass the civil servants and to receive trusted counsel with less bureaucratic formality and delay.

Palace politics, family rivalries and nepotism played a significant role. A family of the nobility could attempt to win influence in the palace by offering a daughter as an imperial concubine. There were thousands of concubines, and so the chances were low, but the 'jackpot' was to bear the emperor's sons and become his favourite. Or a fortunate marriage could result in a family's elevation as in-laws of a future emperor. An empress or empress-dowager wielded significant power, including appointments to senior posts. The most prominent example was Lu Zhi (241–180 BCE), or Empress Lu, the first wife of Liu Bang/Gaozu. She played a crucial (and often cruel) role in consolidating dynastic power and inheritance. She elevated members of her own family, the better to control those under her, and if necessary, eliminated rivals. From the death of Emperor Gaozu in 195 BCE until her own in 180, she 'most emphatically ruled while emperors barely reigned.'[78] In spite of the deadly palace politics, Han Gaozu and Empress Lu initiated a period of relative peace and reconstruction, lowering taxes and improving state revenues.

The Empress Dowager Dou (c. 200–135 or 129 BCE), or Dou Yi, was originally a commoner and orphan who was called on to serve Empress Lu. She was sent to the court of one of the vassal-kings of the Han empire, where she found favour and bore a daughter and two sons to the king, Liu Heng (256–195 BCE), son of Gaozu. Due to the deaths of Liu Heng's elder sons, Dou Yi and her sons rose in status. Liu Heng became Emperor Wen, and Dou Yi the empress. She is remembered for promoting Daoism within the court and correcting the rigidity of Confucian and legalist doctrines.[79] Achieving the role of favoured consort or empress, and hence the mother of the heir-apparent, was central to the most intense dynastic politics. For example, violence, executions and witchcraft accusations occurred between the families and supporters of rival consorts during Emperor Wu's (r. 141–87 BCE) final days. This caused tens of thousands of deaths. Both leading contenders were eliminated, and the son of another consort was selected as heir. He was still a minor, so a regency of senior officials was formed.[80]

The political and administrative roles of eunuchs were also important. We may regard eunuchs today as effectively a third gender, not merely anatomically as 'de-sexed' or castrated males.[81] Eunuchs formed the personal bodyguards of the emperors, and there was a small group who managed affairs of state as advisers to the emperor. Men were not admitted into the Inner Palace, and eunuchs were able to perform sensitive household roles. Being deprived of marriage, fatherhood and heirs, they were more dependent upon and loyal to the emperor. While there were prejudices against them, and their privileged status caused resentment, many performed high military and civilian roles.[82]

The civil service

Under the Han dynasty, China developed its famed professional civil service. This was graded into eighteen ranks with corresponding salaries, paid in coin and rice. The basic qualification was literacy but for higher grades, knowledge of the Confucian classics was required. An imperial academy was created under Emperor Wu (r. 141–87 BCE) to train men to respect past traditions of public life based on 'the claim that imperial government rested on the principles of Confucius' rather than legalism.[83] Senior administrators identified recruits, and an examination system was developed. But the selection wasn't purely merit-based: family connections and favouritism played a part. Officials were subject to annual review which, in principle at least, influenced promotion. The civil service thus acquired a high status and self-esteem, with a shared Confucian ideology.

Territorially the realm was divided uniformly into commanderies. The anomalies were the 'kingdoms', but these were brought into line over time as opportunities arose to replace hereditary (and potentially independent) rulers. Some kingdoms came to be governed by sons of the emperor and (from 145 BCE) their senior officials were appointed by the central government, allowing for closer surveillance from the centre. Within each commandery were ten to twelve prefectures. The duties of provincial authorities were law and order, tax collection, land registration, care of granaries, public works and recruitment of corvee labour. The average prefecture may have employed 400–500 staff. Territorial units were further divided into districts, communes and hamlets. Commoners dealt with officials for the purposes of census-taking, tax-collecting and recruitment for the armed forces (two years mandatory service for men) and for corvee labour (one month per annum). It was an increasingly centralised system, with no official scope for local self-governance or customary laws; although imperial rule may not have been respected by non-assimilated peoples in remote and sparsely populated zones. Reports on local government to the centre were done more in writing than through official tours and inspections. The system was thus slow to react and conservative – and corrupt. Over the centuries, however, although dynasties rose and fell, the Chinese meritocratic civil service marched on. (Chapter 8, Part 1 looks in more detail at the bureaucracy and the examination system under the Ming dynasty in the fifteenth century.)

Unlike Rome, the armed forces weren't the favoured career or the support-base for aspiring rulers or governors. The army was 'socially disfavoured and completely under the control of scholar-officials'[84] but was nonetheless formidable. It played more prominent roles when necessary to meet social unrest or conflict with (primarily) northern Xiongnu nomadic raiders. The Xiongnu tribal confederacy defeated the Chinese army and forced the Han government into a 'brotherly' treaty in 198 BCE. This meant a costly tribute in favour of the Xiongnu and the despatch of an imperial bride. The alternative policy was armed raids into the steppe wilderness, which the civil service tended to resist, but which did eventually gain the Chinese a command of the Gansu corridor and the Tarim basin – and hence control over the eastern side of the 'silk road' trade routes.[85]

The state

Han society was primarily peasantry, over which ruled relatively small classes of local nobility and officials. There were few merchants and manufacturers. A more *laissez-faire* policy towards land acquisitions under the early Han rulers allowed local elites to accumulate wealth and land, often at the expense of peasants. The grand families of wealthy educated landowners also supplied and recommended recruits to the imperial bureaucracy. Hence they could influence central government policies but were also integrated or co-opted into the political system. Nonetheless, power relations between the imperial centre and the provincial nobility shifted back and forth over the centuries and weren't always in balance.[86] The existence of the peasantry was precarious and, while the country prospered on the whole, a bad harvest or a natural disaster such as a flood would cause mass displacement and starvation. Peasant revolts and disruptive religious movements occurred from time to time, eventually contributing to the fall of the dynasty itself.[87]

There was no sense of a free 'citizen' with rights within (let alone against) the state, nor civil rights vis-à-vis other individuals. Instead, imperial rule strengthened 'the belief in the essential unity between the family and the state, and between filial piety and loyalty to the sovereign.'[88] The enduring legitimacy of the imperial model since Han times was expressed in ideals of harmonious relations of belonging and dependency. The legal-administrative system reached down to the individual with (in principle) no boundary, rewarding loyalty and punishing disobedience – although laws were poorly encoded and inconsistent at that time. There were harsh methods of judicial interrogation and punishment, including torture and capital punishment, although these were reduced in severity during the Former Han period.

There were land taxes and poll taxes. Under Emperor Wu, the state monopolised iron and salt in an effort to raise revenue for public works and for war with the Xiongnu. A system of granaries provided for the redistribution of grain from areas with over-supply to those with shortages and higher prices.

Policy debates occurred around wealth inequality, the appropriateness of state monopolies, the effect of severe penalties on crime rates, and the level of state expenditures. A record of one such high-level debate in 81 BCE has been preserved.[89] It depicts two differing points of view. The pragmatists wanted to boost productivity and prosperity by retaining the state monopoly on iron for revenue, and to achieve this they distributed iron tools to the peasant farmers and conscripted labour. These officials, who came from provincial elite families, took a *laissez-faire* approach to land sales and were unconcerned about the growth of large estates. The traditionalists were opposed to state monopolies on salt and iron, and to any diversion of labour into manufacturing goods for trade. They sought instead to control the size of, and to redistribute, landholdings to correct the disparity between rich and poor and ensure that everyone could make a living from agriculture. They advocated greater economy and modesty in state expenditure, especially on ceremonial events. The two sides also differed on the role of coined money. The pragmatists were in favour of coin; the traditionalists preferred payments in kind. The latter were concerned about peasants being lured into debt through a greater supply of money, causing them to sell their land. This wasn't a straightforward contest between legalists (harking back to the Qin dynasty) and Confucians (with nostalgia for the ancient Zhou dynasty), but it did continue much the same ideological split. Neither side was completely victorious and actual policies represented shifting emphases and compromises over time.[90]

The Art of Rulership

There were diverse opinions about good or effective rulership, and about the aims and techniques of government, influenced by legalist, Daoist and Confucian traditions (Chapter 2, Part 1). These ideas were synthesised in a scholarly anthology of Former Han times, the *Huai Nan Tzu*, the ninth part of which is *The Art of Rulership*.[91] This advised strict application of rewards and punishments – not used oppressively, but to leave no room for disobedience, and to ensure that ministers will eagerly serve the emperor. Legalist pragmatism was blended with Confucian benevolence, however, as the welfare of the people was seen as essential to the interests of the ruler, and vice versa.

> If the ruler issues commands which brook no disobedience so that those who accord with them will benefit while those who deny them will bring grief on themselves, before there is time for a shadow to move, everyone will be in line with the rule of law. [And yet, if] the ruler prevents that which the people consider injurious while encouraging that which they consider beneficial, his authority will prevail.[92]

Affairs of state should be conducted empathetically in accord with the natural tendencies or predispositions of people and events, 'putting oneself in the place of others and looking inward at one's nature, not imposing on others what one does not desire oneself – putting into effect what benevolence and intelligence are in agreement upon.'[93] Thus the ruler maintained his strategic command of the situation – or political purchase. He would set directions and give rewards, while living a peaceful and frugal life, guided by his ministers. His subjects would 'have no chance to do wrong',[94] as they would see the rewards for their successes and the punishment for disobedience as products of their own actions. Controlling self-interest required clear laws and administration that turned people towards the common good – and the good of the ruler. The two sets of interests were compatible, as 'governmental concession to the interests of the people reinforces the strength and stability of government itself.'[95] *The Art of Rulership* upheld a checks-and-balances explanation of monarchic-bureaucratic government that also mirrored a government of the self.

> The purpose of setting up a bureaucracy in antiquity was to prevent peo-ple from doing just as they pleased. That they set up a ruler was to check the bureaucracy and prevent it from being dictatorial. Law, records, social norms, and a code of moral conduct are to prevent the ruler from making decisions based on his own whims. Where the people are not allowed to do just as they please, the Way will be relied upon exclusively, and the Way being relied upon exclusively, principles are followed through. Thus they return to a state of nonaction. Nonaction does not mean being completely inert, but rather that nothing is initiated from the ego-self.[96]

This gave a well-rounded ethical-political theory of government and legitima-tion of governmental practices. In general, it was during the Han dynasty that the imperial model of government (an emperor served by scholar-officials) and the predominantly Confucian principles of rulership were bedded in. This proved to be an extremely resilient approach to government which we will revisit under the Ming dynasty (Chapter 8, Part 1). Enduring features of the Chinese model of government include the primacy of harmonious relations and service to the state – embodying, rather than standing in opposition to, the interests of the individual – and indistinct boundaries between paternal and imperial powers, or between people and state.[97]

We have considered the Qin dynasty (in the previous chapter) and now the Former Han. The era of the Former and Later Han in full lasted about four cen-turies. This was followed by nearly four centuries of disunion (two or three rival kingdoms at a time) until the Sui-Tang reunification from 580 CE. The Tang dynasty lasted from 618 to 907. This was followed by the Song (960–1279), Yuan (1271–1368), Ming (1368–1644) and Qing (1644–1912). In spite of cataclysmic political changes and popular uprisings, the concept and practice of a unified civilisation and empire, encompassing much the same land mass, survived – and continues to be recognised internally and externally.[98] The disruptions of foreign imperialist interventions into China in the nineteenth and twentieth centuries and the (relatively brief) communist regime from 1949 (Chapter 7, Part 3) may in the future appear to be just another inter-dynastic period of disunion and reconsolidation.[99]

Conclusion

Although the Roman and the Han empires were roughly contemporaneous with similarly sized territories and populations, they were different in almost all respects: the political power of the army, the variability of local governance, the role of the emperor, the turnover rate of magistracies, and so on. While the pathway to a stellar political career for Romans was through the army, in China it lay in scholarship, examinations and the imperial bureaucracy. Military careers were of lower status in China and commanders were subject to civilian control. When compared with China, the Roman empire looked under-governed. Geographically extended, multi-ethnic, multi-lingual empires faced a constant tension between centralisation of power around their monarchs, on the one hand, and the need, on the other, to delegate power and distribute administration across vast distances – but with relatively slow communications. Autocratic rulership had to be tempered by toleration of cultural and religious differences and by concern for the welfare of the people. The pre-Islamic Persian empires set a relatively good example of toleration. They also developed practices of palace-based administration (with provincial delegation) that would incorporate and cultivate waves of invading nomads, including Arabs and (later) Mongols.

The term 'empire' often has negative connotations today. The ancient empires undoubtedly used lethal force to expand and to maintain power, but there are lessons in the arts of government that they have handed down, as they addressed problems that are familiar to us. For instance, they had to protect borders from invaders and maintain internal order. Although borders weren't clearly demarcated, they all maintained the monopoly on the legitimate use of armed force within their territories – to use a Weberian definition of a state. These empires did their best to provide an efficient infrastructure for communication and for distribution of goods, and enforce equitable systems of taxation. They had to account for their lands and populations, grow crops and distribute basic foods, especially grains or rice. They needed to maintain a common ideology of imperial rule and enforce laws, yet they also needed to accept diverse local cultures and social structures. They needed to have a coherent system of divisions into administrative units, down to the level of households, and they had to work with, not against, local elites for enduring collaboration. In these monarchical systems, there was pressure from family members and loyal followers for the inheritance of, or preferment for, desirable posts. The trend towards meritocracy, however, is discernible even in these early empires. Hence officials needed career paths and training. Imperial ruling elites also had to reflect on their own conduct. Although many Roman emperors appeared to have skipped those lessons, the Stoic tradition counselled them to control their anger and to deal with Fortune's fickle nature with indifference. The emperor Marcus Aurelius was an outstanding positive example. The Confucian and Daoist traditions gave the Chinese emperors and bureaucrats a more exacting philosophical and practical set of guidelines in the ethics of self-mastery based on benevolence, respect for tradition and policies that ideally move in accord with the natural courses of events. The ancient empires helped to develop significant and enduring knowledge in the arts of government. While all the empires considered here developed rationally distributed systems, the Chinese government was the most unified, centralised and standardised. The Roman and Persian empires were more diverse and decentralised with relatively lightweight superstructures mainly concerned with order and tribute. None of them, of course, was ever entirely successful. I see no evidence, however, that makes one of them stand out as 'best practice'.

Notes

1 The Lyceum was a public area outside the walls of Athens, devoted to worship, physical exercise and learning.
2 Oakley, 2014, p. 8.
3 Finer, 1999, vol. I, p. 408.
4 Ibid.
5 Cicero was also consul in 63 BCE.
6 Machiavelli, 1996 [1517], p. 14.
7 Oakley, 2014, p. 14.
8 Ibid.
9 Brennan, 2014, p. 24.
10 Ibid.
11 Finer, 1999, vol. I.
12 'On Duties (II)', in Cicero, 1971, p. 141, trans. Michael Grant.
13 Syme, quoted by Finer, 1999, vol. I, p. 430.
14 Beard, 2015; Osgood, 2014.
15 Gaius Gracchus's grain law (*lex frumentaria*) was repealed by Sulla but later restored.
16 Ungern-Sternberg, 2014, p. 86. See also: Beard, 2015; Everitt, 2013.
17 Crassus was given command of Syria and died, in 53 BCE, at Carrhae fighting against the Parthians.
18 Cicero, 1971, p. 135.
19 This brief history of the end of the republic has relied upon: Beard, 2015; Everitt, 2006; Osgood, 2014; Ungern-Sternberg, 2014.
20 Osgood, 2014, p. 319.
21 'Caesar launched a large number of new colonies to resettle the poor from the city of Rome [which] allowed him to get away with reducing the number of recipients of free grain by about half, to 150,000 in all.' Beard, 2015, p. 292.
22 Finer, 1999, vol. I, p. 425.
23 Sallust, quoted by Finer, 1999, vol. I, p. 425.
24 Tacitus, 1971, p. 33, trans. Michael Grant.
25 Ibid., pp. 38–9.
26 Suetonius & Osgood, 2020, trans. J. Osgood.
27 Tacitus, 1971, p. 173.
28 Sailor, 2008.
29 Tacitus, 1971, p. 388.
30 Lucius Annaeus Seneca (the Younger).
31 'On the Shortness of Life', Seneca, 2007, p. 144.
32 Wiedemann, 2000.

33 Birley, 2000.
34 The other four were (all dates CE): Nerva (r. 96–8), Trajan (98–117), Hadrian (117–38) and Antoninus Pius (138–61). See Machiavelli, 1996, Book 1, ch. 10.
35 Aurelius, 2006, p. 42, Book 5, §§21–2, trans. Martin Hammond.
36 Fuhrmann, 2011.
37 Beard, 2015, p. 493.
38 Garnsey & Saller, 2015, p. 40.
39 Fuhrmann, 2011, p. 58.
40 Garnsey & Saller, 2015.
41 Fuhrmann, 2011, p. 152.
42 Finer, 1999, vol. I; Fuhrmann, 2011.
43 It's unclear exactly what became of Valerian in captivity.
44 Ctesiphon is on the Tigris, close to Baghdad. Historical details of the rise of the Sassanids are sketchy. Frye, 1983.
45 Zoroastrianism appears to have influenced the Judeo-Christian tradition. It was suppressed by Muslim rulers from the seventh century CE. It's still practised by Parsees (Persians) in India. Rose, 2011.
46 Finer, 1999, vol. I, p. 295.
47 Quoted in Schwartz, 1985, p. 686.
48 Some of these deities are related to Hindu gods. An important figure was Mithra, who was venerated as Mithras in a widespread western cult.
49 Ancient lists recognise between 23 and 31 ethnicities. Cook, 1985, p. 244.
50 Axworthy, 2010; Schwartz, 1985.
51 Cook, 1985.
52 Brosius, 1998, p. 199.
53 Finer, 1999, vol. I, pp. 298–300.
54 Cook, 1985, p. 267.
55 Finer, 1999, vol. I, p. 296.
56 Meadows, 2005.
57 For example, following the deaths of Alexander, Ashoka, Chingghis Khan and Timur.
58 Finer, 1999, vol. I, p. 298.
59 Ibid., p. 313.
60 Perikhanian, 1983.
61 Lukonin, 1983.
62 Augustine of Hippo was a Manichee before his conversion.
63 Widengren, 1983.
64 Gnosticism entails access to esoteric mystical knowledge.
65 Levirate marriage means that a widow with no male heir is forced to marry a male relative of her deceased husband. See Perikhanian, 1983.
66 Yarshater, 1983. Elements of Mazdakism have survived through the Islamic era in more radical Shia sects
67 Schama, 2013, p. 224.
68 Neusner, 1983, p. 923.
69 Frye, 1983, pp. 139–40.
70 Nestorius drew a radical distinction between the human and the divine natures of Jesus.
71 Asmussen, 1983, p. 946.
72 Frye, 1983.
73 Loewe, 1986a, p. 119. Loewe uses the alternative Anglicised spelling 'Kao-ti' for the first Han emperor.
74 Loewe, 1986c, p. 484.
75 'In 202 B.C. a total of ten kingdoms had been established in a large area lying to the east and north of the fourteen administrative units that lay under the emperor's direct control in the center.' Loewe, 1986a, p. 124.

76 Loewe, 1986b.
77 Pines, 2012, p. 39.
78 Keay, 2011, p. 120. See also: Bennett Peterson, 2000.
79 Bennett Peterson, 2000.
80 Loewe, 1986a.
81 Ringrose, 2003.
82 Finer, 1999, vol. I, p. 495.
83 Loewe, 1986c, p. 465.
84 Finer, 1999, vol. I, p. 513.
85 Finer, 1999, vol. I; Loewe, 1986a, 1986c.
86 Pines, 2012.
87 Finer, 1999, vol. I.
88 Pines, 2012, p. 126.
89 Loewe, 1986a, pp. 187 ff.
90 Loewe, 1986a, 1986c.
91 Ames, 1994.
92 *The Art of Rulership*, in Ames, 1994, pp. 197–8.
93 Ibid., p. 206, abridged.
94 Ibid., p. 193.
95 Ames, 1994, p. 164.
96 *The Art of Rulership*, in Ames, 1994, p. 191.
97 Pye, 1985.
98 One acknowledges controversies over Taiwan and Tibet regarding their sovereignty and independence, and dissent especially in Xinjiang.
99 Although still a one-party state, the People's Republic of China is no longer communist in practice as it has opened its borders and its economy to the capitalist mode of production.

References

Ames, Roger. 1994. *The Art of Rulership: A Study of Ancient Chinese Political Thought.* Albany: State University of New York Press.

Asmussen, J. 1983. 'Christians in Iran.' In *The Cambridge History of Iran: Volume 3(2), The Seleucid, Parthian and Sasanid Periods*, by Ehsan Yarshater, 924–48. Cambridge: Cambridge University Press.

Aurelius, Marcus. 2006. *Meditations.* London: Penguin.

Axworthy, Michael. 2010. *A History of Iran: Empire of the Mind.* New York, NY: Basic Books.

Beard, Mary. 2015. *SPQR: A History of Ancient Rome.* New York, NY: Liveright.

Bennett Peterson, Barbara. 2000. *Notable Women of China.* New York, NY: Routledge.

Birley, Anthony R. 2000. *Marcus Aurelius: A Biography.* London: Routledge.

Brennan, T. Corey. 2014. 'Power and Process under the Republican "Constitution".' In *The Cambridge Companion to the Roman Republic*, by Harriet Flower, 19–48. Cambridge: Cambridge University Press.

Brosius, Maria. 1998. *Women in Ancient Persia, 559–331 B.C.* Oxford: Oxford University Press.

Cicero, Marcus Tullius. 1971. *On the Good Life.* London: Penguin.

Cook, J. 1985. 'The Rise of the Achaemenids and Establishment of their Empire.' In *The Cambridge History of Iran: Volume 2, The Median and Achaemenian Periods*, by Ilya Gershevitch, 200–291. Cambridge: Cambridge University Press.

Everitt, Anthony. 2006. *Augustus: The Life of Rome's First Emperor.* New York, NY: Random House.

————. 2013. *The Rise of Rome: The Making of the World's Greatest Empire.* New York, NY: Random House.

Finer, S.E. 1999. *The History of Government. Vol I: Ancient Monarchies and Empires.* Oxford: Oxford University Press.

Frye, R. 1983. 'The Political History of Iran Under the Sasanians.' In *The Cambridge History of Iran: Volume 3(1), The Seleucid, Parthian and Sasanid Periods*, by Ehsan Yarshater, 116–180. Cambridge: Cambridge University Press.

Fuhrmann, Christopher. 2011. *Policing the Roman Empire : Soldiers, Administration, and Public Order.* Oxford: Oxford University Press.

Garnsey, Peter, and Richard P. Saller. 2015. *The Roman Empire: Economy, Society and Culture.* London: Bloomsbury.

Keay, John. 2011. *China: A History.* New York, NY: Basic Books.

Loewe, Michael. 1986a. 'The Former Han Dynasty.' In *The Cambridge History of China. Volume 1, The Ch'in and Han Empires, 221 B.C.-A.D. 220*, by Denis Twitchett and Michael Loewe, 103–222. Cambridge: Cambridge University Press.

————. 1986b. 'The Religious and Intellectual Background.' In *The Cambridge History of China: Volume 1, The Ch'in and Han Empires, 221 BC–AD 220*, by Denis Twitchett and Michael Loewe, 649–725. Cambridge: Cambridge University Press.

————. 1986c. 'The Structure and Practice of Government.' In *The Cambridge History of China: Volume 1, The Ch'in and Han Empires, 221 BC–AD 220*, by Denis Twitchett and Michael Loewe, 463–90. Cambridge: Cambridge University Press.

Lukonin, V. 1983. 'Political, Social and Administrative Institutions, Taxes and Trade.' In *The Cambridge History of Iran: Volume 3(2), The Seleucid, Parthian and Sasanid Periods*, by Ehsan Yarshater, 681–746. Cambridge: Cambridge University Press.

Machiavelli, Niccolò. 1996. *Discourses on Livy.* Chicago, IL: University of Chicago Press.

Meadows, Andrew R. 2005. 'The Administration of the Achaemenid Empire.' In *Forgotten Empire: The World of Ancient Persia*, by John Curtis and Nigel Tallis, 181–209. London: The British Museum Press.

Neusner, J. 1983. 'Jews in Iran.' In *The Cambridge History of Iran: Volume 3(2), The Seleucid, Parthian and Sasanid Periods*, by Ehsan Yarshater, 909–23. Cambridge: Cambridge University Press.

Oakley, S. 2014. 'The Early Republic.' In *The Cambridge Companion to the Roman Republic*, by Harriet Flower, 3–18. Cambridge: Cambridge University Press.

Osgood, Josiah. 2014. 'The Rise of Empire in the West (264–50 B.C.).' In *The Cambridge Companion to the Roman Republic*, by Harriet Flower, 303–20. Cambridge: Cambridge University Press.

Perikhanian, A. 1983. 'Iranian Society and Law.' In *The Cambridge History of Iran: Volume 3(2), The Seleucid, Parthian and Sasanid Periods*, by Ehsan Yarshater, 625–80. Cambridge: Cambridge University Press.

Pines, Yuri. 2012. *The Everlasting Empire : The Political Culture of Ancient China and Its Imperial Legacy.* Princeton, NJ: Princeton University Press.

Pye, Lucian W. 1985. *Asian Power and Politics: The Cultural Dimensions of Authority.* Cambridge, MA: Harvard University Press.

Ringrose, Kathryn M. 2003. *The Perfect Servant: Eunuchs and the Social Construction of Gender in Byzantium.* Chicago, IL: Chicago University Press.

Rose, Jenny. 2011. *Zoroastrianism: An Introduction.* London: I.B. Tauris.

Sailor, Dylan. 2008. *Writing and Empire in Tacitus.* Cambridge: Cambridge University Press.

Schama, Simon. 2013. *The Story of the Jews: Finding the Words, 1000BCE–1492CE.* London: Bodley Head.

Schwartz, M. 1985. 'The Religion of Achaemenian Iran.' In *The Cambridge History of Iran: Volume 2, The Median and Achaemenian Periods*, by Ilya Gershevitch, 664–97. Cambridge: Cambridge University Press.

Seneca, Lucius Annaeus. 2007. *Dialogues and Essays*. Edited by John Davie and Tobias Reinhardt. Oxford: Oxford University Press.

Suetonius, and Josiah Osgood. 2020. *How to Be a Bad Emperor: An Ancient Guide to Truly Terrible Leaders*. Princeton, NJ: Princeton University Press.

Tacitus. 1971. *Annals of Imperial Rome*. Harmondsworth: Penguin.

Ungern-Sternberg, Jürgen von. 2014. 'The Crisis of the Republic.' In *The Cambridge Companion to the Roman Republic*, by Harriet Flower, 78–98. Cambridge: Cambridge University Press.

Widengren, G. 1983. 'Manichaeism and Its Iranian Background.' In *The Cambridge History of Iran: Volume 3(2), The Seleucid, Parthian and Sasanid Periods*, by Ehsan Yarshater, 965–90. Cambridge: Cambridge University Press.

Wiedemann, Thomas. 2000. 'Reflections of Roman Political Thought in Latin Historical Writing.' In *The Cambridge History of Greek and Roman Political Thought*, by Christopher Rowe and Malcolm Schofield, 517–31. Cambridge: Cambridge University Press.

Yarshater, Ehsan. 1983. 'Mazdakism.' In *The Cambridge History of Iran: Volume 3(2), The Seleucid, Parthian and Sasanid Periods*, by Ehsan Yarshater, 991–1024. Cambridge: Cambridge University Press.

4

RULING BY THE BOOK

Monotheism and government

The three great monotheistic religions – Judaism, Christianity and Islam – propose that there must exist a supreme authority which would (if we obey it) resolve our differences and teach us justice, harmony and righteousness. Similar ideals can be found in Plato's theory of forms and in the Chinese concept of the Mandate of Heaven. The monotheistic faiths, however, take this a big step further by positing a supernatural ruler whose will is revealed in holy scripture and in human history. A local or particular faith emerged, spread beyond its original community, formed a powerful priesthood and legitimised monarchs, asserting its universality over all rival doctrines. Holy scripture set down law and principles of government – but it also produced rivalries around the question, 'Who rules?' Pope or emperor? Caliph or sultan? To examine the effect of monotheism on government and on the education of monarchs, this chapter looks at the Jewish kingdom and at the Byzantine and Islamic empires.

Part 1: The Jewish kings

The earliest widely accepted non-biblical reference to a people of Israel is in an Egyptian inscription dated circa 1220 BCE.[1] Until 586 BCE, Jerusalem was the centre of a small and remote kingdom. The biblical stories of the founding Jewish kings derive from folk traditions that are now lost, but David and Solomon 'probably reigned sometime in the tenth century BCE'.[2] The Old Testament accounts of their reigns were written about four centuries later and aren't accurate historical records, but neither are they entirely mythical. There's some, but very little, corroborating (extra-biblical) documentary evidence of a house of David.[3] And the biblical record, when compared with archaeological evidence, appears to exaggerate the extent of the conquests and the grandeur of that kingdom. The stories that come down to us may be a product of the 'political necessity

DOI: 10.4324/9781003166955-4

of establishing Temple and Dynasty as the twin foundation stones for the [then] new idea of a united Israel' ruled by kings of Judah, the Davidic dynasty.[4] Biblical accounts of events from the eighth century BCE onwards do have some corroborating documentary and archaeological evidence. The reign of the last of this line of Jewish kings, Zedekiah, ended in 586 BCE, on the well-attested conquest of Judah by Babylon. Regardless of their historical accuracy, however, the narratives of Jewish kingship had a profound influence on later political thought and practice. The figure of a messiah, the vision of redemptive social justice and divine judgement, individual moral accountability, and the later concept of 'divine right of kings' derive from the laws of Moses, the legacy of the house of David and the image of an eternal kingdom of God.[5]

The story of David's rise from shepherd to bandit to king is foundational for Judeo-Christian traditions of monarchy. But David usurped and maintained power 'by removing anyone who was in his way', including Saul and his heirs, and even his own sons.[6] The biblical narrative is devised to excuse his actions and legitimise his dynasty. In addition, it exaggerates the extent of statecraft at that time. The books of Samuel and Kings give, for instance, named lists of David's and Solomon's senior officials, including priests and military chiefs of staff, as well as recorders, secretaries and an official in charge of Solomon's palace.[7] These suggest a specialisation of ceremonial, bureaucratic and political tasks, somewhat like a 'cabinet', giving the impression of 'an urban-based state system'.[8] But Jerusalem was then a relatively small, remote and unfortified hilltop village with few natural resources and little strategic importance. There's no archaeological evidence (from that time) of the literacy and record-keeping that underpin a full-fledged statehood. The biblical story that David and Solomon ruled over a grand united monarchy that later divided into two kingdoms, Judah in the south (with Jerusalem as capital) and Israel to the north, may be inaccurate. It may have been 'spun' for the benefit of the later kings who assimilated Israelites fleeing the Assyrian invasion in the eighth century and then asserted a retrospective claim over both territories.[9]

David's Judah was a highland merging into the desert; it was unpromising for settled agriculture. The richer valleys of the north were more productive, more populated and hence more powerful. But the early peoples of these two small kingdoms, Judah and Israel, had closely related polytheistic religions. They were not yet monotheists in the tenth century BCE. A change occurred in the eighth century, however, due to pressure from the north, especially from the Assyrian conquest of Israel in 732–722 BCE. A depopulation of the north and a sudden rise in population and settlements in the south suggest a migration of Israelite refugees into Judah. From that time Jerusalem became a more influential capital with institutions of state, boosted by its usefulness as a vassal of the Assyrians, its position on a trade route from Arabia and its acquired mantle as the remaining capital of a now recognisably Jewish people. There's evidence of literacy and organised public works[10] in Jerusalem around the time of Hezekiah (r. 727–698 BCE). Signs of state administration (standardised weights and measures, royal seals and uniform storage vessels) show up in archaeological finds from this time.[11] Along with the centralised monarchic state went the end of countryside shrines and polytheistic 'idolatry' and the creation of a temple-based, monotheistic religion – although the record in 2 Kings suggests that the commitment of the descendants of David to monotheism was patchy. Under Josiah (r. 639–609 BCE), however, the Israelites were to worship only one God. The lawbook of Deuteronomy was 'found in the temple of the Lord'.[12] It laid down the law for the Israelites – and for their future kings, who must 'follow carefully all the words of this law'.[13] It also made individuals (and not kin groups) the basis of legal rights and responsibilities.[14] Deuteronomy uses the first-person voice of Moses but switches to a third-person narrative as it approaches the time of his death. Textual evidence suggests its actual author(s) also wrote the books that tell the history of the Jewish kingdoms centuries after Moses' time. In other words, Deuteronomy was written in the late seventh century, in a style that made it sound like ancient Mosaic law, to lend it greater authority.[15]

Limited monarchs

It was common for ancient monarchs to act as the link between the earthly and supernatural realms, ensuring the wellbeing of people and land through the observance of rites. The religion of the Jews, as it consolidated under Hezekiah and Josiah, introduced something new. God's covenant is with the people, and the monarch should 'not consider himself better than his fellow Israelites and turn from the law to the right or to the left'.[16] Kings couldn't disobey the received law without dire consequences. Hence those kings who didn't prosper were those who violated the law and/or permitted the people to indulge in pagan practices. Bound by a higher law, the Jewish king is 'history's first *limited monarch*'.[17] The authority of Mosaic law as God's law, and hence supreme, gave licence to the biblical prophets openly to criticise (if not excoriate) the kings and the nation at large. The prophets are often social agitators who expose unrighteous conduct and injustices. They criticise individual kings as well as the institution of kingship itself. This represents a political tension between priests and kings – that is, between theocracy (rule according to religious doctrines as interpreted by priests) and 'caesaropapism' (subordination of religion to the state by concentrating secular and spiritual rule in one person).[18]

The invasion by the Babylonians in 586 BCE and the exile of the leaders of the Jewish communities changed everything, however. Independence was lost, and Palestine was a vassal or province of larger empires. After the fall of Babylon to Cyrus the Great in 539 BCE, Palestine was ruled by the Persians who, by all accounts, treated the Jews relatively well.[19] The conquests of Alexander the Great, however, brought Palestine under Hellenistic rulers, until the latter were forced to recognise the Jewish Hasmonean dynasty as kings and high priests – even though not all Jews regarded them as legitimate.[20] The Hasmoneans gained independence from the Hellenistic Seleucid Empire in 110 BCE but lost it to the

Romans in 63 BCE. Roman 'protection' and the suppression of Jewish revolts meant that the subsequent Herodian dynasty's rulers were clients of Rome. But Jerusalem and the Temple were destroyed by the Romans in 70 CE; the city's Jewish legacy was obliterated and its treasures were looted. This destroyed the institutional and political base for the Jewish doctrines of kingship.[21] A prophecy of a Davidic ruler who would unite the people and restore divine law, however, was not forgotten.

The tension between monarchy and priesthood (or papacy) resurfaced later in medieval Christendom. The examples of Moses, David, Solomon and Josiah that were used by kings and emperors for the purposes of public legitimation of their authority also signified constraints on that authority. The Frankish kings Pepin (714–68 CE) and Charlemagne (742–814 CE) adopted anointment for their coronations in emulation of David and Solomon, lending them 'an almost priestly quality' and enhancing their authority and legitimacy.[22] But if it took a bishop of the church to anoint them, then was the church somehow superior to the anointed ruler? In 756 CE, Pepin proclaimed the popes as rulers of the Papal States (in Italy). But when, after Christmas Mass in Rome in 800, Pope Leo III laid the imperial crown on Charlemagne's head, as if it were his to give, he was 'simultaneously granting himself implicit superiority over the Emperor whom he had created.'[23] In the eleventh century, Pope Gregory VII would further claim 'ultimate superiority over the temporal power.'[24] The lengthy historical struggle between medieval kings and bishops was also about jurisdiction over the people. Vassals of the king paid him homage, but they held jurisdiction over their own subjects, and so on in a hierarchy of feudal 'contracts' down to the level of the peasantry. Churches and monasteries held large properties, so bishops and abbots wielded considerable economic power. The church also had a pastoral concern for the conduct and salvation of all people, including monarchs. The king, in turn, protected the realm as a whole. So the European medieval king as lawmaker and commander was constrained by the bishops (and the warlords) on whom he depended, and legal and fiscal decision-making was consensual within the king's council. The constraining effects of the church on kings were as much a political struggle as a struggle for the welfare of people's souls.

Despite their antiquity, the Old Testament examples of kingship continued to have an effect. For example, the Solomonic dynasty of Ethiopia claimed lineal descent from Solomon and the Queen of Sheba; it commenced in 1270 and lasted until a *coup d'état* in 1974. Justinian I, on entering the newly completed Hagia Sophia cathedral in Constantinople (in 537 CE), is said to have exclaimed, 'Solomon, I have surpassed you!' The quotation may not be reliable, but the grand image of Solomon was still potent.[25] As for Jerusalem, after the turbulent period of post-Alexandrian Hellenistic and then Roman rule, it fell into the hands of the Sassanian Persians, the Islamic caliphates, the Christian crusaders, the Egyptian Mamluks and later the Ottomans. Towards the end of World War I, Jerusalem was occupied by British forces. Palestine was then governed under a League of Nations mandate by the British until 1948.[26]

Part 2: Byzantium

Originally a Greek colony called Byzantion, set on a natural harbour in the narrow straights of the Bosphorus, the metropolis now known as Istanbul was once 'the new Rome', capital of the eastern empire. Its location commands the passage between the Mediterranean and Black Seas and the trade route between Europe and Asia Minor, making it a logical place for the emperor Constantine (r. 306–337 CE) to have founded a new capital city. Constantine was the first Roman emperor to convert to Christianity in 312, causing 'one of history's great surprises'.[27] But it was not until 380 that Christianity became the official religion of state under emperor Theodosius, after whose death in 395 the division of the empire into two – eastern and western – became permanent. Rome itself was sacked by Germanic tribes in 410, and the western Roman empire became defunct by 476, dividing into numerous kingdoms. Constantinople was much less exposed to barbarian invasions, and the weight of Roman rule shifted east. This eastern empire – Byzantium – still regarded Augustus as its first emperor, and its citizens were *Romaioi*. Its official religion was Christian, but theological differences steadily grew between the church patriarchs in Constantinople, the independent churches in Egypt and Syria, and the popes. As bishops of Rome, the latter claimed to inherit authority from St Peter, the recipient of 'the keys of the kingdom of heaven',[28] and didn't concede ecclesiastical authority to Constantinople.

The main rivals of Byzantium were in the east: the Sassanian Persian empire (Chapter 3, Part 2) and later, from the seventh century, the caliphates (see below). Arian and Nestorian Christian sects were deemed heretical but continued to flourish, the former among barbarian tribes, the latter in Persia and beyond. Longstanding disagreements within Christendom led to the Great Schism of 1054 and a permanent parting of ways between the Greek Orthodox and Roman Catholic churches. Constantinople went into decline after being sacked by western Christians in 1204. It was sacked again by the Ottomans in 1453, from which time onwards it has been under Muslim rulers.[29] This section focuses particularly on the times of Justinian I (r. 527–565 CE).

Religion and state

The Roman empire had encompassed culturally diverse cities overseen by military provincial governors who had what we would now regard as a 'skeleton' staff, while continuity of governance was provided by local elites (Chapter 3, Part 1). With the Christianisation of the empire, however, local pagan cultures were violently suppressed, with the destruction of art, literature and architecture.[30] Cities retained a Graeco-Roman character (with public baths, markets and amphitheatres) but temples gave way to churches and civic governance changed significantly. Democratic assemblies were a thing of the past; competitive donation by civic leaders for public entertainments and monuments was rejected as pagan vanity. The treasuries and landholdings of ancient temples were confiscated, local resources were depleted, lawmaking was centralised, and the personal costs and obligations of participation in local governance became burdens. Hence, many of those eligible to become councillors pursued opportunities elsewhere, such as in church or army. By the sixth century, local politics was in the hands of the provincial governor, the bishop and wealthy landowners, while the people at large relied upon petitions, acclamations, demonstrations or riots in order to be heard.[31] 'Over the years the bishop must have become the most powerful individual in many, if not most, cities.'[32]

Emperors were no longer mobile military commanders (as Marcus Aurelius, for example, had been) and their abiding in one seat of government encouraged bureaucracy and archive keeping.[33] Constantinople originally saw itself as a capital city for all Christians – even though not all Christians lived within its realm. Heaven was imagined as a kind of palace ruled by God, and the emperor was the earthly imitation of, and chosen by, God.[34] (Wicked emperors were accounted for as punishment by God and were still to be obeyed.) Byzantine rule was monarchic and palace-based; religious worship and state rituals were combined.[35] Church and state became intertwined under the emperor, and there was no independent class of prophets or philosophers to challenge imperial ideology. This meant little intellectual progress in theological or political terms. The basic principle of rulership was to maintain order while kings and subjects awaited divine judgement. The integration of Christian doctrine and practice into the affairs of state began under Constantine, who convened the Council of Nicaea in 325 to settle theological controversies. The church had turned to the emperor to bring bishops together to resolve disputes, thus setting a precedent in Byzantium for imperial authority over religious belief. Rulers would increasingly – and harshly – impose the agreed doctrine.[36]

In Constantine's time, Christians were a small minority, and Christianity was in its infancy compared with the venerable Greek and Roman traditions. The biblical canon was still being finalised and Christian teachings had yet to construct an edifice of learning comparable with non-Christian literature and rhetoric. By the literary standards of those days, the biblical stories were poorly written and downright illogical.[37] So, although pagan literature was often banned or destroyed by Christians, the educated classes could not afford to ignore pre-Christian philosophy, rhetoric and grammar.[38] As Christian congregations grew and were deterred from contact with 'demons',[39] however, more people refused to participate in pagan civic rites. This challenged local social hierarchies and norms. In pagan cults, the most wealthy civic benefactors were entitled to lead, but in churches, benefaction meant giving to the poor, and bishops weren't necessarily the wealthy. Women and men weren't segregated within, and slaves weren't excluded from, the congregations, thus cutting through social stratification. Although Christian doctrine enjoined obedience to rulers and accepted slavery in the earthly realm, everyone could hope for salvation – and should fear damnation – in the next life regardless of their wealth or rank.[40] So although early Christians (especially the purists who risked martyrdom) had sometimes been executed by Roman governors, their growing numbers challenged and changed civic power structures. Indeed, groups of Christian zealots destroyed many pagan temples.

Constantine's immediate successors didn't all follow his Christian example. Julian ('the Apostate') tried to reinstate pagan rites; two other successors preferred the Arian doctrine that had been ruled heretical at Nicaea. But Theodosius I (r. 379–95) made Nicene Christianity the official religion of the empire and put an end to ancient pagan rituals. A list of heresies was drawn up and banned by law; open dissent was suppressed on pain of death. By the end of the fifth century, 90 percent of the population was Christian, required to follow doctrines adopted at the Council of Chalcedon of 451 CE. Justinian later 'mopped up the residue of pagans'.[41] In 529, pagans were banned from publicly teaching philosophy and law, ending a tradition of Greek rationalism that had begun a millennium earlier.[42] Byzantium aggressively enforced an orthodox faith, and thus reinforced imperial power, even though this was never entirely a success. 'Justinian expected to govern the church in his domain; but he was frustrated by the religious passions of the easterns [especially Syrian and Egyptian Monophysites] and by the inflexibility of Rome.'[43] Nonetheless, Byzantium became a much more centralised and bureaucratic monarchy than the earlier Roman empire.

The Byzantine court

Anyone who visited the imperial court of Constantinople was bound to be amazed and awed by the architecture, the costumes, the theatrical machinery, the entertainers and the sheer spectacle of imperial power. The palace, moreover, was both the household of the emperor and the centre of his government. Protocols were elaborate, guided by eunuchs who held positions close to the emperor and empress. Castration was illegal within the empire, and so there was a lively slave trade in eunuchs.[44] Being infertile, unable to aspire to be emperors, and only passively sexual, eunuchs were considered safe for duties involving close proximity to the imperial family. Indeed they occupied pre-eminent roles in the heart of Byzantine political life, more so than in China. There were also eunuchs in high military, diplomatic and clerical posts. For instance, Narses (c. 478–573), a eunuch from Armenia, led the reconquest of Italy. Such 'manly' achievements were, however, regarded as anomalous for eunuchs at the time, revealing how they were treated socially as a distinct gender, not just as physically incomplete males.[45]

Patriarchal father-to-son inheritance of imperial power became normalised through the notion of 'born in the purple', symbolised by a purple birthing room in the palace. But successions weren't always so straightforward. An emperor could name a male successor or co-regent before his death, but revolts and usurpations also occurred, and election by senate and acclamation by the armed forces (whom the emperor normally led out) were important. An emperor or empress reigned by the will of God, so long as the people received the benefits and acclaimed them.[46]

Several empresses and empresses-dowager ruled in their own right or as regents. 'Although they were always patronized by men and documented only by male writers, [they] evidently shaped and directed imperial power.'[47] Irene, for example, overthrew her own son, Constantine VI, in 797, and was deposed in a palace coup in 802.[48] Other Byzantine empresses such as Theodora (a former actress and reputed prostitute, who married Justinian I)[49] were renowned for their political influence. Families and the court made strategic moves such as marrying into imperial families and exporting brides as diplomatic gifts. The politics of family relations and the management of the royal household were intertwined with the bureaucratic hierarchies of the governmental apparatus.[50] Titles at court that weren't inherited could be purchased, and the title-holders were remunerated in gold and fine costumes. For those who purchased a title, the financial return on investment may not have been high, but any role in the palace conferred honour and status. The court was the ultimate destination of the ambitious, as proximity to the emperor maximised prestige and influence; it attracted a constant supply of new recruits who provided low-interest credit along with their services.

Imperial government

Besides an entourage of courtiers, the Byzantine government required extensive bureaucracy and archiving. This meant centralisation and allowed arbitrary intervention by emperors. Office holding was not entirely meritocratic; it was as much a matter of honour and social rank as actual service. Patronage, office selling and influence buying were accepted norms.[51] The *magister officiorum*, or master of offices, was 'head of the empire's central administration', below whom were palace officials, fiscal administrators and the diocesan and provincial governors.[52] The basis of government was fiscal, tied inextricably to territory and warfare. The primary unit of taxation – and of social status – was land, differentiated according to productivity. Persons and villages were also taxed. Payments were either in coin or in kind and were extracted with whatever force it took. Territorial gains and losses translated directly into fiscal gains and losses. Hence, conquest, defence and reconquest were essential for the accumulative practices that, in turn, sustained the armed forces. A wealthy family's tax liability could be reduced if they equipped and fielded cavalry or militia. The imperial 'business model' encompassed peasantry, landed gentry, tax collectors and soldiers. Surpluses went into imperial buildings, civic infrastructure, monasteries and churches. But the fiscal burden of warfare, especially the reconquest of western territories in the sixth century, led to over-extension. Expansion bore the contingent risks of heavy territorial losses in defeat and potentially crippling economic costs of taxation to fund campaigns. The western reconquests in North Africa (in 533) and Italy (through to 554) aimed to restore Roman imperial authority and eliminate the Arian Christian sect of the Germanic kings. Byzantium remained exposed in the east to attacks from the Persians, however, and in the north from migrating tribes. Plague in 542 reduced the population and its economic productivity. The empire overreached itself fiscally and strategically. The western territorial gains were lost again after Justinian's death, so Constantinople failed to restore the former glory of the Roman empire.[53] Later emperors were more defensive than expansionist, and gradual losses of taxable lands and people compounded their fiscal losses.[54]

The monetary gold standard that underpinned Byzantium's economy was nonetheless remarkably stable. The state issued gold coins to pay its officials and soldiers and to acquire supplies, especially grain, and the coinage in turn gave producers and merchants a means to pay their taxes. The coins that the state paid out thus came back as revenue, and the portrait stamped into each coin reminded everyone of who ruled. The survival of the empire depended on the production and distribution of grain. While merchants and tradesmen were socially disdained by the landowning elite, conspicuous displays of social status used imported goods such as silks and precious stones. These imports also produced public revenues from customs duties at ports or city gates. The government regulated exports, especially those of strategic military importance and/or economic and cultural value. Tradesmen were regulated through guilds.[55]

To sustain this economy required a census, land surveys and records of productive assets and livestock. Monasteries enjoyed tax exemptions, meaning further record keeping. 'The main function of the constantly evolving administration had come to be the assessment, collection, and redistribution of fiscal resources, in whatever form, to maintain the state.'[56] Justinian sought to remedy corruption, speed up judicial processes and address inequity and unfairness in taxation. He sought to improve administrative efficiency and advance the welfare of subjects, and he was supported by able advisers. He abolished some dioceses – a whole layer of regional government. But the slowness of communication, the opportunities for exploitation by soldiers and officials, and the evasion of responsibilities by local landowners impeded solutions. The result was a lessening of the independence of the municipalities and an increase in the authority of provincial governors and central administrators.[57] Byzantium was bureaucratic but constantly under reform; 'it was not a monolithic or petrified structure'.[58] It was governed by one code of law, and yet it permitted informal discretionary decision making.

God's lawmaker

An official but incomplete collection of imperial edicts had been promulgated in 438 CE by Theodosius II. Nearly a century later, in 528, Justinian commissioned legal experts to revive this project and to codify the whole of Roman law for consistency, clarity and compactness.[59] This produced the *Corpus Iuris Civilis* (Body of Civil Law), comprising a complete edition of imperial pronouncements (the *Codex*, or Book); an edition of commentaries by the leading jurists; excerpts of 'new' imperial pronouncements; and, for students, *Justinian's Institutes*, 'a course of legal education which from start to finish proceeds from the Emperor's lips'.[60] This massive collection harmonised and reshaped disparate and inconsistent texts that had accumulated in Roman legal practice and scholarship over more than a millennium, reauthorised in the name of Jesus Christ.[61] The emperor thus asserted himself as 'the source of both secular and ecclesiastical jurisprudence',[62] although the church had its own council of bishops and courts. He claimed a God-given authority to make law. 'Even oral utterances of the emperor (*interlocutiones*) could acquire statutory authority.'[63] He was 'the fountain of law', but nonetheless 'by powerful convention *alligatus legibus*' (bound by the law).[64]

The new lawbooks were technical and hence remote from ordinary people. The language of administration and law was originally Latin, so had to be translated for Greek-speaking subjects.[65] In spite of Justinian's unification of civil law under an immutable divine law, the complexity of social life meant that he often issued exemptions and immunities in response to appeals and unanticipated or local circumstances. The emperor could intervene in administration at any level.[66] Moreover, litigants could settle disputes through out-of-court arbitration, often resulting in decisions that suited those involved, rather than legal compliance. Some arbiters had little legal training and were semi-literate. Women had often acted as arbiters in courts, but Justinian deemed them unfit for this and banned them from doing so.[67] The patriarchal ideal of 'one God, one ruler, one law' didn't represent the complexities of actual social life, and an imposed legal and ecclesiastical uniformity had stultifying social, political and intellectual effects.

Justinian's reform of the law was conservative. The substance and legitimacy of the *Corpus Iuris Civilis* relied on Roman traditions, but Justinian moved even further towards autocracy than the Augustan model. His oversight of civil and ecclesiastic law asserted his own authority as much as it clarified and renovated an untidy set of documents. The *Corpus* re-established the law as *Justinian's* law. By God's authority, the emperor was the legislator and the highest judge.[68] Roman republicanism had made the written law a higher authority than any magistrate, and Augustus established his one-man imperial rule on the basis of republican institutions. Under Justinian, however, 'the pretense of popular participation in government was dispensed with, [and] the notion took hold that the powers formerly held collectively by the Roman people had been duly delegated to the emperors, who exercised sovereignty on their behalf.'[69] Lacking the traditional checks on the magisterial powers of the Roman consuls, subjects had to place their faith in the wisdom and self-restraint of their emperor.

Mirror of a Christian emperor

Imperial succession in Byzantium was often a bloody affair, and not all rulers' lives ended peacefully, but there was little serious disagreement that there should be an emperor or, on occasion, empress. The main constraints on the monarch were religious and moral, however, rather than constitutional. Just as the aim of good government on earth was to imitate the kingdom of heaven, so the emperor was supposedly the imitation of God. And while the average Christian was enjoined to obey and not to sin, the obligations on those who ruled over Christians were greater, encompassing benevolence for humankind, especially the poor and indigent. This at least was the advice to Justinian delivered by the deacon Agapetus in a prime example of the mirror of princes genre. The emperor is to reflect upon himself, as he will be 'most properly called master when he masters himself and is not a slave to unseemly pleasures'. With 'pious reflexion' and temperance he overcomes the passions.[70] As God 'needs nothing', so the emperor, who imitates God, needs nothing; he is 'generous to those who seek mercy [but] without keeping an exact account.'[71] Imitation of God means a paternal benevolence towards subjects, especially the poor. The emperor reserves his wrath for his enemies and is merciful towards his subjects. He could exempt himself from the law, but imposes upon himself 'the necessity of keeping the laws'.[72] As God endowed Justinian with power, the emperor should 'always both wish and do as is pleasing to Him who gave it.'[73] He must consider his own salvation, as ruling well in this world will make him worthy of the next. Agapetus depicts mutual obligations between God and emperor:

> The more you are thought worthy of great gifts from God, the greater is the return you owe Him. Repay, therefore, your debt of gratitude to your Benefactor; He will accept your debt as a favour and return favour in return for favour.[74]

According to Procopius, however, Justinian was an evil and foolish man who systematically robbed the people.[75] Agapetus may have sermonised in vain. Nonetheless, monotheism and monarchy go together in principle – one God, one ruler, one belief system. A centralised administration and an increasingly autocratic rule were consistent with this, as strict orthodoxies in political ideas and religious doctrines converged. At one level egalitarian (as all souls are equal in the eyes of God, and no amount of money can buy you salvation), Christian orthodoxy meant, in imperial practice, the opposite. Emperors were God's anointed rulers on earth, and subjects had to obey even the wicked ones. A similar claim was made in the Latin speaking world by Augustine of Hippo (354–430 CE) as he sought to universalise the Catholic faith on the back of imperial and papal authority and to defend Christianity from the accusation that its adoption by emperors, and the repudiation of pagan deities, had been responsible for the fall of Rome. According to Augustine, all humans, including rulers, are sinners, and government is a necessary evil. Christian emperors would at least maintain order and fear God – while everyone awaited His judgement.

Part 3: The caliphs

The Quran was a new – and, for its adherents, *final* – revelation received and recited by the Prophet Muhammad (571–632 CE), which recognised Abraham, Moses, Solomon and Jesus. The Prophet himself was not literate, however, and dictated no text directly; there's uncertainty about when and by whom the Quran was written. It's thought to have been put into writing during the 650s CE.[76] Moreover, the standard biography of Muhammad doesn't come from first-hand accounts.[77] It's understood, however, that he lived in a diverse community of settled and nomadic tribes, among followers of polytheism as well as Jews and Christians, and that he rose to rule the city of Medina and (later) his native Mecca in the Hejaz region of the Arabian Peninsula. The Quran's commands, along with the *hadith* or recorded deeds and sayings of the Prophet, form the basis of the Islamic law, *sharia*. Muhammad came to be regarded as the supremely virtuous ruler. He was a successful political and military leader whose actions converted tribal solidarity into a universal religion and law, and (posthumously) formed the basis of a new multi-ethnic empire. Early Islamic political thinkers thus assumed that prophecy was a natural and necessary condition for government, and that religious and royal authority should be united in the person of the caliph.[78]

Muhammad died in 632, to be succeeded by four 'deputies' or caliphs, some-times known as 'rightly guided caliphs'. They led further conquests which, by 661, encompassed the Levant, Egypt and Persia.[79] Expansion was motivated by territorial acquisition and wealth extraction, and warfare preserved the unity of the new faith community across disparate Arab tribes. Their stunning successes can be explained by the depletion of Byzantine and Persian forces following dec-ades of warfare and plague, and by the disaffection of Christian communities in Egypt, Syria and Mesopotamia (respectively, Copts, Miaphysites and Nestorians) towards the Byzantine ecclesiastical orthodoxy. Or as the medieval philosopher Ibn Khaldun put it, 'the group feeling of the Arabs was consolidated in Islam through the prophethood of Muhammad with which God honoured them.'[80] The conquerors were followed by Arab Muslim migrants who mixed with exist-ing communities. Bedouin soldiers were prevented from looting and from occu-pying or destroying farms and instead rewarded with incomes from taxation of the conquered peoples. The latter were not converted by force. Jews, Christians and Zoroastrians were tolerated but prohibited from preaching to Muslims, and they had to pay a tax (*jizya*) in accordance with *sharia*. Pre-existing elites were left in place but served new masters.[81]

In spite of its initial unity, however, Islam divided over the question of who should legitimately succeed the Prophet as leader of the Muslim community. 'Who was entitled to the imamate?'[82] The first four caliphs were companions and fellow tribesmen of the Prophet, who would ideally have been chosen by consensus. But not all the community recognised the third, Uthman, as lawful. He was assassinated in 656 by a delegation who were dissatisfied with his gov-ernment. Consequently, the Prophet's cousin and son in law, Ali, whom many regarded as his intended heir and the true caliph, was elevated as successor. This caused a civil war between the followers of Uthman and the followers of Ali. Due to his alleged failure to avenge Uthman's assassination, Ali was challenged by the governor of Syria, Muawiya, a blood relative of Uthman. After the assassination of Ali in 661, Muawiya seized control and shifted the centre of government to

Damascus.[83] This was more than just a political struggle: it was a religious division over what is the righteous path and who is the rightful guide or leader. The party of Ali became the minority Shia branch of Islam.

The Umayyads

Muawiya began the Umayyad dynasty, which lasted until 750. Supported now by non-Arab forces, the Umayyads made further conquests, expanding the empire as far east as the Indus Valley and into Central Asia, including Samarkand in 712, and as far west as Morocco and Andalusia (the Iberian Peninsula). Islamic forces ventured across the Pyrenees but were rebuffed by the Franks at the Battle of Tours in 732. In the meantime, rulership had shifted from a circle of Arab chieftains to a palace-based regime with a professional administration. Initial reliance on Greek and Persian as customary languages of administration in the conquered lands gave way to Arabic. And as non-Arabs converted to Islam, thus avoiding the tax (*jizya*) on non-Muslims, they claimed equal status with Arab Muslims. Caliphs came to resemble kings, and succession normally went to the designated son and heir. The Umayyads were not direct descendants of the Prophet himself, but they were of the Quraysh, the Meccan clan of the Prophet. In many Muslims' eyes they lacked legitimacy, but, in the longer course of history, 'Muslims who stuck to communal unity [and] refused to form separatist communities', the majority *Sunni*, accepted and obeyed their caliphs, sultans and amirs, even those who were less than pious.[84] Many later rulers, such as the Turkic Seljuks and Ottomans, were not even Arabs, let alone Quraysh.

Muslim communities didn't create institutions comparable to the Christian churches. (With the loss of imperial government in western Europe in the dark ages from roughly 500 to 800 CE, the Catholic church institutionally united local warlords and bishops into a form of state.) The *ulema* – a community of recognised religious scholars and preachers – was a looser collective who may (or may not) reach consensus on particular legal questions and controversies. Government may be guided by *sharia*, but the interpretation of God's will, or jurisprudence (*fiqh*), became a specialised scholarly occupation distinct from the palace. This duality of religious scholarship and caliphal rulership underpinned Sunni versions of Islamic government.[85] It meant that caliphs could adjudicate but couldn't issue new law with divine authority. In theory, no Muslim ruler could privately appropriate the throne and its benefits, as all power belonged to God, and the caliph ruled by His will. Moreover, if all of the subjects, as fellow believers, also accepted God's immutable rules, then there should be a concord between subjects and caliphs.[86] Matters became contentious, however, as the Umayyad caliphs assumed greater powers as monarchs, including the development of law. The consultative traditions of nomadic Arabs no longer sufficed and Persian ideas of kingship took hold. The caliphs would become more than just deputies or successors of the Prophet as they were ideologically reframed as deputies of God. This trend alarmed many Muslims as it led to impiety and tyranny.

Those who formed the dissenting minority *Shia* branch recognised Ali as the first ruling Imam. His son, Hussein, began a line of Shia Imams. Ali's grandson, Husayn, rebelled and was killed in 680. The twelfth Imam is believed by most (but not all) Shia Muslims to be the 'hidden' Mahdi, the redeemer who will return and rule with perfect justice. Shia rulership ideally combines the secular and the spiritual in one person – a direct descendent of Ali or, failing that, charismatic rulers who serve until 'the divinely guided one' returns from hiding. The ruler should therefore be a religious figurehead with a special relationship with the divine.[87] A third faction was the *Kharijites*. Their criteria for choosing the ruler were utmost piety and learning, as the divine law itself should rule. The leader should be elected, as his family or tribal origins were of no importance; his only mission was to see to it that *sharia* was observed, for the benefit of the faithful. If the imam erred, he should be removed from office by force or even assassination if need be. Strict piety meant rejection of formal hierarchical government, approaching anarchism, as all the faithful should be capable of obeying the revealed law. Kharijites violently opposed the other branches, whom they considered not to be Muslims, and they caused numerous bloody revolts. They were trying to restore the culture of autonomous tribesmen in which Islam had originated, but they were defeated as Muslim rulers became more powerful and remote. From the beginning, then, the Umayyad caliphate faced dissension and rebellion over the legitimate form of rulership and succession.[88]

The Abbasids

While the house of Ali was unable to raise a successful rebellion, the descendants of an uncle of the Prophet, al-Abbas, claimed that they had been granted a right to restore justice. The Abbasid movement arose from Khurasan in north-eastern Persia, supported by

> Arabized Persians and Persianized Arabs who were ideologically united by their commitment to the family of the Prophet as the only legitimate caliphs and to the idea that Islamic identity should replace ethnicity and nobility as the basic principle of society.[89]

The first Abbasid caliph, Abu'l-Abbas, seized power in 750. One of the finest achievements of the new regime was the new capital city, Baghdad, established by the next caliph, al-Mansur (r. 754–75). Baghdad became a leading economic and cultural centre, with a diverse population.[90] The most renowned of the Abbasid caliphs was Hārūn al-Rashīd (r. 786–809). Unlike Byzantium and China, there were no empresses – although the consorts of the caliphs sometimes wielded considerable influence and wealth. A former Byzantine slave, Shāhān, for example, was a 'gift' to the caliph al-Mustansir (r. 1226–42). According to a thirteenth-century chronicler, she 'went on to hold her own independent court and had a fiscal office, agents, functionaries, servants, and a splendid retinue.'[91]

The Abbasids gradually ended Arab supremacy and sought loyalty to the empire from its diverse communities by allowing equal status to all Muslims. Arabs remained prominent in the military and the administration, but no longer by birthright. A class of religious scholars and educated professionals grew, to help administer the new empire. As administration became routine and bureaucratised, it established itself outside of the households of the caliphs. The three main branches were the chancery (records and correspondence), the tax collectors and the departments responsible for the disbursement of pensions and army salaries and for the courts. The role of the chief minister (*wazir*) grew in importance for its supervision and coordination role across the whole bureaucracy. According to Ibn Khaldun, *wazir* originally means 'help', but 'the wazirate is the mother of governmental functions and royal ranks.'[92] The *wazir* signed correspondence on behalf of the caliph, oversaw the finance departments and reported to the caliph on the treasury's balances. Below him were senior officials or secretaries (*kuttab*) whose positions were virtually hereditary as they were occupied by members of a tight network of families. Their roles evolved from Sassanian and Byzantine models, but they now wrote in Arabic and many had a literary education.[93]

While *sharia* formed one body of law – subject to interpretation – the legal system divided into two: religious, family and most civil matters were handled by courts run by the *ulema*; police, criminal justice, taxation and defence were under the jurisdiction of the caliph. Or one might say it divided into three, as non-Muslim communities were permitted to retain courts under their own customary laws. The main concerns of the caliphs were taxation, maintaining the armed forces and preventing rebellion or other forms of disorder. There were three main forms of taxation: a tithe on Muslims required under *sharia* for charitable purposes (*zakat*), a land tax originally levied only on non-Muslims (*kharaj*), and a poll tax also exclusively on non-Muslims (*jizya*). These discriminatory taxes encouraged a kind of toleration, as they dissuaded the state from forcing conversions; they also created an economic incentive to convert voluntarily, as Muslims paid less tax. As the numbers of converts increased, the state's revenues would decline. The land tax thus came to be applied to Muslims as well as non-Muslims.[94]

For the control of such a vast empire, the flow of information was as important as the flow of finance. The courier system, which used the main highways, was essential for this, and it evolved into a secret intelligence service. Reports were received by an official in the capital, and summaries were made for the caliph. The government of the provinces wasn't consistent across the empire, as it relied on local elites and customs that the Arab conquerors had found in place, and those provinces closest to Baghdad were the most closely supervised. The more distant or highland regions, such as in Central Asia or North Africa, 'were scarcely, if at all, controlled by the central government.'[95] The main administrative problem was ensuring local officials' compliance with the demands for collection of taxes, which was made difficult by locals' lack of knowledge of the capital and its administrative methods. Success depended partly on sheer force or the threat thereof. To maintain obedience to the centre, and avoid excessive loyalty to the locals, provincial governors were appointed on limited terms and rotated from province to province. Nonetheless, compliance also relied heavily on recruitment of the heads of leading families, and collaboration with them as equals, to survey villages and landholdings in order to calculate and collect the taxes. As this was a multi-ethnic empire, the patronage of community leaders of all ethnic, religious and clan affiliations was necessary for effective government. Unsurprisingly, though, there was resistance and hence frequent outbreaks of rebellion, often by Kharajite or Shia groups. Shias had supported the Abbasid rebels at the beginning but were disappointed that they had not installed the 'legitimate' Imams descended from Ali. Major Shia revolts occurred in the early ninth century, and a new branch of Shi'ism, the Isma'ilis, arose and provoked further anti-Abbasid resistance in the provinces, especially the Fatimid dynasty (909–1171) who claimed descent from the Prophet's daughter, Fatima, and ruled North Africa and Egypt.[96]

Political philosophy

Amid all this, what kinds of ideas about good government occurred to the philosophers? One of the most prominent political thinkers was Abū Nasr al-Fārābī (c. 870–950 CE). He hailed from the east of the Abbasid empire and was of Turkic and Persian origin. He was educated in Baghdad and thus benefited from the translation movement that had brought many key works of Greek philosophy to readers of Syriac and Arabic. His philosophical writings are vast and explore a full range of fields. His political thought is more heavily influenced by Aristotle and Plato than by Islam, but he does consider the ruler's responsibilities for upholding religious belief for the benefit of the community. His model of the ideal city thus blends rationalism with faith.

Al-Fārābī compared the city with the human body, each limb and organ of which has its specialised part to play for the health of the person. Like a doctor, the ruler has to treat each household in its specialised role and in its relations with others. The minimal or indispensable city is that which aims to maintain its livelihood and to sustain life. But the ideal city is one in which all inhabitants help one another to achieve excellence and ultimate happiness. It isn't enough to be endowed with a virtue; the perfection of virtue occurs in the actions that perform it. Such a 'first' perfection 'affords us the last perfection which is ultimate happiness, i.e. the absolute good, which is chosen and desired for itself, and not for the sake of anything else' – and this is only found in the afterlife.[97]

Lesser cities regarded greatness, honour, wealth or the enjoyment of pleasure as their goal. The ideal or supreme ruler, such as the Prophet, on the other hand, led a virtuous and happy nation. He possessed all forms of knowledge and didn't need guidance by any other person, as he received revelation through direct acquaintance with pure and immutable truth.[98] Al-Fārābī took a cue from Plato's ideal philosopher kings but added that a ruler should also be an imam, or a scholar who taught and observed religious law and was ready to wage holy war. In the absence of such a wise imam, the next best was a council of governors who comprised the qualities of the ideal ruler, or, failing that, a ruler guided by the rational laws of past wise rulers. As few subjects could study the true philosophy, the city needed a common religion that harmonised the people's beliefs and actions, stimulated their imaginations and symbolically conveyed deeper truths. Ultimate happiness could be widely shared if the people were guided correctly by religion. Philosophy gave a reasoned account of 'ultimate principles', but religion used symbols or likenesses that imitated the higher knowledge of the philosopher.[99] Religion served a second-best function, necessary for the uneducated masses. Al-Fārābī wrote at length about politics and religion without prescribing any particular religion. The true philosopher respected the social value of religious practice but rose above it himself.[100]

End of empire

Neither the religious nor the philosophical ideals were satisfactorily upheld, however. The caliphs suffered from religious dissent over their legitimacy, and there were significant rebellions. They were called upon by theologians to be pious and just, but their powers were often arbitrary and absolute, and public officials could exploit their offices for private gains, making the whole system into a giant extortion racket. The empire's sheer size, moreover, meant that governors of provinces had wide powers to act relatively independently – the obvious temptation being to rule in one's own right. Their fealty to the caliph in Baghdad could become increasingly perfunctory, and the payment of tribute might eventually cease. Large and costly military and police forces were required to keep the payments of taxes and tributes flowing and to maintain obedience – and the soldiers themselves got angry when unpaid. The revenue of some districts was awarded directly to powerful military officers in lieu of salary, but this reduced the treasury's incomes. In some provinces, there were outright takeovers, such as that by the Fatimids in Cairo. The golden age of the caliphate was over by the tenth century, and cynicism about its authority set in.[101] Independent Abbasid rule came to an end in 945 when the Shia Buyid dynasty took over as commanders-in-chief. They, in turn, were supplanted in 1055 by the Seljuk Turks, who were Sunni and ruled as sultans (Chapter 5, Part 2). The Abbasid dynasty struggled on, lending caliphal legitimacy to the effective rulers; it ended with the destruction of Baghdad by Mongols, led by Hulegu Khan, in 1258. This great city was ruined, its people were massacred and its famous library was destroyed.

Conclusion

Monotheism implies (for the faithful) a promise to resolve the manifold problems of politics and government in two related ways: certainty taken from holy scripture, and legitimisation of rulers by the will of God. When rulers do evil things, this can be put down to God's punishment. Political rivals can be expelled or eliminated as infidels and apostates. The political use of religious doctrine represents, however, an unattainable desire for certainty in a world of uncertainty. Instead of delivering harmony, a mandated orthodoxy may accelerate dissent, followed by oppression and schism. The monotheistic monarchies of Byzantium and Baghdad had no parliaments, moreover, and little sense of popular representation (Chapter 7, Part 2). Religious principles that could have been egalitarian were often ignored in practice. Emperors ruled in God's image or as God's deputy. Although God's justice demanded benevolence, earthly administration and defence demanded taxation – and hence obedience, compelled by force if necessary. Although Islam had, in the Prophet, an ideal of a temporal ruler who unifies religion and politics, many Muslims resisted the growth of the caliphate into absolute monarchy, fearing tyranny and impiety. Once combined with the Islamic doctrine of submission to the will of God, however, the establishment of a monarchic government meant strict obedience to sultans.

Christ's kingdom was foretold in the Gospel,[102] although in His lifetime he was a victim of judges, governors and soldiers. Ancient Jewish stories of the House of David exemplified monarchy, and St Paul could be cited to justify obedience.

> Let everyone be subject to the governing authorities, for there is no authority except that which God has established. The authorities that exist have been established by God.[103]

Monarchy would later be argued for on grounds of a universal natural law promulgated by God – for example by St Thomas Aquinas (1225–74) and Francisco de Vitoria (c. 1485–1546).[104] Others used the 'image of God' metaphor. For example, the renaissance scholar Erasmus wrote:

> When the totality of things is in one person's power, then indeed, in so far as he is in this respect in the image of God, he excels everyone else in wisdom and goodness, and concentrates exclusively on helping the state.[105]

The centralised monarchical systems of the Muslims and the Christians nonetheless needed to operate and refine their earthly administration. Their practical model of government was to tax (by land or by heads) and to expand (or, failing that, to defend) their territory. The Christian government of Byzantium grew from Roman roots, while the Islamic dynasties adopted Sassanian Persian methods. Government's enduring gains from monotheism in general are numerous, however. The most obvious is the external higher constraint upon rulers imposed by the will and judgement of God, keeping them from arbitrary, unjust or cruel actions. Rulers were warned that they would be held to account and could face damnation if they failed to limit their actions within the law or to live up to their profound obligations to the people. If even the lawmakers were bound by the law, then surely all were bound by it equally. Models of good rulership and just government could be taken from scriptural edicts and from the examples set by past kings and prophets. And in as much as the community accepted the same faith, there was a congruence between the civil law and the values of the people. If people accept the precepts of a shared religion, then they may also willingly accept and obey the law that derives from it as if it were their own. Indeed, the monotheistic religions prescribed laws and issued prohibitions many of which we still respect. They gave us the concept of individual accountability before God, and hence before the law of the civil government, leading to the elimination of practices such as collective punishment. By embracing all people within their law, they advanced ideals of fundamental equality and social justice.

Notes

1 Wiener, 2014.
2 Finkelstein & Silberman, 2006, p. 20.
3 McKenzie, 2000.
4 Finkelstein & Silberman, 2006, p. 144.
5 Meyers, 1998, p. 222.
6 McKenzie, 2000, p. 188.
7 2 Samuel 8:16–8; 2 Samuel 20:23–6; 1 Kings 4:1–6.
8 Meyers, 1998, p. 269.
9 Finkelstein & Silberman, 2006.
10 Notably the Siloam tunnel and the wall fortifications.
11 Finkelstein & Silberman, 2006, p. 140.
12 2 Kings 23:2.
13 Deuteronomy 17:19.
14 For example, Deuteronomy 24:16. 'Parents are not to be put to death for their children, nor children put to death for their parents; each will die for their own sin.'
15 'The book of Deuteronomy and the Deuteronomistic History, which contains the David and Solomon epic, were written to serve Josiah's cult reform strategy and territorial (or state) ideology.' Finkelstein & Silberman, 2006, p. 203.
16 Deuteronomy 17:20.
17 Finer, 1999, vol. I, p. 239. Original italics.
18 Ibid., p. 268.
19 Stern, 1984.
20 Goldstein, 1990.
21 Schama, 2013.
22 Barbero, 2018, p. 20.
23 Norwich, 2012, p. 55.
24 Finer, 1999, vol. II, p. 885.
25 Alchermes, 2005.
26 Montefiore, 2011.
27 Lane Fox, 1988, p. 609. Already in 301 CE, however, King Tiridates III of Armenia had converted to Christianity, making it the state religion.
28 Matthew 16:18–9.
29 Mango, 2002.
30 Nixey, 2017.
31 Haldon, 2005.
32 Liebeschuetz, 2001, p. 218.
33 Barnish, Lee, & Whitby, 2001.
34 Kelly, 1997.

35 McCormick, 2001.
36 Gray, 2005.
37 If Jesus was sent to redeem humanity, the ancient critics asked (for example), then why did a supposedly benevolent God wait for so many centuries to send Him? See: Nixey, 2017.
38 'For all their declarations on the wickedness of pagan learning, few educated Christians [not even Augustine] could bring themselves to discard it completely.' Ibid., p. 190.
39 The Greek *daimon* was a minor deity.
40 Lane Fox, 1988.
41 Mango, 2002, p. 111.
42 Sheppard, 2001, p. 841.
43 Hall, 2001, p. 735.
44 Some families deliberately castrated boys, however, in the hope of their gaining high-status employment in the court. Castration was also used as punishment or to end an individual's imperial ambitions.
45 Herrin, 2007; Ringrose, 2003.
46 Finer, 1999, vol. II.
47 Herrin, 2007, p. 55, cites Irene (780–90 as regent for her son, and then 797–802), Theodora (842–56), Zoe (914–9) and Theophano (963–9).
48 She wasn't recognised in the west, however.
49 Procopius, 2007, p. 37.
50 McCormick, 2001.
51 Kelly, 1997; McCormick, 2001. This bureaucracy still lacked many principles of the modern bureaucracy.
52 Haldon, 2005, p. 41.
53 Maas, 2005.
54 Finer, 1999, vol. II.
55 Herrin, 2007.
56 Haldon, 2005, p. 42.
57 Ibid.
58 Barnish, Lee & Whitby, 2001, p. 206.
59 Liebs, 2001.
60 Birks & McLeod (translators), 1987, p. 33.
61 The Code of Justinian is still relevant to those European jurisdictions based on Roman law, as contrasted with the English common-law systems.
62 Humfress, 2005, p. 178.
63 Liebs, 2001, p. 243.
64 Finer, 1999, vol. II, p. 656. Later medieval kings read from the Code a principle that the ruler may also be exempt from the law, according to Kantorowicz, 1957.
65 Greek became the official language of government under Heraclius (r. 610–41).
66 Barnish, Lee, & Whitby, 2001; Liebs, 2001.
67 Humfress, 2005.
68 The ancient Roman republic had prevented supreme powers of legislator and judge from falling into one man's hands (see Chapter 3, Part 1). In modern republics, they're strictly separated (Chapter 7, part 2).
69 Pazdernik, 2005, p. 190.
70 Agapetus, 2009 [ca 530 CE], trans. Peter Bell, p. 120.
71 Ibid., p. 119.
72 Ibid., p. 109.
73 Ibid., p. 102.
74 Ibid., p. 101.
75 'It seemed as if nature had removed every tendency to evil from the rest of mankind and deposited it in the soul of [Justinian].' Procopius, 2007, p. 35. Written about 550 CE, Procopius's account is evidently exaggerated.

76 Holland, 2013, takes a more sceptical view that 'different communities of the faithful preserved different versions of the holy text' and that it received little scholarly attention until the ninth century, implying that it was a work-in-progress well after the Prophet's time (p. 335).
77 'The earliest surviving biography dates to the middle of the eighth century,' more than a century after the Prophet's death. Lapidus, 2012, p. 39. For a biography of Muhammad see Armstrong, 1991.
78 Crone, 2004. The medieval historian Ibn Khaldun (1332–406) pointed out, however, that it was only under Islam that prophecy had been integral to the formation of government. Khaldun, 2005 [1370], p. 183.
79 A Byzantine army was defeated at Ajnadayn (in present-day Israel) in 634; the Persians were defeated at Qadisiyya (by the Euphrates River) in 636/7, following which the Persian capital Ctesiphon was taken, and, to the west, Alexandria capitulated in 643.
80 Khaldun, 2005 [1370], p. 162.
81 Lapidus, 2012, chapter 6.
82 Crone, 2004, p. 21.
83 Sluglett & Currie, 2014.
84 Crone, 2004, p. 28. The term 'Sunni' only applied from the eleventh century.
85 Finer, 1999, vol. II, p. 691.
86 Crone, 2004, p. 45.
87 The Supreme Leader of the contemporary Islamic Republic of Iran stands in for the Mahdi, as guardian, awaiting his return.
88 Black, 2011.
89 Lapidus, 2012, p. 90.
90 Marozzi, 2014.
91 al-Sāʿī, 2007, p. 71.
92 Khaldun, 2005 [1370], p. 190.
93 Lapidus, 2012, chapter 7; Finer, 1999, vol. II.
94 Finer, 1999, vol. II.
95 Lapidus, 2012, p. 99.
96 Ibid.
97 al-Fārābī, 1961, pp. 39–40.
98 al-Fārābī, 2008, p. 286.
99 Mahdi, 1962.
100 Crone, 2004.
101 Bonner, 2010.
102 Luke 1:32–3.
103 Romans 13:1.
104 'On Civil Power' (1528), in Vitoria, 1991.
105 Erasmus, 1997, p. 37, abridged.

References

Agapetus. 2009. 'Advice to the Emperor Justinian.' In *Three Political Voices from the Age of Justinian*, by Peter N. Bell, 99–122. Liverpool: Liverpool University Press.
Alchermes, Joseph. 2005. 'Art and Architecture in the Age of Justinian.' In *The Cambridge Companion to the Age of Justinian*, by Michael Maas, 343–75. Cambridge: Cambridge University Press.
al-Fārābī, Abū Naṣr Muḥammad. 1961. *Fuṣūl al-Madanī: Aphorisms of the Statesman* (ed. D.M. Dunlop). Cambridge: Cambridge University Press.
———. 2008. 'The Political Regime.' In *The Broadview Anthology of Social and Political Thought, Volume 1: From Plato to Nietzsche*, by Andrew Bailey, Samantha Brennan, Will Kymlicka, Jacob Levy, Alex Sager and Clark Wolf, 283–96. Buffalo, NY: Broadview Press.

al-Sāʾī, Ibn. 2007. *Consorts of the Caliphs: Women and the Court of Baghdad*. New York: New York University Press.

Armstrong, Karen. 1991. *Muhammad: A Biography of the Prophet*. London: Phoenix.

Barbero, Alessandro. 2018. *Charlemagne: Father of a Continent*. Berkeley: University of California Press.

Barnish, Sam, A.D. Lee, and Michael Whitby. 2001. 'Government and Administration.' In *The Cambridge Ancient History*, by Alan Cameron, Bryan Ward-Perkins and Michael Whitby, 164–206. Cambridge: Cambridge University Press.

Birks, Peter, and Grant McLeod. 1987. *Justinian's Institutes*. London: Duckworth.

Black, Antony. 2011. *The History of Islamic Political Thought: From the Prophet to the Present*. Edinburgh: Edinburgh University Press.

Bonner, Michael. 2010. 'The Waning of Empire, 861–945.' In *The New Cambridge History of Islam*, by C. Robinson, 305–59. Cambridge: Cambridge University Press.

Crone, Patricia. 2004. *God's Rule: Government and Islam*. New York, NY: Columbia University Press.

Erasmus. 1997. *The Education of a Christian Prince*. Cambridge: Cambridge University Press.

Finer, Samuel Edmund. 1999. *The History of Government*. Oxford: Oxford University Press.

Finkelstein, Israel, and Neil Asher Silberman. 2006. *David and Solomon*. New York, NY: Free Press.

Goldstein, Jonathan. 1990. 'The Hasmonean Revolt and the Hasmonean Dynasty.' In *The Cambridge History of Judaism*, by William Davies and Louis Finkelstein, 292–351. Cambridge: Cambridge University Press.

Gray, Patrick. 2005. 'The Legacy of Chalcedon.' In *The Cambridge Companion to the Age of Justinian*, by Michael Maas, 215–38. Cambridge: Cambridge University Press.

Haldon, John F. 2005. 'Economy and Administration.' In *The Cambridge Companion to the Age of Justinian*, by Michael Maas, 28–59. Cambridge: Cambridge University Press.

Hall, Stuart George. 2001. 'The Organization of the Church.' In *The Cambridge Ancient History*, by Averil Cameron, Bryan Ward-Perkins, and Michael Whitby, 731–44. Cambridge: Cambridge University Press.

Herrin, Judith. 2007. *Byzantium: The Surprising Life of a Medieval Empire*. Princeton, NJ: Princeton University Press.

Holland, Tom. 2013. *In the Shadow of the Sword*. London: Abacus.

Humfress, Caroline. 2005. 'Law and Legal Practice in the Age of Justinian.' In *The Cambridge Companion to the Age of Justinian*, by Michael Maas, 161–84. Cambridge: Cambridge University Press.

Kantorowicz, Ernst H. 1957. *The King's Two Bodies: A Study in Mediaeval Political Theology*. Princeton, NJ: Princeton University Press.

Kelly, Christopher. 1997. 'Emperors, Government and Bureaucracy.' In *The Cambridge Ancient History*, by Averil Cameron and Peter Garnsey, 138–83. Cambridge: Cambridge University Press.

Khaldun, Ibn. 2005. *The Muqaddimah: An Introduction to History*. Princeton, NJ: Princeton University Press.

Lane Fox, Robin. 1988. *Pagans and Christians in the Mediterranean World*. London: Penguin.

Lapidus, Ira. 2012. *Islamic Societies to the Nineteenth Century: A Global History*. Cambridge: Cambridge University Press.

Liebeschuetz, J.H.W.G. 2001. 'Administration and Politics in the Cities of the Fifth to the Mid Seventh Century: 425–640.' In *The Cambridge Ancient History*, by Averil Cameron, Bryan Ward-Perkins, and Michael Whitby, 207–37. Cambridge: Cambridge University Press.

Liebs, Detlef. 2001. 'Roman Law.' In *The Cambridge Ancient History*, by Averil Cameron, Bryan Ward-Perkins and Michael Whitby, 238–59. Cambridge: Cambridge University Press.

Maas, Michael. 2005. 'Roman Questions, Byzantine Answers.' In *The Cambridge Companion to the Age of Justinian*, by Michael Maas, 3–27. Cambridge: Cambridge University Press.

Mahdi, Muhsin. 1962. *Alfarabi's Philosophy of Plato and Aristotle*. New York, NY: Glencoe.

Mango, Cyril (ed.). 2002. *The Oxford History of Byzantium*. Oxford: Oxford University Press.

Marozzi, Justin. 2014. *Baghdad: City of Peace, City of Blood*. London: Penguin.

McCormick, Michael. 2001. 'Emperor and Court.' In *The Cambridge Ancient History*, by Averil Cameron, Bryan Ward-Perkins, and Michael Whitby, 135–63. Cambridge: Cambridge University Press.

McKenzie, Steven L. 2000. *King David : A Biography*. New York: Oxford University Press.

Meyers, Carol. 1998. 'Kinship and Kingship: The Early Monarchy.' In *The Oxford History of the Biblical World*, by Michael D. Coogan, 221–271. Oxford: Oxford University Press.

Montefiore, Simon Sebag. 2011. *Jerusalem: The Biography*. New York, NY: Vintage Books.

Nixey, Catherine. 2017. *The Darkening Age*. London: Pan.

Norwich, John Julius. 2012. *The Popes: A History*. London: Vintage.

Pazdernik, Charles. 2005. 'Justinianic Ideology and the Power of the Past.' In *The Cambridge Companion to the Age of Justinian*, by Michael Maas, 185–212. Cambridge: Cambridge University Press.

Procopius. 2007. *The Secret History*. London: Penguin.

Ringrose, Kathryn M. 2003. *The Perfect Servant: Eunuchs and the Social Construction of Gender in Byzantium*. Chicago, IL: Chicago University Press.

Schama, Simon. 2013. *The Story of the Jews: Finding the Words, 1000BCE – 1492CE*. London: Bodley Head.

Sheppard, Anne. 2001. 'Philosophy and Philosophical Schools.' In *The Cambridge Ancient History*, by Averil Cameron, Bryan Ward-Perkins, and Michael Whitby, 835–54. Cambridge: Cambridge University Press.

Sluglett, Peter, and Andrew Currie. 2014. *Atlas of Islamic History*. London: Routledge.

Stern, Ephraim. 1984. 'The Persian Empire and the Political and Social History of Palestine in the Persian Period.' In *The Cambridge History of Judaism*, by William Davies and Louis Finkelstein, 70–87. Cambridge: Cambridge University Press.

Vitoria, Francisco de. 1991. *Political Writings*. Cambridge: Cambridge University Press.

Wiener, Malcolm H. 2014. 'Dating the Emergence of Historical Israel in Light of Recent Developments in Egyptian Chronology.' *Tel Aviv: Journal of the Institute of Archaeology of Tel Aviv University* 41 (1): 50–54.

5

RULERS OF NO FIXED ABODE

On 13 October 1806, the philosopher G.W.F. Hegel saw Napoleon Bonaparte riding through the town of Jena. He wrote to a friend:

> I saw the Emperor – this world-soul [*Weltseele*] – riding through the city on reconnaissance; it is indeed a wonderful sensation to see such an individual, concentrated here at one point on horseback, reaching out across the world and being its master.[1]

The following day, in fields close to Jena, Napoleon's armies met and routed the Prussians. A fortnight later Napoleon entered Berlin in triumph. He had already bound the many kingdoms, principalities and duchies of the former Holy Roman Empire as client states, forcing them to supply troops but also to modernise. Hegel saw him as representing historical transformation, ending feudal forms of subjection and advancing freedom through the legal status of citizenship won in the French revolution. But Napoleon depended on success in battle; he ruled 'on the move' so long as he kept the strategic advantage. In his ill-fated invasion of Russia, however, his opponents avoided battle and lured his army 'deep into Russian territory, stretching its supply lines'.[2] Retreat with catastrophic losses became Napoleon's only option.

An equally intriguing encounter between a philosopher and a mobile conqueror occurred in 1401 outside the walls of Damascus in a tent – one must imagine a luxurious tent. The city was under siege by the forces of the Mongolian ruler Timur, known in English as Tamerlane (1336–1405). The philosopher, Ibn Khaldun (1332–1406), was a judge from Cairo who had accompanied Egyptian forces sent to help defend Damascus. He was lowered from the city walls to pay Timur a visit. Timur was a violent and illiterate warrior who loved philosophy, and the two men conversed at length. Ibn Khaldun negotiated safe passage for

DOI: 10.4324/9781003166955-5

the Egyptian clerics and administrators who were trapped in Damascus before its inhabitants were massacred.[3]

Just as Hegel had seen a 'world-soul' in Napoleon, so Ibn Khaldun saw in Timur a man who exemplified or even fulfilled his philosophy of history. Timur was more successful than Napoleon, as he remained 'on the move' prosecuting his own strategic plans until the day he died on his way to invade China. No one defeated or imprisoned him. From his pastoral-nomadic society, he built a large and cohesive force that overcame agricultural urban societies, violently setting in train a new cycle of historical change. Ibn Khaldun's theory assumes that the social characteristics of humans are shaped by their environment and by their material means of making a living, which in turn influence their level of 'group feeling'. The Arabic word used by Ibn Khaldun for this group feeling or spirit, *asabiyya*, is more than a static quality of a community, however, as it has dynamic and strategic effects. Groups with strong *asabiyya* (the nomadic tribes) will defeat and rule over those with weak *asabiyya* (the softer, less courageous urban communities), and the 'natural goal' of group feeling is 'royal authority', which requires that 'one person claim all the glory for himself and appropriate it to himself.'[4] But this monarchic rule will lead the conquerors' descendants into the settled and luxurious lifestyle of the city. They'll then tax their subjects to maintain standing armies to fight for them and to expand and defend their territories. The rulers will employ advisers, ministers and tax-collectors from nations other than those who first won them power, but this 'announces the destruction of the dynasty'.[5] As the soldiers become used to wealth and urban life, their will to endure the hardships of warfare declines. But the cost to the treasury of keeping them rises, and the rulers must either impose excessive taxes or reduce the size of the armed forces. The group feeling and military strength of their forebears is thus dissipated. 'When the roots are gone, the branches cannot be strong on their own.'[6] Once it sets in, this 'disease' invites invasion from rival groups. The *asabiyya* that first made conquest and royal authority possible has been lost and the dynasty will fall. Hence, *asabiyya* is crucial to Ibn Khaldun's understanding of a cyclical theory of conquest, state formation, the rise and fall of dynasties and empires, and their replacement by new rulers who command large mobile groups with greater *asabiyya*. He provides a critical historiography as well as a theory of social, economic and political change. This involves the interactions between nomadic and settled peoples, presenting the former as the initiators of historical change.[7]

We think of government as subsisting in stable institutions based in capital cities. But in practice, government means acting on a defined population to achieve regularity and to avert destabilisation by unexpected events or systemic flaws. This doesn't necessarily mean one has to stay in one place, and the nomadic conquerors are the best examples of mobile rulers. Even today, those who govern are mobile, while also denying mobility to others by means, for instance, of incarceration or border controls. We may think that the government of a state is the prerogative of those born and bred in a defined territory and that peoples who migrate or invade are outsiders or interlopers. But movement may instead be seen as the norm for humans. The longer story of *Homo sapiens*, going back 100,000 years, is dominated by foraging lifeways, migrations and colonisation; whereas agriculturalism and settlements emerged relatively recently, from 12,000 years ago, and only in limited geographic zones.[8] Many groups could have alternated between moving from place to place in pursuit of game, fresh pasture or untapped resources, on one hand, and seeking the warmth and security of settled shelter, on the other. One estimate has it that the urban-based state form has encompassed the majority of the world's population only since 1600 CE, prior to which most people 'had never seen a (routine) tax collector or, if they had seen one, still had the option of making themselves fiscally invisible.'[9] Settled and mobile peoples have meanwhile traded and fought throughout history. The consequent contact and mixture of diverse populations have led to the appropriation and adaptation of techniques of government.

The interventions of nomadic tribes in history are numerous. The ancient Greek colonists around the Black Sea knew the Scythians; the Romans were unable to pacify the Parthians; the Spanish-American governors in Mexico were forced to come to terms with the Comanches of the southern plains in the eighteenth century. In the previous chapter, we saw how Arab and Berber tribesmen, inspired and united by a new religion, defeated Byzantine, Persian and Egyptian armies and built the Islamic empire. In its turn, the caliphate was dominated by Daylamite tribes (the Buyids) from northern Iran, then by the Seljuk Turks from Central Asia, and later ended altogether by the Mongols. The Eurasian steppe, a geographical belt of grasslands and scrublands interrupted by rivers and mountains stretching from Hungary to eastern Mongolia, supported pastoral nomads. These were mobile tribes whose primary resources were horses and domesticated livestock. Survival on horseback produced hardy people skilled with bow and arrow. As every able-bodied man was also a cavalryman, they saw no distinction between civilian and military. Their traditional religions were shamanistic; their politics were relatively egalitarian; their economies had little specialisation. Tribal groups migrated on a seasonal basis and in response to changes in climate or pressure from rival groups. They had strong internal cohesion, and plundering rival tribes was normal and honourable. When many tribes formed an alliance, they could threaten established empires. For example, the Xiongnu alliance of the eastern steppe posed problems for the Han dynasty in China (Chapter 3, Part 3). The historian Ernest Gellner succinctly posed the basic problem of governing nomads:

> Shepherds are hard to govern, because their wealth is on the hoof and they can easily escape authority. Their mobility makes it possible to avoid taxation, to raid, and to elude oppression.[10]

In the absence of police, the obvious way to augment one's wealth is to rob one's neighbour. The basis for doing this, and for preventing others from doing it to you, is group cohesion or *asabiyya*, with a strict customary code of honour based on kinship and loyalty – one that does not, however, rule out treachery and changing sides. State formation requires enforcing law and collecting tax – tasks that are most readily achievable in societies that are settled and that depend on fixed-field agriculture for their staple diet.[11] Nonetheless, nomads have also been capable of multi-tribal unification under a strong leader.

> Nomad empires [of Central Asia] began first by conquering other nomads, incorporating them into often uneasy tribal unions. Ethnically diverse and polyglot, nomadic states were filled with competing forces. There were aristocrats and commoners. Certain clans ranked higher than others. A clan or tribal chief was expected to share some of his wealth with his followers. Stingy leaders lost followers – and sometimes their lives. Unwilling subject peoples rebelled.[12]

What does it take, then, to unite many such tribes under one ruler, and what keeps them in motion under this command? And when they encounter the need for civil government, how do they do it? This chapter considers the Berber Almoravid dynasty, the Seljuks and the Mongols. We begin, however, on sea rather than land. For a maritime example, historians might refer to the Vikings. Instead, we consider the great oceanic migrations across the Pacific Ocean and the first human colonisation of its many islands. How did the Polynesian navigators achieve this feat, and what might their political motives have been? What did an oceanic empire look like?

Part 1: The Pacific navigators

Perhaps the greatest of all human migrations was the discovery and colonisation of the many islands of the Pacific Ocean. This differed from other such migrations because it spanned a vast ocean rather than land, and the settlers were already agriculturalists bringing their crops (including coconut palms) and domesticated animals with them. Elsewhere on earth, the first humans to arrive had been foragers (hunter gatherers), and agriculture was established only later. The most remarkable features of the great Pacific migration were the sailing and navigational technologies that made it possible.[13] The timings and routes taken are not precisely known, but a combination of oral traditions and archaeological, botanical, linguistic and genetic evidence reveals the basic trajectory. The first seaborne migrations from New Guinea westwards across the Bismarck Archipelago and the Solomon Islands began around 1400 BCE, reaching as far west as Fiji by around 1000 BCE. There was a long hiatus until people migrated further to the Society Islands sometime in the first 500 years CE. By around 700 CE, people had colonised Rapa Nui (Easter Island) at the far eastern corner of the Polynesian Triangle, and Hawai'i at the northern-most corner. The last corners to be discovered were in Aotearoa New Zealand including the remote Rēkohu

(Chatham Islands), 800 kilometres east of Te Waipounamu (the South Island of New Zealand) at about 1200 CE.[14] There are remains of human habitation on sub-Antarctic Enderby Island (at 55 degrees south) dated to the thirteenth or fourteenth century.[15] The distribution of the sweet potato (*kumara*) through Polynesia stands as evidence that Polynesian sailors made it to South America, returning with this tuber to cultivate it and share it with other distant communities. The kumara became a staple food in Aotearoa.[16]

This oceanic migration was not the result of sailors going off course and making landfalls by chance. Enough is known about the oceangoing canoes (double-hulled or single with outrigger) and the navigational knowledge to show that people had learned how to sail long distances and return safely home between tiny islands. For example, although the archipelagos of Fiji, Samoa and Tonga are separated by hundreds of kilometres of ocean, for centuries these distinct island realms traded in goods and marriage partners, and they fought one another for dominance. In 1830 a missionary recorded an expedition of seven large Tongan canoes heading to Samoa. Fleets could carry up to 500 men.[17] Frequent reciprocal maritime journeys over long distances were well within their abilities.

Aotearoa New Zealand was reached by numerous independent voyages over a considerable period, as recorded in oral histories and confirmed by the DNA of the introduced Polynesian rat. The existence of this landmass would have been inferred by people in East Polynesia observing migratory birds. Genetic evidence suggests that somewhere in the range of 70–190 women were among the first colonists. Some canoes may have returned to their home islands. Eventually, however, contact with the islands of origin (most likely the Society Islands) was lost. The long-distance navigational techniques were forgotten once the people of Aotearoa settled in, enjoying an abundance of bird and marine life, and cultivating the imported kumara.[18]

Being accustomed to modern navigational technologies, it's hard now to imagine how people can confidently set out across horizons into such vast oceanic spaces – let alone how they can return safely to the island from which they departed. A thorough knowledge of stars, ocean currents, prevailing winds, wave patterns, birds, marine life and cloud formations is necessary – and, of course, sturdy sailing-boats. Acquiring this knowledge or lore takes lengthy education and preparation. Enough of it has been recorded to allow us to appreciate its sophistication.[19]

Oceanic imperialism

There's no compelling evidence that gradual eastward migration of humans across the Pacific resulted from over-exploitation or overpopulation of islands, and hence competition for resources leading to expulsions or searches for new islands. Although the story of the over-exploitation, deforestation and collapse of Rapa Nui is well known, this was exceptional not normal.[20] It represents one tragic consequence, rather than a basic cause, of migration. It was one of the last islands to be reached, and older eastern-Pacific communities continued to flourish. Motives for migration such as sheer curiosity or adventure and the prestige of establishing a new island community may have been more important, as well as the search for unexploited resources. Acquiring the skills of sailor and navigator, and then successes at sea, confer status on an individual, stimulating ambitions to go further.

Settled island realms competed with one another. The economic and political rivalry and exchange that went on between Fiji, Samoa and Tonga for many centuries resulted in Tonga freeing itself and establishing the Tu'i Tonga empire, which reached its peak around 1200 to 1500 CE. Its hegemony encompassed initially all of Fiji and parts of Samoa, and then expanded to the whole of western and central Polynesia including parts of Melanesia and Micronesia.

> The building of the imperial centre was made possible through the enforced extraction and exploitation of both human and material resources such as slave-workers, prestige goods and services and rare material objects, facilitated by the existence of an imperial fleet of sea-worthy, long-distance canoes.[21]

A series of regicides and political turmoil around 1470 led to a diarchy in which the Tu'i Tonga retained the divine rulership while a second dynastic line of kings was created for a secular rule. By the time Europeans began to visit the area, relations between the three main maritime powers had settled into a tripartite exchange arrangement.[22] Although converted to Christianity, Tonga remains an independent kingdom.

Part 2: The Almoravids

We shift now to North Africa, where Arab Muslim rule expanded during the latter decades of the seventh century, meeting resistance from the Byzantines and the indigenous Berbers. Under the Umayyads (Chapter 4, Part 3) Muslims fought against, and at times in alliance with, the Berber tribes. The latter joined Arab military leaders when they saw opportunities to be part of an expanding empire that encompassed the Iberian Peninsula. Roderick, the last Visigothic king of Spain, was defeated by a mixed Arab-Berber force led by the governor of Tangier, Tariq ibn Ziyad, who crossed the Strait of Gibraltar in 710 CE. By 716, most of the peninsula was under Muslim governors answering to the Umayyad caliph in Damascus. Muslim expeditions in France were defeated near Tours and Poitiers in 732. The Franks restricted the Muslims largely to the Iberian Peninsula, and resistance to Muslim rule continued from the north. Christians and Jews retained their faiths, but some high-status families converted to Islam and/or formed marriage alliances with the new rulers. Arabic customs and language became the norms, and some Berbers challenged the Muslim rulers' discrimination in favour of Arabs. When the Abbasids defeated the Umayyad dynasty in 750, Abd al-Rahman ibn Mu'awiya (731–88), a grandson of a former Umayyad caliph, fled to al-Andalus. With the support of Umayyad clients, he defeated a pro-Abbasid faction and declared an independent emirate based in Córdoba. This was elevated to the status of caliphate in the tenth century. The caliphate was abolished in 1031 after Muslim Andalusia broke up into petty independent states (*ta'ifa*) ruled by kings of various origins. These kingdoms were unable to muster forces sufficient to combat the Christian rulers of Castile and Aragon in the north. They were reduced to paying tribute to the Christians; hence they imposed heavy taxes that didn't conform with Islamic law.[23]

Meanwhile, in Morocco, the Almoravid movement was gathering force among Berber pastoralists of the western Sahara. Disparate tribes who had previously raided one another began to unite under the Maliki[24] version of Islamic law and a single leader. This unifying effect of religion was to be an important feature of Ibn Khaldun's theory of *asabiyya* and tribal state-building.[25] The Almoravids expanded across the Atlas Mountains to the north, taking over fertile plains and the trade routes between North Africa and Andalusia, and founding Marrakesh as their capital in 1070. Their realm extended from the Atlantic coast to Algeria as they took over settlements and city-states and subjugated or killed their *amirs*. The Almoravids then crossed the strait to al-Andalus in 1086. They found, though, that the rivalries between, and the alleged self-indulgence of, the Andalusian Muslim kings were as big a problem as the incursions of the Christian King Alfonso VI of León and Castile. Hence the Almoravids had to overthrow the former in order to combat the latter. By the early years of the twelfth century, they had transformed a movement of Saharan nomadic tribes into an imperial rule that encompassed the western deserts, the High Atlas mountains, the North African coast as far east as Algiers, and roughly a half of the Iberian Peninsula.[26]

These successes created the predictable problems of government. For the sake of legitimacy in the wider Muslim world, the Almoravid ruler was 'commander of the Muslims' (*amīr al-muslimīn*) subordinate to the Abbasid caliph in Baghdad (Chapter 4, Part 3). Succession was based on the incumbent ruler's nomination of a son as heir. In relation to the other tribal leaders, the *amīrs* were considered first among equals rather than autocrats.[27] They remained for the most part in Marrakesh and hence relied on messengers for communications with provincial governors who were also urban-based and were responsible for collection of taxes, mobilisation of armed forces and military leadership. The standardisation of the legal framework, based on the Sunni Maliki school, was carried out by a cohort of jurists. The government of the new empire also required secretaries, scribes and financial administrators fluent in Arabic. Many were recruited from the minor states that the Almoravids had conquered. This meant that the new rulers were able to incorporate Arabic-speaking administrative expertise that provided religious and political legitimacy and stable government.

The expense of sustaining the empire and its armed forces led to forms and levels of taxation that were regarded, however, as un-Islamic and hence were resisted. Armed tribesmen are only loyal as long as they are rewarded, moreover, and the nomadic tradition of sharing booty had to be abandoned in favour of salaries funded by taxation. The growing empire had to look beyond the Sanhaja warriors to recruit slave-soldiers and mercenaries including Christians. By Ibn Khaldun's account, recruitment of paid outsiders meant that the rot had set in and the demise of the dynasty would follow. The threat to the Almoravid dynasty came not so much from Christians in the north but from a rival movement of nomadic tribes, the Almohads, who by the 1140s had gained control of the Atlas Mountains and besieged Marrakesh. The Almohads then waged a holy war of conquest to re-establish proper observance of Islamic law in Andalusia. And so began a new Muslim dynasty that had to resist Christian forces in the north.[28] This particular story of rise and fall was one that Ibn Khaldun (whose family hailed from Andalusia) knew well and which contributed to his theory about *asabiyya* in the cycle of political change.

Part 3: The Seljuks

Our attention shifts now to the far north-eastern edge of the medieval Islamic world – to an area of the Eurasian steppe called Transoxiana (today's southern Kazakhstan and Uzbekistan) around the Syr Daria (Jaxartes) River that flows into the land-locked Aral Sea. From the eighth through tenth centuries competition between rival groups of nomads for pastures precipitated migrations in which tribes were forced westwards and Transoxiana became occupied by Turkic Oghuz.[29] These tribal unions couldn't be described as 'states' except in a very loose and decentralised form; neither were they all related by common kinship or ethnicity, as associations between nomadic groups were fluid and opportunistic.[30] Such nomadic peoples (some of whom had converted to Islam) traded livestock and animal products for cereals and manufactured products from towns governed by Iranians. Many Turkic horsemen taken as slaves in frontier skirmishes converted to Islam and were recruited into the Abbasid forces as mounted archers.[31] But the Turkic tribes also invaded the Persian territories for plunder and pasture, especially in north-eastern Iran (Khurasan). Amid this mixture of peoples and rivalries, the Seljuks (a minor Islamised branch of the Oghuz) emerged from Transoxiana to establish themselves in Khurasan.[32] The Ghaznavid rulers in Afghanistan tried to conciliate the Seljuks with landed titles, but the nomadic Seljuks 'were unfamiliar with the concepts of defined frontiers and the sanctity of landed property'. Armies failed to pacify them too, as the Seljuks were hardier and more mobile; they needed little baggage and could move their households when necessary. They had no siege engines, but they besieged fortified cities all the same. In 1040, Khurasan's cities capitulated to them if only to restore economies blockaded by swarms of horsemen with large herds to feed.[33]

The sultans

The Seljuk ruler Toghril (r. 1040–63) established himself in Nishapur, Khurasan's provincial capital, but the tribes didn't adapt easily to the regulated ways and administrative hierarchies of urban peoples. They nonetheless spread through Iran, and in 1055, Toghril deposed and imprisoned the Buyid prince Al-Malik al-Rahim, thus restoring Sunni supremacy, purging Shia influences and asserting control over the caliphate. Toghril was named king (*malik*) in 1058, and marriages between his family and the caliph's were arranged. This led to a diarchy in which the Abbasid caliph-imam was the spiritual head-of-state and the Seljuq sultan was the secular ruler. Toghril's progress from minor steppe chieftain to Iranian ruler was rapid and transformative. His successors Alp-Arslan (1063–72) and Malik-Shah I (1072–92) oversaw the peak of Seljuq rule and territorial expansion from Central Asia to Anatolia and the Levant.[34] The Battle of Manzikert in 1071 was a major victory over Byzantium that gave the Seljuks access to Anatolia (Turkey) and led to the formation of an independent Sultanate of Rum which flourished in the early thirteenth century until the arrival of the Mongols in 1243.[35]

The Seljuks almost restored the Abbasid empire's former territory, but their nomadic culture didn't adapt easily to government in its Persian form. Monarchy wasn't their custom, as they regarded rulership as consensual. Lands and grazing rights were to be shared among tribal subgroups, each with its own leader. To overcome these traditions, the Seljuk sultans reduced their reliance on Turkic tribesmen by recruiting slave-soldiers and mercenaries, but an expensive standing army[36] had to be paid with land grants. These gave soldiers incomes but weren't bequeathable. On occasions when the sultan chose to reduce these expensive forces by dismissing soldiers, he created cohorts of disgruntled veterans many of whom became his enemies. Moreover, there was 'constant competition [for leadership] between members of the [ruling] family'.[37] And the pressure to divide the empire into provinces for the sultan's sons to inherit, especially after the death of Malik-Shah I, led to the disintegration of the Seljuk empire into weaker sub-units.[38] The most powerful of these units centred on the sultan himself in the capital of Isfahan, but the further out one went, the weaker his influence and the greater the autonomy of local princes or governors. The empire was seen as 'a series of political groupings rather than as a unitary state.'[39] From one governorship to another, Seljuk administration was inconsistent, with official titles and roles changing. There was a generally understood division between 'the sword' (Turkic soldiers) and 'the pen' (Persian administrators), but that too wasn't always strictly observed. The main concerns of government were tax collection and security, and the vizier (chief minister) was pivotal. Those aspiring to serve in the senior bureaucracy would acquire a broad education in Islamic jurisprudence and Arabic grammar and literature. But family pedigree and patronage were often the keys to desirable positions.[40]

The Seljuk horsemen were frequently destructive – burning cities and ruining crops – as they moved west to occupy pasturelands in Anatolia and the Caucasus. Nonetheless, the late eleventh-century caliphate was regarded as relatively secure and prosperous.

Seljuk rule integrated peoples of two distinct cultures – Turkic nomadic pastoralists and Persian agriculturalists – while preserving the agrarian basis of the economy and acquiring the administrative skills to govern both groups.[41] The Seljuks were one of many waves of nomadic peoples who migrated, traded and fought with settled peoples throughout Eurasia. In their case, they took effective political power from the Abbasid caliphs, but they governed alongside them for the sake of religious legitimacy. The sultans adopted Persian ways of government under Islamic law. The Abbasid dynasty and the Seljuk rulers were overthrown, however, by a later wave of central-Asian nomads, the Mongols.

Books of government

Given their nomadic customs, the Seljuk sultans required guidance on how to rule an empire. To this end, they were served by first-rate intellectuals and officials, some of whom produced outstanding texts on good government. We pause to look at three examples.

The first slightly predates the Seljuk takeover. Abu al-Hasan al-Māwardi (974–1058) was a prominent jurist and author from Basra. He wrote *The Ordinances of Government* for the caliphs, providing a wealth of religious, legal and practical advice. Its primary concerns are the appointments of the caliphs themselves and their key officials, governors and military commanders. The caliph's duties are described as both upholding the faith and managing public affairs. There must be a sovereign (an Imam). Reason dictates that people will submit to a ruler who can prevent inequity and conflict, while Quranic scripture makes submission obligatory. The ruler isn't absolute, as he has public duties such as enforcing the law and protecting the people; he may be disqualified for either lack of justice or physical disability.

It's up to the caliph to appoint ministers, magistrates and provincial governors and to delegate powers to them. The qualities and virtues of appointees are paramount. For example, an adjudicator of civil litigation ('redress of wrongs') must be 'majestic, authoritative, and imposing, as well as manifestly honest, free of avarice, and eminently pious.' Litigants need to be persuaded by his 'awesome presence and dignity' if they're to accept a settlement and cease their dispute.[42] Nonetheless, the law that derives from scripture and from tradition provides an impersonal foundation for judicial and administrative practices. According to al-Māwardi, subjects of the caliph could sue for wrongs committed by the state or its officials, for instance, maltreatment, wrongful seizure of property, over-taxation or delays in paying pensions. All Muslims pay poor rates or alms, based on what they own and produce, and the means of collecting and distributing them are described in detail. Assistance is given to the poor and needy, the faithful, debtors, travellers, soldiers fighting holy wars and newly freed slaves. Al-Māwardi sets out the distribution of war spoils, land tax, tribute from non-Muslims, land grants, reclamations, public works, criminal law and other administrative practices. This means a rule of law (not only of powerful charismatic men) and a sophisticated system of taxation and redistribution, guided by concepts of social justice, obligation and protection.[43]

The next prominent example is Abu Ali Hasan ibn Ali Tusi (1018–92), known by his title of Nizam al-Mulk ('Order of the Realm'), a native of Khurasan who first found employment in the Ghaznavid government. After the Seljuks expelled the Ghaznavids, he became vizier (chief minister) to Alp-Arslan and Malik-Shah I, serving for 30 years until he was assassinated. Experienced in governing a settled state with an established landowning class, he aimed 'to initiate his still uncultured Seljuk masters into the arts of Perso-Islamic statecraft.'[44] He consolidated a centralised bureaucracy for the sultanate and its provinces, installing his own sons and in-laws as officials while commanding an armed retinue of thousands.

Nizam al-Mulk composed an important contribution to the mirror of princes genre, *The Book of Government, or Rules for Kings*. The ruler, it says, is chosen by God, who 'entrusts him with the interests of the world and the well-being of His servants'; he's ultimately answerable 'for all those of God's creatures who are under his command.'[45] He must keep command over virtually everything and everyone within the realm. 'It is the king's duty to know everything that goes on' within the army and the peasantry, or else the king would be accused of 'negligence, laziness and tyranny'. He must be informed of and remedy every act of injustice. This necessitates postmasters and intelligence agents who are 'directly responsible to the king [and] who are completely above suspicion and without self-interest.'[46] Royal omniscience makes his subjects fear and obey him. The practice of employing internal spies had been abandoned by the Seljuk sultans, who regarded it as unworthy, but Nizam al-Mulk was concerned about dishonesty and extortion among tax collectors and other officials. A cohort of scrupulously trustworthy informants would therefore assist the king to redress all wrongs, no matter how far away they occurred nor how humble the offender. The king is both lawmaker and judge. He should ensure that all subjects always know their inferior position so they 'do not put off the ring of service from their ears nor loose the belt of obedience from their waists.'[47]

The Persian philosopher and theologian al-Ghazali (c. 1058–1111) was a protégé of Nizam al-Mulk. He intellectually reinforced orthodox Sunni belief, putting theology above philosophy, and hence rejected the rationalism of earlier philosophers such as al-Farabi (Chapter 4, Part 3) and Ibn Sina (Avicenna) (980–1037). Al-Ghazali insisted that revealed religion is inaccessible to reason and that nothing exists or occurs unless willed by God. To ensure they follow God's law, the people should know that God knows of their deeds, and that there's bodily reward or punishment in the afterlife. Philosophers who rejected those premises were no longer Muslims but apostates liable for execution.[48] 'Religious and political authorities are twins' – the latter acting as guardian for the former.

In al-Ghazali's time, there were threats from non-Sunni branches of Islam, and the caliph depended on forces at the disposal of the sultan. In effect, the sultan appointed the caliph, but the sultanate gained legitimacy through its allegiance to the caliphate. If a situation arose in which there was no obvious successor as caliph, those who wielded military force pledged allegiance to the most suitable candidate, he said. It was critical to avoid a power vacuum in which the people were left without the stable unifying force of rulers who provided security and reconciled differing opinions. The alternative was discord, violence, theft, famine and death, and people would be unable to apply their thoughts to religion.[49] Such insecurity would be even worse than an unjust ruler; hence

> authority is necessary for the good ordering of this world, and the good ordering of this world is necessary for the good ordering of religion, and the good ordering of religion is necessary for the acquisition of happiness in the hereafter.[50]

That is, political order is a necessary condition for religious order. (This reversed al-Farabi's thesis that the promulgation of religious imagery is a necessary condition for political order.)

All rulers were enjoined to piety and justice, especially as the moral consequences of their actions were magnified by their power. Al-Ghazali's mirror of princes, *The Counsel of Kings*, is a primer in the religious, political and legal duties of rulers. Righteous conduct brings the ruler great happiness; wickedness causes him torment and damnation. He must consult the community of religious scholars and discipline his servants and officers to act with justice. He should control his own passions to avoid being dominated by pride and anger; he should act with humility, pay heed to petitioners and govern with gentleness. Following Sassanian Persian, not Islamic, precedents, he should have a good chief minister (*wazir*):

> For the good minister is the guardian of the king's secrets, and on him depend the orderly handling of business, the revenue, and the prosperity of the realm and of the treasury; through him the monarchy acquires adornment, prestige and power.[51]

Al-Ghazali's reinforcement of Islamic faith supported a political purpose of combatting rival sects and rejected rational philosophy. Nonetheless, important commentaries on Aristotle and on Plato's *Republic* were later produced by Ibn Rushd (Averroes) (1126–98), who was born in Córdoba towards the end of the Almoravid dynasty.[52] He equated the ideal state with one ruled by *sharia*. Socrates' account of the city-state's decline into timocracy, then oligarchy, then democracy and then eventually tyranny (in Book 8 of *The Republic*) supported Ibn Rushd's critique of the Almoravids' decline into hedonism. Medieval Islamic thinkers produced diverse theories of prophecy, revelation and divine law; they built upon and questioned ancient Greek ethical and political philosophy. They produced practical textbooks which combined Persian techniques with Islamic law and which instructed caliphs and sultans in the government of urban societies. And they showed nomadic conquerors how to govern settled peoples.

Part 4: The Mongols

The vast grassland Eurasian steppe was a source of disruptive change. The Seljuks emerged from there, but 'the Mongol expansion was the most important political event between 1000 and 1250.'[53] The empire forged by the Mongol leader Chinggis Khan[54] and his successors was the largest contiguous terrestrial empire in world history.

Chinggis Khan

Clans of warlike horsemen who observed strict codes of honour and taboos, and who were accustomed to raiding and being raided, could only be mustered as a concerted force under certain conditions. First, it took a strong leader. Temügin (1162–1227 CE), later named Chinggis Khan, emerged as a brilliant strategist and tribal leader in the area that today comprises the north-eastern quarter of Mongolia and adjacent regions of Russia and China. Having come out on top in 1206 after a tortuous struggle for tribal supremacy, Chinggis Khan led campaigns into northern China and the Korean peninsula and west through Central Asia, Persia, the Caucasus and into Russia. He died in 1227 while on the verge of destroying the Tangut (Western Xia) empire in northern China.[55]

The word 'horde' comes from Turkic *ordu* for tent or encampment, and especially the royal tent. The Mongol hordes deserve a reputation for mass murder, and they were universally feared. The present narrative, however, concerns their government of vast territories while on the move and how they also learned from and used the traditions of government of settled agrarian and urban peoples. Chinggis Khan had reorganised his followers in a way that cut across their native clan structures. He gave them a law code with severe punishments and bought their loyalty with generous shares of booty. His carefully organised and governed society moved rapidly, conquered relentlessly and thus unleashed long-distance trade and communication. The Mongols connected civilisations previously little known to one another, and they mastered the arts of governing settled peoples.

Underlying the struggle for power among the Mongolian tribes were political and economic conflicts. Chinggis Khan and his followers were initially the mavericks, challenging the old ways. Chinggis Khan wanted a more meritocratic hierarchy than the old order of the steppe, while also preserving many of its customs. He continued, for example, the tradition of princely assemblies (*quriltai*). Social engineering and law were among his first innovations. He mixed the members of clans and tribes, breaking them into structured groups, thus diluting enmities, dismantling traditional loyalties and reducing the ability to reorganise and rebel. He divided his people into decimal units for military and administrative purposes, with a primary unit of one thousand soldiers and their households. These were responsible for supplying fully equipped soldiers, and no one could change units once assigned. Appointment of officers was on merit rather than kinship. An elite unit that eventually grew to 10,000 composed the bodyguard of Chinggis Khan, running his personal household and administration, and training new military and legal talent. These reforms were instrumental in 'revolutionising steppe society'.[56]

Although little of it survives, Chinggis Khan issued a law code, the Great Yasa. This formalised many of the taboos of traditional Mongolian steppe culture, for instance imposing severe penalties for maltreatment of horses or for polluting running water. It also introduced a strict military code and public law designed for the imperial project. Disobedience in the armed forces was a capital offence, making blind obedience the soldier's best option. The death penalty applied to a very wide range of offences, from the most harmful down to some that may not sound so serious to us today, such as failure to share food. The code permitted the great khan to do as he pleased, but it also constrained him to legal formality and public process. Its harshness was not out of line with other medieval legal systems, and it wasn't necessarily applied to subjugated regions outside of Mongolian society. Religious bodies of all kinds were immune from taxation – a concession that was more inclusive and generous than Islamic law, which taxed Christians and Jews.[57]

The Mongols' *imperium* depended on slave labour, foreign troops and administrators from subjugated states. Bureaucrats were moved out of their home states to reduce any local bias. The Uighurs were the first to submit voluntarily to the Mongols. They were employed in the full range of administrative and judicial roles, their script was adopted for correspondence and their skills 'allowed the Mongols to administer sedentary populations without chaos.'[58] Imperial government also depended on an efficient 'pony express' for rapid communication across great distances, supported by a strictly regulated system of stations. The horse was thus essential for war and for government. Trade was also an important factor. For a mobile ruler, social distinction wasn't signified by monumental architecture but by fine textiles such as gold brocade, and silk was used for currency as well as dressmaking. Hence Chinggis Khan needed control of trade routes across Central Asia to keep a flow of goods into his capital Karakorum. Mongolia was open for business with peoples of diverse religions and languages, including Chinese, Tibetans, Uighurs, Khitans and Persians.[59]

Conquest and division

Maintaining the political consent and unity of powerful generals and soldiers meant supplying them with generous quantities of booty. 'A critical part of Chinggis' new order was that he extended redistributive rights to all his retainers, not just to the leadership, as in the past.'[60] Keeping dangerous armed men busy and under command required ongoing conquests of exploitable peoples.

At the height of their empire, 'the ratio of Mongols to tribute-bearing peoples was about one to one hundred.'[61] But there were still conflicts between the old loyalties of steppe culture and the demand for efficient imperial expansion. Despite Chinggis' efforts to replace kinship with merit and service as the basis for advancement and reward, he was unable to refuse his sons as heirs and beneficiaries. In 1209, he distributed troops and divided the empire between his sons, giving them the revenues from those lands. This may have been one of Chinggis Khan's greatest errors. 'Having created a centralised bureaucracy which threw out all the traditional claims of kinship, he allowed them back in again under pressure from his sons.'[62] But could he have afforded to dishonour and alienate his sons, and risk creating enemies of them and their followers?

Chinggis Khan's second son Ogodei (c. 1186–1241) succeeded him in 1230 and moved against the Jin Empire in China. Another army conquered Iran, Armenia and Georgia. A third conquered the Caspian steppes and the Russian principalities, advancing as far as Hungary and Poland before withdrawing due to Ogedei's death. Chinggis Khan's grandson Mongke (1209–59) seized power in 1250. Mongke's brother Qubilai (d. 1294) led an invasion against the Southern Song in China. Hulegu (1218–65) invaded northern Iran, destroyed Baghdad and ended the Abbasid caliphate in 1258. Due to the Mongols' norms of shared inheritance and rivalry, however, the death of Mongke meant that the divided empire fell into civil war. It split into the Yuan dynasty (1271–1368) in China, commencing with Qubilai; the Persian Il-Khanate under Hulegu; the Chagatai Khanate in Central Asia; and the Golden Horde in Russia.[63] The Mongols stopped at Poland and Hungary, but Europeans lived in fear of them.[64]

In the end, the taxman tamed them. As they increasingly taxed farmers, the Mongols needed literate tax collectors. But Mongol horsemen couldn't adopt such occupations without losing their honour and their strategic advantage of mobility. Conquest and plunder required mobile men of the sword; taxation called for administration run by literate and numerate urban-dwelling officials. And conquered peoples (those who survived the onslaught) couldn't be robbed repeatedly. It made more sense, and more long-term profit, to keep them under relatively predictable and peaceful regimes of tributes, taxes and trade. Such was the advice of the talented Khitan official and Confucian scholar Yelu Chucai (1190–1243) to Ogodei when the latter was contemplating genocide in the conquered Jin empire. Ogodei was persuaded that one can't tax the dead, and Yelu was given the chance to prove the point in practice.[65] Impartial, merit-based administration created a rift, however, with the Mongolian warriors who were eager to acquire land in China for their own benefit and who rejected Yelu's taxation policies. Yelu fell out of favour after Ogodei's death, but bureaucracy outlasted the rule of nomads. The vast Mongol empire required government over widely dispersed localities with many different languages and economies. Having transformed the world, the Mongol dynasties were eventually absorbed into bureaucratic forms of government in China and Persia. The Mongol empire was later reunited by another mobile leader, Timur.

Timur

While Chinggis Khan has become a household name,[66] Timur (1336–1405) is less well known today but was no less terrifying in his time. (He was depicted in Christopher Marlowe's play of 1588, *Tamburlaine the Great*.) Timur was born in the south of today's Uzbekistan, in what was then the Chagatai Khanate. Chinggis Khan's second son Chagatai (1183–1242) had inherited Central Asia, but, by the 1340s this had split in two. Transoxiana in the west was dominated by Muslim tribes and its rulers preferred the settled way of life. Moghulistan in the east was dominated by nomadic Mongols, some of whom followed Buddhism and others shamanism. The eastern nomads had largely gained the upper hand. In the 1360s, Timur emerged as a tribal leader who gained mastery over Transoxiana, deftly playing one side off against the other, defeating a major rival and taking the city of Balkh (now in northern Afghanistan). He installed a descendant of Ogedei as his puppet khan and married a descendant of Chinggis Khan, Saray Mulk-Khanum (c. 1343–1406), the widow of his defeated rival, to legitimise his rule.

Timur's successes arose from military brilliance, violent plunder and generous sharing of spoils with his followers. In 1380, Timur campaigned against the city of Herat, a vassal state of the Mongols since 1221. His forces massacred an outlying garrison-town, and so the governor of Herat decided it was prudent to surrender. Timur 'pardoned' him and then took possession of the treasury and all moveable property of any worth. This was not undisciplined plunder; it was carried out by tax collectors backed by torturers. Any soldier who breached the ban on unauthorised looting would pay for it with his life. The poorer suburbs were set aside for the soldiers to plunder only after the choicest treasures were accounted for and distributed. Undisciplined plunder would lessen Timur's revenue. He took 'human capital' as well. Scholars and artisans were rounded up and sent to Samarkand to glorify Timur's capital. Herat's city walls were demolished to make it defenceless, in case anyone should be minded to rebel. By contrast, Zaranj in the southwest of Afghanistan decided to resist and paid the price. Everyone was killed; nothing was left standing; even the irrigation system was destroyed.[67]

Timur went on to reconquer and reunite a large portion of the former Mongol empire, including defeating the Golden Horde in Russia. He sacked Delhi in 1398 and inflicted a major defeat on the Ottoman emperor Bayezid I in 1402. Aside from wintering over in various places or visiting his capital Samarkand, Timur was constantly on the move and planning his next siege or campaign. Having amassed loyal forces, there was no time for inaction if he was to keep them loyal and supplied with booty. He died undefeated, probably due to poor health and snowy conditions, on his way to a planned invasion of China. Due to the loss of his two sons and dynastic infighting, however, Timur's empire soon crumbled after his death. But a direct descendant of Timur was Babur (1483–1530), the founder of the Mughal dynasty of India, which lasted until 1858 (Chapter 6, Part 2).

Timur exemplifies the waves of nomadic warriors that swept from the Eurasian steppe and united diverse peoples into empires. While often destructive to a degree that is hard now even to comprehend, once they had won territories, nomadic conquerors worked constructively with peoples of differing cultures and religions. They gained from the literacy and administrative skills of urban dwellers. The Mongols themselves were gradually 'conquered' by Uighur, Persian and Chinese bureaucrats, and 'tamed' by Muslim merchants. Incongruous though it may sound, Chinggis Khan favoured (what we would now call) religious toleration, multiculturalism and open borders. His conquests freed the Eurasian peoples for continental trade and migration. He valued artisans, scholars and officials, regardless of their cultural background, and his policies actively mixed peoples of different kinds – often, it must be said, by force. But he and Timur faced resistance from some of their kin who resented the dilution of their warrior culture, the spread of Islamic law and the intrusion of meritocracy into traditions of honour and inheritance. It was no easy task balancing the diverse skills and demands of settled and nomadic peoples. By the time Ibn Khaldun met Timur face to face in 1401, he had already written his account of the historical and political dynamics of nomadism versus sedentarism and its implications for royal authority and policymaking.

Conclusion

We've now seen how mobile conquering peoples ruled and governed. Leading large forces of horsemen was like riding a tiger: to prevent it from turning on him and destroying him, the ruler had to keep moving it and feeding it. Other than when wintering down, Timur did that until the day he died. In contrast, the Turkic Seljuk rulers were content to settle into an urban existence and to rely upon established Persian methods of government, while letting their tribal followers continue their nomadic-pastoralist ways. Relations between settled and mobile peoples in the course of history have been more complex than portrayed above, however. Nomads sometimes were rulers; other times they had to be ruled. For example, the Ottoman dynasty emerged in Anatolia in the fourteenth century from a 'statelet' of frontier warriors after the Mongols destroyed the Seljuk Rum sultanate. They had roots in the nomadic Turkmen culture. The Ottomans developed a bureaucratic government and a military machine sufficient to sack Constantinople in 1453, obliterating the vestiges of the Byzantine empire. By the seventeenth century, Ottoman territory encompassed Hungary, the Balkans, Crimea, Anatolia, Mesopotamia, Egypt, North Africa and the holy cities of Medina and Mecca. This required recognition of many different religions, ethnicities, languages and ways of life, including pastoral nomads and gypsies. Nomads made excellent cavalrymen, and their seasonal occupation of pastures supported claims to marginal territories where borders were poorly demarcated. Some nomadic leaders gained titles, acted as representatives and influenced imperial policymaking. Peasants and nomads maintained mutually beneficial relations through trading manufactured implements for animal products. Sometimes nomadic groups were forced by governments to move from place to place or to assist in moving supplies to areas suffering from famine. Thus nomadism was institutionalised by the Ottomans – and inevitably nomads were taxed. At other times, nomads were at the heart of disorder and dissent, or they eluded government by disappearing into mountainous or desert zones. Incorporation into the state wasn't entirely congenial to the nomadic way of life.[68]

Even those most powerful of nomads, the Mongols, weren't invincible. Led by Hulegu and his successors, they made several unsuccessful attempts to invade Egypt between 1260 and 1312.[69] The sultanate in Cairo had come under Mamluk rule in 1260. The Mamluks were trafficked from non-Muslim Turkic-Kipchak, Circassian or Armenian peoples and then forced to convert. Boys were trained for elite military regiments; girls became domestic servants, musicians and concubines.[70] The purpose was not to enslave them, according to Ibn Khaldun, but to import their nomadic spirit and 'to intensify their zeal and solidarity and strengthen their prowess.'[71] They became a political force in their own right, to the extent that eventually they chose sultans from among their cohorts. Their Mongol enemies had adopted Islam and taken in defectors from Egypt, posing the legal problem of Muslims potentially killing fellow Muslims in battle. This matter was put to Ibn Taymiyyah (1263–1328), a Syrian jurist in Cairo. He held an uncompromising interpretation of *sharia*, undiluted by Greek rationalism or other foreign sources and inspired by the *salaf*, the first three generations of Muslims including the Prophet. (Salafists are Muslim scholars faithful to original or pure versions of Islam.) Ibn Taymiyyah reasoned that, although the Mongol rulers were Muslim converts, they didn't conform with Islamic law, as they preserved their pre-Islamic traditions and the code of Chinggis Khan. The Mongol invaders were condemned as apostates and adversaries. The Mamluks succeeded in fending them off.[72]

Nomadism is less prominent today. Displacement, migration and statelessness caused by war and famine, however, are all too common, along with intolerance for those who are habitually or involuntarily mobile. The worst example was the extermination of gypsies under the Nazi regime. But the spirit of rulers of no fixed abode hasn't died. In June 2014, mobile forces of the Islamic State in Iraq and the Levant (ISIL) captured the strategically located city of Mosul. Driving Toyotas rather than riding camels, they forced regular soldiers to retreat, ISIL's leader, Abu Bakr al-Baghdadi (1971–2019), then declared a caliphate and a holy war, claiming religious and political authority over all Muslims. Almost all Muslims worldwide disagreed with him, and ISIL was condemned as a terrorist group due to numerous atrocities. Nonetheless, until its eventual defeat in 2018, ISIL held territories in Iraq and Syria. To outside observers, ISIL represented only religious fanaticism and terrorism, but they did have to govern. They had to register births and marriages, operate telecommunications, issue vehicle licence plates, distribute funds to the poor and take care of public sanitation as best they could. Their theory of government derived from none other than Ibn Taymiyyah. This was not 'history repeating itself', but some of the concerns and ideas from the history covered in this chapter resurfaced in different configurations and conflicts. While Ibn Khaldun may not have been surprised by ISIL's savagery, religious zeal and *asabiyya*, he couldn't have imagined the modern air power that drove them out.

Even in more civilised settings, there's tension between settled and mobile groups: between those who belong in a particular place, put their own nation first and resist immigration, and those who will go anywhere, prefer open borders and love cultural hybridisation. It would be a step too far to call the latter nomads. Nonetheless, one can discern a similar dynamic between (metaphorically) those who prefer to stay by the hearth and those who prefer to be on horseback – or in a canoe or an aircraft. The premise of this chapter was that government isn't necessarily conducted in fixed urban locations. The conclusion was that rulers of no fixed abode eventually bowed to those who stayed put and wielded the pen. But that was when the fastest thing they had was a horse. Today, government depends on sedentary work, often without leaving home, but equally on the ability of leaders to move rapidly between locations. We also see a major political division between nationalism and globalism, or populists versus neoliberals. The Khaldunian dialectic reappears in new guises.

Notes

1 Letter from Hegel to his friend Friedrich Immanuel Niethammer, quoted in Welsch & Vieweg, 2003, p. 233.
2 Roberts, 2014, p. 581.
3 Alatas, 2013; Marozzi, 2005, pp. 301–6.
4 Khaldun, 2005 [1370], p. 164.
5 Ibid., p. 147.
6 Ibid., p. 140.
7 Adamson, 2016.
8 Reich, 2018; Sykes, 2020.
9 Scott, 2017, p. 253.
10 Gellner, 1988, p. 144.
11 Scott, 2017.
12 Golden, 2011, p. 16.
13 Howe, 2006.
14 Ibid.
15 Anderson, 2005.
16 Howe, 2006, p. 135.
17 Gunson, 1990.
18 Howe, 2006, pp. 90–91.
19 Ibid.
20 Diamond, 2007.
21 Mâhina, 2004.
22 Howe, 2006, pp. 230–36.
23 Bennison, 2016; Moreno, 2010; Phillips & Phillips, 2010.
24 The Maliki school is one of the four major schools of Sunni jurisprudence.
25 Bennison, 2016, p. 29.
26 Ibid.
27 Ibid., p. 50.

28 Ibid.
29 These invasions 'led to the formation of Turkish populations in Anatolia, Azerbaijan and the Caucasus that exist there today.' Peacock, 2010, p. 1. See also Findley, 2005.
30 Peacock, 2010, pp. 58–60.
31 Findley, 2005.
32 'By origin, the Seljuq tribes were not purely nomadic, but comprised sedentary and semi-sedentary elements. Among the tribes there was a constant tendency for groups to break off and form new units.' Peacock, 2010, p. 71.
33 Bosworth, 1968, p. 20.
34 Ibid.
35 Findley, 2005. Rum is Arabic for Rome.
36 'Reliance on a professional army instead of on tribesmen or local levies has in the course of human history generally meant a rise in state expenditure, resulting in fresh taxation and an increase in the central power of the state.' Bosworth, 1968, p. 80.
37 Peacock, 2010, p. 68.
38 Lapidus, 2012, Chapter 20.
39 Bosworth, 1968, p. 78. See also Peacock, 2010, Chapter 3, who differs regarding the Seljuks' siege capabilities.
40 Peacock, 2015.
41 Findley, 2005.
42 al-Māwardi, 2000, p. 87.
43 Ibid.
44 Bagley, Introduction, in al-Ġazālī, 1964, pp. xxviii–xxix.
45 Nizam al-Mulk, 2002, pp. 9, 13; trans. H. Darke.
46 Ibid., pp. 63–4.
47 Ibid., p. 186.
48 Griffel & Adamson, 2013.
49 Hillenbrand, 1988.
50 al-Ghazali, quoted by Hillenbrand, 1988, p. 88.
51 al-Ġazālī, 1964, p. 107; trans. F.R.C. Bagley. Scholars have cast doubt on the authorship of Part II of this text.
52 Aristotle's *Politics* wasn't available to Ibn Rushd but a Hebrew translation (from Arabic) of his commentary on Plato's *Republic* survives, translated into English by Lerner, 1974.
53 Holslag, 2019, p. 391.
54 I've adopted the spelling Chinggis, rather than Genghis, as the former is regarded as more accurate.
55 The cause of his death remains uncertain. McLynn, 2016, p. 378.
56 McLynn, 2016, p. 101. See also May, 2018.
57 McLynn, 2016, pp. 112–24.
58 Ibid., p. 145.
59 Findley, 2005.
60 Ibid., p. 81.
61 McLynn, 2016, p. 506.
62 Ibid., p. 105.
63 May, 2018.
64 In the early sixteenth century Machiavelli commented:

> Very great movements of the Tartars often occur, which are contained by the Hungarians and those of Poland, who often glorify themselves, saying that if it were not for their arms, Italy and the church would have often felt the weight of the Tartar armies.
>
> Machiavelli, 1996 [1517], p. 145

65 McLynn, 2016, p. 417.

66 The expression 'somewhere to the right of Genghis Khan' is a common jibe for those seen as supporting political repression or fascism.
67 Marozzi, 2005.
68 Kasaba, 2009.
69 Neither did Timur succeed in taking Egypt, even though he revealed to Ibn Khaldun an interest in going as far as North Africa.
70 Rapaport, 2007. *Mamluk* means 'owned' or slave. They're comparable to the Ottomans' Janissaries.
71 Quoted in Irwin, 2018, p. 87.
72 Aigle, 2007.

References

Adamson, Peter. 2016. *Philosophy in the Islamic World*. Oxford: Oxford University Press.

Aigle, Denise. 2007. 'The Mongol Invasions of Bilâd al-Shâm by Ghâzân Khân and Ibn Taymîyah's Three "Anti-Mongols" Fatwas.' *Mamluk Studies Review* 11 (2): 89–120.

Alatas, Syed Farid. 2013. *Ibn Khaldun*. Oxford: Oxford University Press.

al-Ġazālī, Abū Ḥāmid Muḥammad b. Muḥammad. 1964. *Ghazālī's Book of Counsel for Kings (Naṣīḥat Al-mulūk)*. Edited by F.R.C Bagley (trans). London: Oxford University Press.

al-Māwardi, Abu al-Hasan. 2000. *The Ordinances of Government*. Reading, UK: Garnet Publishing.

Anderson, Atholl. 2005. 'Subpolar Settlement in South Polynesia.' *Antiquity* 79 (306): 791–800.

Bennison, Amira K. 2016. *The Almoravid and Almohad Empires*. Edinburgh: Edinburgh University Press.

Bosworth, Clifford Edmund. 1968. 'The Political and Dynastic History of the Iranian World (A.D. 1000–1217).' In *The Cambridge History of Iran*, by John Boyle, 1–202. Cambridge: Cambridge University Press.

Diamond, Jared. 2007. *Collapse: How Societies Choose to Fail or Survive*. Camberwell, VIC: Penguin.

Findley, Carter Vaughn. 2005. *The Turks in World History*. Oxford: Oxford University Press.

Gellner, Ernest. 1988. 'Trust, Cohesion, and the Social Order.' In *Trust: The Making and Breaking of Cooperative Relations*, by Diego Gambetta, 142–57. Oxford: Basil Blackwell.

Golden, Peter B. 2011. *Central Asia in World History*. New York, NY: Oxford University Press.

Griffel, Frank, and Peter Adamson. 2013. 'Frank Griffel on al-Ghazālī.' *History of Philosophy Without Any Gaps*. October 13. Accessed September 2020. https://historyofphilosophy.net/al-ghazali-griffel.

Gunson, Niel. 1990. 'The Tonga-Samoa Connection 1777–1845: Some Observations on the Nature of Tongan Imperialism.' *The Journal of Pacific History* 25 (2): 176–87.

Hillenbrand, Carole. 1988. 'Islamic Orthodoxy or Realpolitik? Al-Ghazālī's Views on Government.' *Iran* 26 (1): 81–94.

Holslag, Jonathan. 2019. *A Political History of the World*. London: Penguin.

Howe, Kerry R. 2006. *Vaka Moana: Voyages of the Ancestors*. Auckland: David Bateman/Auckland War Memorial Museum.

Irwin, Robert. 2018. *Ibn Khaldun: An Intellectual Biography*. Princeton, NJ: Princeton University Press.

Kasaba, Resat. 2009. *A Moveable Empire: Ottoman Nomads, Migrants, and Refugees.* Seattle: University of Washington Press.

Khaldun, Ibn. 2005. *The Muqaddimah: An Introduction to History.* Princeton, NJ: Princeton University Press.

Lapidus, Ira. 2012. *Islamic Societies to the Nineteenth Century: A Global History.* Cambridge: Cambridge University Press.

Lerner, Ralph. 1974. *Averroes on Plato's Republic.* Ithaca, NY: Cornell University Press.

Machiavelli, Niccolò. 1996. *Discourses on Livy.* Chicago, IL: University of Chicago Press.

Mâhina, 'Okusitino. 2004. 'Emancipation in Tonga: Yesterday and Today.' *Planet Tonga.* June 11. Accessed May 2019. https://web.archive.org/web/20060305174550/http://planet-tonga.com/language_journal/Emancipation_in_Tonga/index.shtml.

Marozzi, Justin. 2005. *Tamerlane: Sword of Islam, Conqueror of the World.* London: Harper Perennial.

May, Timothy. 2018. 'Central Asia: The Mongols.' In *The Great Empires of Asia*, by Jim Masselos, 27–52. London: Thames & Hudson.

McLynn, Frank. 2016. *Genghis Khan: The Man Who Conquered the World.* London: Vintage.

Moreno, Eduardo. 2010. 'The Iberian Peninsula and North Africa.' In *The New Cambridge History of Islam*, by Chase Robinson, 581–622. Cambridge: Cambridge University Press.

Nizam al-Mulk. 2002. *The Book of Government or Rules for Kings.* London: Routledge.

Peacock, A.C.S. 2010. *Early Seljūq History A new interpretation.* London: Routledge.

———. 2015. *The Great Seljuk Empire.* Edinburgh: Edinburgh University Press.

Phillips, William D., and Carla R. Phillips. 2010. *A Concise History of Spain.* Cambridge: Cambridge University Press.

Rapaport, Yossef. 2007. 'Women and Gender in Mamluk Society: An Overview.' *Mamluk Studies Review* 11 (2): 1–48.

Reich, David. 2018. *Who We Are and How We Got Here: Ancient DNA and the New Science of the Human Past.* Oxford: Oxford University Press.

Roberts, Andrew. 2014. *Napoleon: A Life.* New York, NY: Viking Penguin.

Scott, James C. 2017. *Against the Grain: A Deep History of the Earliest States.* New Haven, CT: Yale University Press.

Sykes, Rebecca Wragg. 2020. *Kindred: Neanderthal Life, Love, Death and Art.* London: Bloomsbury.

Welsch, Wolfgang, and Klaus Vieweg. 2003. *Das Interesse des Denkens: Hegel aus heutiger Sicht.* Munich: Wilhelm Fink Verlag.

6

METASTATIC IMPERIALISM

Global colonial rule

The sixteenth century was an age of great emperors, and in this chapter, we encounter two of them: the Habsburg emperor Charles V (1500–58) and the greatest of the Mughal emperors, Jalal-ud-din Akbar (1542–1605).[1] From the early sixteenth century, new sailing and military technologies made it possible to project power across oceans and into distant continents. If empire is likened to a cancer due to its destructive and parasitic effects, then the modern form of globally extensive imperialism emanating from Europe was metastatic. This chapter considers four examples of colonial government: Spanish America, British India, Aotearoa New Zealand and French Algeria. It takes account of the governments that pre-existed contact and colonisation, and the reciprocal effects on both the colonised and the metropolitan peoples. Modern European nations and nationalism are products of their histories as imperial powers. Colonised peoples, for their part, already had social hierarchies and means of governing affairs and resources, and in some cases complex empires. Indeed, all societies are governed, including those that aren't full-fledged states with literacy, record-keeping, taxation and cohorts of officials. That is, all societies have leaders, social rank, customs, laws (written or oral), myths, taboos, means of common defence, norms of exchange or reciprocity and social obligations that regulate members' lives, guide everyday conduct and preserve social cohesion. Regardless of their technological capabilities, all societies are complex political systems with practices that govern individual and collective conduct. How did trans-continental imperialism transform government?

Part 1: The Spanish-American empire

Isabella of Castile and Ferdinand of Aragon were married in 1469 to rule in unison. In its own right, the Crown of Aragon ruled a sizable Mediterranean

DOI: 10.4324/9781003166955-6

empire, and so after the death of Ferdinand's father in 1479 Isabella and Ferdinand became jointly the monarchs of Castile, Aragon, Catalonia, Valencia, Sicily and Naples. In 1492, after a long campaign against the emirate of al-Andalus, they entered the city of Granada and incorporated it into Castile, ending more than seven centuries of Muslim rule in the Iberian Peninsula. Jews who hadn't converted to Christianity were expelled, finding refuge in various parts of Europe and the Levant. Furthermore, a Genoese sailor called Christopher Columbus (1451–1506) gained Queen Isabella's support to sail uncharted ocean to the west in the hope of reaching East Asia. In four voyages, Columbus explored islands of the Caribbean and some of the coast of mainland Central America. (His commission included administrative titles, but he proved to be 'hopelessly inadequate' in those roles and was soon replaced.)[2] In 1492, the Archbishop of Valencia, Rodrigo de Borja (1431–1503), was elected Pope Alexander VI and confirmed the rights of the Castilian crown to the 'New World' the following year. The crowns of Castile and Aragon remained distinct, and Castile held a monopoly on the Americas. Rulership in Europe was still dynastic, with realms acquired through marriage and inheritance. One monarch could inherit (or lay claim to) titles to numerous domains, as Ferdinand did. The imperial integration of Europe expanded, moreover, with the rise of the Habsburg heir Charles of Ghent (1500–58). He inherited Burgundy from his father in 1506, and Castile and Aragon (including Naples, Sicily and Sardinia) through his grandfather, Ferdinand, in 1516. Then in 1519, he was elected Holy Roman Emperor as Charles V. Following his abdication in 1556, Charles V's Spanish and Italian crowns were bequeathed to his son Phillip II, who died in 1598.[3]

From this background, imperial rule in the New World proceeded. In addition, the Reformation began with the publication of Martin Luther's 95 theses in 1517, following which the House of Habsburg supported the Catholic Counter-Reformation. This era of European religious wars concluded with the Peace of Westphalia in 1648, which affirmed a principle of equal and independent sovereign states. Hence, the beginnings of modern states and international law were contemporaneous with the new transcontinental imperialism.[4] Imperial enterprise helped to form and finance the growth of – and the conflicts between – European nations. Colonial rule and rebellion also challenged and reflexively shaped ideas about government and the law of nations as they evolved in Europe. The political institutions of the imperial centres, as well as the colonised countries, were thus permanently transformed.

The Incan empire

One of the New World empires that flourished before European exploration was the Incan. Signs of human habitation in Andean South America date back to 12,500 BCE, and numerous complex societies rose and fell over the centuries. The Inca dynasty began around 1200 CE, but its main imperial expansion occurred in the fifteenth century, extending from modern-day Ecuador down to northern Chile. It was thus a relatively recently formed empire at the time of the first contact with Europeans. It encompassed many ethnic groups, and it isn't clear to what extent local custom was retained by, or overlapped with, central-ised authority. With neither written language, iron tools nor wheeled vehicles, but with ingenious engineering, the Incans built an efficient agricultural society with irrigation systems and stone terracing. Provincial urban centres were linked by a network of well-constructed roads to the imperial capital of Cuzco. Gov-ernment was palace-based and socially collectivist. There was a strict political hi-erarchy, beginning with a quasi-divine emperor, under whom were four regional prefects, and then provincial, district and local governors. The local census and administration were based on a decimal system of households. The economy lacked a monetary commodity, and 'the revenues of the state consisted over-whelmingly of time spent on the state's behalf in a wide range of enterprises.'[5] Heads of households were conscripted to military service, essential trades and public works on a carefully recorded rotation system. Agricultural labour was divided between allotments of land that produced for the people, the gods and the state. People could be resettled some distance away from their homes to take advantage of differing climates, and large numbers of women lived together as conscripted weavers.

> Being the major Andean art form, cloth also had many political, ritual and military uses which required its weaving for the state on what were truly industrial dimensions. Full-time weaving occupied scores of 'chosen' women separated from their ethnic group and located at every state admin-istrative centre, where soldiers expected rewards in cloth as they marched towards the frontier.[6]

With no written language, record-keeping relied on a threaded textile that used dyes and knots as mnemonic devices. The administrative inflexibility of Incan society, and the correlative inability of individuals to act on their own initiatives, may have created a vulnerability to unexpected external threats.[7] Nonetheless, there was a complex and sophisticated system of government.

The conquistadors

Spanish adventurers overthrew the Aztec and Incan rulers in Mexico and Peru respectively in the first half of the sixteenth century. The newcomers' mari-time mobility, horses, gunpowder, muskets, cannon and literacy all contributed to their effectiveness, along with the epidemiological factor of introduced dis-eases that killed huge numbers of indigenous people, who lacked immunity.[8] The Spaniards formed alliances with local tribes who also wished to overthrow their rulers so that natives often outnumbered foreigners among invading (or rebellious) forces. 'The collapse of a Mexica [Aztec] empire of some 25 million people in the face of an assault by some few hundred Spaniards' was in part due to smallpox and to the tactical ability of Hernán Cortés (1485–1547) to exploit weaknesses; it was also 'a revolt by a subjugated [indigenous] population against its overlords.'[9]

In Peru, the Incans had recently experienced internal strife over succession to the throne which weakened their defences, and about 160 men led by Francisco Pizarro (c. 1471–1541) captured the emperor Atahualpa in 1532. This was facilitated in part by panic among people unfamiliar with musket-fire. Large quantities of gold- and silverware were seized as 'ransom', melted down into ingots and shipped back to Seville. The treasury then took a 20 percent royalty, which maintained the confidence of Charles V's creditors, such as the Fuggers of Augsburg, and helped to finance the war against the Ottoman empire.[10]

The expanding trans-Atlantic empire wasn't easy to govern, however. Rapid and reliable communication at the speed of the horse had been essential for the effective government of empires. But a letter from Mexico to Madrid could take three months to arrive, and in remote areas, a response to an official request could take two years.[11] Conquest, expansion and exploitation in the New World, however, required the invaders to be mobile, adaptable and enterprising. As plantations and mines were established, the demand for labour grew and decisions were needed on the spot. The government of the colonies was cumbersome if not weak and often gave way to unofficial local imperatives. The 1512 Laws of Burgos, which protected indigenous peoples from abuses and reasserted their liberty, 'fell dead from the pens of the legislators [as] there was no authority on the island [of Hispaniola] willing or able to ensure their enforcement.'[12] The enslavement and decline of Hispaniola's native population – to eventual extinction – continued unabated.[13] Even local governors had their limitations. For example, the fleet of eleven ships that sailed from Cuba to the mainland under Cortés in 1519 – leading to the conquest of the Aztecs – did so in mutinous defiance of the island's governor. Ships, muskets and steel may have been effective technologies of conquest, but the techniques of European government struggled to keep up. On the other hand, the Spaniards' rapid takeover of vast territories was facilitated by the effective systems which the Aztecs and Incans had already put in place – and which the conquerors could then utilise. The transfer of control was facilitated by pre-existing government and infrastructure, especially roads, and an obedient populace. Those peoples whom the Incans and Aztecs hadn't already conquered would continue to resist Spanish control.[14]

The first conquistadors and settlers largely acted on their own initiatives, sometimes as small egalitarian bands with little need of investors or administrators. But they weren't entirely ungoverned, as they relied upon legal instruments and charters, and larger expeditions required finance derived from banking houses in Augsburg and Genoa. They claimed to act for the glory of God and monarch, and hence they anticipated royal favour and honour in return for their services. The mutual obligations (services and rewards) between conquerors and monarchs that were observed during the Reconquista were also observed (with modifications) in the New World. The *encomienda*, an official assignment, governed the distribution of land seized from the Moors, and this was recreated in the New World – but for assigning labour as well as land. The assignee, or *encomendero*, was entrusted by the crown with the care and religious instruction of a group of natives in return for compulsory labour. This encouraged the settlement of immigrants in small communities and the resettlement of indigenous labourers. But dispossession, disease and forced labour were diminishing native populations, while Spanish immigrants in search of wealth were increasing. Settlers on Hispaniola resorted to raiding the Bahamas for workers, but this only raised the appalling death toll. Hence, they turned to Portuguese traders of African slaves to redress the labour shortage. The first shipment reached Hispaniola in 1510, and blacks soon outnumbered whites in colonial settlements. Gold and silver mines, sugar plantations and agriculture exploited slave labour. Slaves were also prominent in domestic services and trades.[15]

Metropolitan control

'Not far behind each conquistador was a royal official sent to secure and remit to Spain the crown's share of all treasure.'[16] The early no-frills military model soon gave way to monarchical control under Castilian law and administration. In 1523, a new Council of the Indies, equal to those of Castile and Aragon, was set up to advise the monarch, pass laws, convey executive orders and act as a supreme court for the Americas. The councillors were lawyers who'd never travelled to the Americas. In 1535, the viceroyalty of New Spain was created, followed by the viceroyalty of Peru in 1543. Two more were added in the eighteenth century. The viceroys represented the monarch and, although treated like royalty, they were (in principle) controlled by the Council for the Indies and the *audiencias*. Ten *audiencias* were created in the New World, largely composed of Spanish-born lawyers appointed by the crown, on advice from the Council. They acted as a court of appeal and a political cabinet, presided over by the viceroy, who had no vote and whom the *audiencias* could bypass by appealing directly to Madrid. The numbers varied, but there were up to 35 provincial governors who could also bypass the viceroy. This top-level of colonial government was mostly Spanish-born. Laws were made in and promulgated from Madrid, while large amounts of official information were gathered from the colonies in return. By making viceroys' appointments on a fixed-term basis, the crown prevented the emergence of hereditary landed nobility in the colonies,[17] but at lower levels, many professional bureaucrats, such as judges and treasury officials, held lifetime appointments. A grant of office was a royal gift 'producing a source of income for its recipient that could be held until his death and, at times, passed on to his heirs.'[18] Given the distance from Madrid, however, the system was open to corruption, tyranny and sheer cruelty.

The colonies were founded upon townships with local councils, the *cabildos*, which were run by selected householders (*regidores*), who elected two chief magistrates, the *alcaldes*. Eventually, the *regidores* became life appointments, and vacancies were even put up for sale. The most important local judicial and administrative officer, however, was the *corregidor*, who was appointed by the crown on two- or three-year terms to serve the interests of central government. This wasn't local democracy, and the society was racially and economically stratified. African chattel slaves were at the bottom with indigenous labourers just above them. The *mestizos* (Spanish-Indian) formed the next higher stratum. Above them were the American-born Spanish-descended *criollos*. The wealthiest minority of the *criollos* were the *encomenderos* (owners of ranches and mines), who controlled local workforces, sat on councils (*cabildos*) and appointed the *alcaldes*. The church was also involved in colonisation, seeing itself in a protective and tutelary role for indigenous peoples. The priesthood often denounced abuses of native labour by the *encomenderos* but also used this labour force to build monasteries and work mission farms.

In the seventeenth century, indigenous Americans were ruthlessly exploited through compulsory draft labour (*repartimiento*) and debt peonage. Provincial administrators would force natives to buy merchandise and tools and make them work to pay back their debt. These administrators then acted as middle men for merchants in the capital cities, selling goods produced at below market price. With limited-term offices, they had only three to five years to enrich themselves and did so at the double. The cash-strapped crown began selling minor administrative posts in the late sixteenth century, which only lowered the standard of appointments. By 1677, these sales extended to the posts of *corregidor* and *alcalde mayor*, and appointees became even more exploitative to recover their financial outlay.[19]

It was a cruel and authoritarian but law-bound empire.[20] It had many (perhaps too many) checks and balances, limiting viceregal and gubernatorial powers, but slowing down decision-making often to snail's pace. Administration at such distance meant informal compromises and selective enforcement as execution of the law filtered through district authorities and town councils and mixed with the vested interests of *encomenderos*. The great body of laws and directives from Madrid were often inconsistent or impractical. Hence, there was a 'wide gap between the law and its enforcement',[21] and the maxim 'I obey but do not execute' was often applied. Given the slowness of trans-Atlantic communication, 'by procrastination the unwanted proposals might be buried by bureaucratic inertia.'[22] Despite the formalities of centralised government, then, local oligarchs maintained autonomy by compromising between authority and flexibility, resulting in 'self-rule at the king's command'.[23]

Problems of success

At the end of Philip II's reign (1598), about 20 percent of fiscal revenue came from the Americas, contributing to soldiers' wages, shipbuilding and the like. Silver not taken as royalties or taxes went into the private economy. The influx of bullion and the demand for exports back across the Atlantic drove up prices, but the Castilian economy didn't raise productivity in accord. Spanish manufacturers couldn't meet colonial demand and so trade was picked up by producers in other countries. Variations in the supply of American silver thus affected the whole European economy, not just Spain. It also attracted envious looks from competing nations.[24] The bullion helped to finance wars within Europe. The Ottomans invaded Hungary and besieged Vienna in 1529, but they were halted in the naval battle of Lepanto in 1571. Meanwhile, the Spanish Habsburgs had to defend their Italian territories from the French and fight the Dutch War of Independence (1568–1648). Religious conflicts led to the Thirty Years' War (1618–1648). And the international rivalry within Europe spilled over into the New World and the Atlantic sea-lanes. English and Dutch privateers raided Spanish ships and attacked colonial settlements. Spain had to invest in more warships and fortifications but couldn't defend its monopoly on the New World. For example, the English seized Jamaica in 1655.[25]

Charles II (r. 1664–1700) was mentally unfit to rule and the state faced bankruptcy. His death ended a dynasty and occasioned a war of succession among the European powers, leading to French Bourbon rule commencing with Philip V (r. 1700–46). This stimulated Spain to recreate its armed forces, raise its revenues and build an absolutist bureaucratic state.[26] Under Charles III (r. 1759–88), significant policy and administrative reforms occurred, including 'reliance on career officials subject to regular appraisal and promotion, who lived off fixed salaries instead of gratuities or the fees of office' and ending the sale of public offices.[27] The age of absolutist monarchy in Europe saw the rise of bureaucratic government (Chapter 8, Part 2).

The loyalty of the creole elite in the Americas declined in the long term, in part due to preference for peninsular Spanish appointees at all levels of the colonial governments. Further unrest was caused by the banishment of Jesuits from Spanish America in 1767 and increased state control over the church. The colonies were exploited for basic commodities (principally silver) and as supplementary markets for manufactured Spanish goods, frustrating industrial development in the New World. But as markets in the American colonies grew, they traded among themselves with increasing vigour, and this was accompanied by cultural and political independence. Around the turn of the nineteenth century, Spain was defeated in conflicts with France and Britain, suffered occupation by Napoleon's army, and ceded Louisiana and Trinidad. The fear of French interventions in the Americas, the creoles' desire for greater participation in government, the resentment of imperial taxation and the example of the Thirteen Colonies helped to fuel the conflicts that formed the now independent nations of Latin America.[28]

Part 2: India and Britain

As transcontinental global imperialists, the English made a late start compared with the Spanish and Portuguese. Later still, the Scots made an abortive attempt to found a colonial settlement (see Part 5, 'Sovereignty'). Following the union of England and Scotland in 1707, one may speak of British imperialism. But first, we should take account of the imperial government of India under the Mughals.

The Mughal empire

The name Mughal comes from the Persian for Mongol, as the dynasty was descended from Timur (Chapter 5, Part 4). Setting out from Kabul in 1525, Timur's great-great-grandson Babur (1483–1530), supported by Turks and Pashtuns, invaded Punjab, occupied Delhi and established a capital at Agra. Babur's grandson Jalal-ud-din Akbar ('the Great') (r. 1556–1605) strengthened Mughal rule, expanded the empire to encompass most of the northern and central subcontinent, and reformed its government. A Muslim ruler of a mainly Hindu society, Akbar is remembered for his religious toleration. He neither converted subjects nor imposed the *jizya* tax on non-Muslims. He supported dialogue between the faiths, following an Indian tradition at least as old as Ashoka (Chapter 2, Part 2), and he married a Hindu Rajput princess, Jodhaa Bai (c. 1542–1623).[29] In the early Mughal period, women were active 'not only in issues of family and succession but also in the military and political concerns of the Timurid dynasts as they battled to hold their empire.'[30] By Akbar's time, there was an enclosed harem with apartments for thousands of women, creating a stratified community served by eunuchs and guarded by armed women called *urdubegis*. The selection of wet-nurses for Akbar in his infancy was in itself a political dynastic concern, as it recognised, reinforced and created alliances. The 'milk relationship' between a future emperor and other boys could be just as significant as 'blood'. The harem wasn't cut off from public and economic life, and women of the royal family exercised authority.[31]

Although the Mughals didn't interfere with local legal and religious traditions, their rulership must be described as despotic. They weren't bound by *sharia*, unlike the Baghdad caliphate. They were originally Central-Asian invaders, claiming conquest as a justification. Having plundered cities and provinces, their government was secular and pragmatic (army, police, justice and taxation) but pervasive and exacting. Revenues and expenses were carefully recorded; surpluses were the norm; most spending was on the armed forces. This required tightly organised and ranked bureaucrats and tax collectors, recruited from foreigners and native-born Indians and using Persian language and methods.

The vast imperial household with its ministers, administrators and auditors was mirrored by provincial patriarchal households of sovereign governors and nobility with their own land-based revenues. These provincial revenues were centrally authorised and scrutinised, however, based on land surveys and productivity, commutable into cash. Local revenue collectors were also magistrates and police officers with a general mandate for the wellbeing of the community, including such matters as the administration of estates of those who died without heirs.

A currency based on copper, silver and gold coin was valid throughout the empire. As India had few sources of precious metals, trade surpluses with the outside world supplied specie, including silver from the New World.[32] The economic power of the empire came from plentiful land and labour, with a population of

100 to 150 million, larger than Europe and Britain combined. Economic output in 1700 (under Aurangzeb, r. 1658–1707) is estimated at 27 percent of the world economy,[33] with which only China could compare. Although the Mughal emperors were enriching themselves, their system was economically productive as a whole and attracted foreign traders. Its main flaw was to over-tax the peasantry to pay the salaries of the tax collectors and the soldiers who protected them – not to mention maintain the extraordinary wealth and entourages of emperors.

Akbar acted like a chief executive, with huge personal wealth and an efficient system of communication. Unwilling to apply *sharia* strictly, he made no written law code. But Aurangzeb was not so tolerant and outraged Hindus by imposing the *jizya* tax. He also expanded Mughal territory to the south. But internal rebellions weakened the empire, with Hindu Maratha rulers engaging the emperor in the ongoing conflict and eventually controlling central and western India. The Mughal imperial decline was accompanied by rural unrest, regional governors acting increasingly independently, and a series of short-lived or incompetent emperors after Aurangzeb. Their system depended heavily on the emperor himself; there was no vizier or loyal nobility with authority to make up for a weak monarch. Wars of succession and struggles for provincial autonomy erupted. The severest blow was delivered by the Iranian ruler Nader Shah (1688–1747), who sacked Delhi and looted its treasury in 1739. During the reign of Muhammad Shah (r. 1719–1748), 'the empire slipped into a loosely knit group of regional successor states'.[34] Despite steadily declining status, the Mughal dynasty was recognised until 1858 by which time it was merely one component of British India.[35]

The English East India Company

In 1498 the Portuguese explorer Vasco da Gama arrived in Kerala, having rounded the Cape of Good Hope. This opened a maritime route for the spice trade that bypassed the Persians, Arabs and Venetians. To establish a base in India, the Portuguese seized Goa in 1510. As one of a string of fortified ports at strategic locations around the Indian Ocean and points further east such as Melaka and Macau, Goa became Portugal's Asian headquarters for the next 450 years.[36]

In 1600, Queen Elizabeth of England signed the charter for the East India Company's (EIC) monopoly on English trade in the east. Although 'it took two and a half centuries for the potential to be realised, the wording of the EIC's charter left open from the beginning the possibility of it becoming an imperial power, exercising sovereignty and controlling people and territory.'[37] The charter vested the direction of the joint-stock company's business in a governor and 24 stock owners, or the court of directors, who were elected annually by the court of proprietors. The company was thus self-governing and the assembled proprietors could overrule the directors. In 1612, the Mughal emperor Jahangir (r. 1605–1627) granted the English the right to trade within his territory. At around the same time the first successful English colonies in North America were being established.[38] These would grow into thirteen colonies on large tracts of land, seized with relative ease from indigenous inhabitants, each with a governor, council and legislature.[39] In India, by contrast, the European merchants encountered a wealthy and advanced civilisation that had sophisticated paper-based centralised government and massive armies. The Mughals and the regional rulers confined foreign traders to the coasts.

Competition between the European powers in the region was mainly for control of sea lanes, using heavily armed vessels based in fortified ports. The Portuguese were unable to maintain control over the Indian Ocean, and they allied with the English against the Dutch. The English established a factory at Madras in 1641. The island of Bombay was given to King Charles II in 1661 as dowry for his marriage to Catherine of Braganza; it was rented to the East India Company in 1668.[40] English traders brought economic opportunities to India, but the political and commercial rivalries within and around the company were sometimes unscrupulous and violent. Being so far from London, the actual conduct of business and social life in seventeenth-century Madras and Calcutta was more dynamic and complex than company policies would have permitted. There were intense rivalries between company agents, clashes with local tax collectors, European 'interlopers' (merchants breaching the company's monopoly), powerful local commercial interests and mixed marriages.[41] Back in London, moreover, the company was found out for bribing parliamentarians.[42]

By the mid-eighteenth century, the company was fully involved in Indian political life. The Mughal emperor had lost control over much of the country as a result of regional rebellions. In the chaos and credit crisis that followed the sack of Delhi, first in 1739 by Nader Shah and again in 1756 by the Afghan king Ahmad Shah Abdali (c. 1722–1772), East India Company forces in Bengal took sides among local power-brokers and governors as all parties vied for sources of revenue. The company deposed the Nawab (viceroy or governor) in favour of his military commander Mir Jafar (c. 1691–1765), who defected with his forces to the British at the Battle of Plassey (1757). Jafar was installed as Nawab at the behest of the company, which in return received revenue rights over an autonomous province, along with large payments to its leaders. A foreign power looting a treasury and extracting revenue wasn't unusual for those times, given 'the conventions of power-seeking under the late Mughal empire'.[43] In hindsight, though, 1757 was the turning point towards British rule. According to the 1909 *Imperial Gazetteer of India*, the company had acquired 'full rights of territorial sovereignty over Bengal' by 1772.[44] Run from an office in London, however, this hostile takeover was probably 'the supreme act of corporate violence in world history.'[45]

The company's wholesale plunder and an appalling famine in 1770 in Bengal were causes of grievance in India. They didn't go unnoticed in London, where the government held the company to account and limited its independence. The company avoided 'imminent bankruptcy' through a loan from British taxpayers in 1772,[46] and the post of governor-general was created, to be appointed by parliament. Company officer Warren Hastings (1732–1818) was the first appointee.

He called for a more unified government of British India, staffed by Indian officials and judges following the Mughal system.[47] This was never implemented. Hastings was recalled to London in 1784 and then impeached by the House of Commons on charges of corruption – from which he was acquitted after ten years of hearings.[48] In 1783, the House of Commons put the government of British India and the commercial activities of the company under two separate commissions. Opponents argued that this violated the company's rights as granted by the royal charter. Speaking in favour of the bills, however, Whig MP Edmund Burke (1729–97) argued that the fundamental 'chartered rights of men' enshrined since the Magna Carta didn't include trade monopolies or dispossession of inherited properties, and certainly not the criminal misconduct of which the company stood accused.[49] Parliament sought to prevent further conquests in India, but the company continued to involve itself in conflicts and enlarge its territory.

By the 1820s, the East India Company had mastery of India, but with inconsistent forms of government and no concerted strategy. There were the original fortified port cities of Madras, Calcutta and Bombay, acquired in the seventeenth century, in which judicial and administrative institutions had developed, and around which territory, such as on the east coast, was subsequently acquired. Then there were territories acquired in wars in Mysore and against the Marathas. Finally, there were 'princely states' in which the British maintained a Resident but recognised, by treaty, the traditional rulers. The annexations continued, notably Sind in 1843, the Punjab in 1849 and Burma in 1852.[50] There was no overarching law code, neither indigenous nor imperial, and British judges in India lacked a basis for consistent rulings.[51]

Despite greater political oversight, the East India Company remained a going concern until 1857. Its military expenditures were growing, however, and commercial revenues weren't keeping up; hence, tributes and taxes were essential.[52] This joint-stock company was effectively a government, accountable commercially to its shareholders and politically to parliamentarians as a hybrid 'company-state'.[53] It was 'capable of waging war, planting colonies, raising taxes and exercising sovereignty.'[54] It taxed landowners and peasants at extortionate rates, but not necessarily to return services and benefits to the people. 'The main objectives of the Company were to enrich its officials and finance its exports from the tax revenues of the province instead of shipping bullion to India.'[55] In effect, Indian farmers paid for the merchandise from which the company profited; moreover, the company undermined those Indian manufacturers who were more competitive than the British by dumping goods at below cost.

The Empress arises

The removal of local rulers whom the British had already subordinated by treaty, plus Christian evangelism and utilitarian progressivism, excited genuine fears among Indians that their religious, cultural and (for Hindus) caste traditions and distinctions were at risk of being overridden or obliterated by a foreign imperial government and law. The sense that deeply held values, such as the sacredness of cattle for Hindus and the prohibition on pork for Muslims, were being ignored or treated with disrespect by British administrators inflamed resistance, to the extent of full-blown rebellion (or 'mutiny') mainly around the northern regions in 1857. Efforts to re-establish Mughal rule through the rebels' support of the (now powerless) hereditary heir were ended when the British retook Delhi and plundered it. The last of the Mughals was exiled to Burma and his two sons were killed. The result of the 1857 rebellion against company rule was, however, a confirmation of *imperial* rule, but with some concessions to Indian traditions and concerns. Queen Victoria's Proclamation of 1858 terminated the company's rule but arrogated its powers to Westminster rather than repatriate them to the Indian people. The expanding enfranchisement of the British people during the mid-nineteenth century didn't apply in India. Victoria became Queen of India, later Empress; the governor-general became her executive viceroy; the East India Company's administrative functions were taken over by British civil servants. A secretary of state for India was appointed, supported by a council of fifteen advisers, mostly retirees from the Indian civil service.[56] The Queen instructed British officials to respect native religions and princely succession and cease annexations. The reforms inducted into the British-Indian hierarchy the local minor nobility, landlords and tax collectors, utilising their 'genuine hold on the loyalties as well as the remittances of their subordinates'.[57] Rebellion hadn't engulfed the whole country, and many landowners and princes accepted British rule so long as it provided protection, ended the violence and elevated their status.

The British Raj was administered by a surprisingly small number of officials. Selection for the Indian civil service excluded Indians. Through examinations held in Britain, it recruited officials who were almost exclusively British.

> They formed an administrative cadre that numbered around 1,000 who had signed the "covenant" of faithful service, and for whom the 700 or so most senior posts in the central and provincial governments were reserved, including the key position of district officer in the 250 districts of British India.[58]

A district officer could have jurisdiction over a large territory and population of which he would normally have little local knowledge; he would be strictly guided by rule-book rather than by observation of actual conditions or by nego-tiation with those affected. The welfare of the people wasn't the main objective, and maladministration contributed to famines. 'The untrammelled authority of British officials, not local self-government by elected politicians, became the constitutional rule.'[59] India was considered 'the jewel in the crown' of British imperialism and wealth extraction. Its strategic location straddled the Indian Ocean and South-East Asia, creating a base for British ground and naval forces between the Ottomans and Persians to the west and the Chinese to the east. To the north, it created a buffer against Russian imperialism. India garrisoned and paid for the bulk of the British army. This imperial phase of British rule, however, produced political resistance led by nationalist politicians. The independence of the subcontinent, painfully separating into India and Pakistan, came in 1947.

Gandhi

The best known of the group of educated nationalist pro-independence leaders was Mohandas Karamchand Gandhi (1869–1948). He was born into a Hindu Gujarati family; his father was the chief minister of the princely state of Porbandar. He studied law in London and practised in South Africa. By the time he returned to India in 1915, he had gained a reputation as a civil rights activist and Indian nationalist. His campaign for home rule included the *swadeshi* movement: boycotting foreign-made products, particularly clothes, and returning to Indian-made and home-spun fabrics. Bonfires of foreign-made clothes were organised. Gandhi's method of resistance to imperial rule was non-violent but not passive. *Satyagraha* ('holding on to truth'[60]) meant active conscientious disobedience to imperial authority while accepting the sacrifices and suffering that followed. This demonstrated moral conviction and forced imperial administrators to confront the injustice of their government. It didn't mean the rejection of all things British. Gandhi argued that 'if we shun every Englishman as an enemy, Home Rule will be delayed.'[61] The English didn't take possession of India by force; the Indians 'kept' them for their commerce. But he was critical of the English parliamentary system. The politicians acted in self-interest; their policies always changed; re-election was more important to them than the common good. 'If India copies England, it is my firm conviction that she will be lost.'[62] Gandhi called Indian civilisation 'the best';[63] while 'civilisation' in general meant 'good conduct', 'the path of duty', and an ascetic self-mastery over thoughts and feelings.[64] Armed struggle against British rule would be 'unholy'.[65] But people weren't bound to obey unjust law: they should resist it and suffer the consequences. Gandhi was assassinated in 1948. He's frequently cited as the exemplar of non-violent political action. He didn't represent all Indian resistance to imperial rule, however. Rabindranath Tagore (1861–1941), for example, strongly disagreed with him on many matters, including nationalism, patriotism and economic development.[66]

British India was evidently very different from Spanish America; the consequent mutual transformations of colonies and metropole played out quite differently. The British empire wasn't based on a consistent model; it was a complex improvised system, not a coherently organised polity.[67] There were many different motives and objectives for British colonisation. In Australia, for example, the British established penal colonies to which courts could 'send and forget' convicts whose offences didn't warrant hanging.[68] The next section considers one of Britain's white settler colonies.

Part 3: Aotearoa New Zealand

The year 1840 was a busy one for British imperialism. A large naval fleet set off from India to bombard Chinese ports, seize territory (notably Hong Kong) and reinstate opium imports into China in defiance of a ban. Meanwhile, on the orders of Governor-General Lord Auckland, British-Indian forces were occupying Kabul, Afghanistan, using regime change to tip the regional balance of power against Russia. And Lieutenant-Governor William Hobson, acting as British consul, was in New Zealand gathering signatures for a treaty with indigenous chiefs. These three quite different imperial actions weren't connected by design or strategy; each was in reaction to particular problems and opportunities.

Arrivals

Polynesian sailors first arrived in Aotearoa New Zealand probably in the early thirteenth century (Chapter 5, Part 1). Oral histories trace the first peoples back to more than 40 canoes that made the long journeys. One's *waka* (canoe) is cited to this day to express belonging and common ancestry. Prior to contact with Europeans, the indigenous peoples of Aotearoa didn't see themselves as one people, and certainly not as a 'race' (which is an introduced concept), but as numerous tribal groups. The diverse *iwi* (tribes) had social structures based on interlocking genealogical narratives and mutual obligations of *whānau* (extended family) and *hapū* (sub-tribe). Oral learning preserved knowledge of ancestry, tracing back to the gods and the creation of the natural world. One's position in the social hierarchy was based largely on descent and seniority. The qualities of an *ariki* (chief) were inherited, but 'could be increased by prowess in war, wise rule and generous behaviour to his people.'[69] Customs based on *tapu* (sacredness) regulated conduct and warfare; transgressions or injustices were dealt with on the principle of *utu* (revenge, reciprocity or payment). *Mana* (authority) meant 'the practical force of the gods at work in everyday affairs',[70] established through ancestry and common occupation of lands. No one owned or controlled land individually, but a tribe's identification with and occupation of land was an essential feature of collective belonging, authority and heritage.[71] The government of people entailed hierarchies of status, honour and chieftainship, and an unwritten law (or lore) that proscribed certain actions and required reciprocity and retribution. While there was no monetary or taxation system, there was a gift economy regulated by established customs.[72] Indigenous government would be faced, however, with an overpowering colonial government.

The first British explorer to reach New Zealand was Lieutenant James Cook in 1769.[73] Gradually sealers and whalers of various nationalities and convicts from Australia arrived and sometimes settled. Anglican, Wesleyan and Catholic missionaries weren't far behind. The indigenous peoples traded goods with the newcomers, learned about their religion and interbred with them. The destructive effects of these contacts, however, were caused by introduced diseases, alcohol and muskets. The latter fuelled inter-tribal warfare throughout the country during the 1820s and 1830s.[74] The pre-contact population of New Zealand was about 100,000, and indigenous Māori were the majority until the late 1850s. Their numbers declined to a low of 42,000 in the 1896 census. Meanwhile, the numbers of newcomers skyrocketed due to a gold rush in the 1860s and assisted migration from Britain. Hence, by 1896, Māori were less than six percent of the total population. There was a common misconception among Europeans that their 'race' would die out.

Transplanted government

To understand the colonial government, we begin in 1833 before the colony was formed. James Busby (1802–71) arrived in New Zealand from Sydney, New South Wales, as the first British Resident with instructions to control unruly Europeans, arrest escaped convicts and protect Māori, but with no armed force in support. London's Colonial Office believed that colonisation would be detrimental to the wellbeing of Māori. But the French were also exploring the area, and locally built vessels had no flag for recognition at sea. Busby persuaded 52 indigenous chiefs to approve a national flag and to sign a Declaration of Independence of New Zealand in 1835. One provision of this Declaration was for annual meetings of a lawmaking assembly – which never actually assembled. Although the Declaration didn't take full effect, tribal chiefs had conceived of themselves collectively as independent and as seeking recognition by other nations.

The situation was complicated by Edward Gibbon Wakefield (1796–1862), who formed the New Zealand Company with a plan for 'systematic colonisation' by British emigrants. Wakefield believed that 'waste' lands in the Antipodes could be purchased cheaply, sold to wealthy investors and used to alleviate unemployment and landlessness in Britain. A 'sufficient price' for land would be set to prevent monopolisation by a small minority. Migrant labourers could work, save and purchase a plot for themselves, while also raising a sum to import a replacement labourer. This plan was never fully implemented, but it reproduced British class relations and yet catered to workers who aspired to be proprietors.[75] Wakefield's company provided passage for working-class Britons, but he had to set sail before the British government annexed New Zealand and banned private land sales between Māori and Europeans.[76] The company's barque, the *Tory*, reached New Zealand on 16 August 1839 after more than three months at sea.

A week later, Captain William Hobson (1792–1842) left England with instructions from the Colonial Office to negotiate, as British consul, a treaty of cession.[77] The 1840 Treaty of Waitangi was signed by chiefs of most (but not all) tribes and sub-tribes. It was written in Māori and in English, but the meanings of the two versions differ. In the English version, the signatories ceded sovereignty to Queen Victoria; in the Māori version, they only permitted *kawanatanga* – government. Māori signatories who heard the Māori-language version could only have believed that they would retain their *mana*, their tribal independence and their properties and possessions, while Hobson would provide protection as a governor. They didn't cede sovereignty or the authority to make and enforce law.[78] But Hobson saw it differently. Having gathered signatures, he proclaimed British sovereignty over New Zealand – over the North Island by treaty and over the more sparsely populated South Island by discovery.

In European international law, however, indigenous peoples were regarded as 'entirely lacking in legal status'.[79] They were not cognisable as treaty-making parties as they lacked formal institutions of state. A supreme court decision over a land claim in 1877 reflected this theory, arguing that the British crown had acquired New Zealand by discovery and occupation only, and that 'the Treaty of Waitangi, so far as it purported to cede the sovereignty of these islands, was a nullity.'[80] This reflects a common imperialist paradox (or hypocrisy) wherein European norms of international law could not, according to Europeans, apply to indigenous peoples, and yet were applied anyway for the purposes of ceding sovereignty or transferring property. Britain made law for New Zealand, in spite of the questionable status of its sovereignty. An Act of the British parliament authorised the creation of a colony of New Zealand with a governor, an executive council and a legislative council. Hobson was appointed governor, and in May 1841, New Zealand was proclaimed to be a colony and no longer administered from New South Wales. A supreme court was promptly established, adopting the laws of New South Wales and the English common law.

So there were a governor and two councils but not yet a representative assembly from which to form a responsible government in the Westminster model. For the time being the executive ruled, constrained by instructions from London and by a paucity of arms to enforce law across the colony. The 1835 Declaration's proposal for an assembly was forgotten. Instead, the New Zealand House of Representatives was constituted by an act of the British parliament in 1852, and the first New Zealand parliament assembled in Auckland in 1854. Its representatives, including Wakefield, were all immigrants from the British Isles. Māori were still then the majority of the population, but they hadn't consented to this lawmaking institution nor were they represented in it. The 1852 Act had permitted self-governing Māori districts, but they were never created. Māori had no parliamentary representation until 1867 when they were granted four seats on the grounds of 'no taxation without representation'. On behalf of all inhabitants, however, this parliament of immigrants had already adopted England's laws as New Zealand's, until such time as it passed its own. Moreover, representatives of settlers tended to further the interests of settlers. For example, a law of 1863 authorised, without compensation, the confiscation of the lands of 'natives' who were opposing European settlements and were deemed, by the government, to be in 'open rebellion'. Māori leaders petitioned Queen Victoria (to no avail) to redress breaches of the 1840 Treaty and to establish a Māori parliament. But by this time the British government viewed relations with the indigenous people of New Zealand as the affair of the New Zealand government.[81] Collective indigenous ownership of land was unravelled, with alienation into private hands, one block at a time in native land courts or by wholesale confiscation.

Having acquired a Westminster-style government, New Zealand introduced, through gradual changes, some significant variations. The four Māori seats have already been mentioned, and this entailed a separate electoral roll. Women acquired the vote in 1893; the parliament abolished its own upper house in 1950. Meanwhile, the country progressed in status from colony to dominion to an independent nation with its own foreign policy, although it unquestioningly followed Britain's lead into the two world wars. By the end of the nineteenth century, governors-general had a constitutional, ceremonial and strictly apolitical role. They were normally minor members of the British aristocracy or distinguished military officers appointed by the British monarch – until 1967 when the first locally-born governor-general was appointed on the recommendation of New Zealand's prime minister. It wasn't until after World War II that prime ministers were consistently New Zealand-born. Independence came slowly and even reluctantly as an evolving sense of nationhood was coupled with an enthusiasm for participation in empire.[82] There was also a desire, however, to build a nation that was free from the social evils of 'Home', especially Britain's rigid class structure and poverty. This ideal was never really achievable, but innovations in industrial policy in the 1890s, labelled as 'state socialism' at the time, and improvements in social security from 1935 moved the country towards the social-democratic category. The attachment to private land ownership, however, so dearly held since Wakefield's first European settlers, was never threatened.[83]

Reluctant independence

The settlers saw no cause to sue (let alone fight) for independence, they chose not to federate along with the Australian colonies in 1900, and hence they never adopted a written over-arching constitution. New Zealand is now one of only three countries (including the United Kingdom and Israel) that lack one. The single house of parliament reigns supreme, by convention, constrained largely by the fear of negative public opinion and the next election. Governments are served by a loyal, meritocratic and (relatively) independent public service. The Treaty of Waitangi was an instrument of foreign policy between a distant state and many independent tribes. It has recently been accepted as the country's 'founding document' and as grounds to redress injustices suffered by the indigenous people.

New Zealand was a relatively late and remote addition to Britain's empire; it offered no special economic or strategic advantage. The desire of many Europeans to hunt, trade, evangelise, escape and settle there led to colonial government all the same. And then the settlers wanted both responsible government and participation in the global empire. London was disinterested in deeper involvement in New Zealand's affairs, but drew upon its troops to defend the empire when it needed them. New Zealand prime ministers – at least until 1935 – were keen imperialists, but their British counterparts paid them little attention. Once Britain joined the European Economic Community (now European Union) in 1973, the imperial relationship was well and truly over.[84]

India, unlike New Zealand, was already the site of ancient civilisations and empires well before the British arrived (indeed, since well before the Romans arrived in Britain). India's economic and strategic value to Britain was immense. British settlers in New Zealand adopted a Westminster-style government, as granted by British law, without permission of the indigenous majority. India's constituent assembly, in contrast, chose for their post-1947 independent state a British form of parliamentarianism with an independent civil service (as compared with, say, an American-style congress and executive president), in spite of their resistance to British imperialism.[85]

We could, of course, compare historical experiences between many countries affected by British imperialism. These two examples alone show how diverse those experiences were, including the differing histories of their government. What they do have in common is that they were haphazard and opportunistic projects. The British ruled pragmatically and with a presumption of their own superiority. The Spanish-American example highlights further differences. The Spanish Empire began with the crown and applied one basic model across different territories, whereas the English crown licensed a joint-stock company that took the lead in India. Viewed as government imposed from across oceans, inter-continental imperialism is 'metastatic' – but diverse. It's not the same pathology in all instances. Diverse political and cultural systems in the imperial and the colonised countries shape the possibilities and the results.

Part 4: Algeria and France

On today's map, Algeria encompasses 1622 km of Mediterranean coastline, a huge portion of the Sahara desert, and mountain ranges in between. Indigenous peoples are Berber, but Phoenicians, Arabs, Jews, sub-Saharan Africans and others made Algeria their home. The long history of the region includes rule by Carthaginians, Romans, Abbasids and Ottomans, among others. In late antiquity, it was Christianised.[86] Indeed, the hometown of the theologian Augustine of Hippo (354–430 CE) is today's Souk Ahras in eastern Algeria.[87] Muslim Arabs of the Umayyad empire swept across the region in the early eighth century and the people were gradually Islamised. The territory of the early twelfth-century Almoravid dynasty (Chapter 5, Part 2) extended as far as Algiers. This region, the Maghreb, was swallowed up as a far western province of the Ottoman Empire in the sixteenth century under Suleiman the Magnificent (r. 1520–1566). Algerian privateers cruised waters off the coast of North Africa, fuelling conflict between the Ottoman and Habsburg empires. The naval battle of Lepanto in the Gulf of Patras (1571) dealt a major blow to Ottoman ambitions, but it didn't stop the privateers. Algerian government settled into a system in which the *divan*, the council of oligarchs, elected one of their own as *dey* ('uncle'), who would be confirmed by the Ottoman government in Istanbul. The *dey* was thus recognised as ruler of the Regency of Algiers, governing with varying degrees of force across fertile coastal and mountainous provinces with grain-producing communities. Between Istanbul and Algiers and its provinces, then, there were varying degrees of autonomy and negotiable power-sharing and taxation. In the eighteenth century, grain exports to Europe grew and diplomatic relations with France were relatively cordial. Nonetheless, privateering and slave trading off the so-called Barbary Coast continued to be a problem for European coastal communities and maritime traders. Political stability in Algiers declined from 1791 due to food shortages and plague. An English fleet bombarded it in 1816, seeking to end the enslavement of Christians. And then in 1830 the French invaded, exiled the *dey* and ended Ottoman rule over Algeria.[88]

France

France meanwhile had been through its revolution (1789–92), the Napoleonic wars and First Empire (1804–14) and the Bourbon restoration (1814–30). The principle of (male) equality before the law established by the revolution hadn't led to much greater equality in real political and social terms. The execution of one monarch, Louis XVI in 1793, was followed by Napoleon's coronation as emperor in 1804. After Napoleon's military defeat and exile, Louis XVIII, the closest heir to Louis XVI, assumed the throne with the nobility's support in 1814. Louis XVIII granted a constitution establishing a limited monarchy that shared power with a bicameral parliament consisting of the hereditary Chamber of Peers and the elected Chamber of Deputies. The franchise was tightly restricted on a property basis. Some of the civil and religious freedoms fought for in the revolution were maintained, with constraints; some of the privileges of the nobility were preserved, without returning to the pre-revolutionary order. The constitution sought a balance between king and legislature, between monarchy and representative government. This compromise only set the scene for a further struggle between anti-revolutionary Catholic conservatives and enlightenment freethinkers.[89] Louis XVIII died in 1824 and was succeeded by his brother Charles X, who took a more conservative line.

The French invasion near Algiers on 14 June 1830 was followed, only six weeks later, by a popular insurrection in Paris and the flight of Charles X. This is not to say that the former event led to the latter. The king's attempts to muzzle the press and to alter election laws (to ensure that fewer liberal candidates could win seats) polarised the political situation, leading to the July 1830 insurrection. Charles X went into exile and Louis-Philippe, the head of a lesser branch of the Bourbons, was installed as king. He promised a constitutional monarchy, satisfying the demands of bourgeois revolutionaries. The more idealistic republicans were disillusioned, however, as the right to vote was still restricted to the wealthy.

The decision of Charles X's ministry to invade Algeria in 1830 was a failed effort to 'boost the regime's popularity'.[90] And it left Louis-Philippe's new government with a problem – which they addressed by getting more deeply involved.[91] If imperialism was meant somehow to restore French national pride after the loss of the slave-plantation colony of Saint-Domingue (now Haiti) in 1805, and after the defeats of Napoleon in Russia (1812) and at Waterloo (1815), then pulling out of Algeria wasn't an option. Only a minority of French politicians argued for withdrawal; France's aim became total domination. Even the liberal thinker Alexis de Tocqueville (1805–59) supported the annihilation of any Algerian tribes that resisted French occupation, if necessary by destroying their agricultural base.[92]

Colonial government

There were differing ideas in France about what kinds of people should emigrate to Algeria. Settling soldiers as colonists didn't work well. Social groups regarded as undesirable or as surplus labour were targeted by some authorities, if only to rid their cities of them. An alternative plan preferred settlers who were morally respectable and who could become self-sufficient small landholders. This meant also ensuring sufficient numbers of 'honourable' migrant women to form families, along with which went concerns about the numbers of prostitutes. On the other hand, joint-stock companies acquired large estates, but preferred Algerian over French workers. In any case, settlers called for systematic suppression of the native Algerian peoples and dispossession of their lands.[93] So colonial government evolved from 1830 on, but not according to any consistent plan. The French disagreed over how to govern Algeria. Opinion polarised around two sets of issues: military or civil administration; colonial autonomy or integration into France.

Indigenous Algerians who survived the French onslaught[94] suffered dispossession and discrimination – French rule with exclusion from French civil rights, along with exploitation of their labour by settlers. Lands that hadn't been confiscated during military actions were gradually broken up and alienated into European hands by legal-judicial means. Algerians responded to the French invasion sometimes by attempting to accommodate it, to maintain the relative autonomy they had enjoyed under the Ottomans, and sometimes by armed resistance. By 1848, the strongest leader of resistance, the *amir* Abd al-Qadir (1808–83),[95] had surrendered, and most of Algeria was under direct French military control. Resistance nonetheless sprang up from time to time for the remainder of the nineteenth century.[96]

In 1841, the French government decided to annex Algeria as French territory. General Bugeaud (1784–1849), a veteran of the Napoleonic wars, was appointed as governor to quell resistance, consolidate French rule and re-establish *le Bureau arabe* (the Arab Bureau) as a military colonial institution.[97] Officers of the Bureau grew in number and were distributed throughout the colony. They were mostly educated military officers supported by local indigenous chiefs as their subordinates. Their roles included local intelligence, social order (including exemplary punishments and summary executions), welfare of tribes and acquisition of knowledge of their origins. The settler demand for civil rather than military government eventually prevailed, however. Following the 1848 revolution, the constitution of the Second Republic (1848–51) created three *départements* within Algeria, like those of mainland France, each administered by a prefect who reported to a minister in Paris. Later, they came under the governor-general of Algeria, who was supported by an elected *conseil général*.

The political turmoil associated with France's defeat by Prussia in 1870, the revolutionary Paris Commune of 1871, and then the re-establishment of order under the Third Republic (1870–1940) formed a backdrop to the gradual replacement of military government in Algeria by civilian colonists. The republican movement among the colonists pushed for the fulfilment of promises made in 1848 for full assimilation into France and full French citizenship for European Algerians so that Algeria would no longer be 'considered a colony'.[98] This was accompanied by the suppression of another Muslim uprising. A French statute of 1865 had declared native Algerian Muslims to be 'French' but governed by Muslim law and hence legally not French citizens. They were 'legislated into a false promise of emancipation that in fact created the legal space of their oppression.'[99] There were also anti-Semitic protests by settlers against a law of 1870 that had granted French citizenship to Algerian Jews.

From 1881, each of the Algerian *départements* returned two elected deputies to the legislature in Paris, and from 1884 one senator. Below the level of the *départements*, there were municipalities with full civic authority. The zones under civil administration grew, and those under military rule in the Sahara declined accordingly. A political movement for greater autonomy for the European settlers was coupled with anti-Semitic protests in 1898. Conceding to these pressures, the French government granted budgetary autonomy to the colony in 1900 through an elected assembly in Algiers. This assembly included indigenous Algerian delegates but was dominated by the European agriculturalists and urban property owners.[100] The European settlers were then largely able to run their own government and dominate the Muslim majority.

Incompatible laws

French imperial policies were supported by the idea of a 'civilising mission' (*mission civilisatrice*): the belief that, thanks to liberty and rational republican government, the French 'were particularly suited, by virtue of their revolutionary heritage and their current industrial strength, to carry out the task of liberating all of humanity – beginning with the peoples they were colonizing.'[101] In the Maghreb, the study of ancient Roman ruins contributed to a view of the region as originally European but overrun by Arabs.[102] Assimilation of indigenous Algerians as equals into French society was resisted by colonists, who wanted to monopolise the benefits provided by the state. For Muslims, assimilation into

French citizenship was undesirable as it meant estrangement from their community and a renunciation of Islamic law which amounted to apostasy.[103] From 1854, while northern Algeria was still being subjugated by French forces, colonial policy attempted to subordinate Islamic law to secular bureaucratic control by creating 'a unified, centralized Muslim court system'.[104] French administration meant that the traditional consensual process of appeal from a local judge or *qadi* to a *majlis* (a council of religious scholars) was abolished in favour of appeal to French courts. It was unrealistic, however, to expect Islamic judges willingly to separate civil from religious law as European courts did. And the *majlis* was the principal institutional protector of Islamic identity and practice as against colonial assimilation. The *qadis* were among the few respected leaders who were able to speak to colonial authorities on behalf of Algerian Muslim communities. But the bureaucratisation of their roles meant 'desacralisation' within a foreign system of 'rules and decrees, fixed salaries and fee schedules, exactly ordered ladders of promotion, inspection tours, and reports in quintuplicate.'[105] The underlying problem was the incompatibility between Islamic and French concepts of what law actually is.

The Quran is both revealed scripture and law code. It's more prescriptive, as law, than the Bible, and yet Muslims never developed separate institutions that resemble the Christian churches. Beginning with Constantine, emperors who adopted Christianity and imposed it on their subjects had inherited civil law from ancient Rome. The Bible might modify Roman law, but didn't supplant it. For the emperor Justinian, ecclesiastic and civil law were distinct and applicable in the distinct institutions of church and state (Chapter 4, Part 2). This wasn't so in the Muslim world. Islamic law applies to the faith and civil conduct. Its arbiters are a community of scholars versed in theology and jurisprudence. Religion and law aren't separable. Sultans and emirs may appoint individuals as judges, but judges belong to a community that seeks consensus about difficult legal questions or judgements. They could 'mobilize popular protests to pressure a ruler into revoking an action which did not conform, in their view, to Islamic principle.'[106]

The Napoleonic code had reformed post-feudal civil and ecclesiastical systems in Europe, making them internally consistent, eliminating local customary privileges, instituting equality before the law (for males) and building secular systems with rights of appeal to higher courts. But a post-Napoleonic French colonial government couldn't readily impose its law on an Islamic society. The French considered their system to be superior, but Islamic scholar-judges were unable to assimilate it – not simply because of differing religions and cultures, but also due to their fear of apostasy, punishable by death. By imposing the force of French law over a pre-existing and incompatible legal code, but excluding Muslims from full citizenship, the colonial system was systematically and violently unjust.

> Colonial rule, imagined as a patient work of peaceful progress, was in fact a routinised infliction of low-intensity warfare: criminalisation, collective punishment, denial of due process and of an effective right of appeal, the

slow, continual erosion of property and the grinding effects of impoverishment, the arbitrary and stingingly disproportionate exercise of everyday 'ordinary violence' characterised Algerians' experience of their subjection to the state up to 1944.[107]

Gandhian non-violent political struggle had no impact on the anti-colonial struggle in Algeria. The Martiniquean psychiatrist Frantz Fanon (1925–61) collaborated with, and became the leading intellectual for, the Front de Libération National (FLN) during the Algerian war of independence. He argued for the necessity of armed violence in anti-colonial struggles. 'The terror that France imposed upon Algeria from 1954 to 1962 represents one of the gravest crimes against humanity of the twentieth century.'[108] The war ended with a treaty in 1962.

Part 5: On imperialism

In the Peace of Westphalia of 1648, the Spanish Habsburgs conceded, among other things, the political and religious independence of the Dutch. The 1648 treaties signify Europe's shift from dynastic kingdoms and empires towards the recognition of sovereign states demarcated by permanent inviolable borders, each of which is free to determine its own religious and political affairs. It inaugurated an era in the law of nations, or international law, especially in the regulation of war and peace. Sovereign states would be juridically equal, even if they were economically and militarily unequal.[109] After the Napoleonic wars, the Treaty of Vienna (1815) produced a model of conflict management based on consensus. A principle of balance of powers emerged to prevent hegemony of one state over others; congresses and treaties were used to conclude wars and manage tensions; permanent mutual diplomatic missions were established. Post-Westphalian Europe didn't put an end to imperial expansion or hegemonic behaviour, however. For instance, Russian imperial expansion into Siberia, Alaska and Central Asia continued through the nineteenth century until the 1867 sale of Alaska to the United States and, in 1907, the Anglo-Russian Convention that defined borders with Persia, Afghanistan and Tibet. Lawless annexations by a certain Third Reich were direct causes of World War II. There was at least a law for the conduct of international relations in peace and in war, but it wasn't the only model.

Throughout history, rulers and peoples of the world made agreements based on various principles and customs other than the (relatively recent) Westphalian system. For example, in the Chinese sphere of influence, a tributary model prevailed in which 'a central power used its domestic rules for regulating foreign relations'.[110] And Islamic jurisprudence set out principles for the justification and conduct of war and for relations between communities of believers and of non-believers (*siyar*). An early contributor to this Islamic tradition was Muhammad ibn al-Hasan, or al-Shaybani (750–804 CE). One special concern was 'Muslim fighters crossing the borders in an effort to "open" non-Muslim territory to the civilizing influence of Islam.'[111] Neither system was exactly a law of nations, as now understood, but different civilisations employed different models to govern relations with other peoples.

The Westphalian-European model nonetheless became the source of modern norms of international society, advanced by the League of Nations after World War I and institutionalised now in the United Nations. The European state system became 'the model for the entire contemporary world.'[112] After all, 'the coming together of numerous and extremely diverse political entities' into an international society required that the parties possess some basic resemblances, with common criteria by which to recognise one another as members.[113] *International* law presupposed a shared understanding of 'nation'. The presumption of European norms arose from the happenstance that the emergence of an international society followed the ascendancy of European imperial powers and the United States. In turn, those European norms were the historical product of the transcontinental imperial experience and the wars within Europe. It was not simply that the competing European nations agreed on a set of legal norms for recognition among themselves and then imposed them upon others, resulting in the international society of today. 'The evolution of the European system of interstate relations and the expansion of Europe across the globe were simultaneous processes, which influenced and affected each other.'[114]

Nonetheless, those Euro-American norms also underlay subsequent distinctions between a 'developed' world and a 'developing' or 'third' world. The aims of 'development' thus had a Catch-22 effect, setting developing countries an almost impossible task of achieving the political-economic standards of former colonial masters to be regarded substantively (not just formally) as equals in the international community. The political reactions against imperial domination have had to struggle within and against this paradox of 'exclusion by inclusion'.[115] Newly independent postcolonial nations rejected European colonial government, but they also had to utilise the rights and protections of an international society governed by European standards.

Race

Ideas that one's own people, culture of social stratum may be inherently superior to others have been around since ancient times. People have often attributed any social, cultural and economic advantages to a 'natural' superiority of their own kind, rather than seeing political domination as the source of historically contingent advantages. An ancient example is Aristotle's idea that the slave is 'by nature' a slave. Later, the monotheistic religions brought about expulsions of heretics, wars against 'heathens' or 'infidels', and persecution of Jews. But the ancient and medieval worlds were largely devoid of systematic discrimination based on skin colour as an imagined 'marker' between different kinds of humans. Early curiosity about the causes of differing skin colours often took climate as an explanation. Writing in the late fourteenth century, Ibn Khaldun, for example, noted that the hot, temperate and cold climates at differing latitudes appeared to correlate with differing skin colours, and he saw 'composition of the air' as the basic cause. His remarks about 'Negroes' we would call racist, but he had no biological theory of 'race' as such.[116] He acknowledged the cultural advancement of black Africans in Abyssinia and Mali who followed monotheistic religions. He often generalised about the societies he knew, but differing skin colours were products of differing environments, he believed, and weren't innate. His main concern was the historical dialectic between nomadic and settled ways of life. Nomads such as Berbers may have been uncivilised, as he described them, but they were stronger and more cohesive than urbanised people, and hence they became conquerors. He didn't make an issue of their colour.

Arabs and Berbers together conquered the Iberian Peninsula in the eighth century, and the last of the Muslim rulers was expelled in 1492. Christians in Spain were thus conscious of ethno-religious distinctions, and they expelled non-Christians including Jews. Spanish and Portuguese colonisation in the Americas then brought together many more religions, cultures and peoples. Power relations between European colonial masters and imported African slaves and indigenous peoples were fixed in principle, but they were unstable in practice due to intermarriage and social exchanges. A conservation of racial distinctions was sometimes seen as necessary, and this generated concerns about the offspring of mixed couples. In the eighteenth century, after many generations of intermarriage, Mexican artists produced a visual archive of mixed-racial categorisations in hundreds of so-called caste paintings (*pintura de castas*).[117] These canvases were normally divided into sixteen vignettes, each depicting parents and a child with a caption such as, 'From a Spanish man and an Indian woman is born a *Mestiza*', progressing to nuances such as, 'From an *Albarazado* man and a *Mestiza* woman is born a *Barcino*.' One apparent concern was whether a mixture of black (as compared with Indian) 'blood' into a white lineage, initially producing a *mulatto*, could return to pure 'Spanish' after sufficient generations of 'dilution'. The depiction of dark-skinned 'throwbacks' suggested that blackness was ineradicable. These racial categorisations did, however, dismiss an old theory that a *mulatto* ('mule') would be sterile.

The caste paintings also indicated, by dress and occupation, the presumed social status of each mixture, declining with successive dilutions of whiteness. Any administrative uses these paintings may have had are unclear, and the nomenclature and lineages weren't uniform across examples. In everyday life, moreover, one's socially reputed or perceived racial classification was influenced by familial and contextual factors, and could change over a lifetime. The real-world uses of such terms were more fluid than depicted. Audience responses to the caste paintings aren't well documented, but seem to have ranged from 'enthusiastic appreciation, to studied skepticism, to criticism'.[118] The *pintura de castas* was more than just visual art; it was one of the techniques that reconfigured superficial human characteristics as 'racial' characteristics and as signifiers of socioeconomic stratification. Today, we see them critically as products of ignorance and pseudo-science; in their time, they represented, like natural history, a way of classifying and hence of *knowing* people by race, gender and class.[119]

By the time of the independence movements of the early nineteenth century, this genre of painting had ceased. During the nineteenth century, pseudo-scientific theories about 'races' and their role in history flourished, however, based on bodily shapes and skin colours. Anywhere from three to eleven races were proposed, with hierarchies placing whites above others.[120] Great civilisations were the work of superior races, it was argued, and hence interbreeding with inferior races would endanger them. Europeans thus perceived themselves as a 'race' (or 'races') distinct from and elevated above others. Race became a category in law and government, enforcing slavery and segregation or *apartheid*, and reinforcing informal exclusion and discrimination.

The late twentieth century's science of genetics refuted categorisations of humankind into biologically distinctive groups. Racial categorisations, as constructs, had differed from place to place; they were products of imperialism in local political manifestations. No one is inherently a member of a race; nor were there pre-existing and distinct races that then met and mixed. The idea of 'race' emerged retrospectively from violent trans-regional encounters, subjugation of indigenous peoples and a demand for slave labour. It was a pseudo-scientific category used to explain, and to attempt to justify, colonial domination and exploitation, especially as imperialism reached a high point in the latter half of the nineteenth century. Racial identification, differentiation and hierarchy reinforced colonial government and imperial ideology.

Sovereignty

The conceptual and practical effects of imperialism rebounded back on and changed the metropolitan centres. Conquest and colonisation were central, not peripheral, to the emergence of European international law, as evident for example in the controversy within the Spanish world regarding relations with the peoples of the New World. 'The Spaniards' justification for conquering the Indies was morally dubious on their own terms [and] was not covered by the ordinary rules of just war.'[121] The theologian and political philosopher Francisco de Vitoria (c. 1483–1546) argued that indigenous Americans exercised reason and had proper dominion over their own people and territories; they were also bound by God's (supposedly universal) natural law. That they weren't Christians, and that some of their practices may have been sinful (in the eyes of Christians) didn't however justify conquest and dispossession by the Spanish. Vitoria argued against many of the means of and rationalisations for Spanish rule over indigenous peoples. Nonetheless, he recognised the rights of the Spanish to explore and travel in the Americas, trade freely and convert those people who were willing. But he remarked that 'these barbarians are by nature cowardly, foolish, and ignorant'. Out of fear, 'these barbarians' might attack law-abiding Spanish soldiers, traders and preachers, and hence give the Spanish crown just cause to wage a defensive war against them.[122] In addition, the Spanish would be obliged to protect native converts to Christianity from efforts to lure them back into 'idolatry'. Thus, he argued, war could be justified against indigenous Americans in some circumstances, and consequently they could legitimately fall under Spanish rule. This led Vitoria into wider reflections on just and unjust conduct of war, within the framework of Christian doctrines and European norms. But he had assumed that culturally particular European concepts were universally applicable or 'natural'. Once these supposedly universal norms were applied to them, native Americans appeared 'ignorant' of those norms, and hence fell outside of them. Natural law did, and yet didn't fully, apply to them. Vitoria's work illustrates how the law of nations (*ius gentium*) was not simply 'invented' in Europe and then transposed onto a non-European world. Instead, the modern understanding of national sovereignty in part 'acquired its character through the colonial encounter'.[123] These cross-cultural encounters challenged and developed European ideas of sovereign rights and just war.

Colonial enterprise and misadventure had profound practical effects on sovereignty and nationality back in the European world. An example is found in the events that led to the union of Scotland and England in 1707. Under the Stuarts, the two nations shared the same monarch, but each had its own parliament and law. William of Orange reigned as William II of Scotland and William III of England from 1689 to 1702. When the Scottish Parliament launched 'a Company of Scotland trading to Africa and the Indies' in 1695 to profit from transcontinental trade – like many Europeans before them – William found himself in a dilemma. The plan was resisted by the East India Company, and the efforts of the Scots to raise capital were blocked by the English parliament. So, the Scots decided to go it alone, and subscribers, including small investors, were found. A fleet set sail for Darién in Panama (not Africa or the Indies) with a plan to open a trading route across the isthmus to the Pacific and thence to the East.

They were apparently kindly received by the indigenous people and began work on a fortified settlement, but climate and disease were against them. The Spanish, moreover, treated them as hostile intruders, and English authorities in Jamaica received orders from their government to give the Scottish colonists no assistance. With war over the Spanish succession looming, the English didn't wish to upset the Spaniards. The Darién expedition became a disaster due to disease, attacks and shipwrecks, and colonists were literally 'left for dead'. Some survivors sold themselves into indentured labour; only a few made it back to Scotland. By 1700 it was clear that the Scottish company had lost almost everything, including more than £150,000 sterling. This damaged the national economy as well as national pride, and Scottish anger was aimed at the English for treachery.[124]

One possible avenue still open to the Scots was a political separation from England by repudiating William as their monarch and reverting to the Stuarts, namely James Edward (1688–1766), who still claimed to be James VIII of Scotland.[125] But the price of independence would have been prolonged poverty, loss of trade and eventual war with England. Instead, a treaty united the two as the

Kingdom of Great Britain under Queen Ann (r. 1702–14). This meant the Scots accepted the Act of Settlement 1701, which ruled out Catholics (such as James) as heirs to the throne and opened the way for the Hanoverian succession.[126] The Scottish parliament was wound up and representatives were sent to Westminster. For taking on their share of England's debt, the Scots were paid almost £400,000 sterling to cover the losses incurred in Darién. The deal was arranged among elites and was bitterly resisted; people rioted as the legislation passed through the Scottish parliament. Their efforts to form a Scottish mercantile empire had backfired and contributed to the conditions that produced union with England. But union also opened trade and career opportunities within a now *British* Empire.[127] Neither Britain nor Spain was a united sovereign entity, as known today, before they initiated transcontinental imperial projects. Rather than nations that formed empires, they were nations formed (in part) as *consequences* of imperial projects.

Independence

Colonisation led to struggles over the correct form of government in the centres and at the peripheries of empires and over independence. The relations between Britain and its former American colonies are an example. No imperial constitution was written for Britain's haphazard empire, and so the degree of independence of the colonies' assemblies from the British parliament and crown was undefined. The colonies mostly had bicameral legislatures with representative lower houses; their upper houses and governors 'tended to advance royal interests'.[128] The English constitution was itself undergoing significant change. The Glorious Revolution of 1688 installed William of Orange and Mary (daughter of the deposed James II) as constitutional monarchs and shifted the balance of power definitively towards parliament. The Bill of Rights curtailed regal authority, making it illegal, for example, for the monarch to suspend or ignore laws without the consent of parliament. And the Act of Settlement 1701 subordinated the royal succession to the law.

Many American colonists asserted the rights of their own representative assemblies rejected laws passed (without their consent) by a distant parliament in London in which they had no representatives, and questioned 'despotic' instructions from the crown. In the 1740s, when the House of Commons considered 'legislation to make royal instructions law in the colonies', the colonies protested that this was unconstitutional and inconsistent with liberties that should apply to 'Englishmen' wherever they lived.[129] Even if parliament had the *power* to pass laws without the consent of the affected colonies, it lacked the *right* to do so. The Stamp Act of 1765 imposed a direct inland duty on the colonies and caused an outcry against 'taxation without representation'. It was later repealed, but Britain's parliament held to its rights to legislate for the colonies.[130]

Many communities within Britain lacked 'actual' representation at that time,[131] and yet, it was argued, parliament provided a 'virtual' representation for them, so the same principle might be applied to the Americans. The proposition that colonies might be 'virtually' represented in the House of Commons naturally found little support in America. Instead, colonial assemblies 'actually' represented the colonists, and, by law and custom, had the sole prerogative to approve internal taxation. A fundamental rift in understandings of the legitimate powers of the British and the colonial legislatures was exposed, especially regarding the supposed 'supremacy' of the former outside of Britain. This challenged the sovereignty of Britain over its colonies, questioning whether the colonists could be fully subject to British law. Did the liberties that the colonists claimed, then, imply nothing less than their full independence? Or was there a constitutional middle way where the colonies could legislate for their internal affairs, while the British crown and parliament controlled external affairs including navigation and trade? Matters came to a head in the 1770s over taxes, duties and shipping – famously over tea from the British East India Company – arousing popular resistance to London-made laws in favour of local laws and liberties.[132]

The colonists had developed administrative systems based in local courts and assemblies.[133] It only remained then for the several colonies to assemble as a 'Continental Congress' in Philadelphia (1774) and to unite around their common cause.[134] The colonies had played no direct part in the 1688 Glorious Revolution, but the same theory of natural law and popular consent by which John Locke (1632–1704) had justified it was reused in the US Declaration of Independence of 1776. After winning that independence, the Americans then had to address, in a new context, a problem similar to the old one: 'how, in an extended polity, to distribute authority between the centre and the peripheries'[135] – this time between a federal government and the states' governments, expressed in a written constitution.

It isn't simply that the British had a settled system of government and law that they tried (and failed) to impose on their American colonies. The British system itself was undergoing change; there was no well-established model for governing their empire; the key concept of representation was still evolving. The revolt of the Americans forced the British to reflect more deeply about representation, government and sovereignty. Edmund Burke was the most prominent statesman in this debate in Britain. He spoke for 'conciliation' with the American colonies, rejected the idea of their 'virtual' representation and saw the impracticability of their having any 'actual' representation, given the distance.[136] In doing so, Burke was helping to form the very meaning of representative government (Chapter 7, Part 2).[137]

Conclusion

Metastatic imperialism – a vector of modernisation and racism – produced its own violent and hypocritical, and also creative and adaptive, forms of government. Incalculable human suffering and loss, and a legacy of global inequality, discrimination and exploitation followed in its wake. Some may count the global spread of representative government as an advance for the former colonies in the long run, but colonial government did inestimable harm along the way. The idea that imperialism brought benefits of civilisation to the uncivilised, outweighing the costs, is unconvincing. Colonised peoples had already been self-governing in various forms, but were often reduced to forced labour, or treated as heathens in need of religion or as obstacles to be swept aside. They were largely not treated as dignified or equal subjects with rights, nor as initiators of their own futures, other than through rebellion against colonisation. There were bound to have been more peaceful and respectful ways of sharing the achievements of one's civilisation – without resorting to *un*civilised mass murder and theft.

Without the evolving model of the sovereign nation, there'd be no inter-*national* law to speak of. But nations, states and the concepts of sovereign na-tionhood and representative government, as we know them now, were in part formed from the struggles and consequences of transcontinental imperialism. Colonisation has been central to the development of the law of nations, even though the colonised were systematically excluded from – or more recently treated as inferior participants in – this modern international order. The prob-lems of governing distant colonies occasioned in return some profound changes in the metropolitan nations. The challenges of empire forced the imperialists to rethink the government of their own homes. Often the imperial project was haphazardly implemented and even the colonisers disagreed among themselves about it, let alone the understandable resistance from indigenous peoples. There were principles and methods of governing people and relations between peoples other than the European ones that we may happen to have grown up with and assumed were unquestionable norms. And in general, successful government has at least tolerated, at best encouraged, diverse communities' own traditions and hierarchies. This is as important a message today as at any time in history.

Notes

1 In the Middle East, Sultan Suleyman I (1494–1566) ruled the Ottoman empire; the Ming dynasty ruled China.
2 Burkholder, 1998, p. xv.
3 Davies, 2011; Kamer, 2005.
4 'The European colonization of the world and the development of the sovereign states system went hand in hand.' Onuma, 2000, p. 25.
5 Murra, 1984, p. 85.
6 Ibid., p. 69.
7 Ibid. See also McEwan, 2006; Ross & Steadman, 2017.
8 Diamond, 1998, develops a historical-causative theory (with technologies such as gunpowder as proximate factors) to explain the defeat of the Incan emperor. This commits a logical fallacy, however. It supposes that, because event A was preceded by B and C, then B and C *caused* A. Undoubtedly, the Spaniards made tactical use of their muskets, but the causative hypothesis is only superficially 'scientific'. One can't submit unique historical events (as recorded by biased witnesses who were also plunderers) to the scientific test of falsifiability. Diamond's idiosyncratic con-clusion that human history can be studied 'as scientifically as studies of dinosaurs'

(p. 425) relies on 'natural experiments', such as Incans versus Spaniards. It overlooks the complexity of human culture and politics, economic motives and the reflexive paradox of 'the human being' as both subject and object of knowledge. I avoid such evolutionist, developmentalist or causative theories, and Darwinian ideas about environmental adaptation and fitness.

9 Elliot, 1984a, pp. 182–3.
10 Kamer, 2003.
11 Ibid., p. 158.
12 Elliot, 1984a, p. 167.
13 Numbers and death-tolls of indigenous peoples are hard to estimate. Concerning the native Taíno of Hispaniola, a balanced estimate of the 1492 population is in the range from 400,000 to two million, with only 16,000 surviving by 1518. Dunn, Kelly & Keegan, 1992.
14 Elliot, 1984a.
15 Kamer, 2003.
16 Burkholder, 1998, p. 84.
17 Elliot, 1984b; Finer, 1999, vol. III.
18 Burkholder, 1998, p. 82.
19 Ibid. See also the testimony of Gabriel Fernández de Villalobos (1642–1702) in Keen, 2018.
20 Finer, 1999, vol III, p. 1384.
21 Burkholder, 1998, p. 54.
22 Ibid., p. 59.
23 Elliot, 1984b, p. 338.
24 Ibid.
25 Gibson, 2014: Kamer, 2003.
26 Kamer, 2003, p. 450.
27 Brading, 1984, p. 395.
28 Lynch, 1973.
29 Their marriage is romantically depicted in the epic movie *Jodhaa Akbar*, dir. Ashutosh Gowariker, 2008.
30 Balabanlilar, 2010, p. 133.
31 The royal women

> counselled Akbar and mediated between dissenting kinsmen. Akbar and other royals sought their advice, and they frequently arbitrated and made suggestions on public matters. The emperor's mother enjoyed an especially honored position during Akbar's reign. Her tenure as the governor of Delhi in 1581 is only its most striking illustration.
>
> Lal, 2008, p. 108, abridged. See also Sharma, 2009

32 Richards, 1993, chap. 3; Finer, 1999, vol III.
33 Angus Maddison, cited in Tharoor, 2017, p. 3.
34 Richards, 1993, p. 281.
35 Keay, 2010, p. 363.
36 Disney, 2009.
37 Dalrymple, 2019, p. 9.
38 Jamestown in 1607 and Plymouth in 1620.
39 By 1660 all thirteen settled American colonies had their own representative assemblies. Greene, 2011.
40 Wilson, 2017; Judd, 2004.
41 Veevers, 2017.
42 Dalrymple, 2019.
43 Keay, 2010, p. 382.
44 Secretary of State for India, 1909, p. 9.
45 Dalrymple, 2019, p. xxvii.

46 Keay, 1991, p. 383.
47 Wilson, 2017, p. 130.
48 The Company was undoubtedly rife with corruption, but Hastings was attempting to clean it up and was framed by his enemies.
49 'Speech on Fox's India Bill' (1783) in Burke, 1981.
50 Judd, 2004.
51 Wilson, 2017, p. 195.
52 Ibid.
53 Stern, 2011.
54 Veevers, 2017, p. 177.
55 Maddison, 2006, p. 111. See also Tharoor, 2017.
56 Darwin, 2009.
57 Keay, 2010, p. 446.
58 Darwin, 2009, p. 187. See also Tharoor, 2017, p. 51.
59 Darwin, 2009, p. 18.
60 Tharoor, 2017, p. 123.
61 Gandhi, 1993 [1909], p. 8.
62 Ibid., p. 15.
63 Ibid., p. 37.
64 Ibid., p. 35.
65 Ibid., p. 40.
66 Sen, 2005, Chapter 5.
67 Darwin, 2009.
68 Hughes, 1987.
69 Walker, 1990, p. 65.
70 Salmond, 1991, p. 44.
71 Ibid.
72 Firth, 1972.
73 A Dutch expedition led by Abel Tasman visited in 1642. Cook was promoted to first lieutenant in 1768 in advance of his first voyage to the Pacific. He is normally known as Captain Cook.
74 Crosby, 2001.
75 Wakefield's 'systematic colonisation' was satirised by no less a critic than Karl Marx in his *Capital*. Duncan, 2007, p. 93.
76 Temple, 2002.
77 Ibid., p. 242.
78 Orange, 1987. In 2014, the Waitangi Tribunal found that, in 1840, the indigenous chiefs did make an agreement, but they 'did not cede their sovereignty to Britain. That is, they did not cede authority to make and enforce law over their people or their territories.' Waitangi Tribunal, 2014, p. 529.
79 Anghie, 2006, p. 745. See also Onuma, 2000, p. 3.
80 *Wi Parata v Bishop of Wellington*, 1877. See Williams, 2011.
81 King, 2003.
82 Darwin, 2009.
83 Duncan, 2007. 'Social-democratic' in the typology of Esping-Andersen, 1990.
84 Some supporters of Brexit promoted 'Empire 2.0'. They also revived a mid-1960s idea about a CANZUK (Canada, Australia, New Zealand, UK) union, with greater freedom of movement and trade between these countries. Wellings & Mycock, 2019.
85 An Indian MP argues that the British system is unsuited to Indian society. Tharoor, 2017, pp. 86–8.
86 Exactly how and by whom Christianity was brought to the region is unclear. Lane Fox, 1988.
87 Brown, 2000.

88 McDougall, 2017.
89 Price, 2014.
90 Popkin, 2017, p. 71.
91 Goubert, 1991, p. 244.
92 Pitts, 2000.
93 McDougall, 2017.
94

> The losses suffered [by Algerians] by the 1870s, in land and lives, were and remain incalculable. Hundreds of thousands of hectares, including much of the country's best agricultural land, had already passed into colonial hands. Algerian direct "combat deaths", sustained in the field and subsequently of wounds, numbered perhaps 650,000, perhaps 825,000, between 1830 and 1875. Famine and disease killed at least as many, very possibly many more.
>
> McDougall, 2017, p. 80

95 Abd al-Qadir was exiled to Damascus. He received international acclaim after saving many Damascene Christians from a massacre in 1860.
96 McDougall, 2017.
97 Hannoum, 2001.
98 Popkin, 2017, p. 155.
99 McDougall, 2017, p. 123.
100 Ibid.
101 Conklin, 2011, p. 174.
102 Hannoum, 2008.
103 Christelow, 2014.
104 Ibid., p. 20.
105 Ibid., p. 266.
106 Ibid., p. 270.
107 McDougall, 2017, p. 127.
108 Hudis, 2015, p. 73.
109 Simpson, 2004.
110 Onuma, 2000, p. 18.
111 Kelsay, 2003, p 66. See also Bsoul, 2008.
112 Finer, 1999, vol. I, p. 94.
113 Bull, 1984, p. 121.
114 Bull & Watson, 1984, p. 6.
115 Pearcey, 2016.
116 The black Africans allegedly had 'a disposition and character similar to dumb animals'. In contrast:

> The inhabitants of the north are not called by their colour, because the people who established the conventional meanings of words were themselves white. Thus, whiteness was something usual and common to them, and they did not see anything sufficiently remarkable in it to cause them to use it as a specific term.
>
> Khaldun, 2005 [1370], pp. 59–61.

117 Examples are readily found online.
118 Deans-Smith, 2006, p. 171; see also Earle, 2016.
119 Foucault, 1994.
120 Robert Knox, *The Races of Men*, 1850, and Arthur de Gobineau, *Essai sur l'inégalité des races humaines*, 1853, are examples cited by Garner, 2017. An example of crude classification of races by intelligence is Sir Francis Galton, *Hereditary Genius*, 1869.
121 Donelan, 1984, p. 81.
122 Vitoria, 1991 [1539], p. 282.
123 Anghie, 1996, p. 332.
124 Davies, 1999; Mitchison, 2002.

125 James Edward was the son of King James II and VII of England, Scotland and Ireland, who was deposed and exiled in the Glorious Revolution of 1688.
126 After Ann's death, the crown went to George I of the House of Hanover.
127 Mitchison, 2002.
128 Postell, 2017, p. 14.
129 Greene, 2011, p. 58.
130 Kuklick, 2009, p. 57.
131 Industrial cities that were growing rapidly had no MPs because they weren't registered as boroughs in the late seventeenth century. In stark contrast, the so-called 'rotten' boroughs had very few voters, but were entitled to representatives.
132 'The American Revolution started as a tax revolt.' Finer, 1999, vol. III, pp. 1490–91. 'The popular uprisings [by American colonists, harassing those charged with enforcing unconstitutional statutes of parliament] described by earlier historians as expressions of lawless violence actually functioned as the police unit, the *posse comitatus*, of local law.' Greene, 2011, p. 144.
133 Postell, 2017.
134 Kuklick, 2009, p. 63.
135 Greene, 2011, p. 190.
136 'Speech on Conciliation with America' (1775) in Burke, 1996.
137 Pitkin, 1967.

References

Anghie, Antony. 2006. 'The Evolution of International Law: Colonial and postcolonial realities.' *Third World Quarterly* 27 (5): 739–53.
———. 1996. 'Francisco de Vitoria and the Colonial Origins of International Law.' *Social & Legal Studies* 5 (3): 321–36.
Balabanlilar, Lisa. 2010. 'The Begims of the Mystic Feast: Turco-Mongol Tradition in the Mughal Harem.' *The Journal of Asian Studies* 69 (1): 123–47.
Brading, D.A. 1984. 'Bourbon Spain and its American Empire.' In *The Cambridge History of Latin America*, by Leslie Bethell, 389–440. Cambridge: Cambridge University Press.
Brown, Peter. 2000. *Augustine of Hippo: A Biography*. Berkeley: University of California Press.
Bsoul, Labeeb Ahmed. 2008. 'Historical Evolution of Islamic Law of Nations/Siyar: Between Memory and Desire.' *Digest of Middle East Studies* 17 (1): 48–67.
Bull, Hedley. 1984. 'The Emergence of a Universal International Society.' In *The Expansion of International Society*, by Hedley Bull and Adam Watson, 117–26. Oxford: Clarenadon Press.
Bull, Hedley, and Adam Watson. 1984. *The Exapnsion of International Society*. Oxford: Clarendon Press.
Burke, Edmund. 1996. *The Writings and Speeches of Edmund Burke, Volume III*. Oxford: Clarendon Press.
———. 1981. *The Writings and Speeches of Edmund Burke, Volume V*. Oxford: Clarendon Press.
Burkholder, Mark. 1998. *Administrators of Empire*. London: Routledge.
Christelow, Allan. 2014. *Muslim Law Courts and the French Colonial State in Algeria*. Princeton, NJ: Princeton University Press.
Conklin, Alice L. 2011. 'The Civilizing Mission.' In *The French Republic: History, Values, Debates*, by Edward Ducler Berenson, Vincent Duclert and Christophe Prochasson, 173–81. Ithaca, NY: Cornell University Press.
Crosby, Ron D. 2001. *The Musket Wars: A History of Inter-Iwi Conflict, 1806–45*. Auckland: Reed.

Dalrymple, William. 2019. *The Anarchy: The Relentless Rise of the East India Company.* New York, NY: Bloomsbury.

Darwin, John. 2009. *The Empire Project : The Rise and Fall of the British World-System, 1830–1970.* Cambridge: Cambridge University Press.

Davies, Norman. 1999. *The Isles: A History.* London: Macmillan.

———. 2011. *Vanished Kingdoms: The History of Half-Forgotten Europe.* London: Penguin.

Deans-Smith, Susan. 2006. 'Creating the Colonial Subject: Casta Paintings, Collectors, and Critics in Eighteenth-Century Mexico and Spain.' *Colonial Latin American Review* 14 (2): 169–204.

Diamond, Jared. 1998. *Guns, Germs and Steel: A Short History of Everybody for the Last 13,000 Years.* London: Vintage.

Disney, Anthony R. 2009. *A History of Portugal and the Portuguese Empire: Volume 2, The Portuguese Empire : From Beginnings to 1807.* Cambridge: Cambridge University Press.

Donelan, Michael. 1984. 'Spain and Indies.' In *The Expansion of International Society*, by Hedley Bull and Adam Watson, 75–85. Oxford: Clarendon Press.

Duncan, Grant. 2007. *Society and Politics: New Zealand Social Policy.* Auckland: Pearson Education.

Dunn, Oliver, James Kelly, and William Keegan. 1992. 'Beachhead in the Bahamas: Landfall.' *Archaeology* 45 (1): 44–56.

Earle, Rebecca. 2016. 'The Pleasures of Taxonomy: Casta Paintings, Classification, and Colonialism.' *The William and Mary Quarterly* 73 (3): 427–66.

Elliott, John H. 1984a. 'The Spanish Conquest and Settlement of America.' In *The Cambridge History of Latin America*, by Leslie Bethell, 147–206. Cambridge: Cambridge University Press.

———. 1984b. 'Spain and America in the Sixteenth and Seventeenth Centuries.' In *The Cambridge History of Latin America*, by Leslie Bethell, 287–340. Cambridge: Cambridge University Press.

Esping-Andersen, Gøsta. 1990. *The Three Worlds of Welfare Capitalism.* Cambridge: Polity.

Finer, Samuel Edmund 1999. *The History of Government.* Oxford: Oxford University Press.

Firth, Raymond. 1972. *Economics of the New Zealand Maori.* Wellington: Government Printer.

Foucault, Michel. 1994. *The Order of Things: An Archaeology of the Human Sciences.* New York, NY: Vintage.

Gandhi, Mohandas Karamchand. 1993. 'Hind Swaraj.' In *The Penguin Gandhi Reader*, by Rudrangshu Mukherjee, 3–66. London: Penguin Books.

Garner, Steve. 2017. *Racisms: An Introduction.* Los Angeles, CA: Sage.

Gibson, Carrie. 2014. *Empire's Crossroads: A History of the Caribbean from Columbus to the Present Day.* London: Macmillan.

Goubert, Pierre. 1991. *The Course of French History.* London: Routledge.

Greene, Jack P. 2011. *The Constitutional Origins of the American Revolution. New Histories of American Law.* Edited by http://search.ebscohost.com.ezproxy.massey.ac.nz/login.aspx?direct=true&db=nlebk&AN=335222&site=eds-live&sco. Cambridge: Cambridge University Press.

Hannoum, Abdelmajid. 2001. 'Colonialism and Knowledge in Algeria: The Archives of the Arab Bureau.' *History and Anthropology* 12 (4): 343–79.

———. 2008. 'The Historiographic State: How Algeria Once Became French.' *History and Anthropology* 19 (2): 91–114.

Hudis, Peter. 2015. *Frantz Fanon: Philosopher of the Barricades.* London: Pluto Press.

Hughes, Robert. 1987. *The Fatal Shore : A History of the Transportation of Convicts to Australia, 1787–1868.* London: Collins Harvill.

Judd, Denis. 2004. *The Lion and the Tiger: The Rise and Fall of the British Raj.* Oxford: Oxford University Press.

Kamer, Henry. 2003. *Empire: How Spain Became a World Power, 1492–1763.* New York, NY: HarperCollins.

Keay, John. 2010. *India: A History.* New York, NY: Grove Press.

———. 1991. *The Honourable Company: A History of the English East India Company.* London: HarperCollins.

Keen, Benjamin. 2018. *Latin American Civilization: History and Society, 1492 to the Present.* London: Routledge.

Kelsay, John. 2003. 'Al-Shaybani and the Islamic Law of War.' *Journal of Military Ethics* 2 (1): 63–75.

Khaldun, Ibn. 2005. *The Muqaddimah: An Introduction to History.* Princeton, NJ: Princeton University Press.

King, Michael. 2003. *The Penguin History of New Zealand.* Auckland: Penguin.

Kuklick, Bruce. 2009. *A Political History of the USA: One Nation Under God.* Houndmills: Palgrave Macmillan.

Lal, Ruby. 2008. 'Mughal Palace Women.' In *Servants of the Dynasty: Palace Women in World History*, by Anne Walthall, 96–114. Berkeley: University of California Press.

Lane Fox, Robin. 1988. *Pagans and Christians in the Mediterranean World.* London: Penguin.

Lynch, John. 1973. *The Spanish-American Revolutions, 1808–1826.* New York, NY: W.W. Norton.

Maddison, Angus. 2006. *The World Economy.* Paris: OECD.

McDougall, James. 2017. *A History of Algeria.* Cambridge: Cambridge University Press.

McEwan, Gordon F. 2006. *The Incas: New Perspectives.* New York, NY: W.W. Norton.

Mitchison, Rosalind. 2002. *A History of Scotland.* London: Routledge.

Murra, John. 1984. 'Andean Societies Before 1532.' In *The Cambridge History of Latin America*, by Leslie Bethell, 59–90. Cambridge: Cambridge University Press.

Onuma, Yasuaki. 2000. 'When Was the Law of International Society Born? An Inquiry of the History of International Law from an Intercivilizational Perspective.' *Journal of the History of International Law* 2 (1): 1–66.

Orange, Claudia. 1987. *The Treaty of Waitangi.* Wellington: Allen and Unwin, Port Nicholson.

Pearcey, Mark. 2016. *The Exclusions of Civilization: Indigenous Peoples in the Story of International Society.* New York, NY: Palgrave Macmillan.

Pitkin, Hanna Fenichel. 1967. *The Concept of Representation.* Berkeley: University of California Press.

Pitts, Jennifer. 2000. 'Tocqueville and the Algeria Question.' *The Journal of Political Philosophy* 8 (3): 295–318.

Popkin, Jeremy D. 2017. *History of Modern France.* New York, NY: Routledge.

Postell, Joseph. 2017. *Bureaucracy in America: The Administrative State's Challenge to Constitutional Government.* Columbia: University of Missouri.

Price, Roger. 2014. *A Concise History of France.* Cambridge: Cambridge University Press.

Richards, John. 1993. *The Mughal Empire.* Cambridge: Cambridge University Press.

Ross, Jennifer C., and Sharon R. Steadman. 2017. *Ancient Complex Societies.* New York, NY: Routledge.

Salmond, Anne. 1991. *Two Worlds: Meetings Between Maori and Europeans 1642–1772.* Auckland: Penguin.

Secretary of State for India. 1909. *The Imperial Gazetteer of India: The Indian Empire, vol 4, Administrative.* Oxford: Clarendon Press.

Sen, Amartya. 2005. *The Argumentative Indian: Writings on Indian History, Culture and Identity*. London: Penguin/Allen Lane.

Sharma, Karuna. 2009. 'A Visit to the Mughal Harem: Lives of Royal Women.' *South Asia: Journal of South Asian Studies* 32 (2): 155–69.

Simpson, Gerry J. 2004. *Great Powers and Outlaw States: Unequal Sovereigns in the International Legal Order*. Cambridge: Cambridge University Press.

Stern, Philip. 2011. *The Company-State: Corporate Sovereignty and the Early Modern Foundations of the British Empire in India*. Oxford: Oxford University Press.

Temple, Philip. 2002. *A Sort of Conscience: The Wakefields*. Auckland: Auckland University Press.

Tharoor, Shashi. 2017. *Inglorious Empire: What the British Did to India*. Melbourne: Scribe.

Veevers, David. 2017. 'India, the Contested State: Political Authority and the Decentred Foundations of the Early Modern Colonial State in Asia.' In *The East India Company, 1600–1857*, by William Pettigrew and Mahesh Gopalan, 175–92. London: Routledge.

Vitoria, Francisco de. 1991. *Political Writings*. Cambridge: Cambridge University Press.

Waitangi Tribunal. 2014. *He Whakaputanga me te Tiriti, The Declaration and the Treaty: The Report on Stage 1 of the Te Paparahi o Te Raki Inquiry*. Lower Hutt, New Zealand: Legislation Direct.

Walker, Ranginui. 1990. *Ka Whawhai Tonu Matou: Struggle Without End*. Auckland: Penguin.

Wellings, Ben, and Andrew Mycock. 2019. *The Anglosphere: Continuity, Dissonance and Location*. Oxford: Oxford University Press.

Williams, David V. 2011. *A Simple Nullity? The Wi Parata Case in New Zealand Law and History*. Auckland: Auckland University Press.

Wilson, Jon. 2017. *India Conquered: Britain's Raj and the Chaos of Empire*. London: Simon & Schuster.

7

THINGS MADE FROM PEOPLE

Republics, representatives, revolutions

For most of history, ordinary membership of a large state or empire meant subjection and obedience to the sovereign, usually a monarch; rarely did it mean a commonly held responsibility for, let alone popular influence over, the government. Sovereignty was granted by God or the Mandate of Heaven or similar. This didn't mean that the ruler should ignore the will or welfare of the people. But an emperor like Justinian I was accountable to God. He, not the people, would be the final judge of an emperor's justice and benevolence. The social value of benevolence was well understood since Confucius, but Chinese rulership derived from the Mandate of Heaven. In general, the foundation-stone of legitimate imperial rule wasn't the will or wellbeing of the people. The ancient Greek philosophers stand out for thinking rationally about how the constitution of a society could be designed and structured to help serve the interests of its people. Their preferred models, however, tended to be neither inherited monarchies nor democracies. There were the wise philosopher-kings proposed by Socrates in Plato's *Republic,* and then Aristotelean mixed government that aimed to balance the competing interests of different social classes (Chapter 2, Part 3). But the idea of a popular sovereignty, the legitimacy of which begins and ends with the people, achieved prominence only relatively recently. When speaking of 'the people', however, those who counted were originally almost exclusively male – and only that minority of males who owned significant property. So why were the propertyless people excluded from participation? And why were women only rarely or marginally involved?

I deal with the latter question first; the former will unfold as we go. The states considered in previous chapters were patriarchies, as the rulers were almost all male, as were their ministers and generals. The need for military prowess and hence physical strength doesn't explain this away. Not all successful monarchs or ministers were capable of leading in battle, whereas many women were. The

DOI: 10.4324/9781003166955-7

intellectual and ethical virtues required of those who govern, as Socrates argued in *The Republic*, are not reserved to one gender. The political inclusion-by-exclusion of women was a norm, however. This needs to be addressed before we speak of 'the people', and two examples follow.

Christine de Pizan (c. 1364–1430) was originally from Venice but lived and wrote in Paris. Her best-known work is *The Book of the City of Ladies* (*Le Livre de la Cité des Dames*) which begins with her expressing despair at the misogynistic depictions of women in classical and medieval literature. Not only was it claimed, following Aristotle, that women lacked the deliberative virtues needed for participation in public life, but worse, there was a prejudice frequently expressed by male authors 'that female nature is wholly given up to vice.'[1] Christine's spirits are revived, however, by the appearance of three female-personified virtues: Reason, Rectitude and Justice. With their help, she sets about building an allegorical 'city of ladies', narrating the lives and achievements of numerous heroines of exceptional virtues: for example Zenobia, Queen of Palmyra in Syria (r. 267–72 CE). During Zenobia's brief reign, Palmyra broke its alliance with Rome as a buffer state bordering Persia and set out to conquer Antioch and Alexandria. She was defeated by the Roman emperor Aurelian and may have been led in triumph through Rome.[2] Given how little reliable information survives about Zenobia, Reason has to embellish her story, but she describes her as physically strong, courageous, beautiful, sober, chaste and learned.[3] As an example of the great intellectual merits of women, de Pizan cites Carmentis, a Greek noblewoman who according to legend settled with her followers on Mount Palatine, one of the seven hills where the city of Rome was later founded. She's said to have given to the indigenous peoples of the area their first laws and to have invented the Latin alphabet for their benefit.[4] De Pizan's work included poetry and assisted her in making a living after the death of her husband. She wrote on the body politic and on just war theory. She argued that women are equal to men in virtue, wisdom and political acumen, and she depicted a women-only *polis* to illustrate this. She didn't take the next step, however, to propose an equal role for women in real-world affairs of state.

Roxolana or Hurrem Sultan (c. 1502–58) probably came from an Orthodox community in Ruthenia, then part of Poland, now in Ukraine. She was likely abducted in her late teens by Crimean Tartars and trafficked to Istanbul, where she was purchased for Sultan Suleyman (r. 1520–66). Given the Muslim prohibition against enslaving other Muslims, the imperial harem imported Christian women as concubines who would then be forced to convert. Once a woman bore the sultan a son, she was removed permanently from his bed-chamber to raise the potential heir. This ensured that Turkish families couldn't vie to marry their daughters to the sultan nor lay claims to the succession. The Ottomans sustained monarchical inheritance this way through many generations, although with ever-decreasing degrees of Turkic 'blood'. Mothers of heirs would remain in the harem after their grown sons had left to govern a province, while royal mothers had important political roles in raising and advising their sons, sometimes acting as regents. The palace mothers held imperial custodianship and the title of sultan. Roxolana upset conventions, however, by becoming Suleyman's favourite and then his lawful wife, bearing him six children including five boys. Suleyman genuinely loved Roxolana, it seems. She also became his political adviser, usurping a role previously reserved for the sultan's mother. She wielded considerable political influence and financed public amenities.[5] But this was largely from the seclusion of the imperial harem and only after the hazards of abduction and forced concubinage. Her 'inclusion' in imperial government, exceptional for women of that era, also meant a radical 'exclusion'.

There were of course outstanding female monarchs: Elizabeth I of England (1533–1603), Catherine the Great of Russia (1729–96) and Empress Dowager Cixi (1835–1908), who governed China for the Qing dynasty from 1861 until her death. The much-admired Isabella d'Este (1474–1539) and her husband Francesco Gonzaga (1466–1519), marquesses of the Italian city of Mantua, may be regarded as a power-sharing couple.[6] These examples proved women's political abilities. But they're remarkable in part because a female ruler was then the exception rather than the rule. In a republic, 'the people' implicitly included all genders, but women were excluded as political actors. The recognised active citizen was male; anointed rulers were male by inheritance. Patriarchal rule and the systematic subordination, exclusion and/or seclusion of women were among the norms of government for most of the history examined in this book. To counter this, Mary Wollstonecraft (1759–97) and John Stuart Mill (1806–73) rightly argued that the subordination of women was unjust and that the removal of legal disabilities from women in favour of equality of rights, especially to education, would benefit humanity as a whole.

Part 1: Republics

The principal alternative to rule by one or by an elite few is the *republic* – in Latin, *res publica*, meaning the people's thing or commonwealth.[7] Early popular ownership and control of states were seen in Athens, Sparta and Rome, as well as the ancient *gana sangha* clan-based republics of northern India.[8] The government of a republic originates in the people and is intended to promote their common good. A republic is neither an absolute monarchy nor a self-serving oligarchy.[9] It's also something more than a large association of free individuals who 'tolerate' government as a necessary evil to ensure security. Ideally, it's a shared public concern, in the government of which its members actively and responsibly participate.

One of the most important republics to emerge in the Middle Ages was Florence. But first, we need to summarise the feudal form of government that was the norm in western Europe, against which Florence can be compared. Feudalism was based on personal allegiances or contracts between local lords (as vassals) and their overlord, practised symbolically by paying homage and materially in fees and military services in return for tenancy. The vassal then exercised his own 'miniature' government over his domain. These hierarchical arrangements gave vassals the right or privilege to be present in the king's court as tenants-in-chief and to advise (even defy) him on law and policy. To counterbalance the king's inner circle of clerks, advisers and ministers, the lords and bishops of the realm were to be present at a colloquium with the king (which was the historical kernel of early modern representation, described below). Feudal government entailed complex interlocking person-to-person arrangements that didn't fall neatly into territorial bounds. It was seen in its classic form in France. Bishops often fell within the feudal model but there was separate ecclesiastical jurisdiction over matters of divine law. Popes were also temporal rulers of the Papal States in central Italy, and there was a long-running political dispute over the scope of his and the church's authority as against kings and emperors (Chapter 4, Part 1).

The bounds of the Holy Roman Empire reached into northern Italy but its actual authority was weak. In many Italian cities including Florence, there were rebellions against those nobles who were supported by the northern emperors; while the Papal States intervened aggressively to augment the popes' temporal power. The major internal political divisions in late medieval Florence were between those loyal to emperors (Ghibellines) and those loyal to the papacy (Guelphs), and also between the old patrician families, a new breed of wealthy mercantile banking families (most notably the Medici) and 'the people'. Consequently, Florence threw off feudal and monarchical government, asserted itself as a self-governing walled city and conquered the surrounding countryside and the city of Pisa. But it had to fight hard for its liberty in an environment of constantly shifting alliances among its neighbours and to deal with factional in-fighting. By the fourteenth century, Florence settled on a constitution with an executive *Signoria* of eight members plus the *gonfaloniere della guistizia* (standard-bearer of justice) served by two colleges, one consisting of sixteen *gonfalonieri* from the city's quarters and an advisory college of ten. The *Signoria* and the two colleges elected two legislative councils (500 members in total) which approved bills sent to them by the *Signoria*. All positions were held for only a few months and were chosen by a complex system of lots (sortition). If necessary a citizens' assembly could be called to approve a course of action. And the state employed educated paid professionals to advise on and execute policies. The overall aims were to avoid tyranny and prevent domination by one faction. But narrow terms of eligibility for office meant that, out of a population of 50,000, 'not many more than about 750 of Florence's 3,000-odd citizens, at the best, were eligible for public office'.[10] The criteria and the determination of eligibility were in themselves highly political, the state became indebted to the new class of financiers, and the wealthiest family gained *de facto* control.

Renaissance humanists

The merits of republics versus monarchies were widely debated during the Renaissance. The basic problem for inherited monarchy lies in reproduction and education; no one wants to be stuck with a ruler who's barbaric, evil or insane. There was a preference for a healthy male heir, but 'the main hope of getting a good prince hangs on his proper education', according to Erasmus of Rotterdam (c. 1466–1536).[11] To avoid tyranny and disorder, much depended on the virtues of the monarch, and the best minds were needed to educate heirs and advise princes. Writing a book on virtuous rulership dedicated to a living prince might even be a bid for employment in his court. Erasmus's *The Education of a Christian Prince* (1516) was a classic mirror of princes intended for Charles of Ghent (later Charles V, Holy Roman Emperor) as instruction in the differences between evil tyranny and virtuous monarchy. The people and their property already belong to the prince, it argued, and hence any harm done to them is in effect harm to the prince himself. The people owe him taxes and obedience; he in return owes them benevolence and vigilance. 'There is a mutual interchange between the prince and the people.' States such as republics can exist without a monarch, but a monarch can't exist without a state. The reciprocal duties of the ruler and the ruled depend on the people's consent to be ruled. To maintain legitimacy, the prince, as 'the chief of the guardians of the laws', must be 'the least corruptible of men'.[12] Erasmus didn't get the job as Charles's tutor, however, and his book is largely forgotten today.

Only three years before Erasmus's *Education*, the Florentine government official Niccolò Machiavelli (1469–1527) wrote what would become an all-time bestseller, *The Prince*.[13] But it wasn't initially intended for publication. After the banishment of the ruling Medici family in 1494, Machiavelli was a busy diplomat and military commander for the Republic of Florence. In 1513 the Medici were reinstated and Machiavelli was imprisoned and tortured on suspicion of conspiring against them. After release he was jobless, so he retreated to his modest country estate and wrote books and plays. *The Prince*'s dedication addressed the new ruler Lorenzo de' Medici (1492–1519) with a plea for political rehabilitation. The book then helpfully described what had and hadn't worked for ambitious new princes (not unlike the Medici) who suddenly came into possession of a state. The prince's unrelenting aims must be the seizure and maintenance of power in order to ensure the security and augment the greatness of the state. In the real world, princes who rely on moral goodness for success will fail when fortune turns against them. If success calls for wicked or violent deeds, therefore, a prince needn't hesitate to abandon moral scruples. But he should act promptly and decisively. He must boldly and violently master fortune whenever necessary so his state can survive turbulent times and achieve greatness. He must impose punishments so that laws are obeyed. People are fickle and untrustworthy and, no matter how well a prince pays his followers, they'll become disloyal and disobedient when it suits them – unless he controls them with fear of punishment. *Il Principe* was written in Machiavelli's native Tuscan dialect, not Latin, suggesting that it was meant only for a small local audience. It was published posthumously in 1532 and soon translated and distributed throughout Europe.[14] It was read with interest as an early statement of 'reason of state': the right of rulers to act, when necessary, outside of law. Others heard in it the voice of the devil, and it was banned by the Church in 1559. Given the pain and humiliation that Machiavelli must have been feeling as he wrote, though, his book may contain a disguised critique of the Medici.[15] He adopted, and yet scandalously subverted, the mirror-of-princes genre – but did he intend his advice to be taken literally?

Machiavelli's full contribution to political thought isn't as 'Machiavellian' as *The Prince*. His *Discourses on Livy* (written in about 1517) is a study of stable republics, primarily ancient Rome. In this more coolly written text he advocated a mixed form of government rather than leaving it in the hands of either a prince or one of the two main social classes. 'For the principality easily becomes tyrannical; the aristocrats with ease become a state of the few; the popular is without difficulty converted into the licentious.'[16] These terms derive from Aristotle's *Politics*. Government that includes all three estates (monarch, aristocrats and commoners) is deemed more stable, as each class can watch over the actions of the others. This didn't imply harmony – indeed, the opposite, as dissent and conflict could be vented openly. The liberty of the state was Machiavelli's main concern. A republic that maintains a broader civic consensus and collective responsibility would be less vulnerable to external forces, as the wider population would be more willing to defend it. Only a small minority 'desires to be free so as to command', whereas the vast majority 'desire freedom so as to live secure'.[17] The inherent antagonism between rulers and ruled will persist, but, for successful government, it's better to include the majority of the common people. 'A people is more prudent, more stable, and of better judgment than a prince. Not without cause may the voice of a people be likened to that of God.'[18] This sounds quite different from *The Prince*, but there's a consistent theme of doing what's best for the state. For Machiavelli, the guiding principle of rulership was *virtù* – although this shouldn't be translated as 'virtue' in the moralistic sense. *Virtù* meant the ability and willingness to act boldly in the interests of civic liberty and the greatness of the state, according to necessity rather than godliness.

Unlike Socrates, Machiavelli didn't aim for a harmonious and unchanging ideal state. Instead, a strong republic was built by managing internal discord and changing with the times. The reason for Rome's greatness, he argued, was the constitutional containment of class conflict achieved by balancing the council of the plebs and the tribunes with powers of veto as against the elite senate (Chapter 3, Part 1). Along with other Florentine thinkers,[19] Machiavelli was more than just a scholar; he was a prominent official in the government. (And he did eventually get his job back.) His primary focus was the human. The state was no longer considered an expression of the will of God – nor the will of an earthly despot. Religious institutions and practices could be useful for social cohesion but were only one part of the social fabric that Machiavelli considered. Indeed, he openly blamed the Church for keeping Italy divided and hence weaker than its neighbours.

Venice

Machiavelli was concerned for the security and liberty of his native state Florence, which was constantly troubled by its neighbours. The Roman republic had lasted for roughly four centuries; it set a historical example of a state that had achieved greatness. He also looked at Venice, *la Serenissima* (the most serene republic), founded more than a millennium before his time. The first Venetians were refugees who occupied islands in a large lagoon to flee from invading tribes in the fifth century CE. They built on sandy islands and elected a Doge (duke) from 697. They were originally subject to the emperor in Constantinople but eventually achieved independence as a maritime trading republic. Venice took a leading role in the fourth crusade and the sack of Constantinople in 1204. By the fourteenth century, Venice had a mature and stable constitution. The extent of her eastern Mediterranean empire waxed and waned, but her system of government proved remarkably durable.

Before the bubonic plague of 1348, the population of the city-state of Venice is estimated to have been about 100,000. The male-only Great Council elected and authorised higher legislative and executive officers, and numbered around 1,200–1,500. In 1297, eligibility to sit in the Great Council was barred to new entrants, with rare exceptions, and so its life members were a wealthy male elite, entitled by inheritance. Their numbers grew to over 2000. This was too large a body to govern effectively. It assembled weekly, with a quorum of 600, for rounds of elections by ballots and/or by lots.[20] Authority was thus delegated upwards to a Senate (*Consiglio dei Pregadi*, council of the invited). The Great Council elected 120 of its members to the Senate for 12-month terms, although re-elections were normal. The Senate eventually grew to 300 in total. *Ex officio* senators included the Doge (who presided), his six councillors, and judges, prosecutors and administrators. The Senate had deliberative and legislative functions and met in secret. It also acquired significant executive functions, including diplomatic, military and monetary policies. As it was 'omni-competent' it created administrative committees to manage its affairs. To one side of the Senate was the shadowy Council of Ten – senators specially elected by the Great Council for one-year terms. The Ten chose their own presidency of three members. It also operated in secret, with powers of investigation, prosecution and execution, as well as censorship and supervision of public morality. It aimed to prevent and punish sedition and corruption and wasn't above displaying corpses to send the people a message. Venice relied heavily on networks of informants and spies; it was the most advanced state in the field of codebreaking.[21]

The Senate assembled two or three times a week; its decision-making was by majority vote after free debates. Its agenda and processes required oversight and regulation from the *Collegio*. The *Collegio* included those senators who held the highest executive (ministerial) and judicial offices, plus the *Signoria*, which consisted of the Doge, who presided, and his six councillors (*il Minor Consiglio*). While the Doge was elected for life, the members of the *Collegio* had short terms, but a small group tended to rotate around these offices, thus preserving institutional knowledge. The *Collegio* could initiate legislation, act administratively and declare emergency powers. It was the engine-room of government.[22]

The Doge was head of state. After the death of a Doge, his six close councillors (*il Minor Consiglio*) remained in office, and the Great Council, through nine rounds of election and sortition, set about choosing an electoral college of 41. This group was secluded under guard until it reached a decision. A majority of 25 in the electoral college was required for the decisive ballot.[23] This complicated process prevented capture by a faction or dynasty. The Doge was more than a ceremonial figure, as he presided over all of the main councils, and, from that height, wielded great influence. On the other hand, he was constantly supervised by his six councillors, whom he didn't hand-pick and who served eight-month terms. And the Doge's proposals had to pass through the *Collegio*. Dictatorial power was impossible; nonetheless, swift and effective action could be taken through emergency powers in the *Collegio* or by the police powers of the Ten. No wrongdoing could escape accountability. As Machiavelli put it, in Venice, 'if an accuser is not lacking, a judge is not lacking to hold powerful men in check.'[24] There were effective 'checks and balances' even though executive, legislative and judicial powers weren't institutionally separated (see next section). The Venetian constitution was the product of a healthy political *dis*trust: no one was trusted with unlimited or unaccountable powers; no one would get away with abusing the limited powers that were entrusted only conditionally and temporarily. From 1297, when *la Serenissima* blocked new entrants to the Great Council, government was reserved for the rich and established families. Machiavelli saw that this caused no 'tumult', as the common people were governed well. But they had no part in governing, unlike republican Rome, and he believed this had cost Venice her potential for expansion and true greatness.[25]

Venice was an exceptionally wealthy city, open to trade with the Levant and continental Europe; hence it was tolerant of the different religions observed by merchants and immigrants. The Catholic priesthood was controlled by the state and Venice sometimes opposed the papacy politically and militarily. In return, several popes formally censured Venice. Interventionist trade, shipping and labour laws protected Venetian interests; industrial policies were advanced through trade guilds; charitable institutions were created by public policy and private philanthropy. Venice was famous for its public health system (probably the world's first), which attracted medical expertise from abroad. Its government was by the rich but not just for the rich. It was the closest (in those times) to a conservative corporatist welfare state. Commoners were protected by due process as equals before the law; the indigent were given care. Although people may have found some regulations annoying, 'if this was the price of living in the richest, safest, best ordered and most beautiful city in the civilized world they were prepared to pay.'[26] In all of Venice's history, there was no major popular uprising; when Napoleon ended the Republic in 1797, the invaders found only 27 people in the city's prisons.[27]

Personal political ambitions in Venice had to be subordinated to constitutional processes and political compromises if they were to succeed. But compromises were also negotiable outside the formal system through informal deals, marriage-alliances between the great families and quiet manipulation of elections. Venice was plutocratic and gerontocratic (ruled by the rich and elderly); the senior magistracies were dominated by elders of a relatively small number of wealthy clans. These qualities seem undesirable today, but the principle that made it work relatively well for all classes was not simply *noblesse oblige*: it was a shared respect for the republic and its laws, a high level of civic participation, and freedom to air differing opinions. The common good and the law stood above individual and dynastic ambitions. Until its decline in the eighteenth century, Venice was, according to Finer, the best-governed place in the world.[28]

Part 2: Representatives

Regardless of how well they governed, the Venetian senate wasn't representative by our standards. The male members of wealthy established families met as a 'closed shop' to elect one another to senatorial and other higher posts. When it came to the election of the Doge, the Great Council excluded members under 30.[29] The highest posts tended to be filled by men in their 70s.[30] Women of even the highest-ranking families were confined to roles in the family – unless, for want of a dowry or 'unfitness' for marriage, they were confined to a nunnery.[31] One Venetian author who suffered such enclosure was Arcangela Tarabotti (1604–52). From the 'repulsive prison' of the nunnery,[32] she wrote polemical texts and corresponded with numerous European intellectuals, attacking involuntary seclusion and the misogyny of male authors. Institutionalised oppression of women reinforced patriarchal government.

For men who were ineligible for the Great Council, there was corporate representation through the *scuole* – the hundreds of brotherhoods or guilds. Each *scuola* was dedicated to a patron saint and served a devotional purpose; its revenues derived from membership fees and donations. Although under the watchful eye of the Council of Ten, it was self-governing and independent from nobility and clergy. Most *scuole* performed the practical purposes of overseeing a craft or accommodating merchants of a particular nationality. They also performed important charitable work. The *scuole* gave wealthy non-noble citizens opportunities to show their civic generosity and social status and gave poorer citizens social belonging and economic security, all within their recognised occupational or migrant groups. They played a prominent role in public ceremonies and vied with one another to patronise the arts.[33] This institutionalised recognition of commoners and protection of poor labourers meant a corporate representation that contributed to the high level of unity in Venice.[34] Similarly, many of us today belong to professional, occupational, sports or business associations that set rules, monitor standards, provide services and represent us or speak on our behalf to policymakers or the media, and hence incorporate us into wider ethical social worlds.

What is representation?

To understand representation we shouldn't limit our attention to elections and legislatures. Representative parliaments, however, evolved out of medieval Europe's feudal arrangements (as described above). In the thirteenth and fourteenth centuries, royal councils supported the monarch with practical aid and advice, but membership widened from a circle of bishops, warlords and barons to include other prominent civic and provincial figures summoned from around the realm. Traditional feudal fees and military services owed by barons and knights became insufficient for larger and more expensive campaigns. More people had to be induced to contribute – ideally by consent. So assemblies were called to raise revenues for waging wars. Those who could speak and give consent on behalf of their communities were summoned, and hence regular parliaments arose, based often on three 'estates': clergy, nobility and property-owning commoners. The royal court then had to deal with assemblies that *represented* or stood for the communities that the sovereign needed to tax.

European parliaments differed greatly in how such representation was practised. The geographical division of the represented communities often reflected particular local circumstances or customs. England's first representative assembly, the Model Parliament of 1295, was summoned by Edward I. Elected representatives included two knights from each county, two burgesses from each borough and two citizens from each city. But by the eighteenth century, many representatives were elected in 'rotten boroughs' that had become depopulated, while large new urban areas, if not yet incorporated as boroughs, had no representatives. The powers of the three estates in relation to one another, and over taxation, law-making and judicial decision-making, also varied between countries.[35] In Poland, the assembly of the nobility (the *Sejm*) by the late sixteenth century dominated the monarch, whom they elected, producing a parliamentary aristocracy or 'a nobiliary republic with a royal figurehead'.[36] At the other extreme, France's Estates-General was easily ignored by monarchs, didn't assemble regularly and indeed ceased to do so from 1615 until the crisis of 1789. In between these extremes stood what was to become the most influential exemplar: after the seventeenth century's civil war, restoration and Glorious Revolution (1688), the English reached a compromise by which the executive (the crown) would respect parliament, putting an end to absolute monarchy and constraining monarchs from dictating or suspending law.

In some parliaments, members held wide mandates to speak for and to bind their constituencies, while in others the mandate was more restricted. Underlying this were differing ideas about representation. In seventeenth-century English, the verb *represent* could mean 'to act or speak authoritatively for others in their absence'. Political philosopher Thomas Hobbes (1588–1679) wrote that a person may '*represent* himself, or another; and he that acteth another, is said to bear his person, or act in his name as a *representative*.'[37] An attorney may represent a plaintiff; a sovereign king or assembly may represent a nation. They needn't have been elected; it was enough that they were given authority by those who had the liberty to do so.[38] There are then no strict limits on the sovereign's authority, provided they can protect and defend the people; neither is the sovereign strictly accountable to the represented for actions taken in their name. Hobbes held a strong view of representation-as-authorisation.

When a representative was authorised (by birth, wealth or election) to attend a parliament, in some cases it may only have been to voice the pleas and petitions of their community, as a 'delegate', with little authority to act independently. And yet the monarch, as the executive, may have wanted binding and urgent commitments to raise taxes. As parliamentary business became more complex and fast-moving, an effective representative would need to judge and act independently – albeit with accountability to constituents at the next nomination or election. Measures to make representatives' actions closely align with constituents' wishes were often demanded. One method was an enforceable requirement for the representative to follow instructions, or 'imperative mandates'; another was a right of recall, or 'permanent revocability', of representatives by their constituents. Such electoral provisions haven't commonly prevailed at national or federal levels of government.[39] Given the pace and complexity of parliamentary business, modern representatives mainly act independently 'on trust' as lawmakers, unable to consult constituents directly on many issues other than the most high-profile – and yet they must pay attention to public opinion, with a view to being returned at the next election. If a representative acts independently, moreover, is their best judgement to be employed in the interests of the particular community that he or she formally 'stands for', or in the interests of the government of the nation as a whole? Edmund Burke (1729–97) spoke in favour of the latter view: 'Parliament is a *deliberative* Assembly of *one* Nation, with *one* Interest, that of the whole.'[40] Since his day, however, the locus or responsibility has shifted from the individual representative to the political party. As autonomous organisations, political parties select and put forward candidates for election; if voting for a party, voters place their trust in a group of representatives who act in concert. Members normally fall into line with their party, sometimes not even understanding what they've voted for. As representatives' personal judgement is subordinated to and not free to differ from the policies of their party, so the party incorporates representation.[41]

There was moreover the problem of 'actual' versus 'virtual' representation (already briefly discussed in Chapter 6, Part 5, 'Independence'). Communities or sectors of communities who couldn't vote were supposedly represented anyway, albeit *virtually*. They were bound by 'majority' decisions and yet excluded from the decision as to who will represent the community in making the decisions. Up until the nineteenth century or beyond, the franchise was restricted to property-owning males, being the people liable for tax. But there was also the idea of 'descriptive representation': just as a portrait-in-miniature should accurately represent the facial features of its subject, so the representatives should resemble the represented in terms of their political sentiments, values and ideologies.[42]

The historical trend has been towards universal adult rights to vote and to stand for election, such that (ideally) all are represented and any citizen could aspire to become a representative.[43] This has decreased the extent of virtual representation (especially regarding women) and advanced the cause of descriptive representation. Increasingly, the composition of the legislature should resemble, culturally and demographically, the adult population that's represented, particularly in terms of gender, race and ethno-religious heritage. As we shall see below, however, some past theorists argued that representative legislatures should consist of members of a social minority that's superior to, and hence does *not* resemble, the majority. Rousseau even argued that representation is bad for us.

What's wrong with representation?

Jean-Jacques Rousseau (1712–78) rejected representation altogether. The only assembly that could produce valid laws, he said, was an assembly of the whole (male) public. Only thus could the 'wills' of private individuals, publicly voiced, coalesce around the common good and express 'the general will', so that whatever law I will for others I also will for myself, and vice versa. From such an assembly the execution of law can be delegated to an administrative government. But the citizen has a public duty to participate in the passage of law itself. The will, Rousseau argued, can't be represented. Hence deputising our responsibilities of lawmaking to a small minority produces invalid law. He was scathing of the English nation 'that thinks that it is free, but is greatly mistaken, for it is so only during the election of members of Parliament; as soon as they are elected, it is enslaved and counts for nothing.'[44] From this viewpoint, the term 'representative democracy' is an oxymoron as it means that the general will is overthrown by a tiny minority.

On the other hand, representation in England was advanced by Edmund Burke and John Stuart Mill (1806–73), both of whom favoured a model in which the elected representative acts independently 'on trust' for the people, and not at their behest. For Burke, all political power was a 'trust', regardless of whether the office was inherited, appointed or elected. Those with 'no connexion with the interest, sentiments and opinions of the people [should not be] put forward into the great trusts of the State.'[45] Representation was a responsibility for the good government of the nation as a whole, however, and not for particular communities or electors; legitimate government acted for the people, but not for factions or local constituencies. Burke's model meant 'an elite caring for others'.[46] The type of government he defended wasn't 'by the people, but government for the people by the qualified few'.[47]

Mill also saw representation as a form of trust in an elitist sense, but with some accountability to voters. That is, the voters should elect cultivated and educated people whom they can trust 'to carry on public affairs according to their unfettered judgment; [people] to whom it would be an affront to require that they should give up that judgment at the behest of their inferiors in knowledge.'[48]

The elected representatives should be 'entrusted with full power of obeying the dictates of [their] own judgment.'[49] In turn, the electors 'are the judges of the manner in which [a representative] fulfils his trust.'[50] The catch is that, as a trust, the franchise must therefore be a civic duty and not an individual right, and so Mill argues that ballots should be made public and transparent. He was afraid that the choices of 'the majority' would mean that ignorance and class-based self-interest would drive the government. He preferred that the majority should elect their 'betters' from among the educated minority, or that the common voter should elect an informed representative to an electoral college which in turn would elect the governors or legislators.

So there was a non-egalitarian strain in representation. Indeed, systems of political representation that emerged following revolutions in England, France and America were originally designed in part to *avoid* democracy, in the sense of 'majority rule by the people'. Election of representatives was preferred over sortition (drawing lots) because the former favoured a 'natural aristocracy' while the latter favoured democracy or 'ordinary' people getting an equal chance to hold office. Instead of democracy, electoral franchises were restricted to property-owning males who would recognise and vote for the 'best' citizens, not just for ordinary ones.

In Europe and America – and subsequently much of the rest of the world – representation came to dominate, with election (not sortition) as the preferred method for choosing and authorising representatives. While election may once have been associated more with aristocracies than democracies, it triumphed over sortition partly because it supported the natural law principle that power should derive from the consent of the governed.[51] Drawing lots randomly selects any qualified citizen as a representative or magistrate and evens out the chances; voting requires the governed actively to choose candidates whom they believe to be the best qualified. Voting thus signifies a rational consent of the governed to the process and hence the results of elections. Those who are disappointed by the results are said to have consented to be bound by the decisions of the majority.[52] In ancient Athens, sortition gave every active citizen who wanted office an equal chance. Modern elections, on the other hand, create a wide division of political labour between a minority put forward by parties for elections and the mass of citizens who remain mostly passive observers.

The right to vote was often restricted to men who met property or tax quali-fications. But tighter restrictions on the right to stand for election also limited the pool of candidates and further entrenched the social distinctions between electors and elected. The framers of the US Constitution intended their electoral system to ensure that representatives, due to superior talent, virtue and wealth, would differ from (and not *too* closely resemble) the represented. In a republic (neither an aristocracy nor a democracy) the people would look for outstanding candi-dates who would remain accountable through regular elections.[53] According to James Madison (1751–1836), the republic would be better than a democracy. Democratic government could only work in a small community, he argued, and it is prone to factionalism. A large republic with 'delegation of the government to a small number of citizens elected by the rest' can contain the rivalries. 'The chosen' would be so for their wisdom, patriotism and love of justice. A multi-level system of elections would winnow out the coarsest factions without restricting day-to-day liberties.[54] The people at large can sometimes be misinformed and misguided, it was thought; so cooler rational deliberation in a legislature was needed. Elections would ensure that lawmakers maintain awareness of and sympathy for the interests of the people, but the republic's 'elite' would be 'elected' (the two words share the same Latin root) and entrusted to decide on behalf of the people. Even today elections put power in the hands of the people only momentarily; while their choices get structured in advance by political parties' candidate selection processes, campaign messages and policy manifestos. Once the people have voted, they've entrusted the powers to make law and govern to a small minority – who are then accountable to opposing parties and a free press and, at the next election, to voters.

Separation of powers

We can't leave the history of representation without considering separation of powers, the great proponent of which was the French judge and author Charles-Louis de Secondat, Baron de Montesquieu (1689–1755). Montesquieu was more sceptical than Machiavelli about the Venetian constitution.[55] He described the Council of Ten's police powers, for example, as 'despotic'. Venice's legislative, executive and judicial powers were all combined in its senate, which he called a 'mischief'.[56] People invested with powers will often take them as far as they can, and hence abuse them and bring an end to liberty – unless constitutions ensure that 'power should be a check on power'.[57] No person or body of persons should exercise more than one of the three institutional forms of governmental powers: 'that of enacting laws, that of executing the public resolutions, and of trying the causes of individuals.'[58] To limit political power, it must therefore be divided. This means separating three vertical branches of government: legislative, executive and judicial. The legislative assembly should be representative and divided into two chambers that deliberate separately: a higher one for the hereditary nobility and a lower for 'the people'. The two classes can then act according to their distinct interests, but with a check on one another, so neither can pass laws that harm the other's interests. The executive, acting within the law, should come under the monarch for quicker decision-making. The monarch may have a veto over laws passed by the assemblies, in case they encroach on royal prerogatives; the assemblies, in turn, should approve taxation and public spending to keep a check on the executive. Furthermore, if judges who apply the law were also lawmakers, then 'the subject would be exposed to arbitrary control'; if judges also belonged to the executive branch, then 'the judge might behave with violence and oppression.'[59] Hence the judiciary must be independent of both other branches of government.

Montesquieu's principle of separation of powers had a big influence on the framers of the US Constitution – save that the Americans chose to have neither a monarch nor a nobility, but an elected president and senate instead. The British and other Westminster-style governments have developed conventions that do respect the separation of powers – but not as strictly or clearly as America. In Westminster governments the crown acts on the advice of ministers who are drawn from the legislature; so there's a large overlap between executive and legislative powers.[60] Ministers can introduce bills to parliament that give themselves lawful executive powers and finance – a huge conflict of interests that Montesquieu feared would bring an end to liberty!

Democratising representation

Originally the election of representatives was intended for government by an elite minority of the people. Such a government acts *for* the people but isn't conducted *by* the people. Nonetheless, the historical universalisation of the franchise, the widespread use of proportional representation (although not in the United States and the United Kingdom), and the contemporary push for a greater diversity of candidates make representation less undemocratic – or if you will, more democratic. Today the gold standard of what we call 'democracy' applies a universal adult franchise to regular competitive election of representatives. Hence those who vote determine which of the candidates or parties on offer will represent 'the people' as lawmakers and governors. The tendency today is still to elect representatives who are older, wealthier and more highly educated than the average citizen. The internal processes of political parties select most candidates presented for election. The high costs of election campaigns make the barriers to election insurmountable for citizens of lower or middle socio-economic status, unless they join a party and distinguish themselves as activists first. Other characteristics of democracies include respect for human rights, civilian control of armed forces, freedom of political opinion, public consultation, and so on. A more thorough-going democratic ideal holds that 'all affected by collective decisions should have an opportunity to influence the outcome.'[61] Elections alone don't meet that ideal, however, as legislators act largely 'on trust', often without the awareness, let alone influence, of 'all affected'. More diverse and inclusive forms of representation are desirable; but to develop genuinely democratic practices, alternatives to representation are often called for, such as deliberative citizens' assemblies.

Part 3: Revolutions

So far this chapter has looked at practices that permitted and yet moderated dissent, disobedience and resistance within a community. Mixed government and republics gradually gained favour over monarchies, allowing for a wider range of participation and hence broader popular acceptance. Dissent could be aired, class compromises achieved and the diverse needs of the people met. Representative parliaments signified popular consent; the separation of powers clarified and limited 'who can lawfully do what to whom'. But compromise and obedience may break down. History is punctuated with moments when resistance and disobedience grew into open rebellion, as enough people overcame their fear of the forces of the state and combined against incompetent, oppressive or exploitative rulers. This sometimes included action by anarchists who rejected any imposition of law and government in favour of self-responsible action and fluid association. But anarchism hasn't ever been realised. If a revolutionary movement prevailed, it overthrew one political order and replaced it with another. Amid such disruptive events, then, how does one redesign government?

The modern idea of revolutions as transformative historical events that overturn unjust government, and that give or restore some political power to previously excluded groups, derives from the examples of England's decisive shift to constitutional monarchy (1688), the American war of independence (1775–83) and the French revolution (1789–92). These revolutions had repercussions, however. The Chartist movement in Britain demanded (among other reforms) universal male suffrage, and caused uprisings in the 1830s and 1840s;[62] the Americans fought a civil war over slavery and states' rights (1861–5);[63] the French restored monarchy and wrote twelve different constitutions between 1791 and 1870.[64] So revolutions may not resolve underlying social and political problems. The Russian revolutions (1905, 1917) overturned Tsarist absolutism but led to Stalinist totalitarianism, so one oppressive type of government followed another (Chapter 9, Part 1). Revolutions produce (or simply *are*) radical change, but not necessarily change for the better. They tend to be bloody and violent, but there are exceptions. The communist regimes in eastern Europe fell relatively peacefully after the Berlin Wall was destroyed and control from Moscow ceased in 1989. But rebuilding may be harder than destroying. The following examples recount overthrow, but also renewal of government, thus restoring predictability and regularity amid uncertainty – or the bureaucratisation of revolutionary charisma. We thus consider two post-World War II revolutions: China (1949) and Iran (1979).

China

The events leading up to China's communist revolution in 1949 were complex, violent and chaotic. The last emperor of the Qing dynasty was deposed in 1912 amid plunder and occupations by various imperial powers including Japan. From then until 1949 China was a conflict zone only partially governed by a series of republican leaders and by local warlords. Two major internal forces emerged. One was the nationalist Guomindang, which governed, to the extent that it could, from 1928 to 1946, led by Sun Yat-sen (1866–1925) and then Chiang Kai-shek (1887–1975). Their main rival was the Communist Party of China (CPC) founded in 1921 and led by Zhou Enlai (1898–1976) and Mao

Zedong (1893–1976). In 1937, based initially in the north-east of China, the Japanese launched merciless assaults on Shanghai and Nanjing, commencing a war that continued until Japan's surrender to the Americans in 1945. The CPC restructured its forces as the People's Liberation Army in 1946 and pushed the nationalists south, forcing Chiang Kai-shek's army to retreat to the island of Taiwan. From there Chiang Kai-shek ruled the Republic of China as president until he died in 1975. As the leader of the victorious communists, Mao Zedong proclaimed the mainland People's Republic of China (PRC) from Beijing in October 1949. He remained in office as chairman of the central committee, or executive president, until his death in 1976.[65]

In September 1949 the CPC convened a Chinese People's Political Consultative Conference to prepare for the establishment of a 'new democracy' and to approve an interim constitution. They aimed to eject imperialists and end the 'feudalism' of landlords and the 'bureaucratic capitalism' of the former nationalist regime. The common programme guided the subsequent period of consolidation and transformation. A new constitution was adopted at the first meeting of the National People's Congress (the supreme legislature) in September 1954.

The goal was to re-establish stable and orderly government and national unity following decades of invasions, conflict and disorder. This was an enormous task given the size and diversity of China and the remaining pockets of armed resistance.[66] The CPC's 'norms of collective leadership and democratic discussion' along with Mao's 'unchallenged authority' made for stability and unity at the top.[67] This new government saw itself as a dictatorship of the revolutionary classes (agricultural and industrial workers) and as a 'new democracy' that would adopt a universal franchise to elect local people's congresses which would in turn elect a national congress. It would introduce incremental reforms based on the Soviet model (Chapter 9, Part 1) with adaptations to Chinese conditions, reaching deeply into everyday community practices. This meant dictatorship by the CPC as the vanguard of the revolutionary working class and centrally planned economic policy. Ownership structures had to change, meaning confiscation of land from landlords for redistribution and local peasant collectives with productivity targets.[68] Rapid industrialisation was coupled with state ownership of enterprises.[69]

A bureaucratised governmental apparatus, distinct from the party, had to be developed to manage these enormous efforts. Beginning as a peasant-based movement, however, the rapid expansion of the CPC's rule meant a shortage of skilled urban personnel. Existing officials were largely retained, but the communists had to project an agenda of national reconstruction, not revolution, to gain support in the cities. By 1949, the CPC had experience in controlling some urban areas and running industry, but it had to restructure many large enterprises and deal with existing managers and owners. Some private enterprises and local services were left to run as before, for the time being, with tolerance for deviations from central policy. But economic productivity was restored, unemployment reduced and inflation brought under control. The CPC's legitimacy depended upon its ability to restore order and national unity and to eject foreign imperialists.

The transition from a revolutionary and militarised party to a stable civil government was consolidated and codified in the 1954 constitution. Local people's congresses would 'elect' deputies to the National People's Congress (NPC), the supreme legislature that met annually. The NPC would 'elect' the chairman of the PRC (that is, Mao) and the president of a theoretically independent supreme court. The chairman would preside over the NPC's standing committee, which convened the congress itself and appointed the members of a state council directed by a premier. The standing committee effectively ruled on a day-to-day basis and exercised civilian control over the military. A state council included the heads of ministries and commissions: it administered the state apparatus and coordinated the efforts of local governments. The NPC's standing committee, however, could rule by decree, veto decisions of lower bodies, appoint or remove officials and judges, and conduct international relations including declarations of war. On paper, any citizen of 35 or older was eligible for election as chairman of the PRC for a term of four years. In practice, it was Chairman Mao until his death. Moreover, the constitution concentrated the powers of the NPC's standing committee into the hands of the chairman, giving him supreme administrative and military powers and appointing him as the republic's representative in foreign affairs.

The 1954 constitution proclaimed a set of fundamental human rights, including the equality of women in all spheres, freedoms of speech and assembly, freedom from arbitrary arrest and the right to work. But in this one-party state, the 'shadow' power of the CPC undermined such rights. The CPC was mentioned in the constitution's preamble but not in its formal articles. Nonetheless, the party became 'the ultimate locus of authority', from the top level of its politburo and secretariat down to local levels.[70] The constitution's description of the PRC as 'a people's democratic dictatorship' captures the paradox. The democratic classes and popular organisations were 'led by the Communist Party' in a 'common struggle' to build a socialist society and defeat enemies of the state.[71] The party would continue to rule, however, as a highly centralised and ideologically disciplined 'state' within, if not above, the state.

Although it lacks formalised constitutional recognition, the CPC remains 'the center of power, while the function of government is to implement the party's political guidelines and policies.'[72] The state, the people's congresses, the military and the local authorities are all subject to the leadership and policies of the Communist Party. It was this system that restored (with important exceptions[73]) national unity to China after 'the century of humiliation' that began with the opium wars of the 1840s. Under Mao's authoritarian rule, China closed itself to the capitalist world; after Mao, it re-emerged as the world's economic powerhouse. China is now showing that success in the capitalist world can be achieved without a multi-party representative government. Its aim of national unification is still not complete, however, and conflict over Taiwan persists.

Iran

From 1925 until the revolution in 1979, Iran was ruled by the Pahlavi shahs, who were modernisers but authoritarian and anti-communist. Mohammad-Reza Shah (r. 1941–79) made himself unpopular with the educated middle-class and with communists by abuses of human rights, and also unpopular with conservative clerics who resented modernisation and non-Islamic influences. Iran's post-war relationship with Britain was problematic too, as the agreement with the Anglo-Iranian Oil Company[74] meant that the British government was earning more than Iran in royalties. The nationalisation of Iran's oil industry turned into the major post-war political issue, pushed for by the highly popular but controversial reformer Mohammad Mossadeq (1882–1967) and by a loose coalition of deputies of the Majles (national assembly) called the National Front.[75] In 1953, however, a CIA-directed[76] *coup d'état* restored and strengthened the monarchy. Mossadeq was tried for treason and put under house arrest until his death, and the National Front was banned. The result was an autocratic monarch and a 'reign of terror',[77] but also a more equitable revenue-sharing arrangement with a consortium of British Petroleum (BP) and American oil companies. Iran became dependent on the US for military aid and equipment and was influenced by American culture. The shah was perceived by many Iranians as an American puppet who encouraged westernised affluence but within a police-state.[78]

The strongest resistance to the shah came from neither the supporters of representative government nor the communists, however. It came instead in the form of political Islam – the use of Islam for concrete political aims. The ayatollah Ruhollah Khomeini (1902–89) arose as an influential *marja* (a top-ranked Shia cleric highly learned in Islamic jurisprudence), speaking out against the oppression and corruption of the shah's government and against American influence. He was exiled to Iraq in 1964 and went to France in 1978, but his writings and speeches made him increasingly influential.[79] He developed a theory of Islamic government based on the Shia belief in the 'hidden' twelfth imam. In the absence of the imam, Khomeini argued, the clerics were legitimately delegated the tasks of interpreting and applying *sharia* through the control of governmental institutions. This implied the constitutional principle of *velayat-e-faqih* (guardianship of the jurist): the head of state would be a senior and revered cleric, chosen from among his peers, who substitutes for the hidden imam while the faithful await his re-emergence from occultation as the redeemer who will establish justice. The distinction between revelation and real-world politics was thus eradicated by Khomeini[80] – although the concept of *velayat-e-faqih* remained unpopular with many high-ranking Shiite clerics who opposed this conflation of politics and religion.[81]

In early 1978, a rolling sequence of demonstrations against the shah's rule began. Repressive state violence peaked on 8 September, known as Black Friday. The shah was ill with cancer and gave an unconvincing appeal for conciliation, but it was too late and the protests continued. On 16 January 1979, the shah fled the country; two weeks later Khomeini flew into Tehran from Paris to be greeted by ecstatic crowds. The incumbent prime minister resigned; Khomeini appointed a provisional government and headed a revolutionary council. Committees were set up around the country to organise supporters and to round up those connected with the Pahlavi regime – and then the executions began. Secular liberals and moderate Islamic jurists were intimidated into silence as the constitution was rearranged.

In March 1979, a referendum approved the establishment of an Islamic republic.[82] Initial drafts of a new constitution were much like the 1906 constitution, with limited roles for clerics. Khomeini did not initially push for a guardianship of the jurist, and there was much public debate about alternative models, some more secular, others more Islamic. An elected assembly of experts with 73 members was established to consolidate the new constitution. Thanks to gerrymandering, secularist boycott, low turnout and voter intimidation, the newly-formed Islamic Republican Party, loyal to Khomeini, won 50 of its seats. The assembly then set about significantly redrafting the constitution in line with Khomeini's model of Islamic government.[83]

More dramatic events then intervened. The exiled shah was admitted into the US for medical treatment in October 1979. Protests against this led to the storming of the US embassy in Tehran, the occupants of which were taken hostage. Khomeini supported the hostage-takers, forcing the resignation of the provisional government, which had been negotiating with the Americans. While that was going on, the assembly of experts approved an absolutist version of *velayat-e-faqih*. A heightened sense of threat from American imperialism dominated public awareness; debate and dissent over the new version of the constitution were silenced for fear of appearing pro-American. Many leading critics were either in exile or eliminated anyway. The moderate ayatollah Mohammad Kazem Shariatmadari (1906–86) supported the revolution but was against clerical involvement in government, and he called for a boycott of the constitutional referendum.[84] But on an even lower turnout than the previous referendum, 99.5 percent voted in favour of this new version of the constitution. 'The people' had legitimated the supreme leadership of the jurist, Khomeini.

The elected *majles* would remain as the legislature; public administration would continue on a secular basis. Monarchy was ended, however, in favour of an elected president, sharing power with a prime minister, guided by the legislature. To that extent, it resembled the French Fifth Republic.[85] Above the elected representatives, however, there was now a council of guardians consisting of six jurists elected by the parliament and five (later six) senior clerics appointed by Khomeini as supreme leader. The council of guardians would pre-approve candidates for election. In the first election for president of the republic, any candidates who had stood against the new constitution or boycotted the referendum were disqualified. Abolhassan Banisadr (b. 1933), who had worked closely with Khomeini in Paris, won overwhelmingly.[86] The supreme leader would appoint the head of the Revolutionary Guard (an armed national-security force), the heads of other armed forces and the head of the judiciary.

So in this constitution, the assembly of experts consists of pre-approved and qualified Shia jurists, elected by the people on an eight-year term. Women and non-Shi'ite Muslims need not apply.[87] The assembly's main purpose is to elect and advise the supreme leader. At the time of writing it has only ever elected one successor, Ali Khamenei (b. 1939), following Khomeini's death in 1989. The succession caused a crisis, necessitating a revision of the constitution itself, as Khamenei hadn't attained the highest rank among Islamic scholars and was reluctant to accept the office. A referendum approved constitutional changes that would legitimise Khamenei as supreme leader and also abolish the post of prime minister in favour of an enlarged presidency.[88]

The supreme leader has ultimate religious and political authority. He appoints half of the council of guardians. This council pre-approves (or rejects) candidates for election and has used this power aggressively to ensure that conservatives win. It can, like an upper house, veto laws passed in the *majles* on grounds of being unconstitutional or un-Islamic. The supreme leader also appoints, for a five-year term, the head of the judiciary – a senior cleric who, in turn, appoints and dismisses judges including the head of the supreme court and the attorney-general.[89]

Although Iran has retained the elected legislature (*majles*) formed in 1906, the revolution produced a canopy of unelected, or indirectly elected, Shia clerics who ensure that law and administration conform with their interpretation of *sharia*, often regardless of public opinion. These bodies are theocratic and patriarchal, excluding women from the highest offices and passing laws that systematically subordinate Iranian women in social and family life.[90] A 'limited democratic promise' expressed in the election of presidents and representatives is combined with the religious authority of the supreme leader, the power of the council of guardians to control eligibility of electoral candidates, and the unconcealed use of the Revolutionary Guard and Basij forces to influence voters.[91] Nonetheless popular uprisings, especially following the 2009 election, and the fear of another revolution, do cause moderation among the ruling clerics. This means a 'pendulum swing' between conservatives and reformers, evident in the elections of the reformist Mohammad Khatami (in office 1997–2005), the conservative Mahmoud Ahmadinejad (in office 2005–13 thanks to vote-rigging), followed by the incumbent at the time of writing, Hassan Rouhani, who sought conciliation with western powers. Post-revolutionary Iran combines a French republican model which accepts the people's choices and an Islamic theocracy which may ignore them. It is a thing of the people and yet also an instrument of God's will.

Conclusion

Revolutionaries may overthrow a system of government, but they must perforce rebuild government. The reader may have expected greater attention to the two seminal revolutions of the modern era, the American and French. With admittedly much less than universal or immediate effect, these revolutions instantiated enlightenment ideals of the 'natural' liberty and moral autonomy of the individual;

they overturned unjust privileges or oppressive rulers in favour of rational law and government; they aimed for government by consent. They gave the nation and its government back to the people from whom they were made. Those entrusted with changing the law, as citizens, would now abide by that law. Indeed, those revolutions instituted an understanding of citizenship itself as a fundamental right to enjoy the full range of rights codified in law. The aim of government would be 'the general happiness', as Thomas Paine (1737–1809) put it, and no longer just the happiness of a privileged elite.[92] The Republic would be 'the common weal' or 'commonwealth' – *weal* having connotations of worldly wealth, prosperity, well-being, spiritual happiness and the welfare or good of a community or state. Republicanism would also advance the common self-identification of a people as a *nation*, by virtue of (real or imagined) shared origins, heritage, language or religion. A people could be inspired to support a new kind of government on the grounds of their being members of a nation, rather than subjects of a multi-ethnic empire, as occurred for example in the post-World War I break-up of Austria-Hungary into numerous 'nation-states'. Conversely, peoples governed under many different polities could be inspired to join together as one nation, as occurred in 1861 with the unification of the Italian peoples, 'by nature, language, faith, traditions and culture for millennia united in the sacred name of Rome'.[93] Nations proud, or defensive, of their heritage, might export their systems, such as the Napoleonic code, to other peoples, or they might try to prevent outsiders from joining the nation, as in recent anti-immigration policies that have been applied in republics such as Hungary.

Modern revolutionary republicanism initiated an awareness of rights that ultimately led, following crimes against humanity during World War II, to a declaration of *universal* human rights. These rights pertain to us simply for being human, not as members of particular communities or nations, while including the right to have a recognised nationality. To the three R's in the title of this chapter, one could add a fourth, rights.[94] The multitudes of rights to do, to be or to have certain things that are claimed by or on behalf of individuals, classes of people, states, organisations, animals and so on, are bound up with the 'things made from people' – the republics, representatives and revolutions – that developed the modern arts of government.

Somewhat pessimistically, then, the two more recent revolutions considered above resulted in authoritarian regimes that have not upheld universal human rights. China is a one-party state that uses intrusive systems of surveillance and persecutes dissidents and minorities;[95] Iran is a theocracy that (by force of law) discriminates against women and religious minorities, and which uses state violence to suppress dissent.[96] One may question whether their governors 'represent' the people they govern and, if not, what it is that they do represent. The clerical government of Iran doesn't truly represent the values or aspirations of a large proportion (I daresay majority) of its people. Although they may be afraid to say so publicly, many Iranians don't want the mullahs running their country, and they wish for greater religious, cultural and political freedoms. And yet China and Iran are republics, or 'things made from people' and made from past popular uprisings.

While many republics may fail fully to recognise, respect and represent their own people, the ideals and the practices of representative government in other countries with otherwise very good human rights records have been challenged almost to breaking point. The anti-establishment sentiments that swept across Europe and America after the 2008 global financial crisis, in particular in 2016, contended that parliaments and governments no longer represented the values and wishes of the people. For many citizens, political leaders appeared out of touch, arrogant and self-serving. Alternative populist leaders who claimed that they spoke for the people (the 'real' people or the 'true' nation) enjoyed a surge at the polls. The very idea of representation – to speak for and to act on behalf of a multitude of absent others – was at stake in this contemporary struggle over the arts of government.

Notes

1 de Pizan, 1999 [1405], p. 6 (abridged), trans. R. Brown-Grant.
2 Andrade, 2018; Dignas & Winter, 2007.
3 de Pizan, 1999 [1405], pp. 46–9.
4 Ibid., pp. 64–6.
5 Peirce, 1993; Yermolenko, 2005.
6 Cockram, 2013.
7 Schultz & Ward, 2019.
8 These arose from relatively egalitarian societies with consultative assemblies of clan or family heads. Thapar, 2002, p. 146.
9 Today most countries call themselves republics. Constitutional monarchies, such as those in the British Commonwealth, have the basic features of republics, as they're governed by elected representatives who should act in the interests of the nation, under public scrutiny by opposition parties and a free press.
10 Finer, 1999, vol. II, p. 983.
11 Erasmus, 1997 [1516], p. 5, trans. N.M. Cheshire & M.J. Heath.
12 Ibid., see pp. 43–5 and 89–90.
13 Machiavelli, 1999 [1513].
14 Soll, 2010.
15 Benner, 2017; Lee, 2020.
16 Machiavelli, 1996 [1517], p. 11, Book I, §2.2.
17 Ibid., p. 46, Book I, §6.5.
18 Ibid., p. 117, Book I, §58.3.
19 Notably Coluccio Salutati (1331–1406) and Leonardo Bruni (1369–1444).
20 Finer, 1999, vol. II, ch. 7. The electoral processes are too complicated – some might say absurdly complicated – to describe in full here. See Finer for details.
21 Andrew, 2019.
22 Finer, 1999, vol. II.
23 Norwich, 2003, pp. 166–7 describes the electoral process introduced in 1268.
24 Machiavelli, 1996 [1517], p. 101, Book I, §49.3.
25 Ibid., pp. 20–21, Book I, §6.1. Machiavelli's case about Venice isn't very thorough or convincing, however.
26 Norwich, 2003, p. 276.
27 Ibid., p. 638.
28 Finer, 1999, vol. II, p. 1016.
29 Norwich, 2003, p. 166.
30 Finer, 1999, vol. II, p. 1011.
31 Chojnacki, 2000.

32 Tarabotti & Panizza, 2004, p. 42.

33 Howard, 2005; Norwich, 2003.

34 'The Venetian government ensured that those who were excluded from government, the "plebes", were not misused by the nobles, and that there was equality of justice; that sufficient corn was provided; and that poor relief was available.' Bowd, 2000, p. 89.

35 Finer, 1999, vol. II, Ch. 8.1.

36 Ibid., p. 1049.

37 Hobbes, 1998 [1651], p. 107, Ch. XVI.3, abridged.

38 'Men who are in absolute liberty, may, if they please, give authority to one man, to represent them every one; as well as give such authority to any assembly of men whatsoever; and consequently may subject themselves, if they think good, to a monarch, as absolutely, as to any other representative.' Ibid., p. 123, Ch. XIX.3, abridged.

39 Manin, 1997, pp. 163–7. The UK's Recall of MPs Act 2015 provides for a recall petition and has been used effectively.

40 Burke, 1996 [1774], p. 69.

41 Manin, 1997; Pitkin, 1967.

42 A representative legislature should be 'an exact portrait, in miniature, of the people at large, as it should think, feel, reason and act like them.' John Adams (1735–1801), quoted in Pitkin, 1967, p. 60. See also Manin, 1997, pp. 110–12.

43 There are still debates about the boundaries of representation, for example concerning the rights of convicted prisoners to vote, or of citizens living overseas to have seats reserved for them. Children are still unable to vote, and so they seem to be 'virtually' represented, as parliaments pass laws 'in their best interests'.

44 Rousseau, 1998 [1762], p. 96.

45 Burke, 1981, pp. 279–80, abridged.

46 Pitkin, 1967, p. 172.

47 Bromwich, 2014, p. 159.

48 Mill, 1991 [1861], p. 380.

49 Ibid., p. 382.

50 Ibid., p. 376.

51 Locke, 1980 [1689].

52 Manin, 1997, ch. 2.

53 Ibid., ch. 3.

54 Madison, *Federalist* 10 [1787], in Jay et al., 2008, pp. 52–3. Historical accounts nowadays tend to focus on the gradual extension and universalisation of the franchise, but socio-economic distinctions between electors and elected have not gone away.

55 Carrithers, 1991.

56 Montesquieu, 2001 [1748], p. 174, XI.6.

57 Ibid., p. 172.

58 Ibid., p. 174.

59 Ibid., p. 173.

60 Moreover, the UK's highest court resided in the House of Lords (the upper house of parliament) until 2009 when the independent supreme court was created.

61 Urbinati & Warren, 2008, p. 395.

62 Royle & Lockyer, 1997.

63 Tucker, 2017.

64 Fitzsimons, 2015, p. 213.

65 Keay, 2011; van de Ven, 2017.

66 Most of the country was cleared of such resistance by 1951, but 'mopping-up actions' continued until 1954. Teiwes, 1987, p. 70.

67 Ibid., p. 61.

68 'Land reform succeeded in redistributing about 43 percent of China's cultivated land to about 60 percent of the rural population.' Ibid., p. 87.

69 '70 to 80 percent of heavy industry and 40 percent of light industry were state owned in late 1952. State trading agencies and cooperatives handled more than 50 percent of total business turnover.' Ibid., p. 93.

70 Ibid., p. 107.
71 Preamble to the Constitution of the PRC, 1954.
72 Guo, 2013, p. 139.
73 One acknowledges, at the least, the struggles of ethno-religious minorities in Tibet and Xinjiang.
74 Later to become British Petroleum (BP).
75 'In March 1951, the Majlis had approved the recommendation of the Special Commission on the oil industry, of which Musaddiq was the chairman, in favour of nationalization, and with that as the principal objective of his administration, Musaddiq became prime minister. The Majlis voted Musaddiq into the premiership on 30 April; on 1 May, he announced the nationalization of the A.I.O.C., promising compensation.' Hambly, 1991, p. 258.
76 The CIA has since confirmed that it directed the coup under US foreign policy.
77 Hambly, 1991, p. 265.
78 Ibid.
79 'Anyone who approaches [Khomeini's book *Islamic Government*] expecting to find coherent political philosophy and logical, factually informed scholarly argument is likely to be severely disappointed. Nonetheless, Khomeini does not seem to have disavowed any part of the text, and it is certainly a blueprint for what he would do following the revolution.' Daniel, 2001, p. 179, abridged.
80 Axworthy, 2010; Hambly, 1991.
81 Pirsoul, 2018.
82 Ninety-eight percent of votes were in favour.
83 Ackerman, 2019.
84 Shariatmadari's moderate approach was arguably more 'traditional' than Khomeini's radicalism, which was not universally accepted by clerics. Menashri, 1980.
85 Ackerman, 2019.
86 Banisadr was dismissed as president by Khomeini in May 1981 and then dismissed by the parliament. He fled Iran and returned to Paris. Sreberny-Mohammadi & Mohammadi, 1987, pp. 111–12.
87 Schmidt, 2016.
88 Ackerman, 2019.
89 Kooshesh, 2018.
90 Ibid.
91 Abbas, 2005, p. 24. The Basij is a volunteer paramilitary force, subordinate to the Revolutionary Guard, that enforces state control over society.
92 Paine, 1996 [1790], p. 164.
93 Translated from an inscription on the Capitoline Hill, Rome, marking the centenary of the unification of Italy.
94 On the nuances of rights talk, see Wenar, 2015.
95 For example, the UN Committee on the Elimination of Racial Discrimination commented on 'the detention of large numbers of ethnic Uighurs and other Muslim minorities [in China], held incommunicado and often for long periods, without being charged or tried, under the pretext of countering religious extremism [and on] the lack of official data on how many people are in long-term detention or who have been forced to spend varying periods in political 're-education camps' for even non-threatening expressions of Muslim ethno-religious culture, such as a daily greeting. Estimates of the number of people detained range from tens of thousands to over a million.' Concluding observations on the combined fourteenth to seventeenth periodic reports on China, 19 September 2018.
96 'Approximately 4,900 people were reportedly detained in nationwide antigovernment protests [in Iran] over the worsening economy and corruption that erupted in late December 2017 and stretched into January [2018]; at least 21 people were killed in clashes with security forces during the demonstrations.' Freedom House, 2019. See URL: https://freedomhouse.org/report/freedom-world/2019/iran.

References

Abbas, Milani. 2005. 'Iran's Peculiar Election: A Historical Perspective.' *Journal of Democracy* 16 (4): 23–34.

Ackerman, Bruce A. 2019. *Revolutionary Constitutions: Charismatic Leadership and the Rule of Law.* Cambridge, MA: The Belknap Press of Harvard University Press.

Andrade, Nathanael J. 2018. *Zenobia: Shooting Star of Palmyra.* New York, NY: Oxford University Press.

Andrew, Christopher. 2019. *The Secret World: A History of Intelligence.* London: Penguin.

Axworthy, Michael. 2010. *A History of Iran: Empire of the Mind.* New York, NY: Basic Books.

Benner, Erica. 2017. *Be Like the Fox: Machiavelli in His World.* New York, NY: W.W. Norton.

Bowd, Stephen D. 2000. '"The tune is marred": Citizens and People in Gasparo Contarini's Venice.' *European Review of History: Revue européenne d'histoire* 7 (1): 83–97.

Bromwich, David. 2014. *The Intellectual Life of Edmund Burke: From the Sublime and Beautiful to American Independence.* Cambridge, MA: Belknap.

Burke, Edmund. 1981. *The Writings and Speeches of Edmund Burke, Volume II.* Oxford: Clarendon Press.

———. 1996. *The Writings and Speeches of Edmund Burke, Volume III.* Oxford: Clarendon Press.

Carrithers, David W. 1991. 'Not so Virtuous Republics: Montesquieu, Venice, and the Theory of Aristocratic Republicanism.' *Journal of the History of Ideas* 52 (2): 245–68.

Chojnacki, Stanley. 2000. *Women and Men in Renaissance Venice: Twelve Essays on Patrician Society.* Baltimore, MD: Johns Hopkins University Press.

Cockram, Sarah. 2013. *Isabella D'Este and Francesco Gonzaga: Power Sharing at the Italian Renaissance Court.* London: Routledge.

Daniel, Elton L. 2001. *The History of Iran.* Westport, CT: Greenwood Publishing Group.

de Pizan, Christine. 1999. *The Book of the City of Ladies.* London: Penguin.

Dignas, Beate, and Engelbert Winter. 2007. *Rome and Persia in Late Antiquity: Neighbours and Rivals.* Cambridge: Cambridge University Press.

Erasmus. 1997. *The Education of a Christian Prince.* Cambridge: Cambridge University Press.

Finer, Samuel Edmund 1999. *The History of Government.* Oxford: Oxford University Press.

Fitzsimons, Michael P. 2015. 'Sovereignty and Constitutional Power.' In *The Oxford Handbook of the French Revolution*, by David Andress, 201–17. Oxford: Oxford University Press.

Guo, Sujian. 2013. *Chinese Politics and Government.* London: Routledge.

Hambly, Gavin. 1991. 'The Pahlavī Autocracy: Muhammad Riżā Shāh, 1941–1979.' In *The Cambridge History of Iran, vol. 7*, by Peter Avery, Gavin Hambly and Charles Melville, 244–94. Cambridge: Cambridge University Press.

Hobbes, Thomas. 1998. *Leviathan.* Oxford: Oxford University Press.

Howard, Deborah. 2005. 'Civic and Religious Architecture in Gothic Venice.' In *Venice: Art and Architecture*, by Giandomenico Romanelli, 88–125. Königswinter: Könemann.

Jay, John, Lawrence Goldman, Alexander Hamilton, and James Madison. 2008. *The Federalist Papers.* Oxford: Oxford University Press.

Keay, John. 2011. *China: A History.* New York, NY: Basic Books.

Kooshesh, Parisa. 2018. *Iranian Women in New Zealand: Their Motivations for Immigration and Trends of Westernisation or Acculturation.* PhD Thesis, Auckland: Massey University.

Lee, Alexander. 2020. *Machiavelli: His Life and Times.* London: Picador.

Locke, John. 1980. *Second Treatise of Government.* Indianapolis: Hackett.

Machiavelli, Niccolò. 1996. *Discourses on Livy*. Chicago, IL: University of Chicago Press.
———. 1999. *The Prince*. London: Penguin.
Manin, Bernard. 1997. *The Principles of Representative Government*. Cambridge: Cambridge University Press.
Menashri, David. 1980. 'Shi'ite Leadership: In the Shadow of Conflicting Ideologies.' *Iranian Studies* 13 (1–4): 119–45.
Mill, John Stuart. 1991. *On Liberty and Other Essays*. Oxford: Oxford University Press.
Montesquieu, Charle de Secondat Baron de. 2001. *The Spirit of the Laws*. Kitchener, ON: Batoche Books.
Norwich, John Julius. 2003. *A History of Venice*. London: Penguin.
Paine, Thomas. 1996. *Rights of Man*. Ware: Wordsworth.
Peirce, Leslie P. 1993. *The Imperial Harem: Women and Sovereignty in the Ottoman Empire*. New York, NY: Oxford University Press.
Pirsoul, Nicolas. 2018. 'Islam and Political Liberalism: A Shi'ite Approach to the Overlapping Consensus.' *The International Journal of Human Rights* 22 (8): 1030–46.
Pitkin, Hanna Fenichel. 1967. *The Concept of Representation*. Berkeley: University of California Press.
Rousseau, Jean-Jacques. 1998. *The Social Contract*. Ware: Wordsworth.
Royle, Edward, and Roger Lockyer. 1997. *Chartism*. London: Routledge.
Schmidt, Patrick. 2016. 'Understanding Iran's Assembly of Experts Vote.' *The Washington Institute*. February 16. Accessed November 9, 2019. https://www.washingtoninstitute.org/policy-analysis/view/assembly-test.
Schultz, Celia E., and Allen Mason Ward. 2019. *A History of the Roman People*. London: Routledge.
Soll, Jacob. 2010. 'Introduction.' In *The First Translations of Machiavelli's Prince: From the Sixteenth to the First Half of the Nineteenth Century*, by Roberto De Pol, 9–14. Leiden: Brill/Rodopi.
Sreberny-Mohammadi, Annabelle, and Ali Mohammadi. 1987. 'Post-Revolutionary Iranian Exiles: A Study in Impotence.' *Third World Quarterly* 9 (1): 108–29.
Tarabotti, Arcangela, and Letizia Panizza. 2004. *Paternal Tyranny*. Chicago, IL: University of Chicago Press.
Teiwes, Frederick. 1987. 'Establishment and Consolidation of the New Regime.' In *The Cambridge History of China, Vol. 14*, by John Fairbank, Roderick MacFarquhar, 49–143. Cambridge: Cambridge University Press.
Thapar, Romila. 2002. *Early India: From the Origins to AD 1300*. London: Allen Lane.
Tucker, Spencer. 2017. *The Roots and Consequences of Civil Wars and Revolutions: Conflicts That Changed World History*. Santa Barbara CA: ABC–CLIO.
Urbinati, Nadia, and Mark E. Warren. 2008. 'The Concept of Representation in Contemporary Democratic Theory.' *Annual Review of Political Science* 11: 387–412.
van de Ven, Hans. 2017. *China at War: Triumph and Tragedy in the Emergence of the New China*. London: Profile.
Wenar, Leif. 2015. 'Rights.' *The Stanford Encyclopedia of Philosophy*. Fall. Accessed November 2019. https://plato.stanford.edu/archives/fall2015/entries/rights/.
Yermolenko, Galina. 2005. 'Roxolana: "The Greatest Empresse of the East".' *The Muslim World* 95 (2): 231–48.

8

LET'S GET ORGANISED

Civil administration

So far we've looked mainly at monarchies and republics. In its pure form monarchy means that the will of one person, once uttered, becomes law. By contrast, in ideal republics, the will, consent or interests of the people authorise the lawmakers and governors to act. Either way, the expression of will is unsuccessful if not *executed* or put into action. The sovereign will of a monarch, an oligarchic council or a representative assembly calls always for implementation. It has to be administered and if necessary moderated through the capabilities and rationalities of civil, legal, religious and military officers, servants or functionaries. Someone has to set goals, make plans, call for finance, keep records and get things done. The early states had scribes, accountants and executioners. Ancient rulers had ministers, generals, emissaries and scholars to advise and act for them, and they couldn't do without tax collectors. This is what we now call public administration or public management, an ideal form of which would be a technocratic rule by expert advisers using the best evidence and experience to identify and solve public problems with proven methods economically, efficiently and effectively, if not scientifically. But do these people exert a political will of their own?

Modern government relied on the evolution of bureaucratic organisation for policy advice and implementation. In the description by the German sociologist Max Weber (1864–1920), bureaucratisation meant that official functions became ordered by rules or laws, delegated in fixed duties assigned to qualified employees who acted within hierarchical command structures. The bureaucracy – which gradually developed from older forms of administration – produced the modern civil service that strictly separated employees' official activities from their private lives. The official no longer possessed the office as a privilege or royal favour; duties of office exclusively occupied the officials' working life rather than being

DOI: 10.4324/9781003166955-8

a 'secondary activity'.[1] The historical champions of civil administration were the Chinese, beginning in the Han dynasty (Chapter 3, Part 3). The Chinese government didn't develop parliaments; it pacified and marginalised the nobility;[2] it didn't foster 'meddlesome priests'. Even the military was under the scrutiny of a scholarly, meritocratic and disciplined civil service. So we turn next to the Ming dynasty (1368–1644) and its record of relatively stable government when bureaucrats (more or less) ruled and China was the world's economic powerhouse.

Part 1: The Great Ming

Chinese dynasties rose and fell, but bureaucracy carried on. The Mongol-ruled Yuan dynasty went into terminal decline in the mid-fourteenth century. A commoner, Zhu Yuanzhang (1328–98) led rebel forces from Nanjing to seize power and declare himself the founding Ming emperor, or Hongwu emperor, in 1368. In 1380, he ordered a purge of the civil service and nobility with tens of thousands of executions, and he 'dismantled all the central government's top-level organs' in order to rule directly.[3] But his system of government over such large territory and population 'was made possible by the *perpetuation* of the regional and local administrations of earlier times.'[4] Ming emperors revived and preserved neo-Confucian education and examinations for appointments to the civil service.

Under the Yuan dynasty, the central and provincial secretariats had leading coordination roles in government alongside the military bureaus and the censorate (the auditing and surveillance branch). The secretariat had overseen six ministries (for personnel, revenue, rites, war, justice and works). The founding Ming emperor believed that this placed too much in the hands of officials and that he was in danger of being usurped by them. The brutal reorganisation of 1380 eliminated the secretariat with its two grand councillors and executive officials, forcing the six ministers to report directly to the emperor, and thus concentrating executive power around him – but also burdening him with a lot more paperwork. He even decreed that any descendant must impose the death penalty on anyone seeking to re-establish the secretariat or to re-create a chief ministerial post akin to the former grand councillor. This left his descendants and their advisers with an awful obstacle to re-establishment of coordinated advice and decision-making. Alternative coordination structures emerged anyway, though not always for the better.[5]

The imperial palace

A Ming emperor normally designated his first-born son by the empress or favoured consort as his heir-apparent once the boy began to read and write. This contributed to the longevity of the dynasty and meant few succession crises. One exception was the sixth, the Zhengtong emperor (r. 1435–49), who was poorly advised to lead troops against the Mongols. Following a humiliating retreat, the emperor was taken hostage. This caused panic in the imperial court, but the emperor's younger half-brother was 'urged to ascend the throne in person [and not as regent], since the emperor was a captive and his infant son incapable of ruling.'[6] This eliminated the Mongols' bargaining power for ransom, and they attacked Beijing, but unsuccessfully. The erstwhile emperor was eventually returned, but only after he'd renounced all claims to the throne. Installing a substitute had been a necessary defensive manoeuvre, but broke constitutional norms. The replacement, the Jingtai emperor (r. 1449–57), unsurprisingly decided to keep the throne; but his son died, leaving him with no successor. When he became seriously ill, a group of palace conspirators (including generals, officials and eunuchs) literally picked the ex-emperor up from his residence and rushed him onto the throne, pulling off a *coup d'état*. Hence, the sixth emperor was rehabilitated as the eighth and renamed the Tianshun emperor (r. 1457–64). The former Jingtai emperor, now demoted to a prince, conveniently died a few weeks later.[7] Most Ming successions went more smoothly, however, aided by the relocation of sons other than the heir to distant specially built palaces. Heirs-apparent were raised by female and eunuch servants and educated by a special branch of scholars.

Imperial wives and consorts tended to be commoners by birth, so the significant political influence that they often wielded came down to personal acumen. The empress Zhang (c. 1384–1442), for example, was the wife of the Hongxi emperor, the fourth in the Ming line, who died after only nine months on the throne in 1425. Her first son thus became the Xuande emperor (r. 1425–35) at the age of 26. She was closely involved in all affairs of state with both her husband and son. Her son died after ten years on the throne when his successor (the hapless Zhengtong emperor mentioned above) was only eight. Ming law had made no provision for managing affairs of state when the emperor was still a child, and the empress-dowager Zhang became the regent. She was supported by a council of respected officials but had the last word on major political and military decisions. She remains to this day highly regarded for her abilities.[8] Had she lived longer, one wonders whether she would have dissuaded her grandson from leading troops against the Mongols.

The imperial palace was strictly secluded. It was staffed by women and eunuchs, mainly the latter, numbering in their thousands. Lower-status families with a surplus of boys could have them castrated and presented to the palace for service, for which they could expect rewards. The founding emperor had banned eunuchs from direct involvement in government business but, given the close personal access eunuchs had, officials had to treat them as conduits to the emperor. Eunuchs weren't scholars, yet they were closest to the emperor and the officials resented them. Some eunuchs were put in charge of important missions, the most famous being the great maritime expeditions commanded by Zheng He (1371–1435), who was originally Muslim and was enslaved and castrated at the age of ten. Palace eunuchs were organised into departments that had critical security, treasury and maintenance duties, with the chief of the imperial household staff wielding the greatest influence. They formed distinct hierarchies to administer taxation, policing, palace management and economic development, as well as controlling the flow of information and personal access to the emperor.[9] 'Eventually, in violation of centuries-old traditions, palace edicts were issued by eunuchs without being proposed, drafted or even seen in advance by court officials.'[10] If the emperor was incompetent, a senior eunuch could seize the opportunity to play the tyrant. The most notorious was Wei Zhongxian who, under the Tianqi emperor (r. 1621–27), conducted a 'reign of terror', banishing and executing his palace rivals.[11] A strong emperor, on the other hand, would find eunuchs more willing to do his bidding than the scholar-officials whose moral duty it was to remonstrate with him.

The inner palace and the emperor's paperwork were controlled by eunuchs, and the external business by scholar-officials. While the latter were schooled in Confucian ethics of piety and service, there was plenty of self-serving ambition and rivalry, sometimes leading to violence.[12] Meanwhile, the emperors' kin and offspring and their many descendants were excluded from imperial politics and government, and so, to pacify them, they were paid generous stipends. This kept nobles away from dynastic intrigue and rivalry. Towards the end of the dynasty, though, they formed an estimated 100,000 imperial beneficiaries doing nothing much while imposing a fiscal burden that exceeded even the cost of the armed forces.[13]

Local government

The Ming dynasty lasted nearly three centuries, during which time the population rose from about 60 million to twice that or more (estimates vary), and yet the number of qualified officials remained relatively steady (although estimates range from 12,000 to 25,000) as did the larger cohort of subordinate clerks (around 100,000).[14] So, the civil servants composed a tiny and declining fraction of one percent of the population.[15] In spite of their rarefied status, however, they were mostly underpaid, and often in debt after years of study. So not only did the numbers competing to pass the entry exams rise, the workload per official and their propensity for 'ticket clipping' did too. Supplementary fees and payments were taken for granted.

The Ming taxation system was top-heavy, encouraged avoidance and evasion, and lacked the capacity to stimulate commerce. The principal currency was rice, but grain redistribution became absurdly complicated, as the infrastructure didn't include large centralised granaries. The Ming emperors inherited a system that surveyed and segmented rural communities and villages by groups of ten households and imposed collective responsibilities on them for tax-collection, corvee labour, justice, care of the aged and security – and collective punishments for failures. Despite increasingly complex and burdensome responsibilities and imposts from above, local administration was supposed to be fiscally self-sufficient and self-governing, which meant that the goods and services needed for local government had to be supplied by communities themselves.[16] The local wealthy landed, literate class worked in administration voluntarily, supported by clerical workers. The official scholarly prefects and sub-prefects were non-native and rotated every three years, and the areas and populations they governed were very large.[17] A local village might never be visited by a county magistrate. So the permanent local clerical workforce, who knew how things really worked, were the ones who controlled (or manipulated) local affairs, under the community leadership of the notables. The system was rational on paper, but written record-keeping often replicated past records rather than up-to-date facts. Inefficient and thinly spread government by scholar-officials would have had to adapt to the messy realities of local customs and loyalties.[18]

Examinations

For academically talented and ambitious young men, and ambitious families, success in the civil-service exams represented outstanding achievement and a pathway towards social prestige. Indeed, from the early 1440s, it was the only path to a first-class civil service career. Schools of many kinds, including village-level elementary schools and more advanced private academies, were officially recognised, but the subsidised Confucian schools established across the country were the most important. Instructors were trained and assigned to the schools, students were regularly examined and the schools were regularly inspected. The curriculum was based on the ancient Four Books and the Five Classics of Confucian literature,[19] as compiled and interpreted by Zhu Xi (1130–1200), and schools trained pupils for success in national examinations. Fixed quotas of graduates who had passed a qualifying exam progressed to advanced study at universities in Beijing and Nanjing, centrally funded by the Directorate of Education. Some places were reserved for sons of high nobility or were purchased, which tended to lower standards, and private academies also operated at this level. 'Once admitted to one of the national universities, students theoretically spent from three to ten years moving through graded stages of study in the six colleges into which each university was divided.'[20] Apprenticeships in government departments were also available. Graduates were sent on to the Ministry for Personnel for consideration in employment.

The recruitment examinations were written and were held in a competitive setting. While they were theoretically open to all, one had to have qualified as a Confucian scholar to be eligible to sit. Local nominees from the prefectures were entered into a triennial 'grand competition' that began at the provincial capitals. The provincial exams were held in three all-day sessions over a week, supervised by an eminent official. Candidates sat in private cubicles under guard, and their papers were coded so as to be assessed anonymously. The questions were on philosophical and literary interpretation and applied topics in contemporary policy and government. There were quotas for the number of graduates from each province. Provincial graduates were eligible for official appointments but could go on to higher-level metropolitan and palace exams in the capital the following year. A qualifying test had to be passed to sit the metropolitan exams, and there were around 1,000–2,000 examinees. Again, there were three day-long sessions, and those who passed were then able to sit a single-question palace exam presided over by the emperor himself. There would have been on average about 90 new metropolitan graduates per year, eligible for immediate appointment to the civil service. Most provincial graduates were unsuccessful at this level, but they could still present themselves for employment or continue their studies. The level at which one graduated would determine the level of appointment in the graded civil service. The top three graduates went to the elite Hanlin Academy, which set them up for promotion to the grand secretariat.[21]

The civil service

Civil servants were subject to triennial merit ratings and to unscheduled evaluations by the censorate. After decades of service, those at the fourth grade and higher could be promoted by the emperor on the recommendation of ministers, and the highest-level appointments were made by an audience of top officials in the capital. Ming government was based on three primary hierarchies: civil administration, military and surveillance. The administrative branch encompassed the six ministries (for personnel, revenue, rites, war, justice and works). The judiciary weren't independent but fell within the administrative system. Similarly Buddhist and Daoist priests were registered and controlled by the administration. Civil and military personnel had quite different careers, as the latter were frequently based on inheritance, but the routine administration of the military, and even its tactical operations, were controlled by the civilian Ministry of War. The five chief military commissioners reported directly to the emperor, however, as did the six chief ministers. Civil servants staffed the third branch, the Censorate, which had intrusive and wide-ranging powers of audit, surveillance and discipline over the other branches.

The daily rounds of a Ming emperor were filled with a tedious sequence of ceremonies and audiences,[22] and later incumbents let others take care of paperwork. They bypassed the founder's interdiction by drawing grand secretaries from the Hanlin Academy, initially as *ad hoc* appointments but eventually as important executive positions within the palace. This led to uneasy relations between ministers who were responsible for operations outside of the palace, a grand secretariat who appeared to represent imperial authority, and the eunuchs who served the emperor personally. Moreover, each of these competing groups had its internal factions. Executive positions within the palace, provinces and military that had been instituted with only *ad hoc* coordination roles gradually became normalised. An apparent lack of formal coordination at the top has sometimes been blamed for the eventual demise of the Ming dynasty, but neither can one deny its relative longevity.[23]

If Ming China was absolutist, then who ruled it absolutely – emperors, eunuchs or scholars? The early emperors were more vigorous and autocratic than the later ones, who were mostly more passive. The balance of executive power swung, depending on the personal characteristics of the emperor, the authority of the grand secretariat and other senior officials and the skills of palace eunuchs. None could function without the others. Nonetheless, Ming bureaucratic government successfully kept China united and relatively peaceful; it presided over demographic and economic growth. Its aim wasn't to improve or innovate but 'to maintain peace and stability'; administration was basically personnel management, or the placement of capable trustworthy men throughout the provinces.[24] But it was neither efficient nor open to reform, and the centralised fiscal system was unwieldy. The extravagant palace, the do-nothing imperial kin, and the decrepit armies were burdens. The latter flaw proved to be fatal when Manchu armies invaded from the north-east, as Ming soldiers were ill-equipped and untested, and the fiscal system too slow to mobilise resources. Nonetheless, the principles of meritocratic civil administration survived, as they had done for centuries, to serve the subsequent Qing dynasty. A change of dynasty didn't mean a major change in the arts of government.

In Confucius' time – an era of warring states – princes competed to secure the brightest of the literati as advisers (Chapter 2, Part 1). Under the unified empire, however, scholars had to compete for offices created by the palace, based on each candidate's mastery of the doctrines of Confucianism and success in invigilated examinations.[25] In their time, the Ming officials were the best-educated workforce in the world. One wonders, though, how useful so many years of orthodox study of centuries-old literary, philosophical and historical texts could have been for employment in government. They were schooled in virtuous conduct, not in the maximisation of utility; the harmonious state and long-lived dynasty depended on moral character and on respect for ancestors and elders. It took a particular historical development to imagine a kind of government based not just on benevolent men but also on rational calculations concerning the welfare of the populace. A modern art of government that saw itself as a *science* had yet to be invented, and it wasn't invented in China.

Part 2: Prussia

The Peace of Westphalia (1648) recognised the sovereign right of the European states, large and small, to govern their own territories and populations. But because of a failure (or unwillingness) to unify the Holy Roman Empire, there were more than 300 territorial rulers in attendance. A map of the empire was an anarchic patchwork quilt. Although the Habsburgs dominated the empire, the German world remained fragmented and vulnerable to invasion by France. Meanwhile, Prussia was an eastern-European dukedom dependent on the Kingdom of Poland. Its capital Königsberg (today's Kaliningrad) lay outside the empire; its duke, however, was also the Elector of Brandenburg (an elector of the empire) and was based in Berlin.[26] The realms of Friedrich Wilhelm (r. 1640–88) thus encompassed several small states that shared no borders. An important strategic question, then, for Brandenburg-Prussia was: How does a small fragmented state, poorly endowed with natural resources, succeed when surrounded by much larger ones? Friedrich Wilhelm and successors used a combination of religious toleration, militarisation and mercantilism,[27] leading to Prussia's rise during the eighteenth century. In 1701, the emperor granted Friedrich I the title of 'King in Prussia'. In 1740, Friedrich II (Frederick the Great, r. 1740–86) seized Silesia[28] from Austria in a surprise attack. At great cost, Prussia then defended herself against an alliance of France, Austria and Russia in the Seven Years' War (1756–63). In the partitions of Poland (1772, 1792 and 1795) she acquired West Prussia (which bridged the formerly separate territories of Brandenburg and Prussia) and provinces encompassing Poznań and Warsaw. Poland, with its unruly parliamentary system, was devoured by its absolutist neighbours. By the end of that century Prussia had become one of Europe's great powers.[29]

Along the way, however, there were struggles in Prussia's disparate realms with landed nobility and city corporations who resisted demands for taxation and defended their distinctive local rights and traditional feudal loyalties. Rather than reach settlements through a representative parliamentary system, Prussian government meant absolute monarchy, an interventionist state and strong armies. Administration was progressively centralised and consolidated; Prussian society was made ever ready for war. Civil administration became indistinguishable from the military, and the main political problem was the need to finance war. In the mid-seventeenth century, the elector had wanted to raise an excise tax with which to build their armed forces but met resistance from the landed nobility – the Junkers.[30] The elector got the revenues he needed, and in return the Junkers got control of the countryside, including over the peasants on their estates, and comprising schools, military service, labour migration and criminal justice. Unlike western Europe's conversions of serfdom into wage labour and free tenancies, the Junkers gained greater political and economic authority – although there was local resistance, and there were many free peasants as well. The landlord's estate 'became an integrated legal and political space',[31] although he didn't own the peasants and the state imposed some standardisation and legal codification on the Junkers' patrimonial courts from 1747.[32] In the towns, however, the elector had greater scope to raise taxes, and paid administrators were appointed to collect them. Excise taxes on goods and services were raised at the point of sale and 'did away with the need for fiscal negotiations with urban Estate representatives.'[33] Disenfranchisement of the towns as bodies corporate and the decline of their traditional privileges and autonomy (which were strongly resisted in Königsberg) accompanied the appointment of paid tax commissioners and the transfer of fiscal and judicial roles to regal officials. The Estates (assemblies of nobles and mayors) were sidelined and the elector arguably became 'fiscally absolute'[34] through standardisation of tax policies, subjection of the nobility to military service and the creation of provincial administrative bodies that answered to Berlin. Such absolutism was not, however, as 'absolute' as we may imagine. Political negotiation and informal power-sharing with local elites and the persistence of diverse local customs – as well as some outright resistance – complicated top-down rule.[35] Officials appointed to serve the monarch in provincial towns could become enmeshed in local oligarchic networks and suborned by vested interests, as civic politics relied on the informal participation of prominent members of the local bourgeoisie.[36]

Concentration of power led, however, to a structure with one overall military board in Berlin, served by provincial boards, in turn served by rural nobility and urban administrators. A General War Commissariat was established in 1655, and gradually incorporated functions in taxation and industry. This 'merging of financial, economic and military administration' wasn't unusual in those times, as it emulated the French example under Louis XIV.[37] Frederick the Great took the throne in 1740 and was a workaholic and micro-manager: he took personal control of the state including foreign policy. As with the Ming emperors, his paperwork grew accordingly. So he gathered around him a non-ministerial *Kabinett* to assist in a secretarial capacity, copying documents and sending out orders. Given the king's personal control over all branches of government and warfare, only he and his small *Kabinett* had an overview of the Prussian monarchy. The king withdrew to his residence at Potsdam, issuing orders directly to departments, provincial administrators and army commanders, and bypassing ministers in Berlin.[38]

The integration of state and army enabled 'a bureaucratic organization of all walks of life, right down to the smallest detail, so that all forces could be mobilized.'[39] Carl von Clausewitz (1780–1831), the Prussian general and military theorist, famously asserted that 'War is merely the continuation of policy by other means.'[40] Conversely, to maintain domestic discipline, public policy was merely the continuation of war by other means.[41] But Prussian absolute monarchy led to rigidity and military incompetence. The civil service was small, and decades of royal dictatorship meant that officials were 'routine-ridden, fearful of taking initiatives, and not very imaginative.'[42] The growth of 'two powerful but rival systems of government' in Potsdam and Berlin meant replication, tension and ultimately crisis for the Prussian state.[43] In 1806, her army was no match for Napoleon's at the dual battles of Jena and Auerstadt.

Cameral sciences

The subtitle of this book refers to the arts of government. But one of the features of modern government is the idea of an administrative *science*, both theoretical and practical. When we talk of science nowadays, we may first think of natural sciences such as physics and biology, but we also have information science and social science. The German *Wissenschaft* translates as 'science', encompassing the systematised fields of research and knowledge. The seventeenth century had produced a political-advisory literature that sought to advance the interests of rulers by first paying close attention to the welfare of subjects.[44] Under the auspices of Frederick William I, this led to the establishment of university studies in 'cameral and police sciences' in 1727.[45] 'Cameral' comes from the German *Kammer*, the chamber or room in which fiscal affairs of state were discussed and administered.

Kameralisten were the officials who worked there and *Kameralwissenschaften* are cameral sciences. Political concepts never translate neatly from theory into practice, but many governmental practices in seventeenth-century Germany, Austria and further afield were generically 'cameralist'.[46] Cameralism flourished among the principalities of central Europe, whose wealth and security depended on their own population, territory, natural resources and industries, and who couldn't emulate the transcontinental imperialism of states such as Castile, Portugal and England.[47] Cameralist science and practice dealt with the crown's management of its domestic domains, finances, industries and resources such as agriculture, mining, forestry and fisheries. The tradition of *œconomy* (household management including rural estates) was inherited from the ancient Greek authors Xenophon and Aristotle, but grew to include princely households and hence the state. The ruler was a householder with large estates; good government attended to animal husbandry, agriculture and forestry. The broader aims were population growth and the happiness or prosperity of the subjects, but 'directed to the increase of the ruler's income'.[48] This included forbidding the export of raw materials to conserve them, and reducing the importation of manufactured goods to protect domestic industries.

Many cameralist ideas were utopian, impractical or unpopular. Those that were put into formal law or regulation may not have been uniformly enforced or observed. Some cameralist writings, such as in forestry, on the other hand, are descriptions of well-established practices and administrative norms, rather than prescriptive or idealistic advice.[49] Cameral science meant 'the rationalisation of state and society' based on impartial expertise and careful organisation.[50] Sure, there were 'bad' (incompetent or corrupt) *Kameralisten*, but professors of cameral science believed that education would improve their skills and their willingness to act in the interests of the people and the prince.[51] Whereas the Chinese trained officials in moral virtue, scholarly excellence and traditional rites in the interests of harmony, cameralism identified problems, resources and potential within the population and the territories of the state, and aimed, with a calculative eye, for a wealthier, more secure state. Cameralists understood that good fiscal policy could stimulate economic activity; they aimed for orderliness (not harmony) through effective 'police' (*Polizei*)

Police meant more than the authority that enforces law: it referred to systematic social regulation and orderliness. Rather than let things take their natural course, the science of police imagined the achievement of happiness through the minutest normalisation of everyday life. This could include public hygiene, flood and fire prevention, care of the poor, security of the streets and so on. It imagined an ever-watchful eye and an ever-ready helping hand. So while cameralism proposed and investigated the objects of government, the science of police put them all in order at the level of villages, pastures, markets and the like.[52] Police represented a world of 'supervision that seeks ideally to reach the most passing phenomenon of the social body: the infinitely small of political power.'[53]

Demise of cameralism

In spite of absolute monarchy and centralised administration, however, the ultimate aims of *Polizei* weren't realised – or simply weren't realisable. State power was limited by slow communications, local customs and the entrenched privileges of landed nobility and urban bourgeoisie – and, one must imagine, by the laziness and unruliness of much human conduct. The cameralist dream of a perfectly administered and regimented society came to an end, moreover, with the assistance of two quite different outsiders: the French emperor Napoleon Bonaparte (1769–1821) and the Scottish moral philosopher and political economist Adam Smith (1723–90).

Napoleon's victory at Jena–Auerstadt and occupation of Berlin in 1806 precipitated a wave of reforms in the Prussian armed forces and government, emulating the new French model. From 1807, these reforms removed restrictions on sales of land, formerly monopolised by the nobility, opened up occupations that were formerly restricted by guilds and corporations, and abolished hereditary servitude, leading to conditions closer to free markets. The franchise was extended to all males who met a modest property qualification, and representative assemblies were summoned at provincial and national levels. The latter dissolved in disagreement, however, rather than in the consensus that ministers had hoped for, and 'no national parliament was forthcoming'.[54] But outdated feudal privileges and protectionist policies were undone in favour of commercial liberty. Political liberty made less progress, but the monarch was constrained by giving greater authority to ministers and bureaucracies. Powers were decentralised.

Adam Smith's *The Wealth of Nations* was translated into German soon after its first publication in 1776, but its reception in Prussia was mixed and slow to take effect. Some Prussian economists were critical of Smith's presumption of a general theory of laws of human economic behaviour.[55] But Smith supported free trade and rejected the protectionist policies of mercantilism. He argued that people are universally motivated to seek economic prosperity, and it wasn't the job of the state to organise it. The idea that a nation needed vaults full of gold and silver to raise armies and wage wars was false too, he said: what really counted was 'the annual revenue arising out of its lands, labour and consumable stock'.[56] This challenged Prussian traditions of fiscal accumulation,[57] and Smith's work was cited in support of deregulatory reform. The cameralists had treated state and society as synonymous: improvements in the welfare and happiness of the populace were matters for good and prudent government in an all-pervasive 'police state'. The new political economy of Adam Smith saw civil society as consisting of people voluntarily interacting in commerce and creating their own prosperity. The state would provide infrastructure such as canals that were beyond the scope of profitable enterprises, and its 'police' would be no more than an enforcer of laws that protected people and property.

This doesn't mean that Prussians were entirely converted to British liberal individualism. Yet neither was Prussia's reputation as an absolutist bureaucratic 'police state' fully accurate. Prussia was socially, linguistically and religiously diverse. Even after the reforms of the early nineteenth century, there were still many different provincial legal systems along with urban self-government. What quality of 'Prussianness' could unite such a diverse population, then? The idea of the state as a unifying force, incorporating the diversity and individuality of civil society, and progressively realising, through law, the rational spirit of freedom, was propounded by G.W.F. Hegel (1770–1831). While not originally from Prussia, Hegel gained a chair of philosophy at the University of Berlin in 1818. Unlike the liberalism of the British – who saw the state as a threat to individuality and economic progress – Hegel elevated the state to a universal, even divine, rational historical vehicle of freedom. His dialectical approach neatly encompassed both conservative monarchism and progressive relativism. He inspired many young intellectuals including Karl Marx; yet he endorsed monarchy and patriarchy. By that time, however, the cameral and police sciences were dusty textbooks. Hegel didn't support the cameralist idea that the future happiness of the people could be 'scientifically' managed through state-mandated activity and orderliness. Historical change and progress, he argued, unfold with a rationality that humans can only dimly perceive in retrospect. We only comprehend the world after the conditions necessary for that moment have slipped into the past. We only understand 'the way we are' once we're no longer that way. So scientific prediction and control of society wouldn't work for Hegel, but the Prussian administration later inspired the US President Woodrow Wilson.

Part 3: American sciences

A revolutionary overturning of government necessitates government's reinvention (Chapter 7, Part 3), the most innovative and enduring example of which was set by the founders of the United States of America. At a constitutional convention – 'establishing good government from reflection and choice [rather than] accident and force'[58] – they chose a separation of powers (executive, legislative and judicial) replicated in each state of a federal system. The Bill of Rights protected a wide field in which the individual would be free from legal constraint and arbitrary coercion; the supreme court would rule on the constitutionality of particular laws or executive actions; the representative congress would pass law and control public finance; the elected president would be commander-in-chief. The constitution also mentioned departments of executive government that might be empowered by law. Ambassadors, supreme court judges and senior public officials were to be nominated by the president but appointed 'with the Advice and Consent of the Senate'. The appointment of 'inferior Officers' might be delegated by law to the president, courts or heads of departments. The latter would report to the president, but not collectively; there was no mention of a cabinet.[59] In 1791, however, President George Washington invited his department secretaries and attorney-general to the first cabinet meeting. The cabinet thus grew organically in response to the real-world challenges of governing.[60]

Unlike the British parliamentary model, the US constitution forbids anyone holding an executive office from sitting concurrently in the legislature. In general, presidents choose their cabinet secretaries and the senate consents.

The constitution left it up to law or convention to specify which officials were the 'inferior officers' that presidents or heads of departments could appoint *without* the advice and consent of the senate. And there was no mention of a presidential power to *dismiss*, with or without the consent of the senate, those officials who had been appointed *with* it.[61] If not for sheer numbers, a new president could have dismissed an entire administration and then begun again with his own followers and sycophants, only some of whom required the senate's consent. Dismissal and replacement of officials by incoming presidents was often justified in terms of democratic accountability: the people had elected a new head of the executive branch and hence also, indirectly, those he selected to implement his policies. Examinations for the purposes of appointments were applied where necessary, such as for military engineers, but they put power into the hands of anonymous examiners rather than publicly accountable officials. The people 'should be governed by political officials chosen through consent rather than competitive examinations.'[62] Selection of administrators by presidents and governors was regarded by many as more democratic. This kind of thinking resisted the growth of an unelected fourth *administrative* branch of government, for fear it would become remote from and unaccountable to the people, like Prussian monarchism. America's founders had debated the balance in the executive branch between energetic and efficient action, on one hand, and responsiveness and accountability to the people, on the other.[63] The constitution mandated a chain of command that unified lawful executive authority and accountability in the president, but it had neither mandated nor prohibited a permanent, unelected and politically neutral civil service.

Patronage

By the mid-nineteenth century, neither the United Kingdom nor the United States had yet developed fully meritocratic civil services. Official obstruction and incompetence were widely discussed, for instance in Charles Dickens's satirical portrayal of the Circumlocution Office in *Little Dorrit* (1857).[64] In London, the Northcote–Trevelyan Report (1854) recognised that a permanent body of officials who provide efficient, informed and politically neutral administration was essential, given that ministers (who advised the Crown and were accountable in parliament) changed from time to time. The report bluntly stated, however, that the civil service had become a haven for 'the unambitious, and the indolent or incapable', while career structures gave officials the message that 'if they work hard, it will not advance them, – if they waste their time in idleness, it will not keep them back.' 'Personal or political considerations' often determined appointments, rather than knowledge and merit.[65] The report recommended a 'central system of examination' for entry, open to all young men, and promotion on merit rather than time in service. This meritocratic ideal was only gradually accepted, let alone implemented, but it supported a permanent, politically neutral and anonymous civil service, independent of ministers and their political staff.[66]

Patronage was even more prevalent in the American 'spoils system'. During Andrew Jackson's presidency (1829–37) the victorious party rewarded loyal supporters with jobs.[67] It's estimated that less than ten percent of federal posts were affected, but public service was partly based on political patronage and partly on non-partisan tenure.[68] For the sake of efficient and effective administration, it was impossible to dismiss all personnel and start again, but new presidents were inundated with pleas for employment. There were however long-standing objections to patronage, especially when nepotism and bribery became more influential than competence. Patronage also concentrated executive powers in the presidency, which aroused many Americans' wariness of anything resembling monarchy. But reformers had to convince the people that non-partisan experts would give them better service than 'spoilsmen'. The movement against patronage, towards a merit-based system, was advanced in the Pendleton Act 1883. Later, in the progressive era, patronage was condemned for failing to insulate administrators from politics, and hence for compromising their objectivity and impartiality as servants of the people. There was a push for a more independent public service, supported for example by the scholar Frank Goodnow (1859–1939):

> In the semi-scientific, quasi-judicial, clerical, and ministerial divisions of the administrative system provision should be made for permanence of tenure, if efficient and impartial administration is to be expected, and if questions of policy are to be determined in accordance with the popular will.[69]

The constitution was written at a time when there were no railroads, aviation or electricity generation, nor large financial institutions or corporate bureaucracies. The only sizeable structures were the churches, the army and the navy; the only federal public service named in the constitution was the Post Office.[70] The constitutional principle of responsiveness to the people and the right to have one's cases heard in court (rather than decided by bureaucrats) stood against the growth of administrative and regulatory agencies. But modern innovations in transport, communications, finance, industry and environmental and social protections made it impossible for state and federal governments to avoid greater administration, regulation and extra-judicial determinations. Aggressive business growth, mergers and takeovers produced large monopolistic corporations that could manipulate prices, deceive consumers and exploit workers. Markets that consisted of small competing farmers, manufacturers and retailers became dominated by big business. New mass-production, transport and energy industries needed large enterprises for sheer feasibility. These corporations thrived on economies of scale but often put small competitors out of business by selling at or below cost. Monopoly economic power was as distasteful to Americans as monarchical political power: anticompetitive tactics of large corporations denied people the prosperity and opportunity that the republic promised. This led to a political reaction against monopolies and to the 'trust-busting' politics of the progressive era.[71] But were the existing monopolies to be broken up, nationalised, regulated or simply monitored? Should grievances against them go before the courts, or a public regulatory agency?

The Interstate Commerce Commission was created in 1887 in reaction to malpractice in the railroads. It was 'authorized to declare certain rates unjust and unreasonable' but went further 'to set just and reasonable rates'.[72] It's regarded as the first institution of America's administrative state. The Sherman Antitrust Act 1890 prohibited anticompetitive agreements, conspiracies and monopolies that fixed prices and disadvantaged consumers. Antitrust laws aimed to ensure fair market competition and to protect consumers from unfair or fraudulent practices. Their enforcement had originally been left to the courts. This changed in 1914 with the creation of the Federal Trade Commission, which could proactively conduct investigations, initiate proceedings against unfair or anticompetitive market conduct, issue 'cease and desist' notices to businesses, seek monetary compensation for consumers and prescribe regulations.[73] In response to financial panics, the Federal Reserve was created in 1913. Public administrative bodies were empowered to regulate finance and business, address malpractices in markets, police food hygiene and (if necessary) discipline errant businesses. These agencies of executive government were creating and executing law, or blurring the separation of powers. They shifted how, and by whom, the interests of the people would be advanced – away from elected representatives and courts, towards permanent bodies of unelected experts.[74] Those who believed in the republic's promise of opportunity and prosperity, but were less convinced that 'a day in court' sufficed to uphold citizens' rights, argued that centralised planning and administrative regulation made better government.

Woodrow Wilson

Woodrow Wilson (1856–1924) was a professor of political science who was actively involved in the Democratic Party. He was elected governor of New Jersey in 1910 and then president (1913–21). The 1912 election was dominated by debate over industrial monopolies and antitrust. Former president Theodore Roosevelt (1858–1919) campaigned for a 'New Nationalism' that would have regulated industry through a centralised administrative commission. Wilson's alternative, the 'New Freedom', offered regulation that wouldn't call for centralised administration but would rely instead on the courts for enforcement. As president, however, Wilson 'pursued a course remarkably similar to the New Nationalism that he denounced on the campaign trail'[75] – and, after much legislative wrangling, the laws of 1914, alluded to above, produced a regulatory commission.

As an academic Wilson had written extensively on the United States constitution, inspired by Hegel's historicism and Darwin's theory of evolution. Wilson argued that the constitution reflected the aftermath of anti-monarchical revolution and was a 'living' document: it wasn't eternal and would eventually be superseded. The transition to the next stage would require a leader who would overcome factionalism, fully represent the will of the people and institute a unified and harmonious form of popular self-government. The constitution had become an impediment to such a transformation. Instead, Wilson admired the 'unwritten' British constitution for its openness to change and its dual role for prime ministers as legislators and heads of executive government. He envisaged a strong presidency, less hampered by formal checks and balances, but mindful of public opinion as the true sovereign.[76] In 'The Study of Administration' (1887)[77] he drew a strong distinction between politics and administration. Politicians compete for office, propose policies and approve laws; hired administrators with defined duties put the policies and laws into action. 'Although politics sets the tasks for administration, it should not be suffered to manipulate its offices.'[78] Administration should be guided by sound rules and expertise without being answerable to partisan political actors. For example, once laws and regulations about building standards are passed by elected representatives, it isn't the role of legislators or courts to certify individual building plans: it's put into the hands of impartial experts within 'the administration of government' to execute the will of the state.[79]

Wilson looked favourably at Prussia's efficient administration, save that it must be Americanised to serve the people, not a monarch. A monarchy and a republic had similar kinds of business to perform; their laws made general provisions which administrators applied impartially to particular instances. Administrators, appointed on merit, who executed political will were equally important in France, Prussia and America. In a democracy, however, 'public opinion' is sovereign as if it were 'a multitudinous monarch'. The American people would therefore need to be educated in 'the right opinion'.[80] Public opinion may then be heeded as an 'authoritative critic'; yet it shouldn't be allowed to 'meddle'. Administration, in return, should be given 'conditions of clear-cut responsibility which shall insure trustworthiness', and yet be neither 'domineering' nor 'officious'.[81] Regulation by the state would equalise conditions, but neither interfere in social life nor diminish diversity and vitality. The state should act to realise opportunities for individual autonomy and self-development. The growth of American society and its desire for equal opportunity would stimulate a popular demand for fair administration.[82]

Wilson's 'Administration' was idealised and exhortatory: it wasn't a description of how American government actually worked. His separation of politics and administration was overdrawn, given that the aims and methods of public administration would always be 'political' in the broader sense. Nonetheless, he saw an important practical distinction between elected politicians and career civil servants, even though their separation was (and still is) clearer in Westminster than in Washington, DC.[83]

Administrative science

As public administration lacked clear authorisation in the constitution, the ideal of a science of administration, by association with the natural sciences, boosted the administrative state's 'respectability' with an aura of objective specialised expertise.[84] This borrowed from the Prussian *Wissenschaften*, adapted to American political norms, emphasising the growing duties and objectives of government regarding the welfare of the people and the fairness of economic conditions for labourers and entrepreneurs. Treating public administration as a science promoted practices that were business-like and which aimed for economy and efficiency. The 'scientific management' of Frederick Winslow Taylor (1856–1915) had been popular in the United States in the late nineteenth and early twentieth centuries. Taylor argued that a systematic analysis of tasks and training of workers would lead to greater industrial efficiency and economic prosperity for all. His methods were initially applied to heavy manual labour, but he argued that they could also be used in government departments.[85] And indeed scientific management found its way into public administration from about 1910.[86] Hence the idea of an administrative science gained further credibility by association with concepts that were prevalent in industrial management and engineering. These new 'sciences' also studied the structures of organisations.[87] Large, geographically distributed organisations with paper-based records and communications needed clear chains of command and delegations within hierarchical bureaucratic structures, in private industry and government. Hence public administration emerged as a science and a profession.

The stock market crash of 1929, however, undermined the idea that government should model itself on business, and stimulated a new wave of economic regulation. The New Deal initiated by Democratic President Franklin D. Roosevelt (1882–1945; Pres. 1933–45) responded to the profound social and economic distress of the Great Depression. It comprised laws and programmes for social security, economic stimulus and job creation – although it didn't overturn fundamental class, gender or racial injustices. The growth of public administration wasn't an aim in itself, but 'the sheer scale of the [New Deal's] legislation and the proliferation of agencies meant a vastly increased bureaucracy.'[88] There are differing views about whether this was an evolutionary enlargement of the achievements of the progressive era or a more profound change. In any case, FDR's vision for an administrative state under a strengthened presidency led to showdowns with Congress (which sought political control of agencies) and with the Supreme Court (which ruled against some new laws on constitutional grounds).[89] But compassionate policies called for a large cohort of dispassionate professionals; experts, often recently graduated, were hired for planning and implementation. The achievement of objectives such as full employment or disease control necessitated governmental action through enlarged bureaucracies. The heritage of American confidence in 'natural' liberty as the source of prosperity was overtaken by expertly planned and administered civic and social improvement. Governmental practises and norms were to be operationally de-fined, measured and evaluated; regularities were to be discovered, resulting in 'reliable knowledge'.[90]

The claim that objective facts and tested methods could be employed effi-ciently to meet determinate ends didn't go unchallenged, however. Dwight Waldo (1913–2000) brought democratic theory back into the debate. He ob-served that the study of public administration had become imbued with 'an almost limitless confidence in whatever bears the label of Science' and a belief 'that morality is irrelevant'.[91] Whereas the Chinese had thought that good gov-ernment required virtuous men, Americans had proposed to remove politics and morality from public administration in favour of impersonal measurement, effi-ciency and expertise. But Waldo noted that this separation from politics was in itself political, being a product of progressive-era ideas.

Public policy

The term 'public policy' was traditionally used in English common law,[92] but expanded to refer to all the practical things that governments do, from goal-setting to legislation to implementation. Public policy also became a branch of academic political science and then a discipline in its own right. The Cold War era witnessed expanding social and economic policy – but also nuclear weapons, the fearful potential of which challenged any 'limitless confidence' in science as a force for good. Leading American scholar Harold Lasswell (1902–78) tem-pered applied social science, or the policy sciences, with a democratic concern for society's values (its 'objects of desire') and real-world decision-making. Concerns about the power dynamics and influences affecting decision-making stimulated the study of (formal and informal) policy *processes*, with the aim of making them more democratic. Lasswell asked how political scientists could 'improve the like-lihood of contributing to the decision process at every level, from the neigh-bourhood to the world as a whole.' Their task was more than technocratic: it was 'to project a comprehensive image of the future' and to clarify 'the fundamental goal values of the body politic'.[93] The growing academic discipline of public policy should train professionals who would mediate between policy scientists and policy practitioners. Charles Lindblom (1917–2018) observed that com-plexity and resource constraints meant that policy formulation couldn't achieve comprehensive scientific analyses of all relevant variables and risk factors. Nor could beneficial ends and appropriate means of policy be linked with certainty. Policymaking was instead a 'science of muddling through' – an imprecise and incremental process.[94] Decision-making occurred through consensus-building based on comparisons between the limited options available. In real life, impor-tant possibilities got neglected and information was lacking; organisational and public decision-making processes were messy and not so rational. Hence the idea of an administrative *science* gave way to efforts to understand, professionalise and democratise policy-making *practices* – or public policy.

The 1960s and 1970s saw another wave of regulation and bureaucracy-building to promote wider public values such as health and safety, non-discrimination and environmental protection. Presidents were frustrated, however, in their efforts to steer their massive and diverse administration. Public agencies developed their own inertia; they became 'captured' by the professionals they employed and the industries they regulated; they weren't sufficiently responsive to the public interest or to those they were supposed to serve. Urban planning disasters attracted critical attention and hence scepticism about rational policymaking. Jane Jacobs's *The Death and Life of Great American Cities* (1961) validated, as an alternative, the spontaneous social interaction and *un*planned development of cohesive and diversified neighbourhoods.[95] Political movements and legal actions fought for greater accountability and responsiveness in agencies' decision-making processes.[96] Claims about 'value-free' scientific and technical rationality failed to persuade protestors, politicians and judges to leave public administration to the technocrats. Scientific methods and economic models were still useful for calculative, evidence-based modelling and evaluation, and academic literature in public policy developed rational-looking models of policy processes. But public decision-making is inherently grounded in, and aims to satisfy, publicly shared values.[97] Policymakers were confronted by the complexity, intractability and uncertainty of 'wicked problems'[98] and by the limitations of organisational rationality and human information processing. Political controversies erupted over taxation, redistribution and market regulation; the Vietnam War and the Watergate scandal eroded trust in government.[99] 'Big government' and its bureaucrats thus became sitting ducks for the 'new right' of the 1980s.[100] As an economic (rather than political) analysis of public services developed, it was argued that, in the interests of efficiency, responsiveness and the equitable distribution of taxes and benefits, 'a better government would be a smaller government'.[101] It was easy then for Ronald Reagan (Pres., 1981–89) to get applause for saying that Americans needed less government[102] – without mentioning who would be made worse off. In practice, though, the managerial reforms for efficiency and market-like competition in public services only proliferated form-filling and centralised bureaucratic controls, as 'strategic planning' and 'accountability' resolved themselves into paper-based, or now online, information-gathering – often serving obscure purposes if any.

Conclusion

New technologies change the ways in which we distribute information and work together. They can't eliminate the administrative state; they do transform it with new capabilities. Digital technologies have created new means for state surveillance, regulation and control that reach further and deeper into our lives than ever. One's location, activities, relationships, personal interests and political opinions can be monitored, and one's choices and preferences can be manipulated more routinely than in the past. In turn, the internet itself needs to be governed, and debate rages over how best to do so. As in the past, the Chinese lead. China's social credit system is a 'state surveillance infrastructure' that collects and analyses data from many government agencies and private organisations (notably Alibaba) to assess the trustworthiness of individuals and to reward and punish by determining who may or may not have access to certain public and commercial services.[103] One survey shows a high level of public approval of the social credit system, as it promotes trust (or obedience) in society. Benefits for individuals can include access to credit, fast-tracked services and a boost on dating sites.[104] Online social media profiling for commercial purposes, or surveillance capitalism,[105] and covert digital surveillance by state agencies[106] are well known in the west too. But China's social credit is an overt state system that seeks to govern personal trustworthiness and to produce social order. The era of big-data analytics means that government reaches even more deeply into everyday life and subjectivity.

Bureaucracy was once a positive advance on the old systems of patronage and favouritism in which officials held office due to pedigree, status, sycophancy or private deals. Bureaucracy improved fair and impersonal implementation of policy, leading to a more just distribution of costs and benefits among citizens. The ideal of a value-free science of administration, driven by technical expertise and isolated from the political fray, was illusory, but the arts of government have benefited from bureaucratic organisation. There are also limits to the usefulness of bureaucratic government, beyond which we should allow for creativity, experimentation, failure and unpredictability. But today we witness a new form of technocratic government by organised and impersonal systems that require neither enclosure within offices nor fixed hierarchies. The prospect of constant surveillance of otherwise 'free' subjects is enabled by digital technologies; it constitutes the biggest single problem that government itself now poses.

Notes

1 Gerth, Mills, & Weber, 2009.
2 'Individual nobles were sometimes prominent in public affairs, but the nobility as a group was not an influential element in government.' Hucker, 1998, p. 29.
3 Ibid. p. 75
4 Ibid., p. 14, italics added.
5 Ibid.; Finer, 1999, vol. II.
6 Twitchett & Grimm, 1988, p. 326.
7 Ibid.
8 Lee & Wiles, 2014, pp. 580–81.
9 Tsai, 1996.
10 Hucker, 1998, p. 24.
11 Atwell, 1988, pp. 606–14.
12 For insight into palace intrigues, see Huang, 1981.
13 Hucker, 1998; Keay, 2011; Roberts, 2018.
14 Hucker, 1998.
15 By comparison, the OECD reports that an average of about 18 percent of workforces (not total population) are employed in 'general government'.

16 Huang, 1998.
17 From historical estimates of one province: 'An average prefect would, in theory, have supervised some 600,000 people occupying some 10,000 square miles, and one of his subordinate county magistrates would have governed some 90,000 people spread across a jurisdiction of some 1,300 square miles.' Hucker, 1998, p. 15.
18 Finer, 1999, vol. II.
19 The Four Books consist of two important texts from the ancient *Book of Rites*, the *Analects* of Confucius, and the dialogues of Mencius. The Five Classics consist of a collection of classical poetry, a collection of writings of ancient rulers and officials, a description of ancient rites, the *I Ching* or *Book of Changes*, and the *Spring and Autumn Annals*, which record the history of the State of Lu.
20 Hucker, 1998, p. 33.
21 Hucker, 1998; Finer, 1999, vol. II.
22 Huang, 1981 recounts palace politics and ritual under the Wanli emperor (r. 1573–1620).
23 Hucker, 1998.
24 Huang, 1981, pp. 51–2.
25 Gerth, Mills & Weber, 2009.
26 The Prince-Electors of the HRE were members of the college that elected the Holy Roman Emperor. By the seventeenth century, however, this normally meant confirmation of the Austrian Habsburg emperor.
27 Mercantilist trade policy seeks to prevent exportation of natural resources and protect domestic industries from foreign competition. Trade is seen as a zero-sum game; a country should export more than it imports and maintain a positive inflow of bullion.
28 Silesia is today the south-western part of Poland that borders the Czech Republic.
29 Clark, 2006; Davies, 2011; Dwyer, 2013; Turk, 1999.
30 The name comes from 'jung Herr', or 'young lord', after medieval noblemen who were granted lands in return for military services. Clark, 2006, pp. 155–6.
31 Ibid., p. 161.
32 Ibid., p. 164.
33 Ibid., p. 149.
34 Finer, 1999, vol. III, p. 1360.
35 Clark, 2006, pp. 111–14.
36 Ibid., pp. 153–4.
37 Ibid., p. 86.
38 Scott, 2013.
39 Schulze, 2013, p. 205.
40 'We see, therefore, that war is not merely an act of policy but a true political instrument, a continuation of political intercourse, carried on with other means.' Clausewitz, 1993 [1832], p. 99.
41 Adapted from: Foucault, 1995, pp. 168–9.
42 Finer, 1999, vol. III, p. 1367.
43 Scott, 2013, p. 199.
44 Tribe, 1995.
45 Today we might call it public policy and administration.
46 Seppel, 2017.
47 In 1680 Frederick William acquired the small fort of Friedrichsburg (in today's Ghana) and engaged in colonial trade (including slavery) and privateering. But the fort was sold to the Dutch in 1721. Clark, 2006, pp. 41 and 93.
48 Magnusson, 2017, p. 30.
49 By the 1750s, 'forestry was becoming a *Wissenschaft* imagined alongside cameralism, and would in subsequent decades follow it into the university.' Warde, 2017, p. 131.
50 'Cameralism posed new questions for the development of the modern state: the abolition of serfdom, concern for public health, schooling, the regulation of internal

security and "good police", actualisation of popular welfare, and the establishment of insurance companies.' Seppel, 2017, p. 16.

51 Wakefield, 2009.
52 Tribe, 1995.
53 Foucault, 1995, p. 214, abridged.
54 Clark, 2006, p. 340.
55 Tribe, 1995, 2003.
56 Smith, 1999, Book IV, p. 17.
57 'In the [1770s], if you except the King of Prussia, to accumulate treasure seems to be no part of the policy of European princes.' Ibid., p. 18.
58 Alexander Hamilton, in Jay et al., 2008, p. 11. Much 'accident and force', including slavery and war, surrounded this fine idea.
59 The Constitution of the United States, II, 2.
60 Chervinsky, 2020.
61 A dismissal controversy underlay the articles of impeachment of President Andrew Johnson in 1868.
62 Postell, 2017, p. 137.
63 Ibid.
64 Banerjee, 2020.
65 Report on the Organisation of the Permanent Civil Service, presented to both Houses of Parliament, 1854. See pp. 4 and 7.
66 Lowe, 2011.
67 'To the victor belong the spoils': New York Senator William L. Marcy in 1832 referring to the election of Andrew Jackson.
68 Leonard White, cited in Postells, 2017, p. 338; see also Roberts, 2009.
69 Goodnow, 2017 [1900], p. 91.
70 The Post Office's inter-state network also made it an instrument for censorship. The Comstock Law of 1873 (named after the anti-vice campaigner Anthony Comstock) criminalised the use of the postal services for the distribution of any sexual information or related items, including birth-control advice. Comstock was employed as a special agent for the Post Office, suborning this vital public service to a conservative moral campaign. Gerstle and Runciman, 2019.
71 From the 1890s to the 1920s.
72 Postell, 2017, p. 160.
73 Winerman, 2003.
74 By this progressive-era doctrine, 'the court does not substitute its judgement [on either the facts or the law] for that of the agency but merely ensures that the agency followed a minimal standard of rationality.' Postell, 2017, p. 214. The courts could still exercise a limited judicial review of departmental actions, to test their reasonableness, but they deferred to the regulators.
75 Postell, 2017, p. 190.
76 Wilson, 2002 [1908].
77 Wilson, 1887. This article has been described as 'the single most important text at the beginning of an academic discipline in America': Thorsen, 2014, p. 118. An article of its kind would probably not be accepted by a peer-reviewed academic journal today, due to its lack of sound empirical or theoretical basis.
78 Wilson, 1887, p. 210. Or, as Frank J. Goodnow (1859–1939) put it: 'Politics has to do with policies or expressions of the state will. Administration has to do with the execution of these policies.' Goodnow, 2017 [1900], p. 18.
79 Goodnow, 2017 [1900], p. 75.
80 Wilson, 1887, pp. 207–8.
81 Ibid., pp. 213–16.
82 Thorsen, 2014.
83 It was estimated in 2018 that a presidential transition nowadays makes 'more than 4,000 presidential appointments, over 1,100 of which require Senate confirmation.'

See the Partnership for Public Service/Boston Consulting Group, 2018, Presidential Transition Guide, p. 3, at URL: https://presidentialtransition.org/wp-content/uploads/sites/6/2018/01/Presidential-Transition-Guide-2018.pdf.

84 Thorsen, 2014, p. 120.

85 Taylor, 2005 [1911].

86 Waldo, 2007 [1948], p. 9.

87 Gulick & Urwick, 2005 [1937].

88 Venn, 1998, p. 68, abridged.

89 'The battle over executive reorganization, which pitted FDR against Congress over political control of the administrative state, was followed by a different conflict between Roosevelt and the lawyers who sought to place the administrative state under legal constraints imposed through judicial review.' Postell, 2017, p. 218.

90 Thompson, 1956.

91 Waldo, 2007 [1948], pp. 20, 23.

92 'The [judicial] doctrine of public policy is commonly invoked when a legal act is deemed to violate a rudimentary public interest.' Ghodoosi, 2015, p. 690. See also: Lowi, 2003.

93 Lasswell, 1956, p. 19.

94 Lindblom, 1959.

95 Jacobs, 1992 [1961].

96 Postell, 2017.

97 Botterill & Fenna, 2019.

98 Rittell & Webber, 1973.

99 Pew Research Center, 2019.

100 This was in spite of evidence that America's public services had in fact 'significantly decreased over the last 50 years', and weren't over-sized compared to other countries. Hill, 2020.

101 Niskanen, 1971, p. 227.

102 'The nine most terrifying words in the English language are: I'm from the Government, and I'm here to help.' Reagan, 12 August, 1986. See URL: https://www.reaganfoundation.org/ronald-reagan/reagan-quotes-speeches/news-conference-1/

103 Liang et al., 2018.

104 Kostka, 2019. Meanwhile, India is developing a biometrics-based identification system, including a card with a unique number, to prove identity and place of residence: Rao & Nair, 2019.

105 Zuboff, 2015.

106 Greenwald, 2014.

References

Atwell, William. 1988. 'The T'ai-ch'ang, T'ien-ch'i, and Ch'ung-chen reigns, 1620–1644.' In *The Cambridge History of China, Volume 7, The Ming Dynasty, 1368—1644, Part I*, by Frederick Mote and Denis Twitchett, 585–640. Cambridge: Cambridge University Press.

Banerjee, Sukanya. 2020. 'Writing Bureaucracy, Bureaucratic Writing: Charles Dickens, Little Dorrit, and Mid-Victorian Liberalism.' *Nineteenth-Century Literature* 75 (2): 133–58.

Botterill, Linda Courtenay, and Alan Fenna. 2019. *Interrogating Public Policy Theory: A Political Values Perspective*. Cheltenham, Gloucestershire: Edward Elgar.

Chervinsky, Lindsay M. 2020. *The Cabinet: George Washington and the Creation of an American Institution*. Cambridge, MA: Belknap Press.

Clark, Christopher. 2006. *Iron Kingdom: The Rise and Downfall of Prussia, 1600–1947*. Cambridge, MA: Harvard University Press.

Clausewitz, Carl von. 1993. *On War.* New York, NY: Alfred A. Knopf.

Davies, Norman. 2011. *Vanished Kingdoms: The History of Half-Forgotten Europe.* London: Penguin.

Dwyer, Philip G. 2013. *The Rise of Prussia: 1700–1830.* London: Routledge.

Finer, Samuel Edmund. 1999. *The History of Government.* Oxford: Oxford University Press.

Foucault, Michel. 1995. *Discipline and Punish: The Birth of the Prison.* New York, NY: Vintage Books.

Gerstle, Gary, and David Runciman. 2019. 'Pornography and the Post Office.' *Talking Politics.* December 26. Accessed December 2019. https://www.talkingpoliticspodcast.com/blog/2019/210-pornography-and-the-post-office.

Gerth, Heinrich, C. Wright Mills, and Max Weber. 2009. *From Max Weber.* London: Routledge.

Ghodoosi, Farshad. 2015. 'The Concept of Public Policy in Law: Revisiting the Role of the Public Policy Doctrine in the Enforcement of Private Legal Arrangements.' *Nebraska Law Review* 94 (3): 685–736.

Goodnow, Frank J. 2017. *Politics and Administration: A Study in Government.* New York, NY: Routledge.

Greenwald, Glenn. 2014. *No Place to Hide: Edward Snowden, the NSA, and the U.S. Surveillance State.* New York, NY: Metropolitan Books.

Gulick, Luther, and Lyndall Urwick. 2005. *Papers on the Science of Administration.* London: Routledge.

Hill, Fiona. 2020. 'Public Service and the Federal Government.' *Policy 2020: Brookings.* May 27. Accessed July 11, 2020. https://www.brookings.edu/policy2020/votervital/public-service-and-the-federal-government/.

Huang, Ray. 1981. *1587: A Year of No Significance.* New Haven, CT: Yale University Press.

———. 1998. 'The Ming Fiscal Administration.' In *The Cambridge History of China, Volume 8, The Ming Dynasty, 1368 – 1644, Part 2,* by Denis Twitchett and Frederick Mote, 106–71. Cambridge: Cambridge University Press.

Hucker, Charles. 1998. 'Ming Government.' In *The Cambridge History of China, Volume 8, The Ming Dynasty, 1368 – 1644, Part 2,* by Denis Twitchett and Frederick Mote, 9–105. Cambridge: Cambridge University Press.

Jacobs, Jane. 1992. *The Death and Life of Great American Cities.* New York, NY: Vintage Books.

Jay, John, Lawrence Goldman, Alexander Hamilton, and James Madison. 2008. *The Federalist Papers.* Oxford: Oxford University Press.

Keay, John. 2011. *China: A History.* New York, NY: Basic Books.

Kostka, Genia. 2019. 'China's Social Credit Systems and Public Opinion: Explaining High Levels of Approval.' *New Media & Society* 21 (7): 1565–93.

Lasswell, Harold D. 1956. 'The Political Science of Science: An Inquiry into the Possible Reconciliation of Mastery and Freedom.' *The American Political Science Review* 50 (4): 961–79.

Lee, Lily Xiao Hong, and Sue Wiles. 2014. *Biographical Dictionary of Chinese Women.* Armonk, NY: M.E. Sharpe.

Liang, Fan, Vishnupriya Das, Nadiya Kostyuk, and Muzammil M. Hussain. 2018. 'Constructing a Data-Driven Society: China's Social Credit System as a State Surveillance Infrastructure.' *Policy & Internet* 10 (4): 415–53.

Lindblom, Charles E. 1959. 'The Science of "Muddling Through".' *Public Administration Review* 19 (2): 79–88.

Lowe, Rodney. 2011. *The Official History of the British Civil Service: Reforming the Civil Service, Volume 1: The Fulton years, 1966–81.* London: Routledge.

Lowi, Theodore J. 2003. 'Law Vs. Public Policy: A Critical Exploration.' *Cornell Journal of Law & Public Policy,* 12: 493.

Magnusson, Lars. 2017. 'Comparing Cameralisms: The Case of Sweden and Prussia.' In *Cameralism in Practice: State Administration and Economy in Early Modern Europe,* by Marten Seppel and Keith Tribe, 17–38. Woodbridge: Boydell Press.

Niskanen, William A. 1971. *Bureaucracy and Representative Government.* New York, NY: Transaction.

Pew Research Center. 2019. 'Public Trust in Government: 1958–2019.' *Pew Research Center.* April 11. Accessed July 2020. https://www.pewresearch.org/politics/2019/04/11/public-trust-in-government-1958-2019/.

Postell, Joseph. 2017. *Bureaucracy in America: The Administrative State's Challenge to Constitutional Government.* Columbia: University of Missouri.

Rao, Ursula, and Vijayanka Nair. 2019. 'Aadhaar: Governing with Biometrics.' *South Asia: Journal of South Asian Studies* 42 (3): 469–81.

Rittel, Horst W.J., and Melvin M. Webber. 1973. 'Dilemmas in a General Theory of Planning.' *Policy Sciences* 4 (2): 155–69.

Roberts, Alasdair. 2009. 'The Path Not Taken: Leonard White and the Macrodynamics of Administrative Development.' *Public Administration Review* 69 (4): 764–75.

Roberts, J.A.G. 2018. 'China: The Ming 1368–1644.' In *The Great Empires of Asia,* by Jim Masselos, 53–77. London: Thames & Hudson.

Schulze, Hagen. 2013. 'The Prussian Military State, 1763–1806.' In *The Rise of Prussia: 1700–1830,* by Philip G. Dwyer, 201–19. London: Routledge.

Scott, H.M. 2013. '1763–1786: The Second Reign of Frederick the Great?' In *The Rise of Prussia: 1700–1830,* by Philip G Dwyer, 177–200. London: Routledge.

Seppel, Marten. 2017. 'Introduction: Cameralism in Practice.' In *Cameralism in Practice: State Administration and Economy in Early Modern Europe,* by Marten Seppel and Keith Tribe, 1–16. Woodbridge: Boydell & Brewer.

Smith, Adam. 1999. *The Wealth of Nations.* London: Penguin.

Taylor, Frederick Winslow. 2005. *The Principles of Scientific Management.* Auckland: Floating Press.

Thompson, James D. 1956. 'On Building an Administrative Science.' *Administrative Science Quarterly* 1 (1): 102–11.

Thorsen, Niels Aage. 2014. *The Political Thought of Woodrow Wilson, 1875–1910.* Princeton, NJ: Princeton University Press.

Tribe, Keith. 2003. 'Historical Schools of Economics: German and English.' In *A Companion to the History of Economic Thought,* by Warren Samuels, Jeff Biddle and John Davis, 215–30. Malden MA: Blackwell.

———. 1995. *Strategies of Economic Order: German Economic Discourse 1750–1950.* Cambridge: Cambridge University Press.

Tsai, Shih-shan Henry. 1996. *The Eunuchs in the Ming Dynasty.* Albany: State University of New York Press.

Turk, Eleanor L. 1999. *The History of Germany.* Westport, CT: Greenwood Press.

Twitchett, Denis, and T. Grimm. 1988. 'The Cheng-t'ung, Ching-t'ai, and T'len-shun reigns, 1436–1464.' In *The Cambridge History of China, Volume 7, The Ming Dynasty, 1368—1644, Part I,* by Frederick Mote and Denis Twitchett, 305–42. Cambridge: Cambridge University Press.

Venn, Fiona. 1998. *The New Deal.* Edinburgh: Edinburgh University Press.

Wakefield, Andre. 2009. *The Disordered Police State: German Cameralism as Science and Practice*. Chicago, IL: Chicago University Press.

Waldo, Dwight. 2007. *The Administrative State*. New York, NY: Routledge.

Warde, Paul. 2017. 'Cameralist Writing in the Mirror of Practice: The Long Development of Forestry in Germany.' In *Cameralism in Practice State Administration and Economy in Early Modern Europe*, by Marten Seppel and Keith Tribe, 111–31. Woodbridge: Boydell Press.

Wilson, Woodrow. 2002. *Constitutional Government in the United States*. New York, NY: Routledge.

———. 1887. 'The Study of Administration.' *Political Science Quarterly* 2 (2): 197–222.

Winerman, Marc. 2003. 'The Origins of the FTC: Concentration, Cooperation, Control, and Competition.' *Antitrust Law Journal* 71: 1–97.

Zuboff, Shoshana. 2015. 'Big Other: Surveillance Capitalism and the Prospects of an Information Civilization.' *Journal of Information Technology* 30 (1): 75–89.

9

ENDS AND LIMITS OF GOVERNMENT

The twentieth century

The early twentieth century saw the end of hereditary monarchy – a form of government that had predominated since the earliest states. The last Chinese emperor abdicated in 1912; the Romanov, Hohenzollern, Habsburg and Osman (Ottoman) dynasties ended with or soon after World War I. Most hereditary monarchs who remained in place were restricted to constitutional and ceremonial roles, with little or no executive power. Instead, there arose dictatorships and representative governments – the former sometimes arising within the latter.

Questions that underlay the great conflicts of the twentieth century included: 'What should be the aim and scope of the government of industrialised society?' and, 'Should social and economic progress be rationally planned by government, or should government only maintain a framework of laws?' The principal models at stake were communist, fascist and liberal-democratic. The latter permitted the greatest freedom of action for capitalist enterprise, of which Karl Marx (1818–83) had been the leading critic. A social-democratic compromise emerged in western democracies, however, in response to the Great Depression of the early thirties, and flourished during the Cold War. It regulated capitalism and defended it ideologically against communist and fascist rivals. After revisiting Marx in 1848, this chapter begins with the Russian revolution of 1917, which instantiated anti-capitalist communist rule but led to dictatorship; it ends with the 2008 global financial crisis and the 2020 pandemic, which punctuate the decline of the late-twentieth century's neoliberal model.

Part 1: Soviet communism

First there was a theory, then came the practice, but the two bore little resemblance to one another. The theorist, Karl Marx, wasn't in favour of centralised

DOI: 10.4324/9781003166955-9

government: 'The executive of the modern state is but a committee for managing the common affairs of the whole bourgeoisie.'[1] The forces of the state defended the property of the rich and oppressed those with nothing to sell but labour-time. Ideological falsification made workers believe that the capitalist order was 'natural' or 'inevitable'. For example, if you're objectively overworked and underpaid, and you say it's because you didn't try hard enough to get ahead, then it appears you've fallen for those 'ruling ideas' that focus on individual merit rather than political economy. You haven't yet identified with a class of similarly exploited workers. To critically understand this falsification, Marx observed that the capitalist mode of production was neither natural nor inevitable: it had a history with a beginning, a middle and hence one day an end.

Anything of economic value is produced by physical and mental labour. According to Marx, the historical development of capitalism entailed alienation of labour in four basic ways. First, labourers produce things that others will own and exchange for profit, rather than things that they use for their own benefit or share with others. They can't see the process through to the final product, nor can they see its exchange-value in the market. Second, most labourers must work under the orders of others, so they don't control their own labour-process. Third, mass industrial work tends to be individualised and competitive, so the labourers are socially divided as a class or alienated from one another. And fourth, workers are alienated from themselves, or from the fulfilment of their own potential as productive and creative beings. Their labour-power is reduced to a mere commodity. Slaves could clearly see the ways in which they were exploited; the modern industrial labourer's exploitation is concealed by the wage-relation, or 'wage slavery'. Given the dreadful conditions suffered by the working-class in nineteenth-century industrial cities, compared with the power of employers and the excessive wealth of the owners of capital, it was reasonable to think that this mode of production had created a conflict between the property-less proletariat and the propertied bourgeoisie that was destined to explode into revolution and social transformation.[2]

Marx never fully explored what a post-capitalist epoch would be like. But if capitalism normalised property, and yet the labouring class lacked property, then the dialectical outcome would be the normalisation of 'propertylessness' – or an end to private property itself. And then production would be 'concentrated in the hands of a vast association of the whole nation'. To get there, the proletariat would realise itself as a class and sweep away by force the bourgeoisie, its mode of production and the very conditions for class conflict. The proletariat would *temporarily* act as a ruling class to seize the forces of production, but it would 'thereby have abolished its own supremacy as a class.'[3] The state would self-destruct; workers would take control of the factories. Marx and his co-author Friedrich Engels (1820–95) hoped that abolition of private property and inheritance rights would result from the uprisings that swept Europe in 1848. That didn't happen. But they also called for progressive income tax, a state-owned central bank, free

public education for children and abolition of child labour, all of which did become normal policy, even in capitalist countries.

The Soviet Union

The communist revolution in Russia (1917) was geographically misplaced, however. Proletarian uprising was expected to occur in the most advanced industrial
capitalist economies, whereas Russia was a largely agrarian, peasant-based society with little heavy industry. The Russian revolution was led by a 'vanguard'
party of intellectuals and political agitators; it wasn't an overwhelming and spontaneous movement of the proletariat. It was expected that revolution would soon
follow in Germany and England. In the post-war chaos of 1919 there were communist uprisings in Germany, but they were violently suppressed, and Russia
was left isolated. Moreover, the Russian Bolshevik – or Communist – Party that
seized power had to contend with a severe post-war slump in agricultural and
industrial output, four subsequent years of civil war, and invasions by foreign
forces determined to wipe Bolshevism out. So the early years of communist rule
necessitated emergency measures. The use of terrorism to defeat enemies, traitors
and rival socialist parties, political centralisation and strict discipline within one
ruling party were deemed essential for the government to survive and achieve
stability.[4]

The word *soviet* is Russian for 'council', and there were local soviets that
during the civil war retained political power and even declared themselves independent. But Russia had a long past of bureaucratic and authoritarian rule, with
only weak forms of popular representation or participation. So centralisation
reinstated a familiar political culture as the soviets came under party control.
They were made financially dependent on, and were required to carry out the
orders of, the central party-state apparatus. The Union of Soviet Socialist Republics (USSR) was founded in 1922, based on a treaty between the republics to
form a federal system that recognised ethno-national differences. The Bolsheviks
'supported the development of non-Russian territories and downplayed Russian
institutions, hoping to create a centralised, multi-ethnic, anti-imperial, socialist
state.'[5] All the republics would be subject to party control, however, and when
the 1924 constitution was approved, authority was centred in Moscow. Nonetheless, the Communist Party's policy of indigenisation meant an ethnically diverse organisation not entirely dominated by Russians. A family code of 1918
commenced the equal recognition of women (extended in 1926), even though it
wasn't welcomed by a majority of women, least of all in Muslim Central Asia.[6]
The Orthodox Church was forcibly separated from the state. Meanwhile, the
Communist Party sought to promote an idealised version of a privileged class of
workers.

Peasant rebellions against grain acquisitions and workers' strikes during the
civil war convinced the communist leaders to relax some policies. The New

Economic Policy (NEP) of 1921 permitted limited forms of private property and commerce, effectively delaying the advent of socialism, especially in the countryside. This addressed the difficulties encountered during the civil war but was accompanied by a famine that lasted until 1923 and took five million lives. The head of government, Vladimir Lenin (1870–1924), defended this pause on the way to socialism on the grounds of securing grain supplies needed for industrialisation. In turn, the potential for mechanisation in large-scale agricultural cooperatives would lure peasants into collectivised farms, rather than traditional labour-intensive agriculture on the small plots allotted to them from the estates of pre-revolution landowners. After Lenin died, however, debate raged about how long the NEP should last. And despite Lenin's disapproval, Joseph Stalin (1878–1953), a Georgian who spoke Russian with a thick accent, succeeded him as leader.

A one-party parliamentary state

The constitution of 1924 confirmed the federal system. Within the Soviet Union, 'each member Republic exerts its public powers independently'. The federal powers of the Union were largely what one would expect (foreign relations, currency, basic laws, etc.), but they included a 'general plan of the national economy' which in practice meant a command economy.[7] The sovereign assembly was the Congress of Soviets, consisting of urban and provincial representatives, but weighted in favour of the cities and towns by a factor of five. The local soviets directly elected representatives to the congress which, in turn, elected from among its members the two legislative bodies: the Council of the Union and the Council of Nationalities. The latter consisted of representatives from the republics (five members each) and associated republics (one each). Together the Council of the Union and the Council of Nationalities formed a bicameral legislature known (confusingly) as the Central Executive Committee of the USSR, with 371 members.[8] The supreme Congress of Soviets also elected a Presidium, the president of which was head of state, and a small ministerial body called the Council of People's Commissars, the chair of which was premier, and which was 'the highest executive and administrative agency of the state.'[9] The president was constitutional head of state, but this post was never occupied by either Lenin or Stalin.

The USSR looked on paper like a representative democracy – except that only one party was permitted, and the Communist Party of the Soviet Union (CPSU) effectively ruled by determining policy, understood as 'democratic centralism'. Given that there was a single party, one asks why people willingly voted for representatives to the Congress of Soviets. There was no alternative, and hence no conscientious consent. But competing parties were seen as factions undermining the state and dividing popular opinion. The claim that the Soviet state was 'democratic' relied on the conviction that 'the party represented the people as a whole, and not merely an interest-group or social elite.'[10] The CPSU had begun as an underground movement, always in danger from the Tsarist police, and had gained power under wartime conditions. From the start, there was limited time and toleration for democratic debate. Once a decision was made, centralised control and party discipline were matters of survival, and factionalism was severely punished.

To understand the real power structure, therefore, we have to understand the party (the CPSU) more than the parliamentary system. The relationship between the party and the constitutional organs of state was obscure but favoured the party. The Congress of the CPSU was in principle the party's supreme decision-making body, but the power structure became increasingly top-down. The Congress first convened in 1898, and annually from 1917 to 1925, but thereafter less frequently, just once every five years. The number of delegates varied, growing from a few hundred to nearly 5000. Party congresses elected the Central Committee of the CPSU, which held full authority over the party between congresses and consisted of about 70 top officials. From 1917 the Central Committee had a small secretariat that kept things running. The first technical secretary was Elena Stasova (1873–1966), a revolutionary or old Bolshevik who was close to Lenin and one of the few women to hold a senior post.[11] This position was renamed responsible secretary in 1919 when the Congress created a political bureau (politburo), originally of five members including Lenin and Stalin, to decide on urgent matters that couldn't await the central committee. The responsible secretary gained the right to attend politburo meetings in 1921 when the post was held by Vyacheslav Molotov (1890–1986). It was renamed general secretary in 1922 when Joseph Stalin took it, giving him bureaucratic control of party appointments and meeting agendas.[12] From technical administrative origins, then, the party's general secretary usurped effective leadership of the Soviet Union. Stalin retained the title until he died, and all his successors held it.

Dictatorship

Stalin's rise from being one member of a team of top party officials to dictator was neither guaranteed nor rapid. It was entangled with controversies about the survival of the revolution and the implementation of socialist policies, and with factional and interpersonal power struggles. But Stalin eliminated rivals, switched allegiances and promoted sycophantic followers. At stake were two fundamental policy issues: the viability of socialism in one country and the fate of the NEP. Stalin's main rival, the war commissar Leon Trotsky (1879–1940), advocated permanent international revolution; he opposed the bureaucratisation of the party and the NEP's toleration of small-scale capitalism. He argued that socialism couldn't survive while surrounded by hostile capitalist nations; hence revolution should be fomented in the advanced industrial countries. He was expelled from the politburo in 1926, forced into exile in 1929 and murdered in 1940. Stalin wasn't opposed to the international socialist revolution but wanted the Soviet Union to plan to go it alone – or 'socialism in one country'. He aligned himself for the time being with Nikolai Bukharin (1888–1938), editor of the official newspaper *Pravda* (Truth), who was against rapid industrialisation at the expense of the peasants and who supported continuation of the NEP. From 1928 Stalin and his supporters ('whose ascent owed much to Stalin's patronage'[13]) did an about-turn and repudiated the NEP. A drop in grain supply convinced them that the relatively wealthy peasants, the *kulaks*, were hoarding in anticipation of higher prices. Stalin set off to requisition grain and then imposed collectivisation of agriculture and rapid industrialisation – with unrealistic production targets. The 'rightist' faction who opposed this, including Bukharin, were expelled in 1929. This was 'effectively the end of NEP [and] Stalin now had complete control over the central leadership of the party.'[14]

The rise of Stalin and his faction utilised his command over the party apparatus, his ability to undermine opponents and foster sycophants, and his policies on the economic crisis.[15] Determined to build a socialist society, Stalin forcibly collectivised farms and deported peasants to slave labour or prison-camps, knowing that millions were dying. Collectivisation was accompanied by poor weather, and by mid-1932, 'famine spanned a wide belt running from the Polish border into Siberia', taking with it five to seven million lives.[16] Stalin blamed mass-starvation in Ukraine on local maladministration and official cowardice. He blamed failures to meet industrial targets on saboteurs, who deserved liquidation. Meanwhile, he enjoyed a fine life and made policy by decree.[17] But demotion, expulsion, arrest, interrogation, show trial and execution became the constant fears of anyone who might be accused of conspiracies against the state or Stalin, or of sabotaging socialist progress. During the great purge of 1937–38, 'nearly 766,000 individuals had been caught up in the police sweeps. Nearly 385,000 were scheduled to be shot, while the remaining arrestees were to receive labour camp sentences from five to ten years.'[18]

Victims included military officers, party members and government officials. Bukharin, for example, was tried and executed in 1938. When the purges subsided in 1939, there were one and a half million people in labour camps.[19] Stalin's inner circle mostly survived the purges, including his successor Nikita Krushchev (1894–1971).[20] Stalin needed willing helpers around him, as even a dictator can't make all the decisions. A federation of republics as large as the Soviet Union also needed some degree of delegation and local autonomy, even though larger industries were centrally owned and planned. What scared large numbers of underlings into obedience, then, was the possible *perception* that they had failed the leader and the state, and hence the fear of denunciation and execution.

Dictators are attributed by followers with the superhuman charisma of predestined saviour-of-the-nation; they harness followers' instinct for self-preservation to engender blind faith. They're nonetheless sustained by mutual recognition between ruler and ruled: 'the power relationship lasts as long as they continue to claim it, and the people continue to ascribe it.'[21] Acceptance of the leader grows well beyond his responsibilities to ensure functional and stable government into deification as the awaited saviour. He issues an implicit promise that, by following him, the people can do and achieve things they wouldn't otherwise have been permitted or able to do – which ultimately encompasses crimes against humanity. The leader's power is neither unlimited nor absolute, as he can't simply do all that he wishes, but he's perceived as exceptional and well above the common person and he acts with impunity above or outside of the law. The people can always explain away any failures by the evil influence or incompetence of his advisers and administrators. Constitutional norms are suspended, and the party, assisted by political policing, commits extraordinary abuses of power. Official forums of collective decision-making meet less frequently or become mere rubber-stamps; actual decision-making occurs increasingly in secret or goes unrecorded. Acquiescence is assured by a popular belief (genuine or manufactured) that the nation or revolution is in danger, and by fear of being accused of conspiracy with the regime's enemies. Citizens are encouraged to inform on one another.

Idolising charismatic leaders is common in mass societies. But dictatorship exaggerates three features of most constitutions, including the most democratic. The first is informal, unaccountable decision-making that operates through friendships, networks and off-the-record understandings. Behind-the-scenes decision-making comes to matter most and public processes are ignored or become devoid of real effect. Second, there is excessive use of 'the rule that suspends the rules'. Powers that should be reserved for national self-defence or emergency become the norm rather than the exception. This gives a perpetual permission to act by force and without law, turning exceptional powers into the ongoing means of government. The labour camp is one grim example.[22] The third is the vision for a better society. A civilised society can debate proposals for progress and wellbeing, but a dictatorship may seize on one such vision and then sweep aside all who stand in the way of progress towards that.

The command economy

The USSR's first two five-year plans (1928–37) set industrial targets that aimed to catch up with the developed economies and control resource use. The high-level economic goals necessitated the co-ordination of data to create annual and long-term productivity and trade plans, and to fix prices and wages. Directives and financial allocations were sent down to ministries to be implemented by the directors and workers in individual enterprises. A command economy worked well to overcome and recover from the German invasion in World War II.[23] In peacetime compliance required some socially shared strategy, such as competition with 'the west', to motivate people in the absence of profit-making incentives. But managers and workers accommodated the pressures to meet targets by sacrificing quality, concealing surpluses and ignoring opportunities for efficiency and productivity gains.[24]

Soviet industrial progress was extraordinary, but the human suffering and loss were appalling. Massive construction works were performed by slave labour, for example. But 'the mechanisms of power, the policies of repression and policing and the bureaucratic apparatus of dictatorship that we know as Stalin-ism were unanticipated by Marxist-Leninist ideology or practice.'[25] The Soviet experiment did industrialise a formerly backward country, but it only changed the structure of, and didn't transcend, the alienation and exploitation of labour. The Soviet Union paid a greater price than any other nation to defeat Hitler in World War II; it then subjected most of Eastern Europe to its communist regime, including the former East Germany. But the challenge publicised by Trotsky in 1925 – who will overtake whom? capitalists or socialists?[26] – received its answer: the capitalist economies were more prosperous. The Soviet Union's efforts to produce a new society with an ideal proletarian citizen, and to defend itself from internal dissent and external rivals, led to an oppressive form of government that failed to sustain the mutual recognition on which political legitimacy depends. Stalin's cruelty (including torture and executions of innocent people) and his cult of personality were denounced by Krushchev in 1956,[27] but authoritarian con-trol continued. By the time of the collapse of the Soviet Union in 1989–90, few people wanted to rescue the command economy. Plenty of people were ready to raid formerly state-owned assets, however.

Part 2: Italian fascism

While communism had a theory that it didn't properly apply, fascism had no theory.[28] Fascist rhetoric condoned action over reflection, showed little concern for logic, and evoked will, struggle and sacrifice through warfare.[29] And there were ideological factions within Italian fascism, ranging from radical modern-ists to conservatives.[30] As for government, fascism reversed Marx's dismissal of the capitalist state as a servant of the ruling class and an oppressor of workers. It demanded instead that both capital and labour should be incorporated into and serve the state. Fascists didn't attack capitalism *per se*. They were critical of the individualism, materialism and disorder of liberal-democratic capitalism. They violently opposed socialist and communist parties, but they used dictatorship, centralised planning and oppressive policing in ways akin to the Stalinist and Maoist governments.

Due to its egregious crimes against humanity, the worst manifestation of fas-cism was Germany's Third Reich, led by Adolf Hitler (1889–1945).[31] For present purposes, however, we look at the Italian fascist regime of Benito Mussolini (1883–1945), partly because fascism originated in Italy. In ancient Rome, the *fasces* was a bundle of rods binding the handle of a ceremonial axe carried by the *lictors* who protected senior magistrates such as consuls, as a symbol of *imperium*. To modern fascists, this binding of many into one symbolised sovereign power and opposed the competitive individualism, factionalism and moral decline (as they saw it) of the liberal-capitalist state. Peasant associations called *fasci*, led by local intellectuals, had appeared in the early 1890s in Sicily and agitated violently for a better standard of living.[32] But Italian fascism arose amid a much more complex set of events.

The unification of Italy (1859–61) was helped along by the French forcibly evicting the Austrians from northern Italy in return for Savoy and Nice. The new Italy brought together many politically and culturally diverse states, including the Papal States, to form a kingdom under Vittorio Emanuele II (1820–78), formerly king of Sardinia, with Turin as the capital city.[33] The Veneto (Venice) seceded from Austria to join Italy in 1866. And Rome was captured by force in 1870 to become the capital of Italy, leaving the Pope with only the tiny Vatican City and setting up a bitter division between the church and the new state. Italy's unification relied on middle-class support for emancipatory nationalism, inspired by the French Revolution and advanced rhetorically by Giuseppe Mazzini (1805–72). Mazzini regarded it as the people's duty to realise Italian nationality, defined by the natural geographical boundaries of the peninsula and the cultural affiliation of communities that were predominantly Catholic and spoke closely related Romance dialects. A 'nation' shares such common features or origins, and should by this theory govern itself as an independent state, protecting the rights of the individual but also invoking a duty to act in unison. Mazzini didn't advocate a chauvinistic or aggressive nationalism. If nation-states mutually respect one another as equals acting in the interests of humanity, he argued, then international cooperation and peace are achievable.[34]

United but divided

National unification didn't however eliminate internal disunity. Italy was a largely agrarian society that needed to catch up with industrialised neighbours. The wealthy ruling class tended to come from the north; the south was poorer and more backward. In 1911 nearly 59 percent of the population depended on agriculture, rural areas were overpopulated, large numbers were emigrating to America and internal migration to Italy's urban industrial zones was sluggish.[35] Nonetheless, industries grew – and so did militant labour movements. Class conflict was alleviated by progressive labour laws and social policies in the early years of the twentieth century. But the Italian left was divided between anarchists and militant syndicalists, who wanted a general strike and trade-union control of factories, and the more cautious wing who argued that Italy needed to fully industrialise before moving to socialist revolution. Many intellectuals who opposed socialism, on the other hand, resorted to nationalism as a critique of the liberal-democratic style of government, which they saw as ineffectual. The unification of Italy should have resolved class conflict, according to nationalists. They often called for war as 'an instrument for galvanising the bourgeoisie and creating a sense of common purpose, to subordinate selfish material desires to the interests of the nation as a whole.'[36] By 1914, the country was polarised between socialists and nationalists, with both sides attacking the liberal centre. Italy joined World War I in May 1915 on the side of France and Britain and fought against Austria. Nationalists welcomed this as a necessary step towards completing the unification process and purifying the country of materialism and corruption. Few socialists wanted war, but one who did was Benito Mussolini (1883–1945), then editor of the Italian Socialist Party's main newspaper. He was expelled from the party, freeing him to promote himself as a populist political voice. He launched the *Fasci di Combattimento* in Milan in 1919 in opposition to parliamentary liberalism.

From a population of about 36 million in 1918, Italy had lost 600,000 soldiers; by 1920, 466,000 more lives were claimed by the influenza pandemic. Those killed by both causes were mostly young or of working age.[37] Centrally planned wartime production had boosted manufacturing, but the post-war switch to civilian production and the return of servicemen meant a threat of unemployment, lower wages and more worker militancy. In 1919–20, 'food riots, lawlessness, industrial conflict, and spreading violence raised the specter of revolution [and,] in the countryside, land-hungry peasants occupied large estates.'[38] There was widespread public dissatisfaction with the relatively small territorial gains achieved by Italy in the post-war treaties. The disputed province of Fiume (in today's Croatia) was occupied by Italians led by the poet and militarist Gabriele d'Annunzio (1863–1938).[39] It declared itself briefly an independent state, until Italian naval bombardment in 1920. Many of the tropes and symbols of Italian fascism, such as black shirts, were invented by d'Annunzio. Mussolini admired him and envied his literary fame and mesmerising oratory.

The polarised nation was ripe for mass radicalisation on both sides. The Bolshevik revolution in Russia had emboldened Italian communists and worker militancy on one side; it provoked fears among employers and industrialists on the other. Given the relative leniency of the state in response to industrial strife, the conservative property-owning elite regarded the thuggish *squadristi* – who attacked socialists and their headquarters and newspapers – as performing a necessary job of restoring law and order. The *squadristi* included many who saw themselves as victims of post-war civil disorder: war veterans, students and public servants from petit-bourgeois families, rural smallholders who feared collectivisation and those who simply hated socialism and loved violence. Local police and military often turned a blind eye. The *squadristi* were fanatically loyal to their local bosses, so Mussolini found it hard to assert authority over them as they grew in 1921, but they recognised him as a national level leader. No fascist candidates had been successful in the November 1919 election. To build support, they resorted to strident calls for war, patriotism, national greatness and opposition to socialism. This gained approval from conservative industrialists and middle-class proprietors. In the May 1921 election, the *Fasci* won seats in the north as part of a right-wing coalition that forced the socialists into opposition. Centrist political leaders thought (wrongly, as it turned out) that the violence could be contained if fascists had a stake in the established system.[40]

The fascist party

Mussolini then formed the *Partito Nazionale Fascista* (PNF). The proportional representation system had delivered a fragmented and polarised parliament, in which the PNF was only a small minority in 1922. As a new deputy, Mussolini displayed contempt for parliament, while also playing parliamentary politics. He conjured the threat of organised violence or a *coup d'état* while positioning himself to gain power by legal means. He courted favour with powerful conservative figures in the army, police, industry and church. Established political leaders had failed to secure majority coalitions, and the king, who may have sympathised with the fascists, refused to sign a declaration of martial law to quell the mobilisation of fascist Blackshirts around Rome on 28 October 1922. The following day the king summoned Mussolini to form a ministry. Crowds of Blackshirts were then allowed to stage a 'March on Rome'. Both chambers of parliament gave Mussolini a vote of confidence. His politics had been pragmatic, manipulative and backed by ultra-nationalist gangs, but his rise was (so far) constitutional and had tacit approval from monarch, church and army.[41]

The path to dictatorship lay open. A national fascist militia was formed to bring the unruly *squadristi* under centralised command and create a parallel armed force. Rural and religious elites were mollified with concessions on land distribution and religious education. And nationalist politicians were absorbed into the PNF. In return for restoring order, Mussolini was able to pass an extraordinary amendment to electoral law which provided that the party that gained the most votes (if over 25 percent) should automatically get two-thirds of the seats. This was a major blow to liberal parliamentarianism. But in an election marred by violence and fraud, the National List – a pre-electoral coalition of fascists, nationalists and others – gained over 60 percent in 1924, or 374 of 535 seats in the Chamber of Deputies. The institutional distinction between the fascist political party and the state was blurred by the creation in 1923 of the Grand Council of Fascism, which took over constitutional functions formerly reserved for the king. Local government was abolished and its functions were centralised.[42]

The murder of the outspoken socialist deputy Giacomo Matteotti (1885–1924) divided Italy and indeed divided the PNF. Six months after Matteotti's disappearance, Mussolini made a speech in parliament in which he accepted 'full responsibility' – without admitting guilt for murder.[43] This moment of open defiance was followed by assassination attempts against Mussolini. These events reunited the Fascist Party under his leadership and created the conditions for dictatorship. The next steps were to ban anti-Fascist parties, establish a secret police and attack the press.[44] For example, in 1925 the communist deputy Antonio Gramsci (1891–1937) debated directly in parliament with Mussolini and the radical fascist Roberto Farinacci (1892–1945) and spoke against a bill that banned 'secret organisations' – ostensibly aimed at freemasons, but really, as Gramsci saw, at communists. He asked why the military police had been 'arresting our comrades every time they find them in gatherings larger than three'. His closing statement was: 'The revolutionary movement will defeat fascism.'[45] The following year, all remaining opposition parties were dissolved by law. Gramsci was imprisoned and remained there until his death.

By the 1929 election, Italy had become a one-party state. A single list of 400 candidates endorsed by the Grand Council of Fascism was presented.[46]

The franchise was restricted to men who were members of an official corporation, the military or the clergy. Voters were given two cards, each of which asked: 'Do you approve the list of members appointed by the Grand National Council of Fascism?' The card that said 'Yes' featured the Italian colours and the *fasces*, and the one with 'No' was left plain. The voter would choose one ballot, present it to the electoral official and discard the other. Almost no one said 'No'.

Mussolini eliminated opponents; he controlled ministerial appointments and bills put before the legislature; he controlled the agenda of the all-powerful Grand Council. His effective use of propaganda and his cult of personality (as *il Duce*) completed a picture of totalitarianism – almost. The monarch remained as head of state, and the Fascist Party saw itself as the servant of the state – unlike the Soviet Union in which the Communist Party controlled the state entirely. And whereas the Soviet Union was officially atheist, Mussolini was forced to deal with the Catholic Church, popular loyalty to which fascism could never have broken. The Lateran Pacts of 1929 settled ongoing disputes between church and state, especially regarding Rome.

Fascist rhetoric and policy were fixated on loyalty to and advancement of the nation, rallying all political, social and economic forces to that cause. But its image of the nation was distorted by hatred of communist workers' movements and by violent exclusion of those who opposed the new order. 'Fascism managed to either incorporate within itself or destroy all other political alternatives.'[47] It regarded the nation as an 'organic' whole – not an economy of competing individuals and firms, nor a polity of competing parties or classes. It needed, however, to be about more than just street-level thuggery and dictatorship and to develop definite social and economic policies. Its mode of government was corporatism.

Corporatism

In a corporatist state, many industrial, social and political groups are legally recognised with monopoly representation of, and control over, particular spheres of responsibility. Viewed from the bottom up, society functions by virtue of its constituent organs – families, civil associations, guilds, industrial associations and so on. Recognised social groups (not individuals) are the basis of representation, while individuals acquire rights and duties through incorporation into such bodies. This contrasts with liberal parliamentary representation, which prioritises individual rights.[48] Corporatist social insurance, for example, emerged from traditional trade guilds in the latter decades of the nineteenth century in Germany, Austria, Italy and France, producing conservative welfare systems that mollified labour movements and rewarded loyalty to the state.[49]

Corporatism in fascist Italy provided 'direct representation of social groups' in the legislature 'to manage both economic policy and the economy itself, and thus protect it from the anarchy of the free market'. This applied especially to industrial relations, through institutions that would resolve disputes between workers and employers, 'to promote a kind of self-government of the production system in order to regulate labour relations and eliminate social conflict.'[50] The legal regime for labour relations introduced in 1926 abolished rights to strike and to lockout and created labour courts to arbitrate disputes. It recognised only one employer association and one trade union for each sector under a Ministry of Corporations and a National Council of Corporations.[51] The representatives of the trade unions were appointed by the Fascist Party, and the National Council of Corporations was headed by Mussolini.[52] This labour-relations system left the employers free to choose who would speak for them, however, while the workers were represented only by government-appointed unionists. Unions lost the independence that some fascist syndicalists had argued for.[53] Neither did peasants benefit from fascism, as they had no representation in the PNF, which was dominated by the large landowners (*latifondisti*). In any case, everyone was adversely affected by the Great Depression, in response to which the Italian government took control of failing banks and firms. Eventually, it owned a greater share of industry and finance than the government of any other European country bar the Soviet Union.[54]

Liberal individualism was seen by many Italians to have failed. Corporatism offered them a 'third way' alternative to liberalism and communism. It appealed to those who abhorred communism's rejection of religion and private property, who wished to re-establish traditional values and hierarchies, and yet who also wished to see social protection for artisans and labourers. Hence it was attractive to church authorities, landowners, industrialists and the petit bourgeoisie. It also appealed, at first sight, to some moderate reformist socialists for its recognition of organised labour and judicial arbitration of industrial disputes.[55] Corporatism was accompanied by accident and sickness insurance (based on wage agreements, not citizenship) and pro-natalist social policy, including a family allowance from 1934.[56] But this also meant bans on contraception, sterilisation and abortion in the criminal code. In line with Catholic doctrine, 'the code entrenched the legal and financial power of the husband over his wife and even made adultery a punishable crime for women but not for men.'[57] Ironically the birth rate declined during the fascist era.

Eclipse of fascism

Not all corporatist regimes and military dictatorships are fascist. Distinguishing features of fascism include the glorification of war, a 'total' state that pervades and militarises society, a goal of uniting 'the people' in an image of 'the nation' or 'race', and promoting itself as 'a way of life'.[58] Fascism is ultra-nationalist and racist, and especially anti-Semitic; it repudiates women's emancipation and Marxist ideas about class conflict. It seeks to overcome individualism and political polarisation through unconditional loyalty to a one-party state. The military and police are used for political goals, and social and industrial activities are required to serve the state. Fascist ideas about national, cultural and racial superiority, and the subjugation of weaker peoples by the stronger, underlay Italy's invasions of Ethiopia and Libya, Nazi Germany's invasions of Poland and Russia and the Holocaust. Both Mussolini and Hitler rose to power through parliamentary systems – which they then usurped, suspending the rule of law, to create socially pervasive single-party regimes violently intolerant of dissent or difference.

Following the 1943 Allied invasion of Italy, the Grand Council voted no confidence in Mussolini, and the king then dismissed him from office. So Mussolini was never entirely above the law. He was captured and summarily executed by Italian partisans in April 1945. Since the defeat of fascism in World War II, there hasn't been another thoroughgoing fascist regime. General Franco's dictatorship in Spain (1937–75) was established with the support of the fascist Falange Española and with military aid from Italy and Germany during the Spanish civil war (1936–39). Franco was a Catholic conservative, however, and 'avoided any clear-cut fascist identity'.[59] Among the authoritarian regimes in Latin America, fascist movements made a mark but weren't politically dominant.[60] Getúlio Varga's regime in Brazil (1930–45) adopted corporatist policies, and the fascist Integralist party was one faction. Neo-fascists are often active outside of institutional politics. For instance, there's the social movement CasaPound[61] in Italy, and Generation Identity operates across Europe. There are many neo-fascist groups and networks in the United States,[62] although fascist corporatism clashes with American competitive individualism. Donald Trump's critics often called him a fascist, but strictly speaking his resistance to the administrative state and dislike of war suggest that he doesn't qualify.

Part 3: Liberalism

The aftermath of World War II left the world divided roughly into three: a liberal-democratic capitalist world, led by the United States; a communist world, led by the Soviet Union and Maoist China; and a 'third' world that fought for de-colonisation and national self-determination – for example, Indian home rule in 1947 and eviction of the French from Vietnam in 1954 and Algeria in 1962. Rivalries between the communist and the liberal-democratic regimes were played out 'by proxy' through postcolonial struggles, from the American-backed mass-murder of communists in Indonesia in the mid-1960s to the Soviet Union's support for the Cuban revolutionary regime. The allied victors of World War II, primarily the United States and the United Kingdom, were faced with two important challenges of government: regulation of international trade in peacetime, and reconstruction in West Germany and Japan. Hence, this chapter summarises the Bretton Woods agreement and West German ordoliberalism. The economic recession of the early 1970s ushered in the neoliberal Thatcher–Reagan era of the 1980s and hence a reconfiguration of the relationship between representative government and market economy. But what made neoliberalism a *new* form of liberalism?

Regulating capital

The rise of Nazism in the 1930s in Germany was precipitated by hyperinflation, unemployment and failure to meet basic human needs. The subsequent war descended into the gravest of crimes against humanity, mass social displacement and wholesale destruction. Recovery necessitated not only concerted humanitarian and construction programmes but also financial policies that would bring the global economy back to steady growth. To prevent the reappearance of fascism and to restore economic confidence, the capitalist states needed to avoid another Great Depression and provide security and stability. Even before the war had ended, the Allies, led by the United States, were preparing multilateral agreements and institutions for reconstruction and trade on a scale that had never been attempted before. The old system of international monetary co-operation based on the gold standard had been disrupted by World War I and found wanting during the Great Depression, to the point that it was ineffective for, if not an impediment to, international trade. The industrialised economies were more dependent on large firms, labour was increasingly unionised, larger proportions of nations had gained the right to vote, but the austere wage and price adjustments often required under the gold standard had provoked social unrest and political turmoil. The pre-World War I model had failed and wouldn't be fit for purpose in peacetime after World War II.[63]

To negotiate a new economic order, a conference attended by delegates from 44 nations was held at Bretton Woods, New Hampshire in July 1944. Its aim was to design 'a set of institutions to regulate the rates at which one nation's currency could be exchanged for another's.'[64] It settled on fixed but adjustable exchange rates. Recognising the dominance of the US economy, other currencies would be fixed against the US dollar, backed by its huge gold reserves priced at US$35 per ounce. The system would be secured and monitored by a new institution, the International Monetary Fund (IMF), which would 'provide temporary credit to states suffering from balance-of-payments difficulties against specifically allocated drawing rights [and would] sanction governments running payments surpluses deemed responsible for destabilising international monetary relations.'[65] This would mean stable exchange rates, which benefited international trade, yet also flexibility for governments to adjust currency values as macroeconomic conditions shifted, thus avoiding the inflexibility of the past gold standard. The IMF would provide bridging finance for countries in balance-of-payments difficulties to soften adjustments, ameliorate economic impacts and hence reduce political strife. But this escalated tension between creditor nations (primarily the United States) and debtors. Bretton Woods also established the International Bank for Reconstruction and Development or World Bank. This would float bonds to provide finance on favourable terms to the governments of developing countries for infrastructural projects such as hydroelectricity generators. These were projects that wouldn't have attracted private investors upfront but would boost economic development as a downstream effect. The Bretton Woods agreement also gave states the right to impose permanent capital controls to prevent 'money for purposes other than trade entering and leaving the country'.[66] This would prevent currency devaluations caused by speculation and capital flight and allow governments to use monetary policy for domestic objectives, notably full employment. Democratically elected left-wing governments with strong social-policy mandates thus wouldn't be at the mercy of 'the markets'.[67]

This new form of multilateral governance encouraged basic economic and social measures to protect industries from foreign competitors and citizens from unemployment or illness and its consequences, expanding the scope and aims of government itself. For many capitalist economies, it meant a 'social-democratic' political compromise in which socialists who had dreamed of 'a post-capitalist utopia' accepted the need 'to live and work in a capitalist world'. They forgot about revolution and 'accepted the rules of the democratic game', in return for which they gained a peaceful path to material security for workers.[68] Large land-owners and capital owners gained greater stability and predictability in the trading environment, with less political risk that socialist parties would threaten private property or foment revolution. This social-democratic compromise meant stable economic growth in capitalist countries and rising government expenditures[69] as states took on wider and more complex responsibilities in education, health care and social security. The British economist John Maynard Keynes (1883–1946) had argued that the 'central controls' needed to achieve full employment would expand the functions of government, but only to foster conditions for 'individual initiative'. Keynes aimed to maximise the volume of employment, not to direct what the labour-force should produce.[70] Under welfare states, the health, education and productivity of the individual and the *re*productivity of the family became objects for wider intervention and taxation.

Bretton Woods was bold but not perfect. In its full convertibility phase, it only lasted from 1959 to 1971, when the United States stopped paying for gold at the fixed price. Most advanced countries then adopted 'a managed floating exchange rate system' with the US dollar as the standard or reserve currency.[71] Soon after, the oil-producing countries began to flex their muscles by raising the price of oil, leading to inflation and global recession. The 1970s were also marked by the Vietnam War and then the Iranian Revolution (Chapter 7, Part 3). Economic and political turmoil and the end of Bretton Woods meant that the club of rich nations needed a new model for policymaking and governing.

Liberating capital

That new model is properly described as 'neoliberal'. This term arose in the 1930s, but its underlying theory emerged from Vienna in the wake of World War I. A German version was adopted as part of de-Nazification, while an American version made a debut after the 1973 military coup in Chile. The neoliberal policies of President Ronald Reagan and British Prime Minister Margaret Thatcher in the 1980s attacked 'big government'.[72] Such varied histories should warn us not to over-simplify neoliberalism. After the Bretton Woods era, however, a wider neoliberal policy orthodoxy supported floating exchange rates, central bank independence, strict price control and removal of cross-border capital controls. This would mean acceptance of a 'natural rate of unemployment' in a free market and hence the abandonment of full employment as a policy goal.

The original Viennese neoliberals wanted to promote Austria's economic competitiveness through lower wages – which meant controlling the demands of workers, using force if necessary – and through removing the trade barriers that had been erected following the post-World War I break-up of imperial Austria-Hungary into nation-states. The Austrian economist Ludwig von Mises (1881–1973) regretted the loss of the relatively stable globalised economic system of pre-war imperialism and the gold standard. War had accustomed governments to emergency powers and invasion of property rights. A wider electoral franchise and the wartime sacrifices made by working-class people emboldened socialist parties in countries like Germany, Austria and Italy to demand better standards of living and social security provisions. To counteract all this, Mises recommended greater openness to international economic competition and measures that would 'push down wages, and cut taxes on industry'.[73] He and Friedrich von Hayek (1899–1992) applauded the Austrian state's use of lethal force to suppress a worker uprising in 1927. But the global economic collapse of 1929 and the abandonment of gold convertibility in 1931 meant defeat, for the time being, for their 'proto-neoliberal' model. Moreover, the rise of communist and fascist economic planning defeated liberalism of all kinds. Numerous pioneers of neoliberalism, including Mises, were forced into exile to escape Nazism and anti-Semitism. They were painfully aware of the political threats Europeans faced.

Against this backdrop of totalitarian government and imminent war, a colloquium of neoliberal thinkers (including Mises and Hayek) convened in Paris in 1938, featuring the American journalist Walter Lippmann (1889–1974).[74] In his speech, Lippmann remarked that the totalitarian governments of Italy, Germany and the Soviet Union were beyond the pale of civilisation. They had 'overthrown the principle of the State in all its forms, monarchical, aristocratic, parliamentary, and democratic.' Their rejection of norms of political conduct necessitated, in response, 'a universal philosophy that, by its total humanity, will be able to maintain the tradition of civilization in spite of a totally inhuman enemy.'[75] This shouldn't mean a return to the economic liberalism of the nineteenth century with minimal government, but instead a renewed liberalism or neoliberalism. Adam Smith's ideal free markets were characterised by specialisation and competition among relatively small producers and merchants. This called for a government that would be prudently self-limiting and *laissez-faire* (let markets do their thing). Smith had aimed to eliminate outdated feudal tariffs and trade controls, but during the industrial revolution *laissez-faire* had become an economic dogma that treated all government and law as 'interference'. Lippmann pointed out, however, that 'private property and contract, the whole system of enterprise by individuals, partners, and corporations, exists in a legal context.'[76]

As we're always 'under the law' anyway, the questions should be what kind of rule of law, and when and why the state should intervene.

Neoliberal thought coalesced around two premises. First, the principal features of a market economy – private property rights and competition – aren't the products of a spontaneously arising order of nature. Nineteenth-century economic liberalism had relied on ideas of natural rights to justify private property and on Darwinian natural selection to justify competition. The neoliberals argued instead that these things are only made possible by a particular kind of social order with a limited but strong state that enforces an appropriate rule of law. Second, human knowledge is limited. Neoliberals 'did not share the belief of their opponents on the left that the economy could be seen and counted',[77] nor did they accept the assumption of classical economic theory that all actors in a market possess perfect knowledge. No individual or institution – no matter how many statistics they gather – could comprehend, let alone predict or control, the functioning of markets. There's no Archimedean or omniscient position from which to view, let alone manage, a market economy. The neoliberals vigorously rejected communist command economics and fascist corporatism. They also disapproved of America's New Deal (Chapter 8, Part 3), which advanced a 'paternalistic' administrative state that undermined the rule of law.[78] Instead, the proper – and limited – role of the state was to establish institutions that would 'produce and sustain [the] market pricing mechanism'.[79] The kinds of laws that the neoliberals saw as essential, then, protected private property and freedom of contract, maintained fair competition, prevented monopolies and cartels, and punished crimes against persons and property. The neoliberal rule of law is 'strictly formal': it doesn't seek to shape economic choices.[80] Neoliberals weren't uniformly against state intervention or regulation. They would make concessions for public services, such as education and social insurance, if they helped lift the standard of living and if private enterprise would be unable to provide them to the necessary level. The public policy question of how to draw the appropriate line between that which should be provided by the state and that which should be left to private enterprise would become a major controversy, especially in the 1990s.

In 1947, Hayek and others formed the Mont Pèlerin Society, one of the stated aims of which was 'redefinition of the functions of the state' in favour of 'minimal and dispersed government'.[81] They opposed the Bretton Woods arrangements that enabled full employment, capital controls and trade barriers. They objected to governments going beyond their 'minimal' function (enforcement of the rule of law) to redistribute resources by means of, say, subsidies or welfare payments. The pursuit of distributive justice would be inefficient and discriminatory, as it would require 'that people be told what to do and what ends to serve.'[82] It would lead, Hayek warned, to a command economy and hence totalitarianism.

Ordoliberalism

Neoliberals in the 1930s had seen themselves as fighting against overwhelming forces of totalitarianism and, in democratic countries, against the administrative state. They became influential, however, in the reconstruction of West Germany. A group of economists critical of Nazi Germany's centralised economic planning had gathered around Walter Eucken (1891–1950), an economics professor at Freiburg University. Freiburg was isolated from the main political centres of Germany, and this (at the time) heterodox group explored ideas about market competition and the constitutional and legal frameworks needed to sustain it. Following Germany's defeat, the occupying Allied forces wanted to see economic reforms that would replace Nazi-era industrial cartels and state planning. The Freiburg School 'were not tainted by ties to Nazism';[83] they had an 'ordo-liberal'[84] model that was German-made and which met with American approval.

Monopolies are inimical to competition, yet firms that succeed in a free market tend towards monopolisation, as the Americans knew (Chapter 8, Part 3). Through below-cost pricing and mergers and acquisitions, large firms control markets and then set the prices they want, if they can. Thus, competition risks undermining itself unless there's suitable regulation. The neoliberal theorists of the twentieth century, and the German ordoliberals in particular, realised that effective competition doesn't occur naturally, and that *laissez-faire* cannot be relied upon for the smooth operation of the pricing mechanism. What was needed was more than a mere 'night-watchman' state, but a constantly active and vigilant state tasked with creating and maintaining 'the conditions of existence of the market', or the legal 'framework' that makes competition possible.[85]

An analogy is with competition in sport. Left to themselves, people enjoy competitive sports, but to reach the highest performance, complex *government* is essential: rules, codes, referees, organised tournaments and, of course, governing institutions such as FIFA and the IOC. Within this quasi-legal framework, competition occurs, players strive for the best results, cheating can be detected and punished – and a price mechanism arises for tickets, broadcasting fees, merchandise and salaries. The competitive game creates the need for enforceable rules which, reciprocally, improve conditions for elite performance. Similarly, high-performing competitive markets don't just 'happen', they're 'formed' through the 'political and legal decision-making' that makes up a nation's 'economic constitution'. According to the ordoliberals, this required law and policy that 'structure the conditions for economic conduct'.[86] Such policy, however, needed to prevent monopolisation by dominant firms and by the state. Both private and public power, if unrestrained, were capable of distorting the price mechanism. Hence clear competition law should guide private enterprise and public administration with an impartial application of rules.

Democratic political competition, moreover, limits the acceptable forms of government. It rules out fascist and communist one-party states. But neoliberals put more faith in the 'democracy', or the freedom of choice, to be found in markets. Representative parliaments were too prone to 'capture' by interest groups, professional bodies and bureaucrats. But the ordoliberals claimed that 'economic action is not an end in itself; rather, the ultimate aim is human well-being';[87] hence, West Germany's 'social market economy' combined private enterprise and social protections. Post-war recovery, strong export-led growth and a 'conservative' social security system were underpinned by restrictive fiscal and monetary policies and competitive markets.[88] The growth of the European Union into a borderless multi-state entity, stretching from Portugal to Finland, and especially (in 1989) the fall of the Berlin Wall, partially vindicated the neo-liberals who had initially bemoaned the break-up of the Austro-Hungarian Empire.[89] Overarching EU standards of law and economics upheld free movement of capital, goods, services and labour. These standards reflect ordoliberal ideas: 'good rules' overseeing a diverse and competitive market, with conservative fiscal and monetary criteria.[90] And yet the European Union also created a large trade barrier around itself and used agricultural subsidies to protect its members from global competition: hence it blocked progress towards the world economic integration which was the neoliberals' ultimate aim.[91]

Chile

In 1973, a *coup d'état* in Chile ousted an elected socialist president, Salvador Allende (1908–73), and imposed a dictatorship the illegality and brutality of which was unexpected and shocking in a nation with a record of multi-party representation. Headed by General Augusto Pinochet (1915–2006), this military regime was motivated by fear of communism, frustration with electoral outcomes and opposition to state intervention and land reform. Pinochet's anti-Marxist dictatorship, in league with vested interests, opened Chile to neoliberal reform aided by the Chicago School of Economics and its professors Milton Friedman (1912–2006) and Arnold Harberger (b. 1924).[92] The generals left technical matters of public policy to a team of business, legal and economic advisers. A prominent minister, José Piñera (b. 1948), who drove the privatisation of social security, described the main policy points succinctly: 'cut the fiscal deficit to reduce inflation and stabilize the economy, free prices to be set by the market, sell off the state-owned enterprises, open the economy to trade with the rest of the world.'[93] Pinochet kept the lucrative state-owned copper-mining company but allowed private miners in by other avenues. The privatisation of public health, education, pensions and transport services, and the reduction of trade barriers did away with many jobs and other sources of social and economic security – and protest was violently suppressed.[94] The number of public employees had risen by 38 percent under Allende, and fell again under Pinochet – although the figures were never out of line with other Latin American countries.[95]

Chile's neoliberal policies were the opposite of fascist corporatism. They produced instead a radical disjuncture between human rights and economic freedoms. American-trained economists gave 'technical' advice on *market* freedoms to a government that trampled on *political* freedoms. Behind this was a belief that economists applied value-free scientific models of human economic behaviour and macroeconomics that should be useful anywhere. But their moral-political dilemma was pointed out by the deposed Allende government's former foreign minister Orlando Letelier (1932–76) – himself a victim of Pinochet's violence.

How could economic freedom and political terror be made to 'coexist without touching each other'?[96] Chile was an egregious example, but political-economic crisis or state violence was used elsewhere to advance market liberalisation and privatisation, from South Africa to Poland.[97] One advocate of neoliberal policies suggested that, if faced by political opposition, then 'deliberately provoking a crisis so as to remove the political logjam to reform' may make sense; indeed, 'reform will be easier where the opposition is discredited and disorganized (or repressed).'[98] Neoliberal reformers recommended 'shock therapy' or such rapid implementation of policies that opponents had no time to organise effective resistance.[99]

What put 'neo' into neoliberalism?

The Pinochet regime came to an end in 1990. For neoliberals like Hayek, this dictatorship was tolerable while it implemented their preferred economic policies. Dictatorship should have a sunset clause, after which a renewed representative government is permanently limited by entrenched economic freedoms.[100] Neoliberal reforms were thus intended to be hard to undo, despite their unpopularity:[101] they're deliberately 'baked in'. Popular demands for a return to social democracy (welfare, subsidies and public services) are the very 'problem' that neoliberalism addresses. The free flow of capital across borders smooths the way for foreign direct investment; it also discourages governments from adopting social policies that investors dislike and which cause capital flight. Countries therefore have to compete over investor-friendly policies, such as low corporate tax rates or loose regulations that are less favorable for workers and the environment. Moreover, once sold, assets are hard to buy back. Policies that permit the competitive provision of services by private enterprise, once embedded, are hard to reverse, even if they don't deliver the promised improvements.

The neoliberal reforms that swept the world in the 1980s and 1990s were responses to post-World War II growth in governmental programmes. Advanced capitalist countries were spending a greater proportion of their annual economic output on public services than ever before. Public investment had been necessary to create airlines, telecommunications, high-tech hospitals and the like, and to meet the correlative demand for highly skilled workforces through expanded public education. While state monopolies were often needed to set up such services, private investors later sought to open them up as new sources of revenue. Important components of the neoliberal policymaking consensus were therefore privatisation (the sale of state-owned assets to private investors) and deregulation (the removal of barriers to the entry and exit of providers competing for publicly funded service contracts). This Anglo-American version of neoliberalism spread from Latin America to many other developing and developed countries, under governments of the left and the right.[102] In New Zealand, for example, a rapid neoliberal reform process commenced in 1984 under a government of the traditionally left-wing Labour Party; it was then advanced by the centre-right conservative National Party after it took office in 1990.[103]

Viewed as government, and not just 'the market model', neoliberalism represented a permanent reflexive critique of government itself. Governmental institutions were seen as having inherent biases towards empire-building and budget-maximising, making them inefficient, wasteful and unresponsive to consumers. Public-sector employees acted, like all humans, out of self-interest, and hence recommended inflating budgets. Interest groups and voters put pressure on politicians to provide more of what they wanted, and politicians had electoral incentives to respond sympathetically, commonly known as 'pork-barrelling'. Representative government itself looked flawed, then, so neoliberal reformers limited public consultation and consent if they could. In the neoliberal world, the individual finds freedom of choice in markets and our spending decisions are often likened to votes, while public services are uniform, often coercive, and unaccountable to consumers.[104] Those services that the state must nevertheless mandate or make compulsory, for sociocultural, national security or environmental reasons, should be funded and contracted out on a competitive basis, treating all tenderers equally. In private enterprise, self-interested behaviour (rational utility maximisation) leads to efficiency through competition; in the public sector, it encourages inefficiency. Therefore public policy should favour free markets, or at least emulate market conditions through competitive contracting-out.

Neoliberalism was 'new' precisely because it didn't seek a return to nineteenth-century *laissez-faire*. Strong government was needed to self-critically reform government itself, to break down trade barriers, regulations and monopolies, and to design and enforce appropriate laws. That meant curtailing workers' rights to strike and to economic security. The late twentieth century's Anglo-American neoliberalism responded to post-World War II expansion of public services and high taxes: hence it was critical of the very institutions in which the policy technocrats worked. The neoliberals wanted more than just tax cuts and budget surpluses, however. They argued for reordering spending priorities, for example moving away from 'non-merit subsidies' and towards 'basic health and education and infrastructure'.[105] The unplanned decision-making within global free markets would constrain government spending while competition and fair trading laws would set rules for market players. Models of economic behaviour were generalised to explain political and social concerns that had formerly been treated as 'non-economic', such as elections, crime, marriage and 'welfare dependency'. Once the theoretical principles of individualism, self-interest and contractual freedom were applied to politics and public policy, then anything publicly-owned looked prone to 'government failure' – such that private enterprise would surely do better thanks to competition and innovation. Where public service organisations were still needed, in those limited fields where private enterprise can't take over, such as the courts, 'traditional' bureaucratic administration (Chapter 8) should make way for the management techniques of private enterprise – a shift known as 'new public management'.[106] There was no 'invisible hand' at work here. Instead, a very visible hand of law and administration restructured governmental bodies into systems resembling markets, separated funders from providers, and contracted services out on a competitive basis. Neoliberalism, then, isn't just a self-limitation of government to protect the freedoms of individuals; it's a critically reflexive *government of government itself.* Liberty becomes more than just a principle to guard against abuses of state power, as in classical liberalism; it's adopted as a principle of government so that the state can redesign the state.

The end of neoliberalism

The late twentieth century's globally integrated markets bore little resemblance to Adam Smith's late eighteenth-century Britain, with its parishes, small traders, merchants and farmers. Smith opposed the mercantilism of the absolutist and imperialist states; he had no idea, however, of complex trade agreements as negotiated between governments today. He didn't imagine a 'world economy' as we can. And today's so-called 'free trade' agreements are highly regulated international treaties; they aren't particularly *free*, even though they normally reduce barriers such as tariffs and quotas.

In its Hayekian version,[107] the neoliberal idea of the market is comparable to a language. A language isn't created or planned by laws and edicts from above; we know it only through many instances of speech and writing; it arises spontaneously from innumerable conversations. As the spoken word expresses meaning, the price expresses value; both are subjectively judged according to the intentions of the actors. Like dictionaries, economic statistics are only retrospective records of features of an evolving system – not a complete description. A language and an economy are what people say and do in real time. The phenomena that lend an order to languages and to markets aren't fully comprehensible to human knowledge let alone planning. We can record the words or prices that pass between people, but we can only *infer* an order (a grammar or price mechanism) underlying the uncoordinated messy lives of millions of people trading and conversing. Meanings and prices aren't sitting there waiting for humans to pick them up. It's as unjust and futile for governments to control what people say (other than prohibiting criminal threats, defamation, plagiarism and so on) as it would be to control their exchanges of goods and services (other than prohibiting theft and fraud). A limited rule of law that enforces such basic prohibitions is the only kind of 'government' called for. Law should leave the rules of grammar and of supply-and-demand to emerge spontaneously from what people actually do and say, in accord with their changing circumstances and needs (l'Académie Francaise notwithstanding). There may be normative understandings of 'correct' uses of words and 'natural' or 'fair' prices; but meanings and prices vary anyway, they change over time, and government should let them be. Wittgenstein's principle that 'the meaning of a word is its use in the language'[108] is akin to the Austrian

School's principle that economic value is what the economic actors make of it: the subjective theory of value developed by Carl Menger (1840–1921). Ludwig Wittgenstein (1889–1951) and Hayek not only grew up in the same Viennese intellectual culture but were second cousins.[109]

With the collapse of the Soviet Union in 1990 and the opening up of China to the world economy, neoliberalism reached an ascendancy, promising reinvented government, competitiveness, individualism, economic growth and 'millions lifted out of poverty'. The twentieth century's global struggle between communism, fascism and (neo)liberalism was partly about the ends and limits of government. It culminated in victory for a liberal international order with fiscally responsible national governments. The global financial crisis of 2008 dealt a cruel blow, however. Suddenly financial institutions and big businesses turned to governments for massive bailouts. Meanwhile China's 'socialist market economy' grew rapidly. Its mixed model of state ownership of major assets, 'collective bargaining between capital and labor', and 'a mechanism where prices are determined by the market'[110] didn't follow the neoliberal pathway. In 2016 the disruptions of Brexit and the Trump presidency signalled a return to nationalism and protectionism, along with populist leaders in Poland, Hungary, Turkey, India, the Philippines and Brazil. These developments were reactions against the 'ordoglobalism' of the neoliberal era that had prevailed roughly from 1980 to 2008. Neoliberal reforms of government had had profound and lasting effects, but that era of reform had come to a close. The pandemic of 2020 sealed the lid on neoliberalism as governments were forced to restrict civil and economic liberties, close borders, subsidise incomes and prop up businesses.

Part 4: Democracy

After the defeat of fascism and then the collapse of communism, it was often thought that a combination of free markets and elected representative government was the winning formula. Neoliberalism, however, had an authoritarian streak, as revealed in Chile, and it was always sceptical about the motives of voters, politicians and public servants. The wave of populism around 2016 was a reaction to the inequalities produced under neoliberal policy, and an attack on liberal norms (the 'political correctness') of public life. Populist leaders claimed that they understood 'the will of the people' better than others and that they would fight for traditional values that many feared were under threat. Democracy seemed to have reached a crisis in the second decade of the twenty-first century. But what is commonly called 'democracy' is basically representation with a universal franchise (Chapter 7, Part 2). Contemporary representative systems don't often reach a democratic standard whereby 'all affected by collective decisions should have an opportunity to influence the outcome.'[111] Representation with a universal adult franchise isn't authentically 'democratic' in the sense of decision-making by and for all people affected. More than a crisis of democracy, then, perhaps what we have witnessed is a crisis of representation.

Back to Italy

To appreciate the recent history of representation, one might look again at Italy. After the defeat of fascism, Italians chose by referendum (in 1946) to end the monarchy and become a republic, and they elected representatives to a multi-party constituent assembly. This assembly drafted and approved the new republic's constitution and then dissolved. Competitive elections with proportional representation to a bicameral parliament became the norm. In the first general election in 1948, the conservative Christian Democracy (DC) party won majorities in both houses.[112] From 1953 to 1994, DC-led coalitions governed, keeping the second-largest party, the Soviet-aligned Communist Party (PCI), permanently out of office. The smaller Socialist Party (PSI) split with the PCI over the USSR's invasion of Hungary in 1956. The PSI was then able to form coalitions with the DC and to advance social reform. Due to the collapse of the Soviet Union in 1989, however, the PCI disbanded in 1991. The DC, in contrast, had traditionally consolidated support by state clientelism and patronage – rather than efficient meritocratic public services. Following the *Tangentopoli* (Bribesville) scandals, the DC disbanded in 1994, and its successor party was decimated in the election that year. Within half a decade, the two major parties of left and right had been obliterated.[113]

Out of the ashes emerged *Forza Italia*[114] and a centre-right coalition government led by media magnate and shameless vulgarian Silvio Berlusconi – a forerunner of Donald Trump. Berlusconi entered politics on the back of his record in business but was, from the start, embroiled in allegations of sexual impropriety, corruption and links with organised crime. He largely controlled the media and used it to project positive images of himself. He served, all told, nine years as prime minister. Meanwhile, the *Lega Nord* (Northern League) had appeared in 1991, initially as a regional secessionist movement. It stoked up anti-Rome and anti-immigrant sentiments – and it signed up to coalitions with Berlusconi.

The 5-Star Movement (M5S) was founded in 2009 by the comedian Beppe Grillo. It claimed not to be a political party, but instead a movement based on participative online policymaking. In Italy's 2018 election, M5S gained the largest vote of any party (32 percent), followed by the Lega. Although both had been openly contemptuous of governments, the Lega and M5S had little option but to form one in a coalition, and it proved to be short-lived. When Matteo Salvini, the leader of the Lega, called for fresh elections as his party was high in the polls, the M5S pulled out of their coalition and formed an alternative government with the Democratic Party, forcing the Lega into opposition. The Lega then declined in opinion polls, losing supporters to the right-wing nationalist *Fratelli d'Italia* (Brothers of Italy) led by Giorgia Meloni. In sum, the decline of traditional left- and right-wing parties began earlier in Italy than in comparable countries such as Spain and France; while Berlusconi's ascendency preceded Trump's by more than two decades. Far-right populism is now well established in Italy. If this country may be seen as a barometer, then its populist parties, political fragmentation and unstable coalitions warned of stormy weather. The rise of far-right populism raised fears about a return to authoritarian government.

Much of Europe had only recently emerged from authoritarianism. Military regimes had lived on into the 1970s in Portugal (1933–74), Spain (1936–75) and Greece (1967–74). Communist regimes controlled the whole of eastern Europe from the end of World War II until 1989. The post-communist era of the 1990s may have been a high tide mark for liberal representative government. Since then representation has been challenged by party fragmentation and by leaders who gained support through breaching democratic norms. Hungary's 'illiberal democracy', for example, was popular from 2010 thanks to strong family welfare policies, but also because it challenged constitutional norms of the European Union. The EU itself is perceived by most Europeans as promoting 'democratic values', but a survey in 2018 reported that '62% say it does not understand the needs of its citizens.' Unfavourable views of the EU were especially common among those who supported right-wing populist parties.[115]

It used to be assumed that democratisation and representative government were inexorably spreading and consolidating globally at the expense of authoritarian and monarchical regimes. The demise of communism in eastern Europe and the spread of multi-party elections across Africa meant that 'the global population of people entitled to vote more than doubled in the four decades to 2010.'[116] Some argued, dangerously, that 'spreading democracy' was such a good idea that it might even be done by armed force.[117] But 'democratic consolidation' went into reverse in the mid-2000s when countries undergoing setbacks began to outnumber those making gains, while surveys suggested a decline in people's commitment to and satisfaction with 'democracy'.[118]

Twentieth-century representative government was, however, neither a direct democracy nor a straightforward majority rule by the people at large. Mass societies were simply too large for the level of public participation necessary for a thorough-going direct democracy. Some electoral systems produced disproportionate results in which minorities of voters (not majorities of the people) determined the outcomes. Global voter turnout 'fell sharply in the 1990s' and declined to 66 percent in the 2011–15 period.[119] In Europe, this decline was deeper in the post-communist east. Even in a proportional representation system, then, if only two-thirds of registered voters (on average) actually voted, then only a minority of the total eligible population would have voted for the parties who controlled the legislature. The majority of 'the people' would not have chosen 'who governs', as the majority may have either voted for opposition parties or not voted at all.

Modern 'democracy' was always a *representative* system that relied on a division of labour between 'the people' and those who actually governed. Representation meant a trust in the elected few who, in turn, relied on technocratic administration by their *un*elected public servants. Originally an aristocratic principle (rule by society's 'best'), representation was made more inclusive by progressive universalisation of the franchise and by a gradual diversification of the representatives, their advisers and administrators. When people have critiqued representative systems, they've often asked for more or better representation – but less often asked for alternatives to representation *per se*. Alternatives may include direct democracy, such as referendums, or deliberative democracy 'in which people come together, on the basis of equal status and mutual respect, to discuss the political issues they face and, on the basis of those discussions, decide on the policies that will then affect their lives.'[120]

The universal franchise has been accompanied by other norms of government. These include an open, fair and predictable rule of law, applied by an independent judiciary. Looking from the bottom up, they include responsiveness to the needs and concerns of the people, through access to their representatives, open debate in a free press, and, if necessary, protest. Freedom of political opinion (to openly disagree without violence) and respect for human rights are central qualities. The wishes of majorities should be qualified by recognition of the needs and interests of minorities. An everyday culture of abstract equality, in which adults of differing kinds or unequal wealth and status treat one another as equals, ensures that those of modest means enjoy respect and that discrimination is reduced. Private property and freedom of economic enterprise make for a vibrant consumer society.

Representation and trust

Political stability in western democracies in the three decades following World War II was supported by rising living standards under the Bretton Woods arrangements. Technocratic government with top-down planning by unelected officials was the norm. Competing peak corporate bodies or interest groups, through their spokespeople and activists, could act as lobbyists and influencers, as a form of *corporate* representation. But this was dominated by vested interests with the means to pay for lobbying and public relations firms. Political legitimacy was relying on a relatively passive public with deep (sometimes naïve) political trust in those who walked the corridors of power. A healthy degree of scepticism or distrust was also called for, and this could be addressed by rules about transparency and accountability. At elections, most voters chose one of (normally) two centrist parties, social-democratic or conservative, and then got on with family and work until the next election. Radio and TV brought politicians into living rooms, allowing audiences to judge their personal traits more closely, but this mass communication was one-sided. Political narratives could be controlled through a small number of media organisations and through dominant political parties that pre-arranged 'who represents whom'. Management of media and parties constrained ideological contests to a relatively predictable band of issues and agendas. So when genuine political controversies did erupt, the basic terms of debate weren't as contestable as they are today. Mediated forums of public debate were much fewer in number and simply slower than today's highly diverse social-media environment.

The post-war representative system was far from perfect. It wasn't universal in its application, as witnessed by instances of institutionalised racial discrimination. Apartheid in South Africa, the exclusion from citizenship of Aboriginal and Torres Strait Islander peoples in Australia, and Jim Crow in southern United States are egregious examples, but the exclusion of minority groups from political participation and legal recognition was common. It was during this supposed 'golden age' of democratic consolidation and economic prosperity, moreover, that imperial wars were waged, for example in South-East Asia. Moreover, post-war democratic societies were disrupted from within by a demographically large and culturally rebellious 'baby boom' generation as they came of age in the late 1960s and early 1970s and, in the United States, by the civil rights movement. Alternative and radical forms of democracy were put forward, including democratic socialism, anarcho-syndicalism and varieties of Marxism. This rebelliousness went as far as terrorism by extremist groups such as the Red Brigade in Italy and the Baader-Meinhof gang in West Germany. Many western European communist parties accepted a class compromise, however, provided workers' living standards and social protections were improving. Europe's conservatives and industrialists could accept this compromise too, as educational achievement, skill levels and productivity rose and there was stability in the international trading environment. The advent of the European Economic Community helped to free up trade and mobility within western Europe and fostered Franco-German peace.

The United States had emerged from World War II as the global hegemon, and its currency underpinned markets, notably oil. Prosperity at home, opposition to totalitarian states and a leading role in post-war reconstruction built significant stocks of moral and political authority for the United States. One could be forgiven at that time for believing the propaganda that the President of the United States was 'leader of the free world'. The decline of this global authority, and the decline of Americans' trust in their own federal government, are often traced back to the Watergate scandal, which led to the resignation of President Nixon in 1974.[121] Illegal bombing raids into Laos and Cambodia, and widespread opposition to the Vietnam War (which ended in 1975) dealt another blow. Americans' trust in government recovered somewhat, according to surveys, during the Reagan and Bush Snr presidencies (1981–93), mainly among Republican supporters. There was a significant spike in surveyed political trust immediately after the 9/11 terrorist attacks in 2001, but trust declined again during the years of the invasion of Iraq (from 2003) and following the global financial crisis of 2008. The downward trend continued, reaching historic lows, under presidents Obama and Trump,[122] accompanied by an increase in partisan polarisation.[123] This reached a peak that can only be described as mutual hatred across the partisan divide.

A long-term decline in 'trust in government' wasn't confined to the United States; neither was it a uniform trend across all liberal-democratic countries.[124] Smaller democracies tend to report lower levels of dissatisfaction and higher trust. And we don't know whether the high levels of Americans' political trust in the decade from 1958 to 1968 were a historical norm or an exception, as there's no comparable pre-war data. Nonetheless, this long-term downward trend was about more than people's dissatisfaction with particular presidents or parties in office at the time: it was also a growing distrust in the *system* of representation and liberal-democratic government itself. Systemic distrust underlay the disruptive anti-establishment ethos of the first two decades of the twenty-first century, provoking questions about the future of representation itself.

In the 1990s, it had appeared to some that nation-states and nationalism were in decline as countries opened borders and relinquished sovereignty to global economic integration and multilateral institutions.[125] A global 'solution' to the problems of political economy, it was argued, had emerged: competitive elections nationally, consumer choice in free markets, and discipline on governments from open economies and mobile capital. Or to quote a pre-digital-era portrayal, 'liberal democracy in the political sphere combined with easy access to VCRs [video cassette recorders] and stereos in the economic.'[126] But this proved to be a false dawn. Certainly, eastern bloc communism collapsed in 1989, hailed by many as 'the death of Marxism'. But communism was replaced by a kleptocratic and authoritarian regime in Moscow that ran a pretence of democratic elections and gradually spread its influence back into eastern European countries and others such as Ukraine, Georgia and Syria. In the affluent western countries, moreover, neoliberal policies had exacerbated economic inequality and insecurity, contributing to popular dissatisfaction and distrust. Neoliberalism hadn't served the interests of all; governing liberal elites had become out of touch with many communities. But the targets of popular unrest were all too often the migrant workers who had availed themselves of the opportunities presented by relatively porous borders. Powerless groups often bore the brunt of the political backlash against neoliberal economic policy. The aftermath of the 2008 global financial crisis helped to boost 'strong' nationalistic leaders who defied the norms of the representative systems that brought them to power. One such norm is the respect for one's political opponents. But opponents were increasingly treated as traitors, infiltrators or conspirators who sought to undermine state authority and national identity. Those opposed to populists might say, for instance, that 'there is no place in our country' for politics like that – even though there clearly was. Donald Trump's election in 2016 and his policies and rhetoric perpetuated this polarisation. Reputable political scientists began to ask if 'the end of democracy' was nigh.[127]

Pandemic policy

Emergency measures taken by many countries in response to the Covid-19 pandemic were contrary to a liberal-democratic and neoliberal status quo. Strict border closures, confinement of people to their homes and massive state subsidies were unthinkable in the 1990s. And even though governments were armed with statistics and public health advice, in 2020 the leading western economies (the United Kingdom, European Union and the United States) didn't control the Covid-19 pandemic as quickly and effectively as did East Asian countries. Taiwan, for instance, had an extremely low infection and fatality rates. Disease control required authoritarian measures of a kind that paternalistic states were readier to undertake – and their populations readier to accept. Temporary dictatorial government in the face of a genuine emergency and risk to human life (e.g., in wartime) isn't necessarily undemocratic, however, provided it's in the interests of, and understood by, the majority of people. Such emergency measures should be grounded in law, temporary, necessary in the circumstances, aimed at the protection of the state and its citizens, and proportionate to the potential for harm. But there were no verses in the neoliberal hymnbook about dealing with a global pandemic. Numerous social and economic norms of a free democratic society were suspended. Many subnational and national elections and referendums were postponed across all continents – although many went ahead too.[128]

In general, however, these severe restrictions on civil and economic liberties were accompanied, counter-intuitively, by boosts in popularity for incumbent presidents and prime ministers. This included Italy's then prime minister, Giuseppe Conte, even though the virus hit that country especially hard. Before-and-after surveys in a number of countries revealed an initial increase in underlying trust in government and satisfaction with democracy around the time of the lockdowns, especially in countries which more effectively controlled the virus.[129] If people saw the need for the lockdowns, then the Hobbesian imperative (obey or die) led them to conclude, 'We may as well trust and obey.' This sentiment wasn't universally shared, however. Although populist parties generally didn't flourish during the pandemic, neither did they perform badly, and some took advantage of conspiracy theories – for example, the false belief that Covid-19 was a plot to usurp government and subjugate the people. Indeed, those who upheld strong traditions of liberty sometimes declared that they'd sooner die from the virus than sacrifice their liberties – after all, hadn't many given their lives in war for those same liberties? Whether a government should prioritise economic liberties ahead of restrictions to reduce infection and mortality rates, or vice versa, and at what costs, were trade-offs that the pandemic forced policymakers to address.

Conclusion

As of 2020, surveyed 'dissatisfaction with democracy' had been rising, especially in larger countries, including the United States, United Kingdom, Brazil, Spain and Australia.[130] But strictly speaking, people are dissatisfied with *representation* – not necessarily with democracy if properly practised. Have we mistaken representation for democracy? Since the late nineteenth century, reforms have progressively made systems of representation less undemocratic – or more democratic, if you prefer. And, in recent years, the demand for greater descriptive representation has improved gender and ethno-religious diversity in many national legislatures. But a diverse nation, being absent, can't be actually re-presented and fully spoken for in its lawmaking assemblies. Any action taken on behalf of absent others must fall short of the democratic principle, and representation by election is an expedient compromise. Most voters (and non-voters) can get on with their private lives and ignore the government until they notice something wrong. At the next election, voters can 'hold them to account' but without the burden of public responsibilities other than paying tax. It was always practically difficult to build a genuinely participatory deliberative democracy for large populations. Hence we entrust powers to a minority of fellow citizens – on condition that they use those powers within prescribed limits and act in the interests of 'the people'. Representation, in some form, may be a middle way, and most people may be content to call it 'democracy'. But the voters are empowering an elite minority. That minority was an easy target for populist leaders who claimed instead to speak directly to and for 'the people' whose democratic will had allegedly been thwarted. And this long-suffering 'people' could be defined broadly (for instance, 'the 99 percent') or more exclusively (native-born as against immigrant).

The twentieth century showed how representative government can be overtaken from within by elected leaders who later become dictators. The rise of far-right populists in the early twenty-first century evoked fears of a recurrence. Neoliberalism was originally conceived as a force for free trade and against totalitarianism. Following the defeat of fascism and the demise of Soviet communism, the neoliberal governments of the late twentieth century sought to reduce and restructure government itself. Ironically the reappearance of far-right populists can be attributed in part to the social disruption, economic inequality and (for many) loss of status that are consequences of neoliberal policies. Neoliberalism's vision of a seamless global free market looks like another false utopia. So the big question of the proper ends and limits of government is still up for debate, especially since the 2008 crash and the 2020 pandemic brought state intervention back into play. If the twentieth century taught us anything, though, it's not to follow leaders who claim to have a permanent solution to the wicked problem of government.

Notes

1 Marx & Engels, 2008 [1848], p. 36.
2 Engels, 1993 [1845].
3 Marx & Engels, 2008 [1848], pp. 65–6.
4 Raleigh, 2006.
5 Ibid., p. 151.
6 Ball, 2006.
7 Constitution of the USSR, 1924.
8 The 1936 reform simplified this by having direct elections to a Supreme Soviet that consisted of the two legislative chambers, both of which could initiate legislation, which needed a majority of both to pass.
9 Overy, 2005, p. 61.

10 Ibid., p. 59.
11 The proportion of female CPSU members grew from 15.9% in 1932 to 21% in 1950. Overy, 2005, p. 144.
12 Bushkovitch, 2012, p. 321. See also Montefiore, 2003, p. 36.
13 Ball, 2006, p. 186.
14 Bushkovitch, 2012, p. 324.
15 Ball, 2006.
16 Bushkovitch, 2006, p. 355.
17 Montefiore, 2003.
18 Shearer, 2006, pp. 212–13, abridged.
19 Bushkovitch, 2012, p. 362.
20 The head of secret police who oversaw the great purge, Nikolai Yezhov (1895–1940), was himself accused of anti-Soviet activity and executed. His replacement, the psychopathic Lavrentii Beria (1899–1953), organised massacres, serially raped and murdered women, and got the assignment to build an atomic bomb. He was executed after Stalin died. One lesser-known survivor, Alexander Poskrebyshev (1891–1965), was responsible for office administration and handling classified documents for Stalin personally and for the politburo. Montefiore, 2003.
21 Overy, 2005, p. 75, abridged.
22 Agamben, 1998.
23 'By 1950 the national product was 50 percent above the level achieved in 1937.' Barratt Brown, 1995, p. 200.
24 Ibid.
25 Shearer, 2006, p. 216.
26 Trotsky, 1925.
27 Krushchev, 1956.
28 Fascist documents include some simplistic versions of G.W.F Hegel's theory of the state and Friedrich Nietzsche's call for an *übermensch*. Lyttleton, 1973.
29 Heywood, 2003; Lyttleton, 1973; Passmore, 2002.
30 Garau, 2015.
31 The Third Reich began with Hitler's seizure of dictatorial powers in 1933 and ended in 1945.
32 Duggan, 2014, p. 170.
33 Davies, 2011, pp. 419–29.
34 Urbinati, 2008.
35 Duggan, 2014, p. 177.
36 Ibid., 2014, p. 187, abridged.
37 Fornasin et al., 2018.
38 Killinger, 2001, p. 140.
39 Hughes-Hallett, 2013.
40 Duggan, 2014; Killinger, 2001; Neville, 2015.
41 Neville, 2015.
42 The Council was the only institutional check on Mussolini's powers.
43 'If Fascism has been a criminal association, then I am the chief of this criminal association!' Mussolini, Speech to the Chamber, 3 January 1925. Quoted in Pollard, 1998, p. 53.
44 Duggan, 2014; Pollard, 1998; Neville, 2015.
45 Gramsci, 2007 [1925], pp. 790, 794.
46 Pollard, 1998, p. 54.
47 Garau, 2015, p. 117.
48 Costa Pinto, 2017.
49 Esping-Andersen, 1990.
50 Pasetti, 2017, p. 63.
51 Ibid., p. 64.

52 Cerasi, 2017.
53 Garau, 2015.
54 Duggan, 2014.
55 Cerasi, 2017.
56 Duggan, 2014, p. 223.
57 Pollard, 1998, p. 82.
58 The supposedly 'new' fascist Italian would display

> obedience to authority and respect for the existing social hierarchies; courage to the point of risking his own life to the fatherland's greater good; loyalty to his country and its traditions, and the defence of socially conservative values, including women's traditional role in society.
>
> Garau, 2015, p. 121

59 Payne, 1999, p. 269.
60 Bethell, 2008; Passmore, 2002.
61 Named after the American poet Ezra Pound (1885–1972) who was a vocal supporter of fascism.
62 In 2018 the Southern Poverty Law Center tracked 112 neo-Nazi groups in the USA. See URL: https://www.splcenter.org/, accessed 14 February 2021.
63 Frieden, 2019.
64 Lamoreaux & Shapiro, 2019, p. 2.
65 Thompson, 2008, p. 78, abridged.
66 Ibid., p. 78.
67 Frieden, 2019. Some legislators in both Washington DC and London resisted signing up to the agreement. American sceptics saw it as creating credit-lines that lacked market disciplines; the British as loosening existing imperial arrangements. But in the end it was agreed. China and the Soviet Union had delegations at the conference, but neither ratified the treaty.
68 Judt, 2010, p. 73.
69 As measured by percentage of gross domestic product. International Monetary Fund, see URL: https://www.imf.org/external/datamapper/exp@FPP/, accessed 14 February 2021.
70 Keynes, 1964 [1935], pp. 379–80.
71 Frieden, 2019, p. 232.
72 Reinhoudt & Audier, 2018.
73 Slobodian, 2018, p. 43.
74 Lippmann, 1937.
75 Lippmann in Reinhoudt & Audier, 2018, pp. 106, 108, abridged.
76 Lippmann, 1937, p. 189.
77 Slobodian, 2018, p. 86.
78 'Fully convinced that he knew best what was needed, Franklin D. Roosevelt conceived it as the function of democracy in times of crisis to give unlimited powers to the man it trusted.' Hayek, 2011 [1960], p. 283.
79 Reinhoudt and Audier, 2018, p. 24.
80 Foucault, 2008, p. 172.
81 The Mont Pèlerin Society, 1947. See URL: https://www.montpelerin.org/statement-of-aims, accessed 14 February 2021.
82 Hayek, 2011 [1960], p. 341.
83 Gerber, 1994, p. 31.
84 'Ordo' refers to 'natural order' and was adopted as the title of the journal *ORDO*, founded by Franz Böhm and Walter Eucken in 1948. Gerber, 1994, n. 25.
85 Foucault, 2008, p. 140.
86 Gerber, 1994, p. 44–5.
87 Dold & Kreiger, 2020, p. 9.

88 Esping-Andersen, 1990.
89 '[An] Edenic Habsburg Empire [that] was largely a fantasy, a wishful construct of their own theories'. Slobodian, 2018, p. 144.
90 Admittedly the 'euro convergence criteria' aren't always observed by members in practice.
91 Dold & Kreiger, 2020. More recently, following the global economic crisis of 2008, German ordoliberalism was blamed for austerity policies. Ordoliberals replied that member-states hadn't abided by fiscal responsibility criteria.
92 Harberger was a frequent visitor to Chile. Friedman visited in 1975, not as a guest of the government, but he wrote to President Pinochet regarding economic reform. Friedman & Friedman, 1998.
93 Piñera in Williamson, 1994, p. 225.
94 Riesco, 1999, 2007.
95 Whitehead, 1995.
96 Letelier, 1976, p. 137. The article is dated 28 August. Letelier was working in Washington DC at the time and was assassinated by a car bomb on 21 September 1976.
97 Klein, 2007.
98 Williamson, 1994, pp. 20–21.
99 For example, Piñera in Williamson, 1994; Douglas, 1993.
100 Farrant, McPhail, and Berger, 2012.
101 Riesco, 2007.
102 The term 'Washington consensus' was coined in 1989. It wasn't intended to be a complete description of neoliberal reforms, but is sometimes used to refer to the same. Williamson, 2009.
103 Duncan, 2007.
104 Niskanen, 1971.
105 Williamson, 2009, p. 9. Non-merit subsidies benefit particular interest-groups, such as farmers, rather than society as a whole.
106 Hood, 1991; Hughes, 2018.
107 Hayek, 2011.
108 Wittgenstein, 2009, p. 25e.
109 Hayek recalled that he and Wittgenstein 'disagreed politically': Hayek & Klein, 1992, p. 180. But 'Wittgenstein's philosophy of language and Austrian economics are both applications of the same distinctively Austrian paradigm for thinking about a wide variety of human phenomena'. McDonough, 2014, pp. 9–10.
110 Xinhua, 2013.
111 Urbinati & Warren, 2008, p. 395.
112 There has been no single-party majority since.
113 Duggan, 2014.
114 Roughly translatable as 'Go Italy!'
115 Wike, Fetterolf, & Fagan, 2019.
116 Solijonov, 2016, p. 23.
117 Hobsbawm, 2004.
118 Abramowitz, 2018; Foa & Mounk, 2017; Foa et al., 2020.
119 Solijonov, 2016, p. 24.
120 Bächtiger et al., 2018, p. 2.
121 A failed attempt to break into the Democratic National Committee's headquarters in 1972, and the Nixon administration's efforts to cover up its involvement, led to impeachment proceedings against the president, which were pre-empted by his resignation.
122 Pew Research, 2019.
123 Hetherington & Rudolph, 2015. The impeachment proceedings against President Trump in 2019 further exemplified political polarisation.
124 Foa et al., 2020; Norris, 2011.

125 Ohmae, 1996.
126 Fukuyama, 1989, p. 8.
127 Applebaum, 2020; Mounk, 2018; Runciman, 2018.
128 International Institute for Democracy and Electoral Assistance (International IDEA), 2020.
129 Bol et al., 2020; Goldsmith, Gauld, & Taplin, 2021.
130 Foa et al., 2020.

References

Abramowitz, Michael J. 2018. *Freedom in the World 2018*. Washington, DC. Freedom House.

Agamben, Giorgio. 1998. *Homer Sacer: Sovereign Power and Bare Life*. Stanford, CA: Stanford University Press.

Applebaum, Anne. 2020. *Twilight of Democracy The Seductive Lure of Authoritarianism*. London: Penguin Random House.

Bächtiger, André, John S. Dryzek, Jane J. Mansbridge, and Mark Warren. 2018. *The Oxford Handbook of Deliberative Democracy*. Oxford: Oxford University Press.

Ball, Alan. 2006. 'Building a New State and Society: NEP, 1921–1928.' In *The Cambridge History of Russia, Vol 3*, by Ronald Suny, 168–91. Cambridge: Cambridge University Press.

Barratt Brown, Michael. 1995. *Models in Political Economy*. Harmondsworth: Penguin.

Bethell, Leslie. 2008. 'Politics in Brazil Under Vargas, 1930–1945.' In *The Cambridge History of Latin America, Vol. 9, Brazil Since 1930*, by Leslie Bethell, 1–86. Cambridge: Cambridge University Press.

Bol, Damien, Marco Giani, André Blais, and Peter John Loewen. 2020. 'The Effect of COVID-19 Lockdowns on Political Support: Some Good News for Democracy?' *European Journal of Political Research* 60 (2): 497–505. https://doi.org/10.1111/1475-6765.12401.

Bushkovitch, Paul. 2012. *A Concise History of Russia*. New York, NY: Cambridge University Press.

Cerasi, Laura. 2017. 'Rethinking Italian Corporatism.' In *Corporatism and Fascism*, by Antonio Costa Pinto, 103–23. London: Routledge.

Costa Pinto, Antonio. 2017. *Corporatism and Fascism*. London: Routledge.

Davies, Norman. 2011. *Vanished Kingdoms: The History of Half-Forgotten Europe*. London: Penguin.

Dold, Malte, and Tim Krieger. 2020. *Ordoliberalism and European Economic Policy: Between Realpolitik and Economic Utopia*. London: Routledge.

Douglas, Roger. 1993. *Unfinished Business*. Auckland: Random House.

Duggan, Christopher. 2014. *A Concise History of Italy*. Cambridge: Cambridge University Press.

Duncan, Grant. 2007. *Society and Politics: New Zealand Social Policy*. Auckland: Pearson Education.

Engels, Friedrich. 1993. *The Condition of the Working Class in England*. Oxford: Oxford University Press.

Esping-Andersen, Gøsta. 1990. *The Three Worlds of Welfare Capitalism*. Cambridge: Polity.

Farrant, Andrew, Edward McPhail, and Sebastian Berger. 2012. 'Preventing the "Abuses" of Democracy: Hayek, the "Military Usurper" and Transitional Dictatorship in Chile?' *American Journal of Economics and Sociology* 71 (3): 513–38.

Foa, Roberto Stefan, A. Klassen, M. Slade, A. Rand, and R. Williams. 2020. *The Global Satisfaction with Democracy Report 2020*. Cambridge: Centre for the Future of Democracy.

Foa, Roberto Stefan, and Yascha Mounk. 2017. 'The Signs of Deconsolidation.' *Journal of Democracy* 28 (1): 5–15.

Fornasin, Alessio, Marco Breschi, and Matteo Manfredini. 2018. 'Spanish Flu in Italy: New Data, New Questions.' *Le Infezioni in Medicina* 26 (1): 97–106.

Foucault, Michel. 2008. *The Birth of Biopolitics: Lectures at the College de France, 1978–1979*. New York, NY: Palgrave Macmillan.

Frieden, Jeffry. 2019. 'The Political Economy of the Bretton Woods Agreements.' In *Bretton Woods Agreements: Together with Scholarly Commentaries and Essential Historical Documents*, by Naomi Lamoreaux and Ian Shapiro, 21–37. New Haven, CT: Yale University Press.

Friedman, Milton, and Rose Friedman. 1998. *Two Lucky People: Memoirs*. Chicago, IL: Chicago University Press.

Fukuyama, Francis. 1989. 'The End of History?' *The National Interest*, 3–18.

Garau, Salvatore. 2015. *Fascism and Ideology*. New York, NY: Routledge.

Gerber, David J. 1994. 'Constitutionalizing the Economy: German Neo-Liberalism, Competition Law and the "New" Europe.' *The American Journal of Comparative Law* 42 (1): 25–84.

Goldsmith, Shaun, Robin Gauld, and Ross Taplin. 2021. 'Trust in Government Soars in Australia and New Zealand During Pandemic.' *The Conversation*. February 12. Accessed February 13, 2021. https://theconversation.com/trust-in-government-soars-in-australia-and-new-zealand-during-pandemic-154948.

Gramsci, Antonio. 2007. 'Occasional Translation: 16 May 1925, Listening to Gramsci.' *Cultural Studies* 21 (4/5): 779–95.

Hayek, Friedrich A. 2011. *The Constitution of Liberty: The Definitive Edition*. Chicago, IL: University of Chicago Press.

Hayek, Friedrich A. von, and Peter G. Klein. 1992. *The Fortunes of Liberalism: Essays on Austrian Economics and the Ideal of Freedom. The Collected Works of F.A. Hayek: V. 4*. London: Routledge.

Hetherington, Marc, and Thomas J. Rudolph. 2015. *Why Washington Won't Work: Polarization, Political Trust, and the Governing Crisis*. Chicago, IL: University of Chicago Press.

Heywood, Andrew. 2003. *Political Ideologies: An Introduction*. Houndmills: Palgrave Macmillan.

Hobsbawm, Eric J. 2004. 'Spreading Democracy.' *Foreign Policy*, September 1: 40–41.

Hood, Christopher. 1991. 'A Public Management for All Seasons?' *Public Administration* 69 (1): 3–19.

Hughes, Owen. 2018. *Public Management and Administration*. London: Palgrave.

Hughes-Hallett, Lucy. 2013. *The Pike: Gabriele d'Annunzio, Poet, Seducer and Preacher of War*. London: Fourth Estate.

International Institute for Democracy and Electoral Assistance. 2020. 'Global Overview of COVID-19: Impact on Elections.' *International Institute for Democracy and Electoral Assistance*. July 8. Accessed July 8, 2020. https://www.idea.int/news-media/multimedia-reports/global-overview-covid-19-impact-elections.

Judt, Tony. 2010. *Ill Fares the Land*. London: Penguin.

Keynes, John Maynard. 1964. *The General Theory of Emlpoyment, Interest, and Money*. New York, NY: Harvest, Harcourt.

Khrushchev, Nikita. 1956. 'The Crimes of The Stalin Era.' In *Special Report to the 20th Congress of the Communist Party of the Soviet Union,* by Boris I. Nicolaevsky. New York, NY: The New Leader. Accessed February 2021. https://digitalarchive.wilsoncenter.org/document/115995.pdf?v=3c22b71b65bcbbe9fdfadead9419c995

Killinger, Charles L. 2001. *The History of Italy.* Westport, CT: Greenwood.

Klein, Naomi. 2007. *The Shock Doctrine: The Rise of Disaster Capitalism.* London: Penguin, Allen Lane.

Lamoreaux, Naomi, and Ian Shapiro. 2019. 'Introduction.' In *Bretton Woods Agreements: Together with Scholarly Commentaries and Essential Historical Documents,* by Naomi Lamoreaux and Ian Shapiro, 1–18. New Haven, CT: Yale University Press.

Letelier, Orlando. 1976. 'Economic "Freedom's" Awful Toll.' *The Nation,* August 28: 137–42.

Lippmann, Walter. 1937. *An Inquiry into the Principles of the Good Society.* Boston: Little, Brown and Company.

Lyttleton, Adrian. 1973. *Italian Fascisms from Pareto to Gentile.* London: Jonathan Cape.

Marx, Karl, and Friedrich Engels. 2008. *The Communist Manifesto.* London: Pluto Press.

McDonough, Richard. 2014. 'Wittgenstein's Philosophy and Austrian Economics.' *Studies in Sociology of Science* 5 (4): 1–11.

Montefiore, Simon Sebag. 2003. *Stalin: The Court of the Red Tsar.* London: Weidenfeld & Nicolson.

Mounk, Yascha. 2018. *The People vs. Democracy: Why Our Freedom Is in Danger and How to Save It.* Cambridge, MA: Yale University Press.

Neville, Peter. 2015. *Mussolini.* London: Routledge.

Niskanen, William A. 1971. *Bureaucracy and Representative Government.* New York, NY: Transaction.

Norris, Pippa. 2011. *Democratic Deficit: Critical Citizens Revisited.* Cambridge: Cambridge University Press.

Ohmae, Kenichi. 1996. *The End of the Nation State: The Rise of Regional Economies.* New York, NY: Free Press.

Overy, Richard. 2005. *The Dictators: Hitler's Germany and Stalin's Russia.* London: Penguin.

Pasetti, Matteo. 2017. 'The Fascist Labour Charter and its Transnational Spread.' In *Corporatism and Fascism,* by A. Costa Pinto, 60–77. London: Routledge.

Passmore, Kevin. 2002. *Fascism: A Very Short Introduction.* Oxford: Oxford University Press.

Payne, Stanley G. 1999. *Fascism in Spain, 1923–1977.* Madison: University of Wisconsin Press.

Pew Research Center. 2019. 'Public Trust in Government: 1958–2019.' *Pew Research Center.* April 11. Accessed July 2020. https://www.pewresearch.org/politics/2019/04/11/public-trust-in-government-1958-2019/.

Pollard, John. 1998. *The Fascist Experience in Italy.* London: Routledge.

Raleigh, Donald J. 2006. 'The Russian Civil War, 1917–1922.' In *The Cambridge History of Russia, Vol. 3,* by Ronald Suny, 140–67. Cambridge: Cambridge University Press.

Reinhoudt, Jurgen, and Serge Audier. 2018. *The Walter Lippmann Colloquium: The Birth of Neo-Liberalism.* Cham: Palgrave Macmillan.

Riesco, Manuel. 1999. 'Chile, a Quarter of a Century on.' *New Left Review I* (238): 97–125.

Riesco, Manuel. 2007. 'Is Pinochet Dead?' *New Left Review* 47: 5–20.

Runciman, David. 2018. *How Democracy Ends.* Chicago, IL: Basic Books.

Shearer, David. 2006. 'Stalinism, 1928–1940.' In *The Cambridge History of Russia, Vol 3*, by Ronald Suny, 192–216. Cambridge: Cambridge University Press.

Slobodian, Quinn. 2018. *Globalists: The End of Empire and the Birth of Neoliberalism.* Cambridge, MA: Harvard University Press.

Solijonov, Abdurashid. 2016. *Voter Turnout Trends around the World.* Stockholm: International Institute for Democracy and Electoral Assistance.

Thompson, Helen. 2008. *Might, Right, Prosperity and Consent: Representative Democracy and the International Economy 1919–2001.* Manchester: Manchester University Press.

Trotsky, Leon. 1925. 'Towards Capitalism or Towards Socialism? The Language of Figures.' *The Labour Monthly* 7 (11). Accessed February 2021. https://www.marxists.org/archive/trotsky/1925/11/towards.htm

Urbinati, Nadia. 2008. 'The Legacy of Kant: Giuseppe Mazzini's Cosmopolitanism of Nations.' In *Giuseppe Mazzini and the Globalization of Democratic Nationalism, 1830–1920*, by C.A. Bayly and Eugenio F. Biagini, 11–35. Oxford: British Academy.

Urbinati, Nadia, and Mark E. Warren. 2008. 'The Concept of Representation in Contemporary Democratic Theory.' *Annual Review of Political Science* 11: 387–412.

Whitehead, Laurence. 1995. 'State Organization in Latin America Since 1930.' In *The Cambridge History of Latin America, Vol. 6, Part 2*, by Leslie Bethell, 1–96. Cambridge: Cambridge University Press.

Wike, Richard, Janell Fetterolf, and Moira Fagan. 2019. 'Europeans Credit EU With Promoting Peace and Prosperity, but Say Brussels Is Out of Touch With Its Citizens.' *Pew Research Center.* March 19. Accessed October 31, 2020. https://www.pewresearch.org/global/2019/03/19/europeans-credit-eu-with-promoting-peace-and-prosperity-but-say-brussels-is-out-of-touch-with-its-citizens/.

Williamson, John. 2009. 'A Short History of the Washington Consensus.' *Law & Business Review of the Americas* 15 (1): 7–23.

———. 1994. *The Political Economy of Policy Reform.* Washington, DC: Institute for International Economics.

Wittgenstein, Ludwig. 2009. *Philosophical Investigations.* Chichester: Wiley-Blackwell.

Xinhua. 2013. 'China Issues Detailed Reform Roadmap.' *Xinhuanet.* November 15. Accessed March 19, 2014. http://news.xinhuanet.com/english/china/2013-11/15/c_132891922.htm.

10
CONCLUSION

This book has looked across a vast expanse of history, but an account of the recent past during which it was written sheds some light on its purpose. My introduction opened with a vignette of events in October 2019 that, taken all together, may have given us to think that 'democracy' was breaking down. At that time no one knew that 2020 would see profound changes in world politics and a shift in the norms of what governments can and should do.

In December 2019, as a novel coronavirus was appearing in China, Boris Johnson's Conservative Party won an overall majority in the House of Commons in an election in which 67.3 percent of those registered actually voted. Conservative candidates received 43.6 percent of total votes, being 29.3 percent of all people registered. Conservative representatives went on to occupy 365 (or 56.1 percent) of the 650 seats. A minority of 'the people' elected a parliamentary majority that would pass law and govern on behalf of all. Whether or not we regard that as 'democracy', Johnson had vowed 'to get Brexit done'. He took the election result as a mandate to fulfil the outcome of the 2016 referendum, cancelling out extreme Brexit positions on both the left and right. The necessary legislation was passed, and the United Kingdom left the European Union on 31 January 2020 with a transition phase until the end of the year to reach a trade agreement. Negotiations went down to the wire, but by Christmas Eve a deal was agreed. It settled cross-Channel trade in goods while granting the United Kingdom the independence to regulate its own affairs, including immigration, as Brexit supporters had largely wanted.

After the American election in November 2020, Donald Trump refused to concede defeat to Joe Biden. Casting doubt on the electoral system was integral to Trump's politics of division. Then on 6 January 2021, as Congress was confirming the electoral college's results, a mob of Trump's followers stormed

DOI: 10.4324/9781003166955-10

the Capitol – but fortunately failed to capture any of the senior political figures whom elements of the mob allegedly intended to murder. Sadly, five people died during that incident, and many suffered serious injuries. Once this violent mob was ejected from the building and its grounds, Congress reconvened to complete its business. There was stirring rhetoric about the republic's constitution, but America's reputation was permanently stained. Far from making America great again, Trump had undermined the republic by promulgating lies and trying to overturn an election.

In Italy, in September 2020, a referendum approved a constitutional proposal, pushed by the M5S party, to cut the number of elected representatives by more than a third. In Chile, a referendum the following month overwhelmingly approved the drafting of an entirely new constitution by an elected assembly of citizens to replace the Pinochet-era constitution. In contrast, Hong Kong police were suppressing protests for human rights and against centralised Chinese rule, and protestors were being arrested. Restrictions on the size of gatherings due to the Covid-19 pandemic contributed to quelling unrest. The pandemic was also used as a pretext to delay elections to Hong Kong's legislative council by one year. In Poland, in July an election did go ahead. President Andrzej Duda, backed by the right-wing Law and Justice (PiS) party, was re-elected with 51 percent of the vote in a second-round ballot, and the supreme court approved the result despite complaints about irregularities.

Was democracy broken? Certainly, some things were malfunctioning. But government's a wicked problem, always on the verge of breaking down, if not already broken. If there was a special problem at that time, then was democracy the problem – or was it a lack of democracy? To be precise, many representative governments that were authorised by elections were apparently performing poorly in many leading countries around the world. The problem could have been that these systems aren't especially democratic, and were jammed by polarised opinion. Many people felt alienated from (or by) their own government, even though (or perhaps because) political leaders were scrutinised daily in the media. People on all sides of political debates were anxious, angry and distrustful, leading to intense polarisation, factionalism and often violence.

No matter what type of government they had, however, all countries were affected by the Covid-19 pandemic. This highly infectious novel coronavirus had appeared first in Wuhan, China, in December 2019 and spread rapidly around the globe. It caused the highest mortality rates in affluent countries, such as Belgium, Italy, the United Kingdom and the United States, which have older, more susceptible populations, and in Latin America. Unlike most such epidemics, the poorer countries, especially those in Africa, weren't as badly affected. But Covid-19 changed the course of history and reshaped the ways in which we are governed. Public policy responses were by no means consistent across countries, but the collective actions taken against Covid-19 showed how extraordinary changes can be made by societies, in spite of economic costs, when enough people see the urgent need to do so. If a similar urgency to change our social behaviour and consumption habits were to redirect our approach towards, say, the obesity epidemic or climate change, then some real progress for the future wellbeing of humanity and the biosphere could occur.

The governmental, economic and social responses to the pandemic were astonishing. Huge sums were mobilised to finance public debt, at very low (sometimes negative) interest rates; central banks created money as needed; compensation was paid to ailing businesses and the unemployed; civil freedoms were curtailed as communities were locked down; people made radical lifestyle changes; rapid innovation and progress occurred in digital communications and medical technologies. This was premised on the sacrifices being temporary, although the consequences would be both permanent and unpredictable. There could be no 'back to normal'. One might say that government was working relatively well under trying circumstances. Much less was done (or could have been done) a century earlier in response to the influenza pandemic in which at least 50 million died.

Could the heroic scale of these governmental and social responses be replicated for other global problems? Possibly, if there were another immediate threat to life, for example, an asteroid heading our way. If we want to prescribe what governments should do, however, it's not necessarily logical or practical to generalise from the pandemic response to a climate change response. Moreover, the most effective pandemic disease-control measures were undertaken by paternalistic or authoritarian East Asian societies, such as Taiwan, Singapore and China, who were better prepared to begin with and whose people were more willing to obey orders. Setting aside the egregious mismanagement of the pandemic under President Trump, there's no evidence that far-right political parties in the west took the pandemic any less seriously, nor that, if in government, they acted any less responsibly than mainstream centrist-liberal governments. Populist leaders weren't afraid to close borders. Some far-right populist parties were, at first, vigorous promoters of stringent lockdown policies, but later adopted anti-establishment rhetoric that saw lockdowns as a state conspiracy to deprive people of freedoms – so they weren't always consistent. Nonetheless, populists performed in general no worse than those centrist governments that ended up with on-and-off lockdowns and high Covid-19 mortality rates. If we generalise from the experiences of 2020, are we willing then to conclude that the governmental 'answer' to the questions posed by global wicked problems could be 'more authoritarianism', as in East Asia, rather than 'more democracy'? Such a conclusion is neither compelling nor inevitable. But as China returns to its place as the world's largest economy, there is a broader question about the extent to which its style of paternalistic government becomes more influential than liberal-democracy, by force of sheer size.

No matter how hard people of different political persuasions may have fought for their own versions of social and political progress, a virus changed everything, including public policy and administration. A virus, however, has neither self-awareness nor moral conscience; one can't reason with it. No one in their right mind would have voted for a pandemic, but Covid-19 didn't need our mandate to stimulate radical change in world politics and economics. However we may style ourselves as strategists or enthusiasts for transformative change, disruption and innovation, government was altered by the effects of complex molecules that knew nothing about our needs or our rules. These effects transformed government, for better or worse, more thoroughly than humans otherwise would have done.

Lessons in the arts of government

So how did world politics get to a stage at which, although there are advanced technologies, expertise, experience and recorded history to inform us, major problems aren't being addressed effectively and so many people have lost confidence in government? A simple answer is: through a series of drastic mistakes and catastrophes, as always. Another response is that the advanced technologies and expertise themselves create as many problems for governments as they solve. Although there's such a thing as good government, even the best is up against complex, uncontrollable and unpredictable change, and leaders can only identify good solutions in retrospect.

This study has reinforced some fundamental points about government: that when things function well, good government is largely unnoticed despite the constant work it requires; that nonetheless government is performed in the face of uncertainty; so that when things do go wrong and uncertainty reigns, measures that were previously unorthodox may suddenly become necessary. Governing entails collective action that can address disturbances and threats, and which, when things go well, reduces events to regulated and patterned conduct. We can't deal with the problems that concern or threaten us collectively without government, but government itself is a problem that concerns us collectively and which we repeatedly try and fail to solve. Reform of any 'broken' system of government requires government, so we have a bootstraps problem: we have to apply the broken system to fix the broken system. We struggle even to reach agreement on what the problem is. It's no wonder that historical change in systems of government tends to occur as a result of violence or unexpected disasters, and isn't normally achieved by reflection and design.

The abiding tasks of government are food distribution, taxation and defence of people and territory. In modern government, the emphasis may have shifted from territory to population, from household economy to political economy, and from material to immaterial things, but the imperatives to feed, tax and defend the people are constants. In affluent countries today we may not regard feeding the people (getting one's daily bread, rice or potatoes) as a major political concern, but this is the gift of good government – that such fortunate citizens don't have to ask, 'Where's my next meal coming from?' In many parts of the world, this is still an urgent problem. Moreover, if we regard grain as the basic currency of most ancient states, then the modern comparator is the stability of money and confidence in financial institutions. Taxation too, of course, is a constant – originally to pay for armies and for conspicuous demonstrations of power, and nowadays to pay for a great range of public services (including defence). Money makes exchange of goods more efficient – enabling us to trade and distribute things – and it's the means for paying tax. (Governments create currency in order to get it back.) So security, taxation and distribution of basic goods (and hence monetary policy) are the core tasks of government. These tasks rely on regulation, ensuring that events happen in commonly understood and more or less predictable patterns.

Although I've offered a critique of historical grand narratives of civilisational progress, there have been some outstanding improvements in government across the centuries. We may extract some essences of government from the foregoing chapters.

Above all, slavery, mass murder and genocide have been outlawed. It looks unlikely that we will ever again see crimes against humanity as open and ferocious as those committed by, for example, the Mongols. Mass atrocities have occurred in more recent times and human trafficking persists, as we well know, but there is now at least international law that prohibits it and licences multilateral intervention. Outright plunder such as that committed by the English East India Company should be preventable now, and one advantage of social media is that the world is watching the criminals. There's a reasonable critique of the UN Declaration of Universal Human Rights that its articles are premised on the individual ('everyone has the right to...') and not the kin group, for example. But at least there's a set of international legal principles to which one may appeal to protect victims of abuses of power including racial discrimination. At a more mundane level, to reap the benefits of global commerce and travel, any government now has to adopt exacting standards of regulation and international cooperation, and this means training people in arts of government.

Women don't yet enjoy full economic and political equality, but they are now included in government (in most countries) as equal participants, if not yet numerically equal at the highest levels. It's widely recognised that full and equal inclusion of all genders at all levels boosts human development, but achieving this is an ongoing political project.

A successful government needs unifying symbols and ideas that are communicated or experienced through religions, philosophies, symbolism, shared activities and media. These may include military service, examinations, elections, broadcasting, currencies and flags. They connect strangers and disparate communities, stitching them together with common themes and careers in the fashion of one polity. This commonality must be balanced, however, with toleration of ethno-religious and local diversity; it must embrace and respect our differing political opinions. Some of the most creative times in the history of political thought were also times of conflict, for example, the kinds of inter-state rivalries that brought Confucius and others to prominence in China, and Machiavelli and others in Italy. Times of strict religious orthodoxy, as in Byzantium, stultified intellectual life. There is an endless tension, or ebb and flow, between centralisation and decentralisation of political power and governmental functions. These matters are socially and historically contingent, and so there is no 'one best way', other than to deal with these real-world tensions openly, recognising the tricky balance between unity and diversity, compliance and autonomy. Neoliberalism's 'promise' of liberty and devolved government was contradicted by its own reforms which were imposed by (often authoritarian) central governments and extorted by the threat of exit by economically powerful producers, investors and financiers. But the pendulum did swing back: curtailment of liberties and massive subsidies became painfully necessary again.

The messy, complex reality of social and economic life will always defeat a governmental plan for complete technical control or universal happiness. The cameralist and legalist dreams were unrealisable. Nizam al Mulk's omniscient monarch never existed. Any dream of uniformity or utopia is ultimately futile and, based on experience, is likely to become a nightmare. Governments need to tolerate differences, experiments and failures to benefit from progress. 'Nudge' techniques (structuring people's choices to increase the frequency of government's preferred choice) are a more subtle form of the dream of control and need to be viewed critically. In general, we have learned that utopian promises may get short-term political support, but they make for ineffective government – and often they lead to catastrophe. Instead, addressing human and environmental needs and taking on the long-term projects of steady progress towards clearly established goals is the rather boring but actually effective framework in which to govern successfully.

The powers of those inherited monarchies that still exist are now normally limited to apolitical symbolic and constitutional actions. Absolute and arbitrary power has been radically reduced, but not entirely eliminated from the world. From the many failures of autocratic or dictatorial rule, we've learned the value of an impersonality of rulership, transcending any individual, achieved through written constitutions and laws, bureaucratic processes and technical expertise. Powers have been limited horizontally and vertically, through federalism and separation into branches of government. New policies are normally required to pass an impartial test based on evidence. But personality still matters in political leadership. The personal qualities, moral conduct and communication styles of political leaders still have real effects, so teaching and learning the ethics of leadership as a reflective practice, akin to the mirror of princes, is still called for. And a balance between personality and impersonality is needed.

The past need for the mirror of princes handbooks showed that relying on inheritance for one's next ruler was risky. It makes sense today that those who acquire office should do so on merit and should act for the common good or face the consequence of removal from office. But this is still no insurmountable barrier to incompetence, dishonesty and corruption. Representation by election helps, in as much as voters are able to judge candidates' merits, however they may judge them, and in as much as the parties select candidates based on merit and not just loyalty. The diversity of representatives is improving in terms of gender and ethnicity, but there's another growing gap between the representatives and the represented: the elected tend to be educated, middle class and middle-aged, with higher incomes and wealth than many of those they represent. Experience (and hence age) and education (which correlates with higher income) may be merit-based criteria for election. But the gap between the affluent class from which representatives are more likely to be drawn and the poorer sectors of society is widening in tandem with economic inequality in general. That many citizens feel alienated from politics and politicians may be attributable in part to this cultural and economic chasm.

The opposite of alienation is belonging. From the start, our belonging and identification with others is also our self-identification (for example, 'our' language is also 'my' language), but it's constituted simultaneously by differentiation from others. There's no knowing one's self without others, both like and unlike oneself. Political belief isn't simply an individual's rational choice; it's more than an acquired value preference. Politics, like faith, is a way to congregate, or to express and maintain belonging to a social group and to differentiate one's own group from others. For instance, I approve of a political idea or proposition partly because people I affiliate with, or look up to as leaders, approve of it. And I'm more likely to disapprove of ideas or propositions that are espoused by opposing groups, simply because those I associate with see them as an opposition.

Many people may disavow this social-belonging view by insisting that one's beliefs are rationally guided by one's inner needs and interests, not by affiliation with or loyalty to others, let alone opposition to others. Moreover, we may well want government and law to be guided by rational thinking, not factionalism. Rational impartial application of law and administration has always been an aim of government – although it can be taken too far, as in the harsh legalist policies of China's first emperor. Some political practices have struggled against the effect of sheer loyalty to leaders or factions while others have utilised it to their advantage. Since the oldest empires many (but by no means all) rulers have rejected entrenched privileges and kinship as criteria for advancement or succession, in favour of meritocratic appointment. In our times a common complaint is, 'It's not what you know, it's who you know.' It appears unfair when the meritocratic principle of promoting people according to their expertise and ability isn't applied, and when non-merit 'political' factors such as old friendships and behind-the-scenes deals take precedence, or worse if unlawful discrimination occurs. Those with reliable knowledge and skill should rise to higher office, either as elected representatives or appointed officials. And once they are in office, the rational use of that knowledge and skill should prevail over partiality to family, gender, race or wealth, or sycophancy. Laws against discrimination and corruption, and principles of transparency exist for this purpose. But I doubt that we'll ever lose the propensity to favour our in-group.

It's often said that power corrupts. In liberal-democratic cultures, truth and state power are often spoken of in opposition to one another. One speaks truth to power. The exposure of the truth holds power to account. Knowledge of the truth means a check on government, preventing abuses of power. If knowledge confers power, then the more widely shared it is, through education and a free press, the more democratic our societies would become. If truth would thus triumph over power, then honest and equitable government would replace partiality, misinformation, discrimination and vested interests.

On questions of justice and public policy, however, the truth is never a solid 'nugget' to be discovered and put on display to end all doubt. We become aware of our political values and form our ideas of what's right or just largely through argument and struggle with others of a different mind. If truth is to be sought, it's by observing the contradictions or oppositions between people and understanding them dialectically. A truth is at work within political contestation itself; whereas the overthrow of one camp by another rarely resolves anything. But the grounds on which people could discern true from false were undermined from the left by relativism (everyone has their own truth) and from the right by conspiracy theories (the state is hiding the truth). Moreover, comprehension of the truth, and wisdom in how to use it for the common good were swept away by a flood of information. For most of history, government suffered from too little information and very slow communication. Suddenly it's the opposite problem: too much information is communicated instantly and globally. Furthermore, the low cost of producing each 'piece' of information means an oversupply of low-quality information, accompanied by 'innovative' tools to draw attention (indeed to create addiction) to such low-quality information. It's sadly unsurprising that this includes deliberate disinformation designed to deceive gullible people.

A basic aspiration of states since early times is to convince people that their government has valid means to distinguish true from false and right from wrong. There have been many methods for doing so, including combat, augury, oath, trial, public inquiry, polling and randomised clinical trials. Even an election could be regarded as the discovery of a truth. The methods may become as politically controversial as the answers, however, and such governmental authority appears to be in disarray lately. Alongside this, a dislocation in the distribution of power has occurred, exemplified by the growth of tech industries and of the gig economy – that is, a growing gap between digital capital and labour. The American deregulated model of internet governance has left powerful social media in the hands of entrepreneurs whose primary motive is profit, not the public good. Social media users are performing free labour for private firms who repackage them as 'targets' to sell to advertisers. In China, by contrast, state control means that social media are used for surveillance and obedience. In either case, the user may treat social media as a public utility or even a kind of 'speaker's corner', but they aren't. Where there's effective online political activism, that too is being co-opted by surveillance for either commercial gain or political purchase. And disinformation campaigns have expanded exponentially. Overall, the internet has become a tool of disempowerment and oppression; its potential for democracy hasn't prevailed; because of it, the field on which we could debate the difference between true and false has become very muddy.

The causes and consequences of the major political concerns of our times, such as pandemics, climate change, economic inequality and online extremism, are borderless. And yet there has been a retreat behind the borders of nationalism, due to populist politics, and there are significant political barriers to multilateral collective action even when most needed. I don't foresee 'one world government' as a necessary precondition or outcome, let alone a solution. The propensity of humans to divide into groups that become mutually hostile would make it politically unachievable. But multilateral policy collaboration is absolutely essential at this stage in world history, and lessons in the arts of government are needed right now if we are to address global and local challenges more wisely in the future.

INDEX

Note: Page numbers followed by "n" denote endnotes.

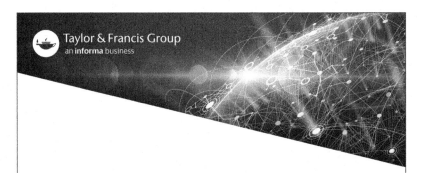

Printed in the United States
by Baker & Taylor Publisher Services